SETTLING THE EARTH

In this worldwide survey, Clive Gamble explores the evolution of the human imagination, without which we would not have become a global species. He sets out to determine the cognitive and social bases for our imaginative capacity and traces the evidence back into deep human history. He argues that it was the imaginative ability to "go beyond" and to create societies where people lived apart yet stayed in touch that made us such effective world settlers. To make his case, Gamble brings together information from a wide range of disciplines: psychology, cognitive science, archaeology, palaeoanthropology, archaeogenetics, geography, quaternary science and anthropology. He presents a novel deep history that combines the archaeological evidence for fossil hominins with the selective forces of Pleistocene climate change, engages with the archaeogeneticists' models for population dispersal and displacement, and ends with the Europeans' rediscovery of the deep history settlement of the earth.

Clive Gamble is Professor of Archaeology at the University of Southampton and is one of the world's leading authorities on the archaeology of early human societies. He is founder of the Centre for the Archaeology of Human Origins at the University of Southampton. Gamble has travelled extensively to see first-hand the evidence for social change from our earliest past, and most recently visited every continent while filming an acclaimed six-part documentary entitled *Where Do We Come From?* for the UK's 5 network. He has held visiting positions at the Australian National University; the Museo de la Plata, Argentina; Boston University; and the universities of LaTrobe and Alaska. He is much sought after as a keynote speaker at international conferences and has been a frequent contributor to national radio. His many groundbreaking books include *The Palaeolithic Settlement of Europe* (1986); *Timewalkers: The Prehistory of Global Colonisation* (1993); *The Palaeolithic Societies of Europe* (1999), the 2000 winner of the Society of American Archaeology Book Award; *Archaeology: The Basics* (2001); and *Origins and Revolutions: Hominin Identity in Earliest Prehistory* (2007). In 2005, Gamble was awarded the Rivers Memorial Medal by the Royal Anthropological Institute in recognition of his outstanding contribution to the field, and in 2008, he won the Henry Stopes Medal from the Geologists' Association. He was elected a Fellow of the British Academy in 2000.

Settling the Earth

The Archaeology of Deep Human History

CLIVE GAMBLE

University of Southampton

CAMBRIDGE
UNIVERSITY PRESS

CAMBRIDGE
UNIVERSITY PRESS

32 Avenue of the Americas, New York NY 10013-2473, USA

Cambridge University Press is part of the University of Cambridge.

It furthers the University's mission by disseminating knowledge in the pursuit of education, learning, and research at the highest international levels of excellence.

www.cambridge.org
Information on this title: www.cambridge.org/9781107601079

© Clive Gamble 2013

This publication is in copyright. Subject to statutory exception and to the provisions of relevant collective licensing agreements, no reproduction of any part may take place without the written permission of Cambridge University Press.

First published 2013

A catalog record for this publication is available from the British Library.

Library of Congress Cataloging in Publication data
Gamble, Clive.
Settling the earth : the archaeology of deep human history / Clive Gamble.
    pages   cm
Includes bibliographical references and index.
ISBN 978-1-107-01326-1 (hardback)
1. Prehistoric peoples.   2. Cognition and culture.   3. Social evolution.
4. Paleolithic period.   5. Anthropology, Prehistoric.   I. Title.
GN741.G357   2014
930.1–dc23   2013027237

ISBN 978-1-107-01326-1 Hardback
ISBN 978-1-107-60107-9 Paperback

Cambridge University Press has no responsibility for the persistence or accuracy of URLs for external or third-party Internet Web sites referred to in this publication and does not guarantee that any content on such Web sites is, or will remain, accurate or appropriate.

For Lewis Binford

Contents

Boxes

Figures

Tables

Acknowledgements

Writing a book about brains and global settlement has to be a cooperative enterprise. I was particularly fortunate in being assisted by Fiona Coward, Peter Morgan, Elaine Morris and James Cole in finding references, correcting mistakes, data digesting, discussing the issues, mapping and illustrating stone tools.

The circle of people that I need to thank for advice, information and argument is wide indeed: James Adovasio, Jim Allen, Nick Ashton, Geoff Bailey, Graeme Barker, Ofer Bar-Yosef, Anne Best, Bill Boismier, Luis Borrero, Ariane Burke, Richard Cosgrove, Iain Davidson, Robin Dennell, Rob Foley, Nena Galanidou, Nigel Goring-Morris, Chris Gosden, Bjarne Grønnow, Rob Hosfield, Geoff Irwin, Marta Lahr, Julia Lee-Thorp, Adrian Lister, Ian McNiven, Paul Mellars, David Meltzer, Steven Mithen, Clive Oppenheimer, Stephen Oppenheimer, Mike Petraglia, Gustavo Politis, Mark Pollard, Matt Pope, Martin Richards, John Robb, Stephen Shennan, Mike Smith, Chris Stringer, Mike Walker, Dustin White and David Yesner.

Participation in three projects helped to structure my excursion into deep history. The British Academy Centenary Project *From Lucy to Language: The archaeology of the social brain* proved immensely stimulating, as it brought evolutionary psychology together with archaeology and anthropology. My co-directors Robin Dunbar and John Gowlett and our steering committee of Garry Runciman, Wendy James and Ken Emond were most influential. While this book was being planned, I also led the NERC thematic programme *Environmental factors and chronology in human evolution and dispersal* (EFCHED). EFCHED had eleven projects that spanned the world and brought quaternary science and Palaeolithic archaeology together, several of which are reported here. My thanks to the NERC team and in particular Chris Franklin and Sally Palmer. Finally, the Radcliffe

Seminar on deep history, hosted by Daniel Smail and Andrew Shryock, made me realise that prehistory had had its day.

During the writing of the book, I travelled from a Geography to an Archaeology Department.

At Royal Holloway, I owe a debt to colleagues who patiently answered quaternary questions, and from the Centre for Quaternary Research these include Simon Armitage, Simon Blockley, Ian Candy, Scott Elias, Rupert Housley, Rob Kemp, John Lowe, Jim Rose, Danielle Schreve and Tom Stevens, as well as Felix Driver, Vicky Elefanti, Hilary Geoghegan, Gil Marshall and Katie Willis. Ian Barnes answered questions about ancient DNA, while Matt Grove and Dora Moutsiou were both very generous in allowing me to use aspects of their doctoral research.

At Southampton, Helen Farr provided information about sea-level change, while William Davies, John McNabb and all the students in the Centre for the Archaeology of Human Origins added thoughts and information.

With great skill, Jenny Kynaston produced all the artwork at Royal Holloway, met every deadline and put up with constant tinkering. I thank her for her patience. Luane Hutchinson also showed remarkable expertise in editing the book for publication. Amber Johnson very kindly provided original data and maps from *Frames of Reference*.

I dedicate this book to Lewis Binford, friend and mentor since we first met in 1980. I'm only saddened that you are not here to see the result. You are much missed.

Glossary

Dates

C^{14}	Radiocarbon dating. All radiocarbon ages in this book have been calibrated.
b2k	Before AD 2000, equivalent to BP (before present)
ka	Thousand years ago b2k, based on science-based dating such as C^{14} and OSL
Ma	Million years ago, based on science-based dating such as K/Ar
OSL	Optically stimulated thermoluminescence dating
K/Ar	Potassium–argon dating
Molecular clock	Estimates based on mutation and coalescent rates
ka molecular	Indicates the basis of the age estimate

Climate

MIS	Marine Isotope Stage, divisions based on oxygen isotope readings of O^{18} (heavy) and O^{16} (light) from foraminifera skeletons in deep-sea cores. Oceans enriched with O^{16} indicate small ice sheets.
Milankovitch cycles	Predictable changes in the earth's orbit (eccentricity), rotation (precession) and tilt (obliquity) that force climate change
Stadial	Cold period, low sea level and ice advance

Interstadial	Warmer interval during a stadial
Interglacial	Warm period with temperatures equal to or above today's, high sea level
GS	Greenland stadial recognised in the ice cores
GI	Greenland interstadial
LGM	Last Glacial Maximum 25–18ka when ice sheets reached their greatest extent
Effective Temperature	A measure of productivity and the length of the growing season based on modern temperature, expressed in ET °C

Genetic

mtDNA	Mitochondrial DNA: only inherited through the female line
MSY	Male-specific segment of the Y chromosome: only inherited through the male line
HLA	A gene family which provides instructions for making a group of related proteins known as the human leukocyte antigen (HLA) complex. The HLA complex helps the immune system distinguish the body's own proteins from proteins made by foreign invaders such as viruses and bacteria.
Ancient DNA	The extraction of DNA from dead rather than living organisms
Haplogroups	Branches of the mitochondrial DNA phylogenetic tree that consist of a collection of related haplotypes and where each haplotype represents a unique pattern of DNA substitutions (Haplo = single)
Clade	A branch on a phylogenetic lineage resulting from a split in an earlier lineage that formed two new taxa
Motif	A distinctive and usually recurrent genetic sequence found in a geographical area and used to distinguish populations and their migration histories
Effective population size	Refers to how many individuals actually contribute alleles to the next generation as opposed to the total number of individuals in a population

Coalescence	When two genetic lineages find a common ancestor
Population bottleneck	Occurs when the size of a population is reduced for at least one generation. When the population is small, this can result in a faster reduction in genetic variation through the process of genetic drift. Such bottlenecks show up in mtDNA and MSY data.

Archaeology

FGH	Fisher-gatherer-hunter; used to describe modern societies and those before the advent of farming
FACE	The social activities of Fragmentation, Accumulation, Consumption and Enchainment that result in patterns in archaeological data
Encephalisation	Growth in brain size
EQ	Encephalisation quotient that scales brain to body size
Mode	Five modes are recognised among stone tools based on techniques of manufacture and dominant artefact type
Technounit	A discrete component of an artefact. When all the technounits in an artefact are added up, it provides a measure of its complexity.
PCT	Prepared Core Technology; e.g. Victoria West, Levallois, Prismatic blade
LCT	Large Cutting Tools; stone picks, cleavers and bifaces
Biface	Any piece of stone worked on both faces; e.g. Acheulean hand axes, Clovis projectile points
Core	What remains after a stone nodule has been knapped
Flake	Less than twice as long as it is wide
Blade	Must be twice as long as it is wide
A-List, B-List	An alternative way to group archaeological classifications
IUP	Initial Upper Palaeolithic

Web resources for skulls and stone tools

These have been selected for the illustrations they contain of stone tools, fossil skulls and climate data that supplement the text figures. There are many more to explore, while search engines will enhance the glossary.

The online *Encyclopedia of Quaternary Science* (2013) edited by Scott Elias and frequently updated is an essential on-line resource for all things ice age, including hominins.

A comprehensive array of hominin skulls can be found at the Smithsonian Institution's Human Origins Program. http://humanorigins.si.edu/evidence/human-fossils as well as some stone tools at its http://humanorigins.si.edu/evidence/behavior/tools.

Many images of Mode 2 artefacts from across Terra 2, and which bring home their variability, are at http://archaeologydataservice.ac.uk/archives/view/bifaces/index.cfm.

Old Stone Age.com has a range of resources in Old World Palaeolithic: http://www.oldstoneage.com/default.shtml.

The Centre for the Study of Human Origins has an interactive Human Evolution Explorer: http://www.nyu.edu/gsas/dept/anthro/programs/csho/pmwiki.php/Home/TheCenter.

For an interactive simulation of changing sea levels with a focus on Sunda and Sahul see Monash University's Sahul-Time: http://sahultime.monash.edu.au/.

Views of the Neanderthals from the Natural History Museum, London, are at http://www.nhm.ac.uk/nature-online/life/human-origins/early-human-family/neanderthals/index.html.

CHAPTER 1

The worlds of deep human history

Going up that river was like travelling back to the earliest beginnings of the world.

Joseph Conrad, *Heart of Darkness*, 1902

Humans Reunited

The prospect of gold had brought them into the mountains. They were pioneers in an unexplored land, and at the end of a day's steep climb, a large fertile valley lay before them. That night the well-armed party of seventeen men grew apprehensive as they saw fires in the far distance. The next day, they met many people who carried stone axes.

This story of encounter could have happened anytime and in many places during the last 600 years. The prospectors could have been Portuguese adventurers, Spanish soldiers, English sailors, Dutch spice-merchants, French trappers, Russian whalers, Danish fishermen, Argentine ranchers or Brazilian loggers. But this was 1930 in the Bismarck ranges of Papua New Guinea (Connolly and Anderson 1988).[1] The two Australian prospectors and their fifteen New Guinean carriers had an official permit to be there. Moreover, they expected to make contact with new people. To help their safe passage, they had brought supplies of trade axes and glass beads. What their leader, Mick Leahy, had not expected were the numbers of people living in the mountains of New Guinea. His small patrol had stumbled across more than a million Highlanders.

This first contact eighty years ago saw two histories moving over and under each other like continental plates: colonial expansion and tribal

---

[1] Subsequent patrols by Leahy and his brothers took cameras providing a full record of this human reunion.

management, fortunes in gold and wealth in shells, rifles and spears, steel
and stone axes, cloth shorts and loincloths, sun hats and feather head-
dresses. But for all the outward differences in ideology and technology,
as well as the skin contrast between northern white and tropical black,
this was a reunion. Both sides of the encounter shared a common origin
in a seed population of Africans that some 60,000 years ago (60ka) began
the process of expansion which settled the whole world. Adaptations to
local conditions followed as new habitats were encountered, while the tiny
numbers, peripatetic lifestyles and frequent separation intensified a variety of micro-genetic changes. These small differences from a remote time
contain an account of humanity's common foundation. The evidence is
accessible through archaeological, genetic and palaeoanthropological[2]
enquiry framed by environmental and climatic data from quaternary science. Together these approaches identify a deep history of geographical
expansion that demands interpretation.[3]

Enter the Hominins

But there is still an older, deeper history which forms the context for
both these historically documented first contacts and the earlier expansion of Africans. The starting point, however, is very different. The people involved were not humans but *hominins*, a grouping that includes
ourselves (humans) and all our extinct ancestors such as the African australopithecines and Eurasian Neanderthals. Yet another taxonomic grouping, the *hominids*, sweeps up humans and hominins together with the
African and Asian great apes. Then the *anthropoids* add in Old and New
World monkeys such as baboons, vervets and capuchins and their fossil
ancestors.

The hominins, like the hominids, inhabited only the Old World. To
be more precise, they were restricted for more than three million years
to particular parts of the continents of Africa, Asia and its European arm.
In contrast to the African expansion starting 60ka, these hominins were
bounded by a reluctance to cross water and climb mountains. They
were also more sensitive to the effects of longitude, latitude, rainfall and

---

[2] Palaeoanthropology combines several fields but is used throughout this book as a synonym
for human palaeontology, the study of hominin fossil remains.
[3] Throughout this book, I use deep history in preference to prehistory. I take the view that
everything about the human past is history.

temperature on growing seasons and the abundance of food. When two species of hominins encountered each other, as is probable, they were distinguished less by what they carried – infants, spears and stone tools for the most part – and more by either the size of their brains or the complexity of their social lives. And during this long period of change and evolution, those brains and social lives were steadily increasing in size and scale. As archaeologist John Gowlett (2010: 357) puts it, there is an eternal triangle in human evolution, and its three points are diet change, detailed environmental knowledge and social collaboration. Some advances, such as fire or domestication, changed these relationships, amplifying them in unexpected ways, some of which assisted the expansion of range and dispersal into new lands.

Any enquiry into the deep history of humans is driven by two themes: on the one hand, brain growth, *encephalisation*,[4] and, on the other, an increase in *global settlement*. The former led to brains three times as large as might be expected for a primate of our size – an encephalisation that occurred long before the global expansion initiated by Africans took place. From our perspective, the latter happened surprisingly late in hominin evolution. Before 50ka, about a quarter of the planet was settled by hominins. The remaining three quarters, when judged against the four million years of hominin evolution, was first occupied in about one per cent of that time. The purpose of this book is to examine these two measures of growth and change in deep human history and to ask how they are linked.

The Evolution of Human Imagination

My theme is an archaeological geography of our deep human history that weaves together time, place and change. Archaeology and geography draw on our ability to imagine other worlds and people them accordingly. And it is this most distinctive human capacity – imagination – that I will explore using material and cognitive evidence set in a global framework. Without imagination, there would be no past, no memories beyond the instant reminders of smell, touch, taste, vision and hearing – the triggers of feeling.

[4] Encephalisation is calculated as a measure of brain to body size, expressed as the encephalisation quotient (EQ). Whales have the largest brains for mammals but they have even larger bodies and so a modest EQ. Compared to the body size of chimpanzees, we have an EQ three times the expected size.

While the human imagination relies heavily on the experience of the senses, it has moved beyond the purely experiential to the relational. It has achieved this by making complex connections through symbols and metaphors. The former substitutes signs for meaning, while the latter expresses how we experience one thing in terms of another. This is how a stone hand axe comes to represent an unseen fossil ancestor and, as Joseph Conrad describes in *Heart of Darkness*, how a journey up a remote river retraces our history to its source.

Several imaginative developments occurred in our deep time history. In no particular order, our imagination began to relate to people when they were not present and to behave as if they were. Then, at some point, we came to treat objects in ways similar to people. Such relations created a two-way agency between the animate and inanimate that amazes us so much, we take it for granted. And finally, an evolving human imagination created geographies of other times and spaces: the Garden of Eden, Swift's Lilliput, Coleridge's Xanadu, Alice's Wonderland, Edward Said's Orientalism, James Cameron's Pandora and a shared Palaeolithic past.

These developments provide the springboard to consider the evolution of human imagination, and three closely connected elements form the core of my archaeological geography:

- the timing of global dispersal and expansion, where archaeology and the genetics that underpin a phylogeography of movement provide the insights;
- the growth in brain size, where cognitive science, evolutionary psychology and palaeoanthropology combine to account for encephalisation;
- the changing environments which frame the process of cultural and biological evolution, the preserve of quaternary science and palaeoecology.

The environments are reviewed in Chapters 2 and 3 alongside evolutionary and cognitive models, while the archaeological, genetic and fossil evidence is presented in Chapters 4–8. The evidence available is set out in Box 1.1, and in Chapter 3, I draw attention to the veneers, the data and assumptions derived from the recent past that cover and colour deep history.

The remainder of this introduction is given over to the cartography of hominin settlement and a route map for extended and expanded minds.

Box 1.1. The sources of evidence for deep and shallow human history

There have been four game-changing moments when the archives available for writing deep history raise new possibilities. These archives are found in artefacts, symbols, genes and digital data. They are applicable to different Terrae (Table Box 1.1).

The first, or artefact archive, contains the evidence for the oldest technologies. It begins with simple implements, often stone which then become more complicated so that we find tools which cannot occur in nature: composite implements such as stone projectile points bound to a wooden haft. We also find during the later stages of Terra 2 and throughout the later Terrae further technological innovation based on the concept of containing things and with which we are very familiar because we live in houses, wrap up warmly on a cold day and drive our cars. One aspect of these changing technologies is to give material form to emotions and bodily sensations through the imaginative device of metaphorical substitution. They are social technologies because they rely on making connections, bringing things and people into association, in order to have both a practical effect and an aesthetic affect.

The second change is a symbolic archive marked by the patchy appearance of literacy beginning in Terra 4. For long the preserve of the very few, basic literacy only became widespread in the last 100 years. Today youth and adult literacy – defined as the ability to read, write and understand simple statements about everyday life – varies greatly between countries and by gender. However, the global estimates are that today eighty-two per cent of adults and eighty-eight per cent of those aged between 15 and 24 years can be classed as literate (Dorling, Newman and Barford 2008: maps 229–232). Traditionally, literacy involves symbols to transfer the sense of spoken language to clay, parchment and textile media. The surviving texts are accorded great significance as a means to record history, amplified at different moments by innovations such as paper, printing presses and keyboards.

The third archive is contained within us. Comparative studies of humans, apes and monkeys have been used for more than 200 years and very successfully by nineteenth-century scientists such as Thomas Huxley and his groundbreaking *Man's Place in Nature* (Huxley 1863). The comparative method has always relied on chains of inference, some of them quite long, to argue for common ancestry and shared capacities. By contrast, the genetic archives, a breakthrough of the last forty years, allow us to go directly to the source to establish lineages and historical

(continued)

Box 1.1 *(continued)*

connections. We can study the DNA of living people and learn about the past movements of the populations to which they belong. Also, we can now obtain ancient DNA data from the teeth and bones of fossil ancestors. Those same bones also provide isotopic data on what food they ate and the geology where they were raised. These direct methods shorten the chains of inference about diet and movement that previously depended on analysing animal bones and raw materials.

The fourth and current game-changing archive is digital, its global impact both astonishing and recent through its manifestation as the World Wide Web. Its significance as an historical archive lies in creating new connections rather than merely storing data. In a sense, the web is the projectile point of the twenty-first century. The addition of sound and moving images is a novelty, and no doubt the other senses of taste, touch and smell will shortly be added. Since 1991, when HTML was written by Tim Berners-Lee in a lab in Cerne, Switzerland, new historically based pathways have become not only possible but virtual. On a personal note, this book has been shaped by these digital archives, and the possibilities they afford, in ways that its predecessor, *Timewalkers* (Gamble 1993), could not begin to imagine.

TABLE BOX 1.1. *The historical archives available for the study of global settlement and encephalisation*

Digital	Terra 5	Shallow history
Text, numeracy and writing	Terrae 4–5	
Personal molecular codes	Terrae 3–5	Deep history
Artefacts and materials	Terrae 1–5	
Skeletal and ancient DNA	Terrae 0–5	
Comparative primate studies	Terrae 0–5	

The point about the three new archives – symbolic, genetic and digital – of Terrae 3–5 is that treated incautiously, they cover the remote past with a veneer, disrupting what should be a continuous record of deep history. These veneers are imposed between us and the older worlds we are investigating. They encourage the unhelpful division between a deep history and a shallow history, according a "greater-truth" to the latter because of what is recorded in the symbolic, genetic and digital archives. But as I have argued elsewhere (Gamble 2007), the commonly made distinction between written history and material prehistory is as false as those Neolithic revolutionaries, such as the archaeologist Gordon Childe, who trumpet the historical importance of agricultural societies against all those that went before.

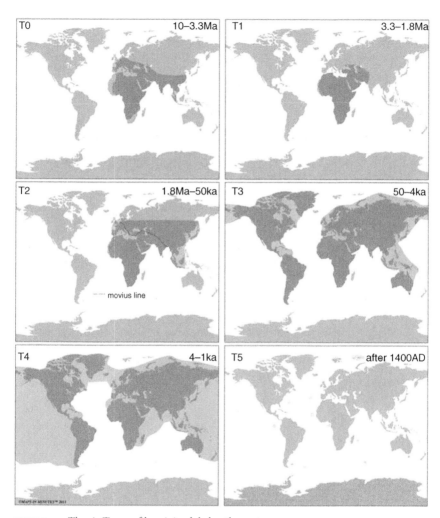

FIGURE 1.1. The six Terrae of hominin global settlement.

The Six Terrae of Deep History

When applied to deep history and the themes of encephalisation and global settlement, our imagination needs boundaries to avoid free fall. Here, I use the changing distribution of archaeological evidence in time and space to distinguish six hominin worlds which collectively I call *Terrae*. Consequently, the boundaries of these six Terrae (Figure 1.1) are drawn by the ages of what has been found, and initially ignore the type of tools their

TABLE 1.1. *The five hominin Terrae*

	Size of Terra compared to present-day land mass 148,647,000 km² (%)	Time from T1–T5 3.3 million years	Duration from T1–T5 (%)
Terra 1	24	1.5Ma	45
Terra 2	44	1.75Ma	53
Terra 3	94	46ka	1.4
Terra 4	95	3ka	0.09
Terra 5	100	600yr	0.02

The current land area of the Earth, whether inhabitable or not, is 150 million km². At times of low sea level, a further 22 million km² became available on the exposed continental shelves. These gains have to be balanced against the continental and mountain glaciations, particularly in the Northern hemisphere. Even at the most equable moments, Terrae would not have been continuously occupied. Rather, their settlement histories express hominin tolerances and preferences to climatic conditions such as temperature and its seasonal fluctuations.

inhabitants made or the shape and size of their skulls. These Terrae are, of course, a snapshot of the current state of research; their boundaries in time and space subject to alteration as new evidence accrues (Tables 1.1 and 1.2). Their purpose is to structure the deep history of a primate that travelled and changed.

Terra 0 10Ma–3.3Ma (Chapter 4 Walking down the evolutionary spine)

This is the world of the Miocene apes, such as the dryopithecines, and the diverse hominids and hominins of the Pliocene that include the australopithecines,[5] the southern apes. The Miocene (23Ma–5.3Ma) began as a period of warmer global temperature with expanded tropical forest habitats across much of the temperate Old World. Fossil apes well adapted to these forest conditions are known from many parts of Africa, southern Asia and Europe. However, after 11Ma, the trend to global cooling sees the reduction of these habitats and the expansion of grasslands.

The key issue in Terra 0 is not encephalisation but bipedalism. The evolution of upright walking marks a significant shift for hominins in habitat

[5] *Dryopithecus* is the Greek for tree ape. *Australopithecus* translates as southern (austral) ape (pithecus) following Raymond Dart's discovery of a fossil child cranium (*Australopithecus africanus*) in the Taung quarry, South Africa, in 1924.

TABLE 1.2. *Geological timescale and hominin Terrae*

Era	Period	Epoch	Division	Age (Ma)	
		Holocene			T5 <1ka
					T4 4ka
				0.01	
			Late		T3 50ka
Cenozoic				0.13	
	Quaternary	Pleistocene	Middle		
				0.78	
			Early		T2 1.8Ma
				2.558	
			Late		T1 3.3Ma
		Pliocene		3.6	
			Early		
	Neogene			5.3	
			Late		T0 10Ma
				11.6	
		Miocene	Middle		
				15.9	
			Early		
				23	

and ecology, and had major ramifications for the structure of social group-ings. There are hints that this novel, at least for the hominids, form of loco-motion takes place towards the end of the Miocene (6Ma), as indicated by the shape of a femur belonging to *Orrorin tugenensis*. In the succeed-ing Pliocene (5Ma–2.5Ma), the fossil record improves, and 4.4Ma-year-old *Ardipithecus ramidus* from Ethiopia was most certainly bipedal but still retained an arboreal adaptation. Bipedalism in the form of a preserved foot-print trail and similar-aged fossil limb bones is known for *Australopithecus afarensis* from Laetoli, Tanzania, from 3.7Ma. Interest also focuses on the transition from an ape diet of fruits and leaves to a hominin diet which includes higher-quality foods such as meat. This shift has ramifications for the size of home ranges from which food is gathered.

To date, all these bipedally competent fossils are exclusively African. However, the evidence is scant, and future discoveries throughout Terra 0 are probable for what seems to have been a highly varied phase of hominid evolution. Finally, close to the boundary with Terra 1 is the australopithe-cine child from Dikika in Ethiopia. The fossil remains come from the same sediments as cut-marked bone which may be the oldest evidence at 3.3Ma for stone tools, although the artefacts remain to be discovered.

Terra 1: 3.3Ma–1.8Ma (Chapter 4 Running down the tectonic trail)

Terra 1 is smaller than Terra 0 (Figure 1.1). Its extent is not confined to Africa alone but includes an extension through the northern Rift Valley into Southwest Asia. This link between tectonic activity and hominin distributions is not fortuitous (G. N. Bailey and King 2011). For hominins, these areas presented advantageous broken topography, while the eroding sediments allow palaeoanthropologists to search systematically for artefacts and fossils.

In the geological chronology, Terra 1 sees the transition from the Pliocene to the Pleistocene, a boundary of some precision now fixed by international convention at 2.558Ma. The significance of this change in geological epochs, and a move from the Neogene to the Quaternary period (Table 1.2), is the continuing cooling and drying trend in global climate. The first small polar ice caps appear at this time.

Terra 1 has stone artefacts. The oldest are those from Gona in Ethiopia dated to 2.5Ma (Semaw, Renne, Harris et al. 1997). However, this baseline will probably move back in time, and may already have done so at Dikika. Hominin brain volumes are now above 400 cm³, a significant threshold, since none of the living great apes, apart from the large-bodied gorilla, exceed this and neither did the Terra 0 hominids.

At least three hominin genera make the grade with attention focussing on the small-brained, less than 900 cm³, *Homo* who co-exists with the australopithecines. The distribution of their fossil remains and stone tools sets the northern limits of Terra 1.

The body size of these earliest *Homo* is large, leading to an increase in the home ranges for food. This combination of large brains and bodies requires a higher-quality diet with some meat.

Terra 2: 1.8Ma–50ka (Chapter 5 Three strides across a bio-tidal world)

The Old World frames the extent of Terra 2 settlement which lasted for almost 2Ma and is crossed in three great temporal strides: 1.8–0.8Ma, 0.8–0.2Ma and 200–50ka. Terra 2 hominins are predominantly from the genus *Homo*, accompanied up to 1.2Ma by the last of the australopithecines. Early in Terra 2, the next significant threshold in encephalisation is exceeded with brains now more than 900 cm³ in volume. Only *Homo* makes this transition, and a further threshold is passed at 600ka when hominins with large brains, more than 1200 cm³, are found.

Carnivory becomes the diet of necessity to meet the energy needs of such large-bodied, large-brained hominins. During Terra 2, a wide range of stone tools are made, indicative of some supple conceptual skills dealing with volume, symmetry and sequence. In the last stride, sets of ornaments and bone tools appear.

But for all these developments, Terra 2 is a world of contradictions and disconnects. Most importantly, there is technological stasis, and hominin settlement rigidly observes environmental boundaries. Technological change occurs, but the pace is slow. There is only limited evidence for crossing water, and none of it opens up the settlement of new continents. Settlement is rarely found above a latitude of 55°N.

However, set beside this stasis is the evidence for a big increase in encephalisation, especially after 600ka. Large-brained hominins are a feature of Terra 2. *Homo sapiens*, our direct ancestor, are just one example. In fact, they are nothing special when they first appear at least 200ka. Larger brains do not automatically lead to geographical expansion or technological innovation. This presents us with a major disconnect between simple expectation and archaeological evidence. The fuss about *Homo sapiens* as something special in hominin evolution comes much later in our story.

Terra 2 sees major changes in Pleistocene climate. These are driven by changes in the Earth's orbit and rotational tilt (Chapter 2) so that, after 1Ma, the long-term cycle between minimum and maximum environmental conditions more than doubles from 41ka to 100ka in length. These contrasted conditions are broadly described as a warm (interglacial) phase and a cold (glacial) stadial. Furthermore, as the length of a full climatic cycle doubles, so the amplitude between the warm–interglacial and cold–glacial phases becomes extremely marked. In the Northern hemisphere, glaciation is now a major factor, and as the ice sheets lock up moisture, the continental shelves in that part of the cycle are exposed. As a result, whole continents appear then disappear. In Southeast Asia, the exposure of the Sunda and China shelves amounts to four to six million km² of additional land. These are then drowned in the next interglacial phase. This pattern of inundation and exposure sets up a strong pattern of bio-tidal geography to hominin expansion; an ebb and flow to settlement that takes place on a Terra scale.

Terra 3: 50ka–4ka (Chapter 6 Going beyond, keeping in touch;
Chapter 7 The call of the north)

What happens in Terra 3 is exceptional in our evolution. In the first place, humans replace all earlier hominins throughout the former Terra 2 so that, by the end of the Pleistocene (Table 1.2), there is only one extant hominin species – *Homo sapiens*, ourselves. Previously there had always been several, often co-existing, hominin species differentiated by region and continent. Some met each other as indicated by genetic histories. However, this ancient pattern ended abruptly as humans moved from their centre of speciation in Africa to settle all of Terra 2 and displace its resident populations.

Then, second, these new humans go beyond the ancient boundaries of hominin settlement into Terra 3. Humans cross to Australia and the islands in Near Oceania. What they encounter is the continent of Sahul formed when low sea levels join up New Guinea, Australia and Tasmania. In another direction, they expand through a very different set of environments to the uninhabited interior of Siberia. This is then the springboard to the 1.5 million km² exposed continental shelf of the Bering Straits and so into the Western hemisphere. A maximum of 42 million km², or nearly thirty per cent of the Earth's land area, is now available for settlement. The people who are presented with this New World opportunity, as indeed is the case for most of the expansion of humans in Terra 3, lived at low population densities depending on fishing, gathering and hunting (FGH).

Mobility and adaptive plasticity are hallmark strategies of Terra 3 humans. Increased mobility adjusts populations to fluctuating resources spreading risk and aiding dispersal into new territory. Adaptive plasticity is reflected in our distinctive geographical phenotypes where skin colour, body shape, hair form, facial architecture and material culture all diversify extremely rapidly as our ancestors disperse.

Terra 4: 4ka–1ka (Chapter 8 Eyes on the horizon)

The landfall gains in Terra 3 are substantial but still fall short of being globally comprehensive. Only the margins of the Pacific had been touched, and the many islands and archipelagos in this 155 million km² ocean remained uninhabited. What distinguishes Terra 4 is the impact of domestic crops and animals on the process of global settlement. These people rely on what they took as their insurance policy against what they might find.

Of course, all the Pacific Islands had to be reached by boat. Some of them such as New Zealand and Hawai'i are substantial. The Indian Ocean, less than half the size of the Pacific, also had uninhabited islands ranging in size from Madagascar to the small islands of the Seychelles and Maldives chains. At a lesser scale, several of the small islands in the Mediterranean, particularly those in the Cyclades, are settled during Terra 4. Iceland in the far North Atlantic is peopled from Norway in 874 AD – another example of domestication-led dispersal.

Terra 4 is the veneer (Chapter 3) through which we see the much older Terrae. Two factors are at play: the preservation of archaeological evidence improves, and it increases exponentially. Part of this is due to the warmer, interglacial conditions of the Holocene that marks the transition from the last cold stage 11.5ka. Terra 4 also sees a massive rise in global population (Chapter 3) based on those same domestic crops and animals that fuel this phase of global settlement. Larger populations will affect the patterns of cultural transmission and diversity, and this is evident in the archaeology of Terra 4. When approaching the earlier Terrae, we have to be aware of this filtering effect and how it can distort the picture of much earlier hominins.

Terra 5: After 1400 AD (Chapter 9 The human reunion in retrospect)

Exceptionally in human history, deep or shallow (Box 1.1), there is now very little left for anyone to inhabit for the first time. From a European viewpoint, Terra 5 begins in the 1430s with Henry the Navigator of Portugal and the discovery of Terra 4 people on the Canaries, while 60 years later Columbus encountered Terra 3 settlers in the Caribbean (Fernández-Armesto 2006). The Atlantic Ocean has few islands, and most of them, like Tristan da Cunha, are extremely remote. The arrival of the colonial powers found them uninhabited: Bermuda, St Helena, Ascencion and the Azores. This is also the case in the Indian Ocean where Mauritius is a Terra 5 discovery. The uttermost ends of the earth as represented by the Antarctic islands of South Georgia, the arctic wastes of Svalbard or desolate Kerguelen in the southern Indian Ocean offer poor pickings compared to those made in Terrae 3 and 4. Instead, the history of Terra 5 is driven by the many instances of politically driven displacement and diaspora within the already settled world.

And finally, to complete this brief survey, I must add the moon landing in 1969. For all those hominins living in Terra 0 to Terra 4, the moon is always visible, unlike Tristan da Cunha in the South Atlantic. And while its pull on human imagination is as strong as the tides, it needed a completed global journey before someone set foot there.

Extended and Expanded Minds

Terrae 0–3 contain a history of expanding brain volumes, the hominin trend of encephalisation that is dealt with as an evolutionary issue in Chapter 2. But my initial concern is how do we turn brains into minds capable of flights of imagination and the complications of social life, one result of which was global settlement?

Two models are on offer. The more familiar is the pragmatic, logical mind which serves us well in Terra 5, since it underpins science, medicine and other measureable advances in health and well-being. This is the rational, thinking mind that the French philosopher and mathematician René Descartes described in the seventeenth century. Descartes established a way of thinking about the world that recognised opposites: mind–body, subject–object, nature–culture to name a few of the dualisms which have subsequently been investigated. At its most extreme, this model of the mind privileges thoughts above emotions which has unfortunate consequences, as addressed by anthropologist Godfrey Lienhardt (1985: 152), by "splitting in two the personal union of mind and body and expelling the instincts of the latter". However, despite pinpointing this analytical schizophrenia, the pragmatic, rational mind lives on. In particular, it is found in the use of computer-based similes to explain its workings as a series of modules, each dealing with different aspects of human activity. This modular approach has been widely applied by archaeologists to their evidence for the evolution of the mind (Mithen 1996).

Set against the view of a mind as a rational machine is a second, relational model that concentrates on making connections and associations in space and time. It stems from the insights of cognitive science which, summarised by George Lakoff and Mark Johnson (1999: 3), provide evidence for the following:

- that the mind is inherently embodied,
- thought is mostly unconscious, and
- abstract concepts are largely metaphorical.

These findings shape the model of the mind I use throughout this book. I view mind as *embodied* and *extending* beyond the boundary of our skin to include objects and environments (Dunbar, Gamble and Gowlett 2010a). In other words, because the mind is embodied, the dualism between brain and body is false, and the way we think is structured by the way we feel. Moreover, because the mind is extended, we have a *distributed cognition* that is not contained, as Descartes proposed, solely within the head of the individual. Rather, as philosopher Andy Clark puts it, "everything leaks" (A. Clark 1997; A. Clark and Chalmers 1998). Instead of being separate from the world, we merge with it – places, landscapes, things, material stuff and people. This starting point produces, as archaeologist Chris Gosden argues, an indivisible trinity of brain–body–world (Gosden 2010a). There are no hard-and-fast boundaries between these components. Mind is as much the tree we sit under, the glass we drink from or the neurons in our brains that appreciate a picnic. The point is that we don't need to privilege the grey matter in our skulls as something special, a mind.

Neither is distributed cognition unique to humans, as psychologists Louise Barrett and Peter Henzi (2005) show for primates. What unites the approach across species is the *social brain hypothesis* (Chapter 2) which states that large brain size in primates and hominins is selected for by social rather than simply ecological factors concerned with getting food. In other words, our social lives drove our remarkable encephalisation. Among these social factors, the size of an individual's personal network and the cognitive load of remembering, interacting and behaving appropriately towards others is seen as critical to encephalisation. Larger group size, or at least network partners, has a pay-off for any social animal in terms of reducing predator pressure which acts as the selective evolutionary force (Figure 2.10; Dunbar and Shultz 2007).

An embodied, extended mind depends for most of its operations on unconscious thought. I have discussed this at length elsewhere (Gamble 1999: ch. 3; Gamble 2007: ch. 4) making the distinction between practical and discursive consciousness and where the wider concept of *habitus*, those ingrained practices and performances of social life, loosely translated as "the feel for the game" (Bourdieu 1977), summarises the position. The essential point is that much of what we do is done unthinkingly. This makes sense. If we had to think consciously about every step we take in order to walk, or every motion of our mouths to chew our food, we would implode under cognitive overload. In his short story *Funes the Memorious*, the author Jorge Luis Borges (1964) considers that if we remembered everything we perceive, every leaf on the tree, every smell from the garden, we would cease to be human. Rather, as he puts it, "to think is to forget differences, generalise, make abstractions".

The final finding of cognitive science that abstract thought is largely metaphorical follows from Borges' point about making abstractions. Metaphors are based on experience. They have three sources: linguistic, musical and material. The first is the most familiar, as in the everyday phrases, "I'm feeling a bit *low* today" or "I'm *in* a good mood", which make sense as metaphors because they refer to our bodily experience of being down and enclosed (Lakoff and Johnson 1980, 1999). By contrast, musical metaphors are highly complex and slippery to define. They have emotional resonance and are described by Claude Lévi-Strauss (Leach 1970: 115) as "being at once intelligible and untranslatable". Music certainly channels our moods in ways that defy a rational explanation but which are understandable as an embodied response.

Material metaphors are less well appreciated (Tilley 1999) but of much greater antiquity than those drawn from either language or music. As we shall see, in the beginning was the object, not the word or the note. I recognise two major sets of material metaphors: implements and containers (Gamble 2007). The former, such as spears and pens, are extensions of our limbs and digits. They change the shape of our arms and hands, and we experience them through these parts of our bodies by holding and touching. Instruments are the oldest artefacts from Terra 1 and, according to William McGrew (1992), make up the entire inventory in chimpanzee technology. Containers are the other large set of material metaphors. Here, the experience is of being enclosed, as in a house or car, or wrapped in clothes. Indeed, wrapping forms a major activity in our cultural worlds, whether it is preparing a Christmas present or enveloping us in collective meanings, both literally in the case of tattoos or jewellery and conceptually with kinship categories and codes of politeness (Hendry 1993). Containers serve as keeping devices in the form of memory boxes and safe places (Hoskins 1998). We derive comfort from their contents and from the experience of well-being that comes from our relationship with well-kept things (Miller 2008).

Containers become important during the third stride of Terra 2, and dominate our material metaphors in Terra 3. One example for global settlement will suffice here – the boat. It was a necessary container to reach Australia 50ka because open water had to be crossed. But the existence of boats was not a sufficient reason for dispersal to take place, as indicated by the much later Terra 4 settlement of Madagascar. It was how they fitted into imaginative concepts such as society that mattered.

Expanding the Mind by Giving it Face

With a model of the mind that is both embodied and extended, we now see that an expanded mind is not simply an outcome of encephalisation, the increase in brain volume, but also of the multiplication of material stuff by which it is extended. This leads us to the sheer scale and variety of the material evidence of the past, let alone the present. We seem to be drowning in the magnitude of our own historical archives (Box 1.1), and yet archaeologists can still make sense of such quantity in terms of spatial and temporal patterns. We have, like Borges, become adept at forgetting in order to classify with the aim of understanding.

The approach I take to the highly structured variety of the past is to examine it as part of the material basis of changing hominin identities (Gamble 2007). Here, I want to replay that argument from the perspective of extended mind/distributed cognition and re-examine the four social practices I previously identified as responsible for the structure in archaeological evidence. These practices are Fragmentation, Accumulation, Consumption and Enchainment, or FACE for short. We construct our identities through close engagement with stuff, artefacts and materials. This cultural stuff is arranged through the four FACE practices into patterned sets and nets of objects that give archaeological evidence its familiar and repeated forms. These patterns are robust in time and space and allow the archaeologist to investigate deep human history. The point about FACE and the extended mind lies in the metaphorical, experiential basis of these practices.

For example, *fragmentation*, as archaeologist John Chapman has shown, employs the metaphorical forms of metonymy and synecdoche where part stands for whole as in a medieval reliquary, an *ex voto* seeking healing or your passport photo (Chapman 2000; Chapman and Gaydarska 2007, 2010). Once fragmented, the opportunity then exists to link, or *enchain*, people through the distribution of those parts, yet at the same time retaining a sense of the whole spread now more widely over space as well as time. *Accumulation* allows similar and dissimilar materials to be drawn together and kept, while *consumption* establishes hominin desire as a motor for the circulation and accumulation of people and stuff. These four principles, when applied to material metaphors, underpin the structure that archaeologists describe from the archives of the past.

A Route Map for Big-Brained Global Humans

If the theme of global settlement needs its cartography (Figure 1.1), so too does encephalisation. A simple route map with five components is presented in Figure 1.2, while in Figure 1.3 a summary of encephalisation in deep human history is provided. Later chapters will explore the evidence for both brain size and cognitive concepts.

My interest here is with the components of the social brain hypothesis that I have already mentioned and will discuss further in Chapter 2. Each of these will be briefly discussed following the linear direction indicated on the route map.

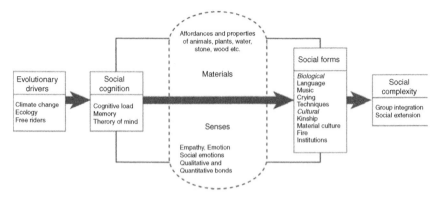

FIGURE 1.2. The social brain route map. The map emphasises the core of materials and senses that form the basis for creating social bonds. This core is under selection from a variety of evolutionary drivers and cognitive constraints. The outcomes, shown here as social forms, are often an amplification of existing cultural and biological features. These provide a qualitative measure of increasing social complexity, as understood through solutions to cognitive constraints. Adapted from Gamble et al. (2011).

Evolutionary Drivers

Underlying all evolutionary drivers is the Darwinian principle of reproductive advantage which operates at the population level. Ecologists describe a population whose numbers increase at a fast rate as being under *r selection*. Humans have this capacity, as reflected in population pyramids that show massive infant mortality and successively fewer individuals in the older age cohorts. This pattern typically occurs in today's Global South and previously in the developing world of Europe and North America in the nineteenth century. But humans are more typically a *K selected* species where the numbers of offspring are reduced and investment is made to get them through to reproductive age.[6]

Which evolutionary strategy is adopted depends on a range of circumstances conditioned by socioecology and sociobiology – respectively, the ecological and biological basis for patterns of social organisation. Some factors remain constant. Among all primates, and indeed social mammals generally, the costs of child bearing and rearing are asymmetrically distributed between males and females. Females bear most of those costs which they mitigate through bonding with other females, especially grandmothers (O'Connell, Hawkes and Blurton Jones 1999) and involving males in the

---

[6] *r* selection is density independent, while *K* strategies are density dependent, usually reflected in population levels levelling out at the carrying capacity set by the environment.

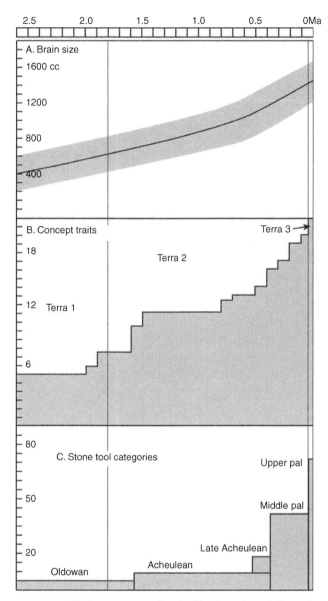

FIGURE 1.3. Brains, concepts and tools. The three charts indicate the changes in complexity from the hominin record for encephalisation (A), the archaeological evidence for technological concepts (B) and the changes in the number of stone tool categories (C). Gowlett (2009) identifies twenty-four concept traits which include tool making, imposing long-axis symmetry, woodworking, fire and burials. Note the shift in brain size at 0.6Ma and the lag in concepts, categories and global settlement that begins in Terra 3.

provisioning and protection of their children. This asymmetry accounts for the primate pattern where the distribution of food resources determines where the females and offspring will be because this gives their offspring survival advantage (Foley and Gamble 2009). Where the males are found is then determined by the location of the females. At some time during human evolution, some hominins broke with this ancestral pattern (Figure 3.10). Males came to control resources and hence the reproductive potential of females. Examples from the modern world abound: the flocks owned by the male shepherd, the granaries of food protected by male farmers even though the crops might have been sown and harvested by female labour. When this fundamental shift in location and access to key food resources occurred will be examined in later chapters.

These evolutionary drivers underpin Gowlett's evolutionary triangle of diet change, detailed environmental knowledge and social collaboration. Bigger brains require higher-quality foods, while larger bodies and larger groups need bigger home ranges. Indeed, a strong relationship can be demonstrated between individual and group body mass and the size of home ranges from which their food comes (Figure 4.3). For comparative purposes, these diets can be compared to those of apes who eat mainly fruit, leaves and nuts, and with those that include ever larger amounts of animal protein. These variable home ranges and their extension under the pressures of encephalisation, group size and dietary needs are the building blocks for geographical dispersal, and I will use them in particular to examine the hominins who lived in Terrae 0–3.

Reproductive advantage, measured by the differential contribution of offspring to the next generation, is also essential in accounting for dispersal into new territories. When considering dispersal, this reproductive motor is usually described in terms of risk. In evolutionary terms, such risk management is described as the failure to meet dietary needs or suffering unacceptable death rates while moving from one habitat to another. For example, when the risk of moving to a new habitat is outweighed by the benefits, then movement is more likely to take place. Risk can be reduced by better information or advances in technology and their transmission within and between generations. Home range size, which depends on the quality of the diet needed by large-size/large-brained hominins, now becomes an important factor in calculating the risk of dispersal.

But there are other evolutionary drivers that apply to the benefits of social collaboration and larger groupings. Responding to predator pressure is one example, while another is punishing society's free riders – those who try to get something for nothing – and where the coordinated sanction of the group is vital to prevent atomisation. And as we will see in the next chapter, climate change and changing ecology also present selection pressures to adapt and change.

These evolutionary drivers can usefully be extended to the demography of populations and where variable density of population sets up different conditions for the transmission of knowledge between individuals. As archaeologist Stephen Shennan (2001) has argued, when population size is small, copying the technology of others invariably leads to the retention of deleterious traits. However, when populations are larger, the advantages of innovation are enhanced because the unwanted effects decline proportionately. This model will be explored in Chapter 3.

Social Cognition

The cognitive processes that underpin our social behaviour have received much attention but little consensus. As explained by psychologist Edwin Hutchins (1995), at issue is the model of the mind: should it be internal or external? The former he labels the "official" history of cognitive science, the one inherited from Descartes. The latter, which he champions, starts from the position that the architecture of cognition, what allows us to cognise, is both internal and external to the individual. To label cognition as *social cognition* recognises the external context (Gamble 2010b).

Earlier, I defined the mind as extended and cognition as distributed. To understand how this capacity evolved, I concentrate here on three concepts. The first is the notion of cognitive load where much larger personal network and group sizes pose a challenge to our cognitive ability to handle and process information. Without such an ability, groups fragment rather than collaborate. As the number of network partners increases for an individual, so the potential amount of information to manage them grows exponentially (Table 2.9). The time available to service relationships starts to become a key issue, and other ways have to be found to cope, or the benefits of larger group sizes, those evolutionary drivers, will not be realised.

Memory, the second concept, is therefore important to social cognition. The evolution of long-term and working memory has been set out by archaeologist Thomas Wynn and psychologist Frederick Coolidge (Wynn 2002; Wynn and Coolidge 2004). For a recent hominin, Neanderthal, they conclude that, on the basis of their technology, Neanderthals relied heavily on their long-term rather than short-term or working memory. They had working memory but with a lower capacity than ours. This distinction in a key cognitive skill surfaced in their reduced attention capacity, as shown by the number of steps involved in making tools.

However, memory is not just a property of the neurons in the brain. In an extended mind, it is also inherent in the artefacts and environments that, as we saw earlier, constitute a social cognition. Neither is human memory necessarily enhanced, as some have argued (Renfrew and Scarre 1998), by developing forms of external storage where information is offloaded from the brain into symbols, texts and digital archives (Box 1.1). Such a situation would return us to a Cartesian model of the mind which creates artificial separations between thought and objects, brains and bodies. Instead, memory, like mind itself, is an extended aspect of our distributed, social cognition. It is indisputable that new archives have been created at different moments during hominin and human evolution (Box 1.1). But these illustrate the process of amplification that characterises an extended mind rather than an internal reorganisation of the brain as something separate from an overarching distributed cognition.

The third element of social cognition is theory of mind – that ability for mentalising that acknowledges that another person views the world from their perspective rather than yours. Children make this leap at about the age of four. Chimpanzees might, but the jury is out (F. de Waal 2006). Having a theory of mind goes well beyond the self-awareness that other animals do possess. It addresses others' beliefs and desires and how these can be accessed. Theory of mind can also be expressed in terms of the levels of intentionality attributed to a social activity (Chapter 2). These build narrative chains by ascribing intentions to the ancestors, gods and objects as well as the living. "Alice *believed* Mary who *maintained* that Guy *thought* he had been *cursed* by his dead father's spirit that was *determined* to revenge the violation of his burial by the bulldozer his father had *meant* Peter, his uncle, to hire". Such mental gymnastics are a part of our imaginative repertoire, and in this example, six levels of intentionality are displayed in italics. In one brief sentence, we deal with personal networks (Alice, Mary, Peter and Guy), add to that a dead ancestor (Guy and Peter's father), an object (the bulldozer) and the property attributed to a person (the spirit), and all made possible because of the theory of mind that underpins our social cognition (Table 1.3).

Theory of mind is an old concept. As long ago as 1759, the philosopher Adam Smith argued in *The Theory of Moral Sentiments* that imagination is the key to sympathy: "We have no immediate experience of what other men feel … By the imagination we place ourselves in his situation " (I.I.2).

TABLE 1.3. *Four levels of intentionality in theory of mind (adapted from Cole 2008, with permission).*

Level 1	Level 2	Level 3	Level 4
Ego is self-aware	Ego recognises another person's belief states as similar/different to theirs	Ego wants another person to recognise Ego's own belief state	Ego believes that the group understands that another person recognises Ego's own belief states
Dave (the re-enactor) *believes* he is a Crusader	Dave *believes* that Ben (a fellow re-enactor) *thinks* he is a Crusader	Dave *desires* that Ben *believe* that Dave *thinks* he is a Crusader	Dave *knows* that the re-enactment group is *aware* that Ben *believes* that Dave *thinks* he is a Crusader

In this example, the use of costume, weaponry and mannerisms would all act to support Dave's intentions, and indeed without such externalism, the different belief states at Level 2 could not be achieved.

Core, Materials and Senses

At the core of the route map of our social brain are two resources: the *senses* with which we perceive and relate to the world, and the *materials* which we engage with and transform. These two elements form the core because they are the resources from which all the many varieties of hominin society, and the six Terrae, are created. They lie at the heart of all hominin and human experience. We negotiate social outcomes by drawing on the experiences of our senses to forge and reproduce social bonds and ties. These bonds vary in intensity and duration, a variety that reflects their significance to us. For example, the most fundamental of dyads, a mother and child, is above all else an emotional, sensory bond, the strength of the tie commensurate with the evolutionary importance of the investment. Casual acquaintances, who might help us in a current activity, need far less emotional commitment, and here the bond might be symbolised by the materials which form the basis of the collaboration (Gamble 1999).

Importantly, both resources are available for *amplification*. The senses can be deliberately heightened, and I will examine a few examples below under social forms. Materials can also be turned to many uses, their affordances and associations made more complex both symbolically and metaphorically. As a result, it is around this core of materials and senses that we

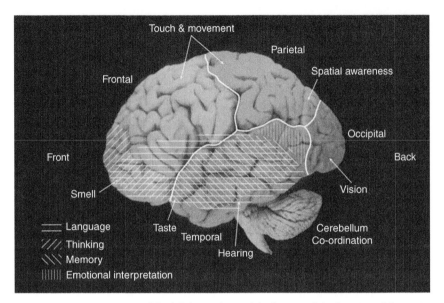

FIGURE 1.4. A map of the left hemisphere of the brain and the location of the major functions in the neocortex.

scaffold our social lives. As the evolutionary drivers select for change in the structure of our social cognition, so the responses are translated through these fundamental resources that are embodied and distributed. The outcomes are new social forms and social complexity.

The dramatic growth in hominin brains is another example of amplification under selective pressure for change. The major difference between the small ape brain and our own large brain is concentrated at the front of the neocortex. The frontal lobes have expanded greatly, and this process is recorded in fossil skulls which show how the brain gradually filled out behind the protective brow ridges and rose above them to create the distinctive human forehead. How this was achieved is the result of differential growth factors described by the process of neoteny, the retention of juvenile features. Human heads and faces are those of young chimpanzees. The large teeth, protruding faces and low foreheads of adult chimpanzees represent the ancestral growth pattern that we have broken with.

A simple geography of the brain is shown in Figure 1.4. The four lobes – frontal, parietal, occipital and temporal that together make up the *neocortex* – are the areas which during hominin evolution see major expansion, while the cerebellum, or little brain, is inherited from a pre-mammalian past although modified subsequently (Weaver 2005).

TABLE 1.4. *Mood, primary and social emotions.*

Social emotions (theory of mind)			
	Shame and guilt (about consequences to self)		Shame and guilt (at self)
Primary emotions (adaptive value)			
	Satisfaction – happiness	Aversion – fear	Assertion – anger	Disappointment – sadness
High intensity	Joy	Terror	Loathing	Sorrow
Medium intensity	Cheerful	Anxiety	Displeased	Gloomy
Low intensity	Serenity	Hesitant	Irritated	Downcast
Mood emotions (affective signals)			
	Calm, safety	Creepy	Friction, tense	Bad vibes

The examples chosen point to the amplification of feelings that are expressed as increasingly complex moods and emotions. How primary emotions vary follows Turner (2000) where the changing descriptions illustrate the process of amplification. However, the point is not to develop a typology of emotions but to indicate the range and nuance of human and hominin emotions that are available for constructing ever more complex social ties.

The technical revolution in imaging techniques has been largely responsible for reintroducing emotion to the study of cognition in the brain. The location of the five senses in the four lobes has been known for many years. But now the advent of magnetic resonance imaging (MRI) traces the neural connections in the lobes between activities such as thinking and language (C. Frith 2007; Figure 1.4). Hearing is controlled through the temporal lobe, while vision is situated in the occipital lobe at the back of the brain. Furthermore, the two halves of the cerebrum are asymmetrical, and functions differ between the right and left hemispheres (LeDoux 1998). For example, the left temporal lobe assists verbal memory, while its right counterpart facilitates visual memory.

The conversion of the senses into what we call *emotions* is a complex process, difficult to define. However, emotions can be usefully divided into three components (Table 1.4). There are mood emotions that provide an affect that comes from living with objects and the feelings about particular places as safe, dangerous or creepy. Then there are primary emotions, for example fear, disgust, happiness and anger, which all animals have because they have obvious survival value as well as being basic to all social interaction. Then, lastly, there are the social emotions such as pride, gratitude, shame and guilt. These are more complex, and only humans among today's primates possess them. The reason for this judgement is that social emotions can only be felt by recognising another's point of view. In other words, someone has beliefs which might differ from yours and which indicate a theory of mind.

Human interaction, even in the climate of texting and social messaging, remains, at heart, an emotional act between small numbers of individuals (Chapter 2). What hominins have developed are ways to ramp up the emotional signal, the process of amplification. For example, singing in a band or a choir amplifies the emotional content of such social activity. In the same way, dancing, team sports, walking clubs or laughing as the member of an audience all strengthen social ties in positive ways. The sociologist Emile Durkheim (1912/1915) stressed the importance of collective action that produced the social benefit of *effervescence*. In other words, people enjoy participating in a group's activities whether a game, performance, ritual or ceremony. Such participation can be measured by psychotropic responses (Smail 2008), the chemical basis for that feel-good factor, and where activity results in opioid surges that reward the brain.

The second resource is the *materials* that hominins use to intensify and extend social bonds. These are the raw materials of wood, stone, water, earth, flesh and many more. These were transformed into many types of foods, artefacts and tools. But animals as varied as chimpanzees and New Caledonian crows also show a capacity for tool making. The hominin innovation was, however, to transfer emotions to objects. These may be treasured possessions kept safe in a memory box. They may be the strong bonds we make with family pets. It can be pride in a well-crafted spear. These materials have aesthetic properties that appeal to our senses – touch, taste, smell and with a pleasing look. These materials are not only turned into better spears to kill more animals more efficiently, they are also examples of a social technology due to the emotional response they engender.

Anthropologist Howard Morphy found just such an aesthetic appreciation of stone by the traditional owners of quarries in Arnhem Land, North Australia (Brumm 2004; Morphy 1989). The owners referred to the sparkling quality of freshly knapped quartzite as *bir'yun*, best translated as brilliance, and this is a property shared with other powerful and dangerous substances such as blood.

Amplification of materials takes many forms. Making tools composed of different materials is one example. Accumulating sets of similar materials such as dressed stones or mud bricks to make houses or pyramids is another. Enchaining, or linking, people by distributing items such as polished axes or shell beads over great distances is a further example. In all instances, amplification is achieved through the diversity and quantity of what has been fragmented, accumulated, enchained and consumed. These are examples of the FACE of the extended mind, a set of common social practices that has the potential to amplify social engagement and interaction using materials and the senses.

Social Forms

For the archaeologist, the most visible aspects of the social brain route map are the social forms. These are the outputs, the adaptive changes, to those evolutionary drivers that pass through the filter of social cognition. They can be divided into two broad categories – biological and cultural – and an example of each is provided here. Many more will follow.

On the biological side, I single out crying and social laughter, partly because they can be closely associated, but more importantly because they are traits unique to humans. Animals do not cry. Neither do they laugh at jokes. Many jokes depend on a theory of mind whether it relates to a slapstick moment, such as a walker so engrossed in texting they are about to collide with a lamp post, or to the bartender who asks his next customer, a horse, "Why the long face?". Laughter can be private, but it is commonly public. As a social form, it leads to the release of opioid surges, the brain's chemical reward system. Laughing together is another form of Durkheim's effervescence comparable to singing and dancing.

What unites laughter and crying is the heightened emotion they achieve in acts of empathy and sympathy. We look at distressing photographs or the memorabilia of an absent loved one and tears can flow. This is due to the amplified basis of our mirror neuron systems – those parts of the brain that respond to what we see, hear and smell as though it was happening to us directly (Freedberg and Gallese 2007). Hence, we can see an image of torture and *feel* another's pain. The fact that we shed tears or laugh out loud is a result of our capacity to amplify this ability to empathise. As a result, we increase the emotional means to make social bonds bind.

Kinship is an example of a cultural form that evolved. At one level, human kinship categories are nothing more than the genetic imperative of recognising close kin and cooperating with them to maximise an individual's Darwinian fitness. This makes socio-biological sense. But it is not the whole story, as anthropologist Dwight Read (2010) has argued. In his scheme, the major evolutionary shift was from a system based on the experience of what happens when individuals interact to one that recognises roles within a relational structure. For example, chimpanzee society has significant social categories such as aggressive males. Outcomes are uncertain for those interacting with them. By contrast, interaction in a human kinship system becomes a matter of social trust prescribed by categories that are not necessarily based on force. Outcomes are more predictable because they are now constrained by moral obligations, for example the requirement of offering hospitality.

Alan Barnard (2011) traces a different historical route with his principle of *universal kinship* that is particularly evident in the small-scale societies that anthropologists study. In such instances, every member of society, genetically related or not, stands in a kin relationship to everyone else. In Barnard's view, this was the original pattern. As a result, a relational form of kinship came first in human history and was then elaborated following the advent of agriculture and the steep rise in population which accompanied it.

Previously, I have argued that the appearance of many artefacts using the container concept late in Terra 2, and dominating Terra 3, is evidence for the appearance of kinship (Gamble 2008). What kinship does is contain and constrain as do nets, baskets, houses and boats, the last as essential for a globe-settling primate as the ability to relate to others would have been. These three scenarios for the history of a social form as basic as human kinship all stress the potential for amplification and change.

Social Complexity

Students of the social brain spend a great deal of time investigating group and personal network size. Essentially, they are exploring complexity, the final leg of the route map (Dunbar, Gamble and Gowlett 2010a, 2010b). As previously mentioned, social complexity can be measured by the increasing scale and cognitive load associated with rising network size. Integrating the members of a group into an effective social unit is time-consuming and hence expensive.

In this regard, effervescence is more than just getting a high from group activity. Durkheim (1912/1915: 29) also stressed the immense cooperation that was needed to produce and maintain the collective representations of society and how this stretched our imaginations in time and space so that the social spirit of the place continued long after the gathering had dissolved.

What humans have done is increase social complexity by extending it through time and across places. We are able to *go beyond* the physical presence of interaction that constrains the primates and so achieve a release from social proximity (Gamble 1998; Rodseth, Wrangham, Harrigan et al. 1991). We stretch social relations *in absentia* through materials linked to the senses and by emotions coupled to objects and cultural forms. We hear a voice in our heads even though we know no one can see us. We can still break the rules, but the important point is that we make that choice through a theory of mind projected over limitless distance and both forward and back in time.

Social extension harnesses the use of the imagination. Two examples will suffice. *Keeping* and *kinshipping* are two concepts that describe the human capacity to go beyond and create imaginary geographies (Said 1978). Keeping not only implies storage for the future but also a sense of possession and control, knowledge about the hidden and a world of secrets. Kinshipping (Shryock, Trautmann and Gamble 2011) describes the human ability to construct relations that are not based on genetic kinship but which nonetheless, as Barnard (2011) argues, allow people to move freely between non-related groups (Shryock, Trautmann and Gamble 2011).[7] The upshot is that social life no longer has to be a face-to-face experience nor one based on genetic imperatives alone.

Thanks to kinshipping, we engage imaginatively and routinely with supernatural beings and ancestors, some of whom ruled the living even though they were dead, like the mummified Incas, or were never alive, like the stones of Stonehenge. To achieve this extension of the social world across space and through time, objects are invested, without thinking, with the attributes of people and in particular their ability to change and transform – in short, their agency (A. Clark 2010; Dobres and Robb 2000; Gell 1998; Knappett 2011).

The sense of extension as an example of social complexity and its material expression is captured perfectly for the Facebook generation by the Greek poet Palladas who lived in Alexandria during the fourth century AD:

> Loving the rituals that keep men close,
> Nature created means for friends apart:
> Pen, paper, ink, the alphabet,
> Signs for the distant and disconsolate heart.[8]

---

[7] Sometimes described as fictive kinship, the point is the ability to create relations outside the genetic pool by using shared concepts.
[8] Translated by Tony Harrison and appearing as a Poem on the London Underground in 2011.

Questions for Deep History

Historian Daniel Smail (2008) has argued that neuro-history provides a compelling narrative for a common deep human history. It offers a welcome alternative to the accounts of the recent emergence of our nation states. I agree, and this allows me to ask if changing brains and global settlement were linked in some way. And if not, why not?

But how can we infer such historical effects from archaeological evidence? We might reasonably expect that increases in brain size, and by inference capacity and potential, should be matched by global expansion. If that were the case, then changes in technology, the stuff that survives so abundantly, should act as a proxy for such potential. Surely there must be a link between encephalisation and technological complexity that made the global getting there both possible and easier? Otherwise, what, from an evolutionary perspective, was the point in enlarging such a costly organ as the brain? Bigger brains, global geography and better stuff should, pragmatically, march together in deep time.

But the problems start at once. Other mammals, including the carnivores (e.g. wolves, lions, leopards and hyenas) and the omnivores (among them bears, pigs, rats and macaques), have achieved impressive distributions, while many herbivores, such as deer, antelopes, elephants and horses, are similarly widespread between major continents and hemispheres. And to this geographical spread, we need to add the extensive migratory patterns of birds, moths, butterflies and marine mammals. Yet none of these animals are encephalised in the way that hominins were before 50ka when their continental range remained fixed while their brains grew. So why should bigger brains and global settlement be linked? Was the latter an unintended consequence of the former? Or did the pressure to disperse partly drive the process of encephalisation?

A brief glimpse at the archaeological evidence instantly points to two disconnects in our deep history. The first saw significant brain growth between 2Ma and 200ka. Yet for much of this period, stone technology stood still, as did global settlement (Chapter 5). A disconnect between expectation and archaeological data is particularly evident in the period 600ka to 300ka.

The second disconnect, named by archaeologist Colin Renfrew (1996) as *the sapient paradox*, occurs with the appearance of people 200ka who looked like us and shared our history-tracing genes. Yet according to his interpretation, they did not realise their human potential until 13ka when plants and then animals were domesticated and settled life appeared.

Renfrew's paradox contrasts the cranial architecture for modern cognitive capacity with the lack of any cultural evidence to indicate that people immediately organised themselves and their worlds in a modern way. In other words, they delayed becoming like us.

I mention these disconnects to allay any fears that what follows will be a simple history of in-step changes. The workings of the evolutionary process were not on a mission to make us like ourselves in the shortest possible time. Evolution is blind to future desires, and teleology is bad history. With that in mind, we can now turn to the environmental context for change and the evolutionary drivers of climate and tectonics.

CHAPTER 2

The drivers of climate and environment: Terrae 0–2, 10Ma–50ka

> *We could not understand because we were too far*
> *and could not remember, because we were travelling*
> *in the night of first ages, of those ages that are gone,*
> *leaving hardly a sign – and no memories...*
> *The mind of man is capable of anything – because*
> *everything is in it, all the past as well as all the future*
> Joseph Conrad, *Heart of Darkness*, 1902

Climate and Brains

At the heart of unravelling the complexities of long-term climate change lies a simple concept: climate is cyclical. The concept draws its inspiration from the marked seasons of wet and dry in the tropical monsoon belts and the contrasts between winter and summer in more northerly latitudes. It establishes an agricultural calendar with times of scarcity and plenty and a timetable for planting, harvesting and moving flocks to fresh pastures. What happens from year to year and decade to decade is a matter of weather. These variable conditions never alter the cyclical pattern but do affect the outputs. Weather marks the difference between famine and feast.

This agricultural concept has been applied to the long-term climates of Terrae 1 and 2 where cycles had a frequency of up to 400ka years. A full cycle moves from predominantly cold conditions through to warmer climates; the classic pattern of glacial to interglacial. This stemmed from the demonstration by geologist Louis Agassiz in the middle of the nineteenth century that extensive glaciations once existed in the agricultural heartlands of Europe and North America. Now the date of 1.8Ma sees the first significant glaciations in the Northern hemisphere. It also marks the boundary between Terrae 1 and 2.

The agricultural metaphor lingers on, even though it is far removed from the first farming late in Terra 3. What persists is a sense that warm climate is good and cold bad. Cold climates, the concept states, lead to extinction and the contraction of global population into settlement refugia where people will sit out this phase of the climate cycle, expanding when the warmth returns. Moreover, this ebb and flow of population at a continental and global scale provides deep history with a motive power. For example, an innovation that occurs in the refuge phase can be exported more widely when climate allows.

In the first part of this chapter, I will explore the modern synthesis of long-term climate change for Terrae 0–2. I will argue that the cold–warm dichotomy is ripe for replacement; not only is it an inappropriate example of agricultural thinking applied to deep history, but it also fails to provide an understanding of how climate contributes to hominin evolution. That climate changed is undeniable. That these changes had an effect on hominins is a reasonable hypothesis. But rather than asserting the fact of change, warm to cold, it is the long-term variability resulting from those changes that provides the current frontier for examining the hominin–climate link.

The second part of the chapter examines the technology and mobility associated with dispersal and sets out some of the terminology used by archaeologists and biologists. I also look in greater detail at the social brain hypothesis: that our social lives drove brain growth. The expense of encephalisation has to be considered, as well as the constraints on hominins such as time available for interaction.

Much happened in these first three Terrae: the appearance of the early hominin pattern of bipedalism, large brains, extended life histories, complex social cognition and the amplification of technology. My question is simple: did climate promote these changes?

The Drivers of Change: Orbital and Tectonic Forcing

The catalysts for change in Terrae 0–2 were twofold: the impact of changes in the Earth's orbit, and tectonic activity at low and mid-latitudes. The impacts of these two processes are felt on climate cycles that in turn influence global productivity and the changing distribution

of major habitat types; for example, the repeated expansion and contraction of tropical rainforests and savannahs and the extent of cold
and hot deserts. These fluctuating patterns of variability in the climate
cycles provide a potentially strong form of long-term selection on hominin physiology and behaviour. On a local scale, these changes affect
the distribution of resources and require mobility to adjust settlement
accordingly.

Measuring cause and effect on a timescale from 10Ma to 50ka will never
be easy. However, in terms of global expansion, the earlier pattern of hominin distribution in Terrae 0–2 can be judged against a series of environmental constraints that had to be surpassed by physical, cognitive, social
and cultural adaptations. Among these checks was the ability, rather than
the desire, to cross oceans, to live at altitude and cope with reduced ultraviolet levels; in short to increase versatility, to become more plastic and
adaptable.

A Cooler Earth

Throughout Terra 0, the trend was towards global cooling that had repercussions for the habitats of the Miocene apes (Elton 2008). This trajectory
is accentuated in Terra 1, as revealed by a series of proxy data for temperature and aridity (Figure 2.1).

When reconstructions of major Old World habitats are compared
(Figure 2.2) between the Pliocene (5Ma) in Terra 0 and a recent interglacial (130ka) in Terra 2, what is apparent is the expansion at this time of the
mid-latitude arid belts, such as the Sahara and Arabian deserts, and the
southward extension of the northern boreal forests. Both changes in habitat
distribution point to lower global temperatures.

The evidence comes from the analysis of oxygen isotopes absorbed by
the skeletons of microscopic marine creatures (Box 2.1). These are incorporated in ocean sediments and recovered in deep-sea cores (Figure 2.1).
These data provide a continuous record of past climate change and typically form wiggle curves of fluctuating isotope values. These curves point
to long-term trends and variation: not only a decline in global temperature
but also an increase in the amplitude of the climate cycles over time and
hence their impact on global habitats and ecosystems. The reconstruction of recent glacial and interglacial habitats in Figure 2.2 illustrates the
differences.

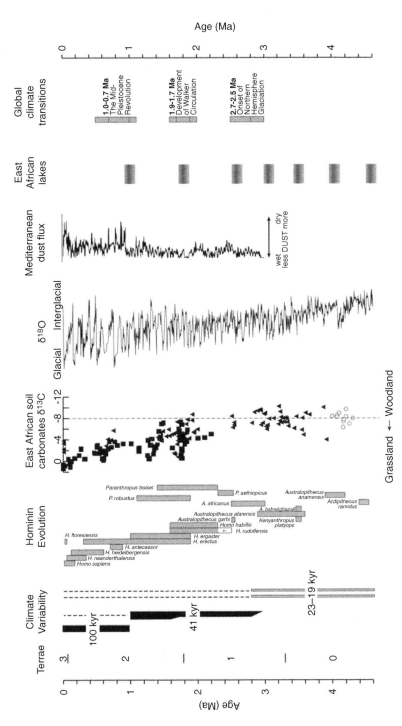

FIGURE 2.1. The lines of evidence that point to colder and drier conditions (soil carbonates, ice volume, dust and lakes) during the last 4Ma. These changes were also accompanied by greater amplitude in the highs and lows of climate and the increasingly longer duration for the cycles. The pattern of hominin evolution is shown, as well as three significant global climate transitions. The positions of Terrae 0–2 are shown when the hominin bauplan evolved (Chapters 4 and 5). Adapted from deMenocal (2004) and Trauth et al. (2009).

35

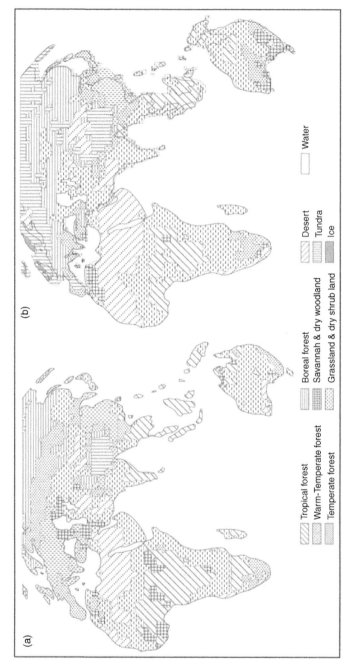

FIGURE 2.2. The vegetation of the Old World (a) during the Pliocene, a warm phase with high sea levels in Terrae 0–1, and (b) in a glacial, low sea-level phase during Terra 2. Note the differences in the size of the mid-latitude deserts, temperate forests and the appearance of dry land on the continental shelves in (b). Adapted from Elton (2008).

Box 2.1. Pleistocene climate curves

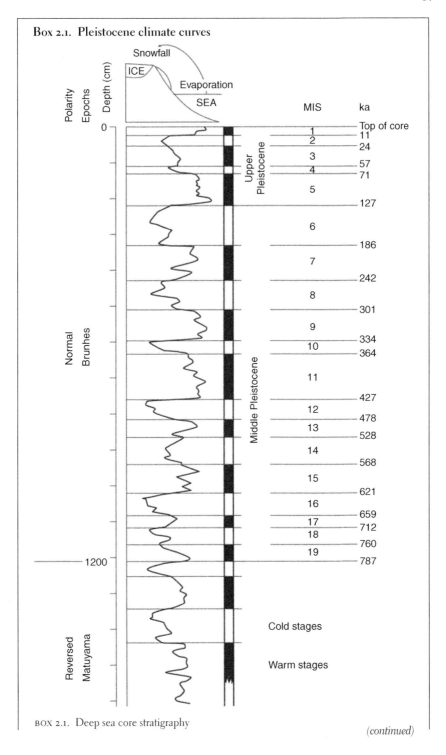

BOX 2.1. Deep sea core stratigraphy

(continued)

Box 2.1. *(continued)*

The variation in ^{18}O and ^{16}O can be measured in the skeletons of forami-nifera, and these provide a proxy for the relative sizes of the oceans and ice caps. When extracted from the sediments into which these marine organisms have been incorporated, it is possible to build up a wiggle curve of changing values through the Pleistocene. Moreover, because these isotopic values are dealing with the global balance of ice and sea, it does not matter, for the general picture, where the core is taken. It is also an experiment in climate change that can be, and has been, repeated many times. The chronology is provided by changes in the Earth's mag-netic field, and one major reversal, the Brunhes-Matuyama, is shown here. This interglacial to glacial chronology can then be compared to the known changes in the Earth's orbit, the Milankovitch cycles, and the explanation tested that these forced climate change.

The changing curves are subdivided into Marine Isotope Stages (MIS), with the odd numbers indicating warmer, interglacial conditions, and the even numbers the cold glacial phase of a full cycle such as MIS19–18 or MIS11–10. This scheme is expanded in the Upper Pleistocene 5–2 and where MIS3 is a period of warmer interstadial conditions between the cold glacial phases of MIS4 and MIS2 which saw the Last Glacial Maximum (LGM).

The ^{18}O curve is not, however, a direct measure of temperature. Rather, it reflects the size of the world's oceans through the measurement in those microscopic marine organisms of the relative abundance of two oxygen iso-topes with different "weights": ^{18}O and ^{16}O (Maslin and Christensen 2007: fig. 8). When the oceans become smaller, they are depleted in the lighter ^{16}O isotopes, and the moisture that is drawn off goes into building continen-tal ice sheets, especially in the Northern hemisphere.

Other records, dust and soil carbonates, confirm this trend (Figure 2.1). Those same cores contain evidence for changing amounts of dust indicative of an increase in drier conditions (Trauth, Larrasoana and Mudelsee 2009). Furthermore, dust from cores taken in the mid-latitude Mediterranean emphasises that other feature from the oxygen isotope record: greater fluc-tuations through time. Similarly, the measurement of ^{13}C soil carbonates in low-latitude environments in Africa points to a long-term shift to more open grassland conditions during Terrae 1 and 2. Corresponding shifts in the abundance of forest and savannah species is therefore anticipated, and found, in the fossil record.

Milankovitch Cycles

The trends can be charted in broad outline, but what accounts for them? Astronomers have known for a long time that the three components of the Earth's orbital cycle around the sun have varied (Figure 2.3). Furthermore, they have varied at different times during the Pleistocene so that, when combined, they have affected the duration and amplitude of the cold–warm climate cycle.

The known changes in *obliquity*, *eccentricity* and *precession* are shown for one million years from the end of Terra 1 and into Terra 2. What these reveal are four dominant lengths to the climate cycle. The two longest, at 400ka and 100ka duration, are driven by the eccentricity of the Earth's orbit that stretches and shrinks around the sun. As the amount of solar radiation decreases due to distance, there will obviously be ramifications for climate. At 41ka, the obliquity cycle, its length determined by the roll of the Earth, is the most stable of all the orbital variations. The least stable is the 23ka-long precessional index that expresses the degree of wobble the Earth has around its axis. These three orbital variations are known as Milankovitch cycles after the Serbian scientist who described them (Imbrie and Imbrie 1979).[1] Their long-term linkages are shown in Figure 2.4, and the pattern is complex.

Terra 0 and the start of Terra 1 are controlled by the precessional 23ka cycle that changes after 3Ma to a pattern dominated by the effects of obliquity, which has a 41ka cycle (Figure 2.1). Then, after 1Ma during Terra 2, the 100ka cycle driven by eccentricity takes over, and with it the severe fluctuations in glacial–interglacial conditions appear (Table 2.1).

The precessional cycle is almost five times shorter than that dominated by eccentricity, and its effect on climate weaker. Even so, the first northern polar ice caps appear during this climate world at 2.5Ma, possibly as a result of either Tibetan uplift or the closure of the Panama Isthmus that provide the moisture to build them (Maslin and Christensen 2007: 455).

The doubling of the cycle length when forced by changes in obliquity has several important developments. There is the appearance at 1.8Ma of

---

[1] Milutin Milankovitch (1879–1958) was a Serbian mathematician, astronomer and geophysicist. Without the aid of computers, he worked out the changes in these three aspects of the Earth's orbit, publishing his findings between 1924 and 1941. He was not the first to suggest the link between ice ages and orbital variation, but it was his insight that glaciation was simultaneous in the Northern and Southern hemispheres which made sense of the data. For a full account see Imbrie and Imbrie (1979).

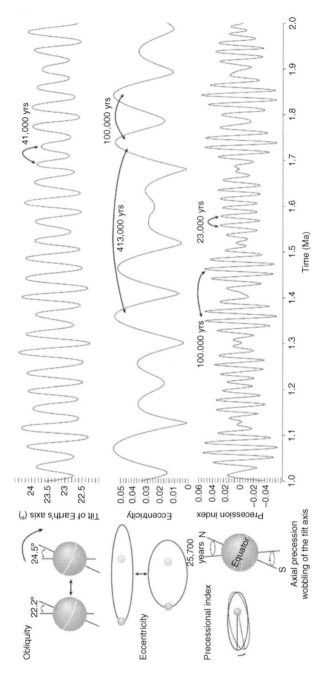

FIGURE 2.3: The changes in the tilt (obliquity), orbit (eccentricity) and rotation (precession) of the Earth during Terra 2. When combined, these factors establish the duration of the dominant signal in the climate cycle (Figure 2.4). Adapted from Kingston (2007).

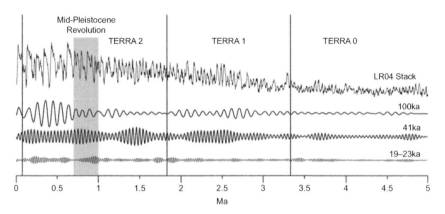

FIGURE 2.4. The stack of deep-sea cores known as LR04 and the changing patterns of eccentricity (100ka), obliquity (41ka) and precession (23ka). These indicate very different patterns of climate variability between the three Terrae 0–2. Data provided by Grove and reproduced with permission. Adapted from Lisiecki and Raymo (2005).

TABLE 2.1. *Terrae 2 and 3 and variation in the scale of Milankovitch cycles*

	Brunhes Chron	B–M boundary	Matuyama Chron
Magnetic polarity	Normal		Reversed
Terrae	2–3		2
Age range Ma	0.012–0.775		0.775–1.636
Number of glacial interglacial cycles	8		22
Dominant Milankovitch cycle	Eccentricity		Obliquity
Length of cycles			
Mean ka	96.88		40.91
Range ka	115–75		45–38
Standard deviation	13.31		2.01

The Brunhes–Matuyama boundary is a palaeomagnetic marker when the Earth's polarity switched from normal to reversed. This can be measured and dated in deep-sea cores and volcanic rocks, and provides a worldwide chronological boundary.

the first, though small, glaciations in the Northern hemisphere (Table 2.2). These increase dramatically in scale when eccentricity dominates, resulting, after 800ka in Terra 2, in eight interglacial–glacial cycles of some 100ka duration each. This is described as the mid-Pleistocene revolution in climate when the Milankovitch cycles change from 41ka to 100ka (Figure 2.1; Table 2.2; Mudelsee and Stattegger 1997).

TABLE 2.2. *Major transition points in the climates of Terrae 1 and 2*

	Variability packets	Precession driven	First and last datums for animal species	Technology	
Transitions in global climate Ma Trauth et al. 2007	deMenocal 2004	African lake phases Trauth et al. 2007	indicating a turnover pulse Vrba 1985	Gowlett 2009	
Mid-Pleistocene "Revolution" 1–0.7	1.2–0.8	1.1–0.9	c. 0.7	0.5 The 'silent' revolution	Terra 2
High-latitude, northern glaciation 1.9–1.7	1.8–1.6	1.9–1.7	1.8	1.6	
Low-latitude Walker circulation cell				Basic cultural package	Terra 1
Northern polar ice cap 2.7–2.5	2.9–2.4	2.7–2.5	2.7–2.5	2.6	

See also Figure 2.1.

The 41ka world of obliquity cycles also sees the appearance of an atmo-spheric system known as the *Walker circulation* (Trauth, Maslin, Deino et al. 2007) that describes the global balance between ocean and air temper-atures in the tropics. This east–west circulation strengthens 2Ma, possibly marking the appearance of the well-known El Niño–Southern Oscillation (ENSO) that has a major effect on the climates of East Africa in Terra 2 (Maslin and Christensen 2007).[2]

A Dry-Land Bonus

The cooling of global temperatures and the severity of the continental ice ages in Terra 2 have dominated discussion of the long-term trend in climate. However, major glaciations, while bad news for the amount of inhabitable land in northern latitudes, had a beneficial effect at low latitudes. Sea lev-els at least 100 m lower occur during large parts of the 100ka long cycles of Terra 2, revealing, worldwide, an additional 21M km^2 of land. By far the largest gains in Terra 2 are on the Sunda continental shelf that extends from Indonesia in the south to the East China Sea in the north. Here, 3.3M km^2 is revealed, an impressive sixteen per cent of the global total.

Most importantly, as Sunda lies between the equator and the Tropic of Cancer (23°N), it is a highly productive zone in terms of plant and animal productivity (Figure 2.2).[3] Reconstructions of the Sunda palaeocontinent are provided in Chapter 3 for the final part of the last cold stage.

Nowhere else in Terra 2 did global cooling result in such a productive habitat for hominin settlement. The exposed continental shelves around southern Africa and in the Arabian Gulf are small by comparison. Moreover, the exposure of the continental shelf off France and Britain is tempered by its mid-latitude position and proximity to the continental ice sheet. While this area supports substantial herds of grazing animals, it could never rival Sunda for terrestrial productivity.

Tectonics and the Geography of Speciation

The ecological importance of the Sunda region today is shown in Figure 2.5 where biodiversity hotspots are plotted. These are areas with high rates of

---

[2] Gilbert Walker was the meteorologist who, in the 1920s, defined the parameters of the cir-culation, or cell, system that is named after him. The cell model accurately predicts regular changes in ENSO pattern, and these occur across the tropics, as described in Chapter 3.
[3] The latitude of the Tropics of Cancer and Capricorn move as a result of the Earth's tilt (precession).

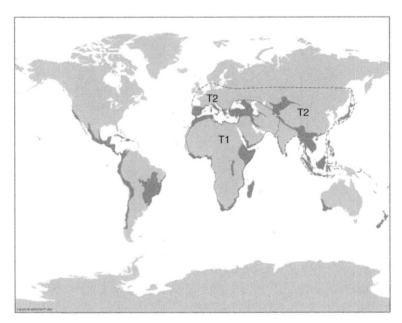

FIGURE 2.5. Biodiversity hotspots (shaded areas) of modern flora and fauna. These correspond to areas of tectonic activity and low latitudes with high primary productivity. Several of these hotspots have been the focus for investigation by palaeoanthropologists interested in Terrae 1 and 2. Adapted from Carrión et al. (2011).

endemism, as indicated by the number of unique plant and animal species. Such speciation centres are found, unsurprisingly, in the areas of highest solar energy, and these are concentrated predominantly between the Tropics.

However, that is not the full story. The biodiversity map also reveals that the mid-latitude hotspots, especially in the Northern hemisphere, are strongly associated with the second driver for change: tectonic activity. The areas of the Sunda shelf exposed today are seismically highly active, and almost forty per cent of the region's tropical rainforest lies in this zone. By contrast, only one per cent of the African rainforest lies in the tectonic zone. In Sunda, tectonic activity combined with the repeated flooding, and hence marooning, of plant and animal communities combines to create its rich biodiversity. But while biodiversity in Sunda outstrips the rainforests of Central Africa, the impact of rifting and tectonic uplift in East Africa has resulted in high rates of speciation. In the same way, the conjunction of several regional and continental plates has made the Western Mediterranean, Turkey and Southwest Asia a highly active tectonic zone, as it has outside

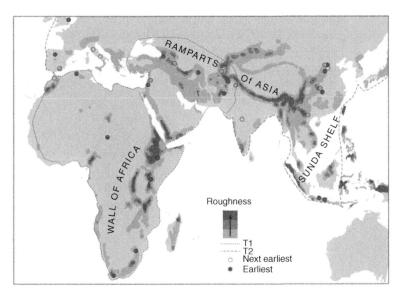

FIGURE 2.6. Tectonic activity shown as a roughness index for terrain. The earliest hominin evidence (filled and open circles) is also shown and in many cases provides a good fit to this geological model of preferred habitats. Adapted from Bailey and King (2011) and King and Bailey (2006).

Terrae 1 and 2 with Japan and New Zealand. Such conditions stimulate habitat fragmentation which, combined with the effect of climatic cycles on mid-latitude vegetation, provides the conditions for geographic, or allopatric, speciation, one condition of which is separation (Table 2.5).

The Tectonic Trail of Evolution

Tectonics provides evolution with a global spine, a tectonic trail for hominins (Figure 2.6). The Wall of Africa runs in a south–north direction for more than 6000 km, is 600 km wide and reaches heights of 5 km. The mountain ramparts of Asia extend west–east over 7000 km, with Mt Everest their highest peak at 8.8 km.

This mountainous backbone links the hotspots of biodiversity and defines a geological track. Along this trail, speciation regularly occurred, and its fossil products are readily recovered due to their exposure in sediments. For example, tectonic activity within the East African segment of the spine produced deep rifting that is essential for creating isolated lake basins, and many of these yield evidence for hominin speciation (Maslin

and Christensen 2007: 448). The tectonic trail sets up two dispersal possibilities for Terrae 1 and 2. First, it links to other seismically active regions with
high biodiversity, such as Sunda, suggesting that this should be a primary
area for dispersal. And second, the lower-biodiversity, low-tectonic regions
away from the trail, such as Northern Europe and West Africa, are potential
areas for secondary expansion.

In another context, geologist Geoff King and archaeologist Geoff
Bailey (2006) have argued that tectonic activity provides hominins with
preferred habitats for both speciation *and* subsequent dispersal. They
argue that the rough, broken topography resulting from volcanic and tectonic activity supplies the evolutionary stimulus. These are ecologically
productive areas rich in the food resources favoured by hominins. To
support their argument, they plot the earliest occurrences of hominins in
Terrae 1 and 2 (Figure 2.6) against an index of rough terrain. One aspect
of that roughness would be to isolate populations and so promote the
conditions for allopatric speciation. Broken terrain also makes it possible for palaeoanthropologists to search for, and discover, fossil remains. I
examine the archaeology of the tectonic trail and surrounding regions in
Chapters 4 and 5.

Monsoon

Tectonics have a direct impact on the global climate system through the
uplift of the Tibetan (Qinghai/Xizang) plateau and the Himalayas that
form its southern ramparts. The plateau has an average altitude of 4000 m
and covers 2.5M km^2. Moreover, these impressive altitudes were achieved
within the timescale of hominin evolution during Terrae 1 and 2. It has
been calculated that the plateau has been rising at the rate of 5 mm per
annum, and if that rate was constant, fewer than 1Ma is required to uplift it
by 4 km (Gansser 1982; Sharma 1984; Wang Chiyuen, Yaolin and Wenhu
1982).[4]

Even allowing for uncertainties in the estimates, the impact of an
uplifted Tibetan plateau on the weather systems of Asia would have been
considerable. Most significantly, tectonic uplift on this scale would realign
circulation patterns and intensify, if not create, the seasonal monsoon climate. At the same time, the tropical and subtropical vegetation belts in
China would be displaced to the south. As a result, any hominin visiting

[4] This means that in my lifetime and since Hilary and Norgay climbed Everest in 1953, the
mountain has risen by a further 30 cm.

this region at 1Ma and then again at 500ka would encounter a different landscape, climate and seasonally driven weather systems. When combined with the effects of changes in the length and scale of orbitally driven climate, which also serve to fragment and coalesce habitats, the conditions exist for allopatric speciation. These circumstances are reflected in the high biodiversity in the Himalayas and the mountains of Central Asia (Figure 2.5).

Tectonic uplift in eastern and southern Africa also impacts on atmospheric circulation (Maslin and Christensen 2007). The region sees continuous rifting and uplift throughout the Miocene, with major uplift 5Ma–2Ma (Sepulchre, Ramstein, Fluteau et al. 2006: 1420). This creates a rain shadow, and the result in East Africa is aridification. Computer simulations suggest that lowering the Wall of Africa in this region by 1 km would allow moist air to circulate from the ocean, and rainfall would result. Instead, the uplift of 2 km during Terrae 0 and 1 favours the spread of dry grasslands over a landscape where trees once dominated (Sepulchre, Ramstein, Fluteau et al. 2006).[5] When combined with orbital changes, this tectonic activity contributes to the alternating process of aridification and lake formation that is seen as a key process in hominin evolution (Maslin and Christensen 2007).

Why This Matters: Models of Selection

The forcing mechanisms of orbital change and tectonic uplift can now be assessed from the perspective of hominin evolution. I will do this by focusing on two major models – *habitat-specific* and *variability selection* – as reviewed by palaeoceanographer Peter deMenocal (2004).

Made by the Environment?

The habitat-specific model stresses the importance of new environments for faunal and hominin speciation in Africa and, in particular, the appearance of savannah grasslands during Terra 1 in the Pliocene, 3.2Ma–2.6Ma (deMenocal 2004; Figure 2.1). The classic case study is provided by the long-established *savannah hypothesis* that links

---

[5] Sepulchre, Ramstein, Fluteau et al. (2006: 1421) model the effects of this uplift for East Africa and South Africa, and the shift to drier conditions at 3Ma that is supported by environmental evidence. Their modelling questions the older view that it was triggered by a cooling of the Indian Ocean. Data from Feature Morgan PDF files.

aridification both to the expansion of grasslands and to the development
of bipedalism, cooperative defence, tools and larger brains (Brain 1981;
Sauer 1967).[6] The evidence for such a close link has, however, not been
confirmed. The move to grasslands, for example, occurs much later
than predicted, and there is no one-way trend leading to drier conditions (deMenocal 2004: 18).

The specifics of habitat also figure strongly in Elisabeth Vrba's (1985,
1988) *turnover pulse hypothesis* that addresses the evidence for sudden speciation across a wide range of animals but principally grazing
ungulates and hominins. She points to bursts of speciation among the
antelopes (Table 2.2), and links these turnover pulses to the abrupt
appearance of new habitats and the onset of climatic rhythms that short-
ened the interval between wet and dry conditions (Gamble 1993: 83).
Vrba draws a distinction between species in the way they adapt to these
habitat shifts through the breadth of their diets. When habitats change
abruptly, and on a massive scale, as seems to be the case in Terrae 1 and
2 in Africa, then generalists are favoured. Generalists eat everything, ride
through the changes and persist. On the other hand, specialists who are
fussier feeders contract. They keep to foods in their preferred habitat
as it becomes a refuge, but are able to expand rapidly when the right
conditions return. Vrba's hypothesis can be summarised as follows: at
the macro-scale, such as Terrae 1 and 2 and the changing Milankovitch
cycles, evolutionary pressures select for an increase in the range of dietary preference so that, down the line, these climate changes are best
met by generalists. The turnover pulse, as indicated by the appearance
of new species, is therefore a result of habitat changes being driven by
orbital changes.

The turnover pulse hypothesis also predicts a distinctive tempo for evolution. It is an example of punctuated evolution, or saltation, where new
forms appear comparatively suddenly. It contrasts with a reading of the fossil record where evolution has a measured, gradual tread – a view favoured
from the outset by Charles Darwin and, it has to be said, most palaeoanthropologists (Gould and Eldredge 1977).

---

[6] Raymond Dart was a strong proponent of the savannah hypothesis to explain changes in
the australopithecines and the appearance of an osteodontokeratic (bone, tooth and horn)
technology to aid predation. But as geographer Carl Sauer pointed out, the savannah was
not a good place for hominins because they were not equipped for concealment, quick
getaways, predation or strength. Sauer regarded coasts and shorelines as the environments
which would favour selection for bipedalism and tool making.

Flexible Plastic

There is an alternative to the habitat-specific model. This is palaeoanthro-pologist Richard Potts' (1998a, 1998b) *variability selection hypothesis* that sets out the adaptive basis, and its genetic consequences, for becoming a more flexible, versatile animal in response to the cyclical changes in climate and resources (Box 2.2). Variability selection applies to both hominins and the wider faunal community of which they are a part. The point about variability selection is that it moves away from making a simple equation between an adaptation and a habitat; for example, savannah hunters or forest gatherers. Rather, variability selection starts to utilise the long-term records of changing climate to understand the complexities of the evolutionary process. Flexibility is the key to that process.

Using a range of palaeoclimate data, deMenocal (2004: 18) identifies three *variability packets* (Table 2.2) that could affect the evolution of hominins and other fauna in Terrae 1 and 2. He stresses their importance for speciation, and this is supported by Vrba's timings for the first and last appearance of fossil species; a measure of speciation rates. Where they disagree is that deMenocal puts this burst down to variability selection, while Vrba argues for the directed, long-term appearance of new habitats that triggered a rapid turnover pulse.

deMenocal explains the timing of these three packets by events in the high latitudes. He interprets the data as showing that African aridity coincides with the onset, and subsequent amplification, of the glacial cycles at the start of Terra 2.

An alternative, low-latitude view is taken by palaeoclimatologists Martin Trauth and Mark Maslin (Maslin and Christensen 2007; Trauth, Larrasoana and Mudelsee 2009; Trauth, Maslin, Deino et al. 2007). They combine tectonic and palaeoenvironmental data, particularly regarding the appearance of lakes in Africa (Table 2.2 and Figure 2.1), to argue that these same three variability packets represent periods of extreme climatic instability with high moisture levels thereby contradicting deMenocal's aridity model. Rather than being driven by Milankovitch cycles that led to significant glaciation in the high latitudes, their preferred interpretation is fluctuations in solar heating at low latitudes (Trauth, Larrasoana and Mudelsee 2009: 410). The effect of those longer eccentricity cycles of 400ka and 100ka duration is to alter the shorter 23ka-long precession cycle that has such an influence on the relative position of the tropics (Trauth, Maslin, Deino et al. 2007: 482). Together these cycles drive the intensity of the African monsoon. As conditions oscillate between wet and dry, and with them the availability

Box 2.2. Why it pays to be versatile

Potts makes the case that what drives hominin evolution is variability in climate rather than its direction of travel, for example towards drier conditions. The diagram (adapted from Potts 1998: fig. 2) shows changing moisture conditions in an East African environment. The variability results from a combination of tectonics and Milankovitch cycles, as explained in the text. What we see is a shift from a wooded lake basin (T1) to a dry grassland habitat (T7). Overall, the period T1 to T7 forms a variability packet, as described by deMenocal and modelled by Grove (Table 2.2; Figures 2.7 and 2.8).

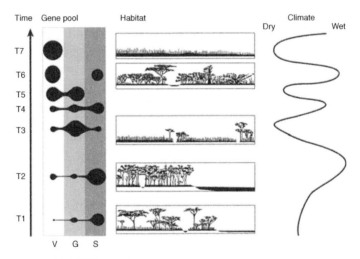

BOX 2.2. Variability selection

The response to this variability is shown by changes in the gene pool. Three alleles for specialist, generalist and versatile adaptations play critical roles, and their relative frequency is subject to environmental selection. The specialists (S) are there at the beginning and well adapted to the moist conditions with tree cover. The first dispersal into this habitat is by generalists (G) during T1 and then versatilists (V) at T2. The size of the shapes is an indication of the relative fitness of these alleles at any one time. Both generalists and specialists do well in some environments. However, contrary to the directional model for changing allele frequencies, we do not see consistent selection from one generation to another. Rather the response to long-term variability, defined as environmental inconsistency and the selective conditions this stimulates, is the success of the versatile allele (T7).

of moisture across the Wall of Africa, so intermittent lakes result. Here, tectonic activity plays its part by creating the basins ready for filling up (Table 2.2).

Trauth and Maslin describe their model as *pulsed variability* which focuses on the causes and consequences of those three variability packets in Terrae 1 and 2 (Trauth, Larrasoana and Mudelsee 2009). The Milankovitch cycle of precession is the forcing mechanism for these pulses. The outcomes are large, deep lakes in East Africa (Figure 2.1), some of them lasting for only a few thousand years – hence the description "pulsed variability".

Palaeoanthropologist John Kingston (2007: 46) narrows the scale of analysis with his *shifting heterogeneity model*. His point is that many species are resilient to change at these long-term orbital scales. What concerns them are the patches of food they can reach and how those shift by season and through time. Such resilience, in his view, leads to a common response to disturbance at the local scale by tracking preferred habitats and resources (Kingston 2007: 48). What matters is the spatial scale and heterogeneity of the environments these hominins and other animals could actually utilise.

Versatile Winners

How best to summarise these models? Archaeologist Matt Grove has examined the proxy temperature records in fifty-seven combined ^{18}O deep-sea cores known as the LR04 Stack (Lisiecki and Raymo 2005). This global archive spans the last 5Ma, and, as shown in Figure 2.4, a complex intertwining, and hence modulation, of the three Milankovitch cycles is revealed.

Two analyses were carried out. The first was a fine-grained approach that models, at a human generation time of 20 years, how two dispersal strategies – *versatile* and *generalist* – compete against the resident *specialists* in a fluctuating environment (Grove 2011a). The outcome is measured by how successful the different alleles for these three adaptations are in becoming fixed at a single locus in the population (Box 2.2).[7]

When this model is run against the temperature data, it is apparent that when variability is high, the versatile strategy outcompetes the other two, generalist and specialist. In other words, its allele becomes fixed at the locus more often suggesting that variability selection is the driver for

---

[7] The single-locus two-allele model can be found in textbooks on population genetics. As described by Grove (2011b: 308), "The frequency of each allele in the next generation is the product of its frequency and its fitness in the current generation, divided by the mean fitness in the current generation of all alleles at the locus".

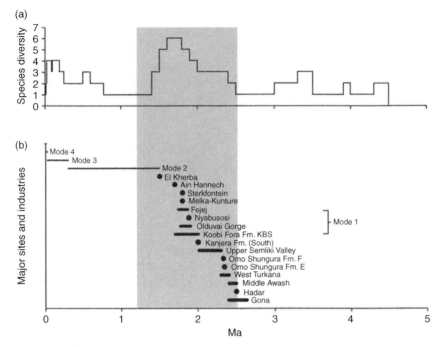

FIGURE 2.7. The variability package (shaded) from 2.5–1.2Ma. It spans Terrae 1 and 2 and corresponds with increased evidence for new hominin species (a), as well as the earliest evidence for Mode 1 stone tools and the beginnings of Mode 2 (b). Adapted from Grove (2011b).

adaptive changes rather than a long-term, directional selection for colder temperatures.

From the LR04 stack, Grove identifies a period of intense variability selection between 2.5Ma and 1.2Ma, spanning Terrae 1 and 2. When this large packet is compared to the archaeological and fossil record, there is both a higher species diversity among the hominins, as well as the earliest widespread use of stone tools, suggesting that selection for greater versatility in both physical and cultural adaptations is standard (Figure 2.7). This supports Trauth's finding that eighty per cent of hominin species first appear when the climate is highly variable (Trauth, Maslin, Deino et al. 2007: 13). Likewise, archaeologist John Gowlett (2009: 74) sees two cultural breakpoints in Terrae 1 and 2. The first between c. 2.6Ma and 1.6Ma ushers in the basic hominin sociocultural–economic package, stone tools and bigger brains, and the second, a largely silent revolution when viewed archaeologically, between 1.5Ma and 0.5Ma, where even larger brains appeared, together with language and fire use. This second change corresponds to the first disconnect between brains and technology discussed in Chapter 1.

In a second analysis, Grove (2011b) uses the LR04 stack to test the evolutionary argument that, according to the dictates of optimality, what will occur in the long term are phenotypes with the highest mean fitness. This time his analysis is coarse rather than fine-grained: the intervals between the data points are at 100,000 not twenty years. But the results again suggest that a versatile strategy will be selected when environments fluctuate widely. Indeed, the key finding from Grove's simulations is that *climatic variability* leads to increasing selection for plasticity, or versatility, in hominin adaptations. Long-term *climate change* in an important variable such as temperature acts differently, resulting in directional selection to colder, drier conditions (Grove 2011b).

But what Grove also finds is evidence for pulses within these packets that for different reasons support Vrba's tempo of evolutionary change as a series of turnover pulses. The coarse-grained analysis identifies, through the standard deviations, a long-term adaptive trend to temperature, while also picking out three significant climatic events, as indicated by the change in the mean values (Figure 2.8). These events occur at 3.3Ma, 1.4Ma and 0.5Ma, the last two coinciding with significant turnover pulses in the faunal record (Table 2.2; Lisiecki and Raymo 2005). The earliest event marks a significant directional shift in temperature as well as the boundary, 3.3Ma, between Terra 0 and Terra 1.

One caveat has to be made. Only one climate variable – temperature – has been analysed, and climate systems are obviously more complex. But even so, when Grove's two analyses, conducted at different scales and with different underlying models, are combined, the conclusion emerges clearly that the *variability* of climate rather than climate *change* is the driving force in hominin evolution during Terrae 1 and 2 (Grove 2011a).

Working with Variability

What are the implications for hominin evolution in Terrae 1 and 2 of accepting variability selection and the long-term success of versatile adaptations? Before reviewing the archaeological evidence in Chapters 4 and 5, I need a vocabulary of terms as well as an understanding of how the chronological cake can be cut in order to answer those questions. My themes of global settlement and encephalisation provide me with an itinerary for deep history: on the one hand geographical expansion and on the other an increase in social complexity (Chapter 1). These two trends structure what follows.

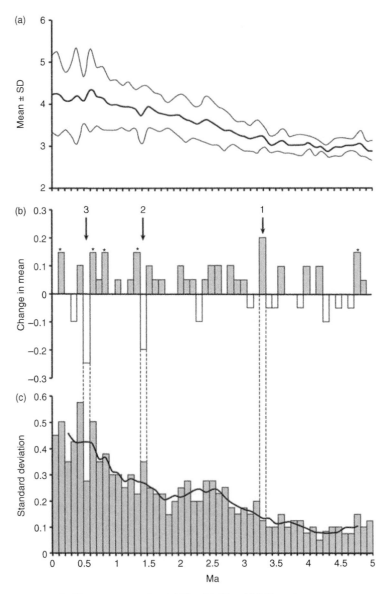

FIGURE 2.8. Temperature and variability. (a) The thick line plots mean temperature
through the period and show that adaptations would be needed to progressively colder
conditions. The lighter lines show the standard deviation and indicate the wider spectrum of temperature conditions that had to be adapted to. (b) The changes in the mean
values for temperature suggest three significant turnover pulses. The asterisks point to
five smaller turnovers. The grey bars show a move to colder and the white bars to warmer
temperatures. (c) The standard deviation of temperature is plotted (thick line). An early
peak at 2.6–2.3Ma is apparent, as is the overall trend towards higher variability in temperature. Adapted from Grove (2011a).

Mobility and Global Settlement

Mobility has always been the hallmark hominin response to environmental variability at the local scale. This adaptation is not exclusive to hominins, but our diverse patterns of socioecology which mobility supports, and which range in scale from a small-world hunting society to industrial economies, most certainly are unique. In particular, our capacity for fission and fusion, whereby group size is rapidly adjusted to resources, remains a potent form of adaptation to many social and environmental situations. For example, fission and fusion underlies Kingston's (2007) model of shifting heterogeneity among hominins, just as socially sanctioned mobility in a contemporary context allows economic migration.

In the long term, our trademark mobility not only adjusts population to resources but also facilitates expansion into new habitats and ultimately new Terrae. Three terms are particularly relevant – dispersal, displacement and diaspora – and these are defined in Table 2.3. A definition of migration is also included and reserved here for broader discussions of seasonal animal movements. These terms carry different weight in different Terrae. In Terrae 1 and 2 dispersal, and to a lesser extent displacement, dominate the description of global settlement, while in Terra 3, the terms have more equal weight. Diaspora and displacement dominate in Terrae 4 and 5.

Dispersal, displacement and diaspora are all elements in the broader evolutionary process of *adaptive radiation*. As discussed by palaeoanthropologist Robert Foley (2002), adaptive radiation describes the process of diversification that stems from dispersal. Crucially, it refers to the adaptive basis of that dispersal: what made it possible. This might be a broadening of diet to include carnivory and so unlock one of the doors to northern dispersal. It might also be the development of kinshipping (Chapter 1) whereby social networks extending over wider areas bring the advantage of a regional insurance policy when local times are hard. Foley's seven adaptive radiations are shown in Table 2.4.

The value for a deep hominin history is that an adaptive radiation identifies a geographical measure of evolutionary success; for example, the archaeological evidence for expansion from Terra 1 to Terra 2, or the displacement of specialists by versatilists within a single Terra. This is all part of adopting a geographical measure, the Terra, as the unit of deep history rather than letting the narrative be led by what we judge as significant instances of speciation and technological advance. When hominins got to different Terrae, and why, are the primary questions. What consequences this radiation had for new hominin species and their adaptive kit is secondary.

TABLE 2.3. *A vocabulary for global settlement.*

Dispersal (Terrae 0–5) is a process that is always in operation. It has the conno-
tation of spreading out by individuals, groups and populations of the same
species. The result can be to fill up the available habitat and reach areas not
previously inhabited. Dispersal may have no lasting consequences for the evolutionary history of that species. Alternatively, if allopatry and founder effect
follow the dispersal event, then it may be highly significant for new variation.
The term needs to consider the environmental controls on dispersal that lead to
extinction and its importance to the concept of adaptive radiations (see below).
Displacement (Terrae 2–5). When dispersal occurs into previously occupied territory, it can lead to the competitive replacement, or displacement, of existing
hominin populations. Displacement is preferred here to colonisation, which
is widely used in deep history; for example, the unopposed colonisation of the
Pacific. In shallow-time history, colonisation exhibits an asymmetry of political
and economic power between donor and recipient societies, as in the colonisation of Australia and the traditional characterisation of Neolithic expansion into
Mesolithic Europe. The term needs to consider that while colonisation can
lead to changes in gene pools, and hence local variation, it is unlikely to result
in speciation and so is not part of the wider concept of adaptive radiations.
Diaspora (Terrae 4–5) involves rapid movements of people as a result of political
economies involving trade, colonisation and slavery. New institutional settings
create spaces and uses for these people in motion, who retain their cultural dis-
tinctiveness but often interbreed with co-existing populations.
Migration can be a confusing term because of its very different use in zoological
and historical contexts. Migration can be seasonal to exploit the geographical
distribution of resources or, in the case of the Viking migrations, a permanent
colonisation in Ireland, Scotland and north-east England. The term should
properly be reserved for situations of movement that demonstrate philopatry, as
in the return of the albatross after a migration of many thousands of miles to the
same nest site, or transhumant shepherds to their winter village.
Adaptive radiation is the process of diversification that stems from dispersal, and
the adaptive basis of that dispersal. Adaptive radiations are therefore not based
on speciation as a mark of evolutionary success but on dispersal that sets up the
conditions for allopatry, local adaptation and genetic drift. From the fossil and
archaeological evidence, Foley (2002) has proposed seven adaptive radiations
during hominid evolution (Table 2.4).
Bio-tidal zone is a region of varying scale where, over time and linked to the
rhythms of environmental change, different biomes successively replace each
other. An example is Northern Europe where interglacial–glacial conditions alternate between deciduous forests and steppe and tundra. The term is
adapted from Vrba (1988).

Refuge area. The scale varies in space and time, but a refuge is characterised as an area of persistence and comparatively little environmental change. It is an area where species are sheltered from the competitive effect of other species (Allaby 1991). Cryptic or hidden refuges (Stewart and Lister 2001) are determined by the distribution of quaternary animals that, on occasion, do not conform to the expectation that particular vegetation habitats were their natural refuges and that such habitats were not continuous.

Home range. The area within which an animal lives and from which it gets food and mates. It may or may not be defended.

Adapted from Earle, Gamble and Poinard (2011) and Gamble (2009).

TABLE 2.4. *The hominin pattern of adaptive radiations.*

Adaptive radiation and innovation	Age (Ma)	Representative hominins		
7 Aquatic foods	<0.1	*Homo sapiens*	Large-brained	Terra 2
6 Projectiles	0.2–0.3	*Homo neanderthalensis*	hominins	
5 Fire	0.4–0.6	*Homo heidelbergensis*		
4 Carnivory	1.5–2	Early *Homo*	Small-brained	Terra 1
3 Megadonty	2.5–2	Robust archaic hominins	hominins	
2 Bipedalism	3.5–6	Archaic and early hominins	Primate size brains	Terra 0
1 African apes	>4			

Adapted from Foley (2002). Megadonty refers to the big teeth of the Paranthropine hominins (Chapter 4) and carnivory to the frequent use of animal foods. The ages are indicative only.

Adaptive radiation is a geographical concept, and once it happens, the possibilities of further diversification, biological and cultural, are increased due to factors such as population size, founder effect, geographical separation and genetic drift (Table 2.5).

Refuge and Bio-tidal Areas

With global settlement as our theme, we also need descriptions of the spatial dimensions of the mechanics of the process. Two terms are particularly useful: *refuge area* and *bio-tidal zone* (Table 2.3). As described by Vrba (1988), the effect of alternating climates is to expand and contract the range available to a species unless it comes up with a novel adaptation. Refuge

TABLE 2.5. *Key terms in understanding the evolutionary effects of geographical changes.*

Genetic drift	Describes the random fluctuations of gene frequencies in a population. This results in the genes of offspring not matching those of their parents, as might be expected under a process of representative sampling. Genetic drift is found in all populations but is accentuated in small isolated populations. This gives rise to the random fixation of alternative alleles so that variation within the ancestral population now appears as variation between reproductively isolated populations.
Founder effect	Occurs in cases of isolation when an individual or very small number of migrants founds a new population; for example the *Bounty* mutineers on Pitcairn Island. These founders represent a very small sample of the gene pool from where they came. Through natural selection the founder population becomes differentiated from the ancestral population in a short time.
Allopatry or geographical speciation	The formation of new species as a result of geographical separation or fragmentation of the breeding population. Many factors can account for this: tectonic activity, habitat change and sea-level rise. Allopatry means "in another place" and is the most accepted form of speciation.
Vicariance	Describes the geographical separation of a species that once enjoyed a continuous range. This can result in two closely related species, evolving each one being the geographical counterpart of the other.

Adapted from Allaby (1991).

speaks to the persistence of preferred conditions, while the bio-tidal zone rolls those out to wider ranges as determined by climatic opportunities.

The Sunda shelf in Terra 2 provides examples of both terms. When inundated, as is the case today, the islands and mainland of Sunda form a refuge. When the shelf is exposed at low sea level, it becomes a bio-tidal zone for expansion. At the other end of Terra 2 in Western Europe, a bio-tidal zone lies to the west of the continental divide. It consists of inundated shelf, glaciated territory and land that was never covered by ice or sea. Its accessibility and composition varies throughout the phases of the glacial–interglacial cycle, and this controls the ebb and flow of population (Gamble 2009).

The fragmentation of a formerly continuous range is described as *vicariance* (Table 2.3). Such geographical separation often involves a barrier such

as water, mountain building or desert. Vicariance can then lead to allopatric, or geographic, speciation that occurs through isolation. Allopatry might
be the least controversial means of speciation, but it is not the only one.
Other modes such as sympatric and parapatric speciation can occur within
the same geographic population.[8] There is also a wider biogeographical
picture that stems from these considerations and which is relevant to the
early Terrae. The dominant model in palaeoanthropology has always been
a dispersal biogeography where a hominin species disperses from a homeland, or refuge area, as far as it is able until it meets a barrier of some sort.
Where a similar environment is rolled out, then the dispersal is continuous
and can be described as a budding-off process driven by population growth,
as shown in Figure 2.9. Continuous dispersal can occur over a wide front
as in a *wave of advance* or along a *corridor* of the same conditions and
resources (Simpson 1940).

An alternative is *leapfrogging*, or discontinuous, dispersal where an innovation leading to an adaptive radiation, for example those in Foley's list
(Table 2.4), jumps across a former barrier. Crossing to Australia in Terra
3 would be one example, while developing ways to deal with ultraviolet B
deficiencies above 46° of latitude is another (Table 2.6). And sometimes on
these geological timescales, as Simpson (1940) demonstrated, the process
of what gets across is random and resembles a *sweepstake*. Even when a
major barrier does not exist, leapfrogging to preferred patches of resources
may still occur, leaving the intervening landscapes to be filled in at a later
date (Figure 2.9).

Vicariance biogeography takes a different position to explain the geographical distribution of plants and animals. The vicariance knife, in the
form of making barriers, is wielded so that a once continuous distribution
becomes isolated and fragmented. Tectonic activity, vegetation refuges and
the flooding of continental shelves are all examples of the vicariance knife
that cuts the geographical cake and separates hominins and other animals
into discrete populations. Dispersal is not seen as a major factor in explaining the present patterns of distribution (Gamble 1993).

One of the reasons for proposing Terrae as a way to study global settlement is to investigate these two processes. Currently, archaeologists
favour dispersal biogeography, as shown by the way they identify hominin
homelands and trace arrows of dispersal away from them. As we shall see

---

[8] Parapatric describes species with separate but adjoining habitats, and speciation occurs
regardless of minor gene flow between populations. Sympatric describes the occurrence of
species in the same area, and speciation occurs despite the presence of an obvious barrier.

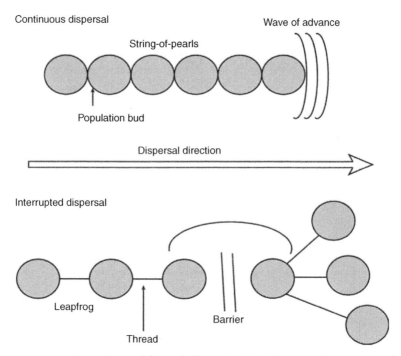

FIGURE 2.9. Two patterns of dispersal. The contrast is between continuous (wave of advance) and discontinuous (saltation or leapfrog) dispersal. The contrast emphasises the importance of staying in touch, either directly or at a distance through the connecting thread, as population buds off. Adapted from Gamble (2009).

in Chapter 5, the Terra 2, Out of Africa 1, model provides a case study to evaluate both biogeographical approaches.

Technology and Dispersal

Technology can be seen as the stuff that makes greater mobility possible. Boats, trains and airplanes have all extended the human reach, while on a simpler scale, bows, houses and clothing make it possible to settle existing Terrae at higher densities and to expand into new ones.

The problem is that archaeologists have not developed a vocabulary for their evidence that addresses the history of dispersal. Our taxonomies range, with many intervening stages, from the chip taken off a flint artefact, a single definable attribute, to an entire period such as the Palaeolithic. Many of the terms remain ill-defined, and several are used interchangeably. What can be said about the three lists in Table 2.7 is that the A-List

TABLE 2.6. *Three health barriers to dispersal in Terrae 1 and 2*

Northern latitudes

The extent of ultraviolet radiation (UVR) depends on latitude. Dispersal from the equator into northern latitudes involves moving from a highly rich UVR environment to a progressively poorer one. Above latitude 46°N, levels of UVB and UVA decrease significantly such that vitamin D levels, produced naturally through exposure to high UVR, have to be supplemented by diet. Vitamin D deficiency leads to bone defects such as rickets in children and adults. Another adaptation to lower UVR leads to changes in skin pigmentation. Recent studies (Jablonski and Chaplin 2010, 2012) report that today's populations with the most depigmented white skins live in areas with the lowest annual and summer peaks of UVB. Getting a good tan is a way of countering the loss of pigmentation that exposes the skin to potentially harmful radiation. Jablonksi and Chaplin (2012) found that seasonal variations in UVB were particularly marked in the mid-latitudes, 23°N–46°N, and well-tanned hominins should be expected (see Figure 3.6).

High altitudes

Hypoxia governs the ability of people to live at high altitude due to oxygen pressure and the challenge this poses to breathing. Anyone who has experienced altitude sickness will know what is involved. At 2400 m, the partial pressure of inspired oxygen is seventy-five per cent compared to sea level. This drops to sixty per cent at 4000 m. Hypoxia has been overcome by several different adaptive patterns, and people live today at altitudes of between 3500 and 4000 m in the Andes, Tibet and Ethiopia (Beall et al. 2002). An upper limit for human habitation exists between 5500 and 6000 m altitude.

Low-latitude disease belts

Reconstructing the incidence of disease in the past is complicated because many vector-borne diseases, such as tuberculosis, depend on the size of the population (Chapter 3). However, putting this important aspect of the Holocene veneer to one side, the geographical distribution of many infectious diseases, including malaria, is restricted to the tropics and mid-latitudes (Cavalli-Sforza, Menozzi and Piazza 1994: 153). The main disease belts lie between 20°S and 40°N, and vary according to moisture, temperature and altitude. Parasite load is also highest in this zone and may have been more important in Terrae 1 and 2 before the larger populations of Terrae 3 and 4 increased our susceptibility to vector-borne diseases such as malaria. In many ways, the low latitudes were good areas to disperse away from, although at some times disease acted as a barrier (Bar-Yosef and Belfer-Cohen 2001).

Other barriers, such as ocean crossings and plant productivity, are discussed in Chapters 3–5. These three barriers deal with biological adaptations to the environment.

TABLE 2.7. *Archaeological terminology simplified*

	Archaeological terms	Examples from all Terrae
A-List	Period	Palaeolithic, Stone Age, Archaic Age, Neolithic
	Sub-period	Middle Stone Age, Earlier Stone Age, Arctic Small Tool Tradition, Upper Palaeolithic, Pre-Pottery Neolithic
B-List	Technocomplex and culture	Core and flake, Backed blade cultures, Large Cutting Tools (LCT), Light duty tools, Ground and polished stone
	Culture and industry	Acheulean, Lupemban, Levalloisian, Clovis, Saqqaq, Aurignacian, Ahmarian, Mousterian, Lapita, Saladoid, Norse
	Industry and assemblage	Defined by presence of regionally and temporally specific tools and techniques
		Victoria West PCT, Quina Mousterian, Nubian Complex, Magdalenian à navettes
C-List	Artefacts and type fossils	Ovate biface, Still Bay point, Levallois point, Denticulate scraper, Thumbnail scraper, Emireh Point, Aurignacian split-based bone point, Prismatic blade core, Cassava griddle, Polished axe
	Attributes that define the artefact	Resharpening flake, Soft hammer flaking, Pressure flaking, Heat treatment, Bipolar flaking, Grinding and polishing, Fingernail impressions on pots

Most of the examples are based on stone rather than ceramic, or organic artefacts such as bone points. There is also some blurring between categories in the B-List. Adapted from Gamble et al. (2005).

is determined primarily by chronology and the B-List by affinity. With the B-List, chronology is still important but is subordinate, as originally proposed by archaeologist David Clarke (1968), to the spatial component that structures the data. Clarke, who gave us the unlovely term "technocomplex", based his terminology on levels of affinity between excavated assemblages of artefacts that recur in time and space. Cultures have the highest levels of affinity, then come culture groups and finally technocomplexes. The level of affinity depends on the intensity of research, and there is an expectation that more work on a technocomplex will result in raising its status in the B-List. Finally, the C-List, artefacts and attributes, is determined by micro-space; for example, the position of delicate retouch

on a stone tool that makes it a recurrent type in a series such as projectile points or scrapers. The chronological significance of such type fossils
only emerges through their repeated association with the B-List (Gamble,
Davies, Richards et al. 2005).

However, affinity means different things to different archaeologists, and
the pages of our journals are full of terminological disputes. What I would
emphasise is that the terms in the B-List have some value if they assist the
deep-history investigation of the spatial organisation of human populations.
I would read them as pointing, however weakly, at demographic possibilities
in the data.

Deep history needs its own terminology, and two solutions have been
proposed to end the nomenclatural nightmare. Grahame Clark (1961), emi-
nent prehistorian and exponent of deep history,[9] simplified the Palaeolithic
for global, comparative purposes into five technological modes (Box 2.3).
As we shall see in subsequent chapters, these have been widely used. The
attraction of Clark's modes is that they lump categories and can be given
first and last datums; in other words, treated like a species. They allow widespread comparisons to be made, and they do encompass a vast amount of
data. They also cleverly sidestep accusations that all he did was describe
progress in five technological steps. He manages this because his modes
are neither sequential nor universal stages. They are instead a homotaxial
scheme and nothing more. Modes allow him to escape the even more tor-
tuous problem of what to call prehistoric hunters and gatherers in different continents. The drawback is that modes concentrate on the stones and
ignore all other materials, and many B-List entities, archaeological industries for example, combine several modes (Gowlett 2009: 70).

As we shall see in later chapters, modes do not map onto the different
Terrae in a simple way. At best Modes 1–3 are primarily those of Terrae 1
and 2, while Modes 3–5 cover some of Terra 3. Once again, while modes
have their uses, they were not designed with global settlement in mind. A
deeper analysis is made by Gowlett (2009) who sets out a list of concept
traits that over time define changes in technology and that match increasing complexity in stone tool categories (Figure 1.2) an approach initiated
by Glynn Isaac (1972).

[9] Clark told me in 1985 at a lecture given by Mary Leakey to celebrate the 50th anniversary of
the founding of the Prehistoric Society, and in which Clark played a seminal role as Editor
and President, that he thought the term "prehistory" was a mistake. "We are all historians",
he said to me as we walked down the stairs at the Royal Society, past the portrait of Darwin
that used to hang there.

Box 2.3. Modes of stone technology

Table Box 2.3 Modes of stone tool manufacture are a widely used way of describing the major direction in hominin technology (Clark 1961; Lycett and Norton 2010). Five are recognised:

Mode		Conventional divisions in Europe	Conventional divisions in Africa	First appearance datum FAD	Last appearance datum LAD
5	Microlithic components of composite artefacts	Mesolithic	Later Stone Age	<25ka	0
4	Blades from prepared cores	Upper Palaeolithic	Later Stone Age	c. 120–50ka	0
3	Flakes from prepared cores	Middle Palaeolithic	Middle Stone Age	c. 0.25Ma	0
2	Bifacially flaked hand axes	Lower Palaeolithic	Earlier Stone Age	c. 1.7–1.4Ma	c. 200ka
1	Simple core and flake		Earlier Stone Age	c. 2.6Ma	c. 0ka

The problem with modes is that they are a blunt instrument when it comes to appreciating the versatility of hominins. Mode 2, for example, the biface, is sometimes described as the Swiss Army Knife of the Palaeolithic – a variety of possible functions in one basic shape. But were such hand-held instruments more versatile than the Mode 5 segments that went into making sickles, harpoons and arrows? Modes also concentrate on stone tools alone. It is more interesting (Table 2.8) to consider broader classes of artefacts such as hand-held instruments and the much later appearance of containers made from perishable materials, as well as artefacts composed of several substances. However, such schemes are in their infancy, and for ease of exposition, modes are used here.

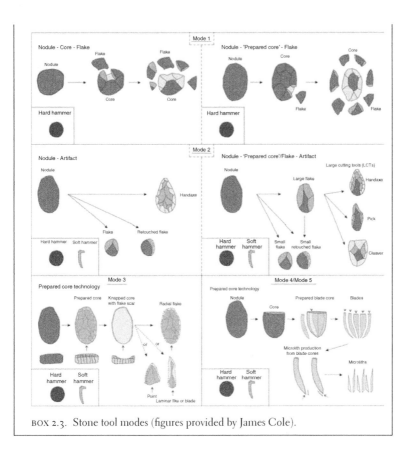

BOX 2.3. Stone tool modes (figures provided by James Cole).

Making Things

The second solution to the problem of what to call things takes another broad brush to the canvas of deep history and global settlement. I outlined in Chapter 1 my reasons for dividing technology into instruments and containers. I now add to this simple scheme the three components of making things from materials: addition, composition and reduction. Technology is created by whittling down, building up, breaking apart, wrapping tightly, gluing together – in short, making relationships between materials and the properties of materials. As a result, all technology is a social technology based on making associations.

Rather than five modes, this scheme recognises three technological movements since the earliest technology 2.6Ma (Table 2.8). The

TABLE 2.8. *Three chronological movements in the early history of technology*

Technological movement			Instruments	Hybrids	Containers	Reduction	Addition	Composition
			%	%	%	%	%	%
3	The short answer	20–6ka	21	7	71	20	55	25
2	The common ground	100–21ka	33	14	52	40	33	27
1	The long introduction	2.6Ma–100ka	72	11	17	72	14	14

These divisions emphasise the changing importance of instrument and container technologies, as well as changes in the making of artefacts by three basic processes. Adapted from Coward and Gamble (2010) and Gamble (2007).

movements are very different in duration, and the overall trend is towards the greater making and use of containers. This is reflected in the increasing importance of additive and composite techniques; for example, twining baskets, coiling pottery and hafting stone tools. It is against this general background of a developing social technology that the specific means to increase our geographical reach occur. The boats, bows and storage bins, as well as the artefacts that serve as memory boxes of all shapes and sizes, are all part of the story of global settlement. In Terrae 1 and 2, the long introduction to technology, the concepts are dominated by instruments and reduction. Why this technology changed will be explored in subsequent chapters.

Expensive Brains

We saw in Chapter 1 that hominin brains become larger through time, and this process accelerates during Terra 2 (Figure 2.1). This increase is due to the expansion of the neocortex that is tightly correlated with total brain size in primates (Lindenfors 2005).[10] Humans are no different except in one crucial respect: our large brains are three times the expected size when scaled against our body size compared with those of apes and monkeys. Moreover, brains are extremely expensive to maintain. Our brain is only two per cent of body weight, yet twenty per cent of the energy we consume goes to feed it. Costly to run, the brain needs eight to ten times more energy per unit mass than skeletal muscle (Dunbar and Shultz 2007; Shultz and Dunbar 2007). The heart is the only organ that is more expensive but shows no long-term increase in size.

In their *expensive tissue hypothesis*, palaeoanthropologists Leslie Aiello and Peter Wheeler (Aiello 1998; Aiello and Wheeler 1995) propose that growing a larger brain necessitates the redesign of the other expensive organs. Their conclusion is that we gain larger brains at the expense of smaller stomachs, since the other expensive tissues – heart, liver and kidneys – cannot be reduced. But the trade-off has consequences. Smaller stomachs mean less digestive capacity. One way to compensate is to up the quality of the diet by moving from plant foods to animal protein (Figure 2.10). Primatologist Richard Wrangham (2009; Wrangham, Jones, Laden et al. 1999) goes further, arguing that cooking is another way to compensate for a smaller stomach. Roasting meat breaks down the enzymes

[10] The correlations are very strong, $R^2 = 0.998$, $p < 0.001$.

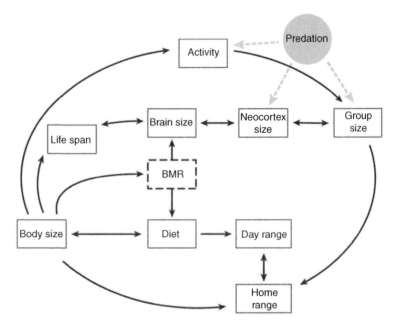

FIGURE 2.10. The expensive tissue model of hominin evolution. Predation acts as the selective force while the interrelated aspects of Gowlett's triangle – diet, social collaboration and environmental knowledge – are also shown. BMR = Basal Metabolic Rate. Adapted from Dunbar and Shultz (2007).

making the food more digestible; in effect, having an external stomach. I will examine the evidence in Chapter 5.

The expensive tissue hypothesis points to the strong selection that is needed for encephalisation to occur. A larger brain might assist in finding food and remembering its seasonal variation in ecologically challenging environments (Gibson 1986).[11] But while foraging for food provides constraints, it does not provide that all-important selection pressure to answer the simple question: why big brains?

The Brain Is a Social Brain

The current best answer looks to the link between brain size and the ability to monitor, co-ordinate and influence the activities of other social partners.

---

[11] Larger brains in larger animals are also known to be metabolically more efficient, although this does not explain their spectacular growth in Terra 2 among hominins who basically remain the same size.

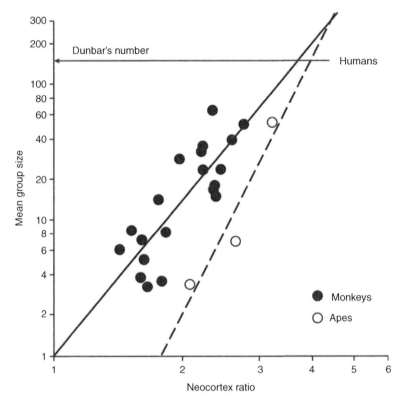

FIGURE 2.11. The social brain. The graph plots brain size in monkeys and apes against their observed group size. Using the same relationship, the expected group size for humans of 150, Dunbar's number, is shown. Adapted from Aiello and Dunbar (1993).

During hominin evolution, the *social brain hypothesis* states that our social lives drove the enlargement of our brains. In other words, compared to apes and monkeys, we have a large example of a social brain. As psychologists Uta and Chris Frith (2010: 165) put it, the social brain allows humans to boldly go where no other species has been. This is accomplished because the human social brain allows us to predict what others will do on the basis of their desires and beliefs (theory of mind), and the brain's neurons comprise a "mirror system" that allows us to understand another's goals and intentions and to empathise with their emotions (Freedberg and Gallese 2007; Gallese 2006; Grove and Coward 2008; Rizzolatti, Fogassi and Gallese 2006).

What is the evidence? Aiello and Dunbar plot brain size against group size among living apes and monkeys (Figure 2.11). The strength of the relationship can be read as a measure of increasing social complexity: from the tiny groups of the nocturnal galago and the monogamous gibbon to the large communities of macaque monkeys and chimpanzees. Even so, a limit of eighty social partners emerges as a threshold that no primate crosses. Some of them, such as gelada baboons, may live in groups of many hundreds, but the number of individuals with which they habitually interact, rather than potentially fight, is limited (Lehmann, Korstjens and Dunbar 2007).[12] The benefits of larger groups when it comes to avoiding predation and defending resources supply selection pressures to drive the trend to more complex groups and the larger brains needed to service them.

But above all, as biologist Patrik Lindenfors (2005) shows, differences in brain size are driven by the social lives of females. The evidence comes from primates and shows that the neocortex in both sexes is larger in those species which have larger female networks. In her study of female baboons, primatologist Joan Silk (2007: 1349) found the following: social bonds enhance the prospects for enlisting support when attacked; such coalitionary support affects the dominance rank of an individual; and this rank influences female reproductive performance.

Time and Cognitive Load

Primate social complexity is an outcome of the number of relationships that have to be remembered and serviced usually on a daily basis. If you live in a group of five or fifteen, the number of potential social relationships you could form between other individuals and between the possible number of subgroups rises from 90 to a remarkable 7,141,686 (Table 2.9) on the assumption that everyone has the same access to everyone else (Kephart 1950). The result can be presented as the problem of *cognitive load* where the amount of information to be remembered and processed, in the absence of innovations such as language or writing, places a constraint on group size (Figure 1.2). Primates are limited in the ways they construct social partnerships. For example, a baboon is best described as "a social actor having difficulty negotiating one factor at a time, constantly subject to the interference of others with similar problems" (Strum and Latour 1987: 790).

One particular problem is the amount of time available to negotiate those social partnerships within ever larger groups. This arises from the

---

[12] Besides forming alliances and coalitions for protection, other social activities include play and mating.

TABLE 2.9. *The structure and size of human personal networks*

Personal networks				Interpersonal relationships	Intragroup personal relationships
Gamble (1999)		Roberts (2010)		(Kephart 1950)	
Intimate	5	Support clique	5	10	90
Effective	20	Sympathy group	15	105	7,133,616
		Band	50	1225	
		Primate limit	80	3160	
Extended	100–400	Active network	150*	11,175	
Global	2500			2500	3,123,750

* *Dunbar's number.*
The intimate, effective and extended networks that everyone has favour different resources that maintain them – emotional, material and symbolic respectively – and these reflect the need to find less expensive ways to deal with larger numbers. Kephart's estimates for the potential number of interactions in networks of different size compares one-to-one interpersonal links with a situation where Ego also interacts with every potential subgroup. While potential is not reality, these figures do point to the increase in cognitive load that arises from social complexity, measured here by increasing numbers.

bonding mechanism in primate societies which is predominantly fingertip grooming. Grooming, as Silk (2007) shows,[13] creates strong social bonds that have big evolutionary pay-offs.

As the number of social partners rises, so too do the demands on time used for grooming. If more than twenty per cent of the daylight hours is spent on this activity, it impacts on the time an individual can devote to finding food, and so a constraint on behaviour arises (Lehmann, Korstjens and Dunbar 2007: fig. 3). When primate group size is fewer than forty, a clear relationship emerges between group size and the time they devote to grooming. Greater than forty, as is the case with chimpanzees and some baboon species, this linear relationship breaks down. The data are open to several interpretations, but it seems that within these larger communities, a pattern of internal fission occurs that reduces the size of the grooming group to meet the time constraint (Lehmann, Korstjens and Dunbar 2007).

[13] Silk shows how the quality of grooming increases the reproductive fitness of female baboons. Equal grooming between females is reflected in the duration of the bond (measured in years), and the social integration such bonding produces results in higher infant survival.

Dunbar's Number

Group size, time constraints, enforced changes in diet – all these point to greater social complexity arising from larger brains. The issue of complexity is starkly illustrated when human brain size is plotted on the primate graph to produce a group size estimate of 150 (Figure 2.11). This figure, known as *Dunbar's number*, is described by evolutionary biologist Sam Roberts (2010) as an individual's active network. As such, it represents the outer limit of four hierarchically organised social networks centred on the individual (Table 2.9) with a scaling ratio of three and four between each level (Zhou, Sornette, Hill et al. 2004).

Dunbar's number represents nearly a doubling of the upper limit of group size found in primates (Figure 2.11). The active networks for large-brained hominins in Terra 2 would be at least 120, so that methods other than fingertip grooming would be needed. Candidates include language, that acts as an efficient form of vocal grooming (Aiello and Dunbar 1993), and the importance of materials and artefacts in creating and maintaining relationships, as described in Chapter 1.

One example of this is the *ostensive signals* we use to attract attention deliberately; the eyebrow flash is a visual example, while the sound of a ringtone or a stone tool being made is another. What ostensive signals do is indicate the intention to communicate in culturally nuanced ways. We use many culturally loaded signals when we initiate interaction. Primates do not, relying instead on automatic ostensive signals such as body motion (U. Frith and Frith 2010).

The human capacity for highly focused attention is a critical gift. It acts as a strong bonding mechanism between partners, as in the love-struck gaze (Dunbar 2010). Close attention is also a necessary skill for making many forms of stone tools, especially those that exhibit symmetry and finely controlled flaking. This emphasises the social nature of technology and may well have arisen as higher levels of attention amplified the bonding mechanisms between individuals.

Amplifying emotions (Gamble, Gowlett and Dunbar 2011) is another possibility, for as Dunbar and Shultz (2007) note, social bonding is an explicitly emotional experience which we try to put into words, often with limited success. Emotions, as we have seen, are difficult to quantify (Table 1.4), but as psychologists Daniel Gilbert and Timothy Wilson (2007) argue, our cortex uses simulations of what might happen to guide social decisions. Accordingly, "the cortex is interested in feelings because they encode the wisdom that our species has acquired over millennia about the adaptive

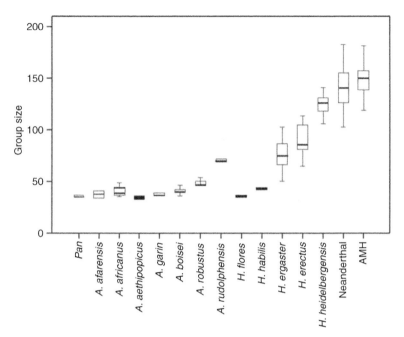

FIGURE 2.12. Estimates of group size for extinct hominins using the brain to group size equation shown in Figure 2.11.The ranges result from variations in skull sizes that are in part due to environment as well as age. Adapted from Gamble et al. (2011).

significance of the events we are perceiving" (Gilbert and Wilson 2007: 1354). Much better, they argue, to simulate meeting a bear in your imagination than learn about it the hard, unprepared, way. Hence, imagination, and its realisation through emotions and feelings, is critical to humans. Moreover, judging by the group-size estimates for hominins (Figure 2.12), such imaginative capacity would have been selected for at an early stage.

The emotional basis of these simulations can also be applied to those future social encounters. A series of tests conducted on great apes to assess their ability to think and plan ahead indicate they have some skill in this domain (Mulcahy and Call 2006). However, and perhaps unsurprisingly, cognitive tests on great apes and children aged two-and-a-half years reveal that they have comparable skills for dealing with the world but that the children far outstrip their primate cousins when it comes to social skills (Herrmann, Call, Hernandez-Lloreda et al. 2007). However, at the age of two and a half, children do not have a theory of mind and the mentalising skills this permits.

Wandering Feet, Wandering Minds

In response to the question of whether climate played a role in the evolution of hominins, the answer must be a resounding yes. But the cause and effect was more complicated than aspects such as bipedalism, technology or encephalisation being driven by the alternation of cold–warm climates of increasing duration. Environmental selection operated through variability to produce versatile hominins who coped better with the conditions, as indicated by their history of dispersal rather than their patterns of speciation.

The costs of being versatile should not be underestimated. Larger brains needed bigger home ranges and higher-quality foods. Larger personal networks posed issues for integration and the efficient maintenance of bonds. Strong selection was needed and the evolutionary pay-offs had to be apparent. When these changes occurred becomes relevant, and this will be looked at in Chapters 4 and 5 where the archaeological evidence for Terrae 0–2 is reviewed.

Changes in social cognition, such as theory of mind, illustrate these costs. Matthew Killingsworth and Daniel Gilbert (2010) have pointed out that the ability to think about what is *not* happening is a cognitive achievement which comes at an emotional cost. The cognitive load of living in larger personal networks is partly met by allowing the mind to wander, to imagine encounters before they happen and to work out what to do when "she'll probably say that" or "he'll think this, won't he". But they found that a wandering mind is not a happy one because it tends to dwell on negative emotions. Using a specially developed smartphone app, participants in their study were able to register their emotions as they went about their daily lives. Mind wandering was very common (forty-seven per cent of the sample), and when wandering, people are less happy. Overall, their major finding is that what people are thinking about is a better predictor of their happiness than what they are doing. By contrast, the benefits of activity, and in particular co-ordinated ones such as singing, dancing and playing sports, are known to release opioids and reward the brain with a high (E. E. A. Cohen, Ejsmond-Frey, et al. 2010). The solitary nature of mind wandering, only possible with a theory of mind, probably accounts for the negative feelings it produces. The social brain is exactly that: a complex package enmeshed in relationships and dependent on common feelings. The globe-settling hominins of Terrae 1 and 2 may not have always had joy in their step.

CHAPTER 3

The recent veneers of climate, environment and population: Terrae 3–5, 50ka to the present day

> *The earth seemed unearthly. We are accustomed to look*
> *upon the shackled form of a conquered monster,*
> *but there – there you could look at a thing monstrous and free*
> Joseph Conrad, Heart of Darkness, 1902

Holocene Veneers

A constant challenge for archaeologists is to avoid making the past look like the present; in Martin Wobst's (1978) trenchant phrase, committing ethnography with a shovel. But besides being alert to the issue, there seems little option. In order to animate, rather than merely describe, archaeological evidence, there have to be references to examples of how people act and behave. When it comes to deep history, the reference points have always been those who live by fishing, gathering and hunting (FGH). However, from the perspective of global settlement, the choice seems artificial. These peoples were already there when, during the great human reunion, the previously populated world was rediscovered by Europeans and other nations. As a result, geographical dispersal by hunters and gatherers that settle new, unoccupied lands is a skill that cannot be observed today. Instead, what can be generalised from the present are two features: mobility and small populations that would have played a major part in such a process. Together they open up a very different world from the well-known one of settled farmers and city dwelling.

The capacity for mobility, and the variety of adaptations this allows, is a most significant hominin skill. When combined with small population sizes, we have the two components that start to explain, without having to draw close parallels to ethnographic instances, the long-term success of hominins and their achievements in dispersal during deep history.

Archaeologists are not the only ones bound by these principles of *uniformitarianism*[1] to make sense of evidence from the past. The same applies to quaternary scientists and archaeo-geneticists. In Chapter 1, I discussed the filtering effect of the Holocene on our understanding of the older Terrae 1 and 2, and described these as veneers. Climate, ecology and population are three significant veneers in Terrae 3–5. They need to be acknowledged if we are to realise a seamless deep history with the older hominins in Terrae 1 and 2.

These veneers belong to the current interglacial: the Holocene[2] warm period beginning in Terra 3 some 11,000 years ago. Proximity in time results in higher resolution and better-dated information on past climates and modern human behaviour. And while it is not possible to trowel these veneers away to reveal a pristine past beneath, we can recognise the filter they impose on the way we imagine that deep history. In this chapter, I begin by examining the higher resolution of the climate record in the last 50,000 years. I then turn to the use of ecology to understand behaviour and cultural diversity on a global scale. This leads to estimates of population and the data now available on regional rates of growth from genetic evidence. Importance is attached to migration distance and kin dispersal.

Running through this chapter are the evolutionary currencies of *energy* and *information* that shape the variable outputs that are the stuff of historical interpretation. These outcomes are stored in ecological, cultural and genetic archives in the form of technology, social forms and biological variation.

Veneer One: Climate

Terra 3 Pole–Equator–Pole Climates and Environments

The data explosion about past climates and environments led in the 1990s to international efforts by quaternary scientists to synthesise the results. The world was divided into three transects which run from pole to pole (Figure 3.1), and all have now reported their initial findings (Batterbee,

[1] James Hutton set out the principle of uniformitarianism in 1795 whereby geological processes such as tectonics and weathering observed today were also responsible for changes to landforms in the past.
[2] Holocene translates as whole (*holos*) and new or recent (*kainos*).

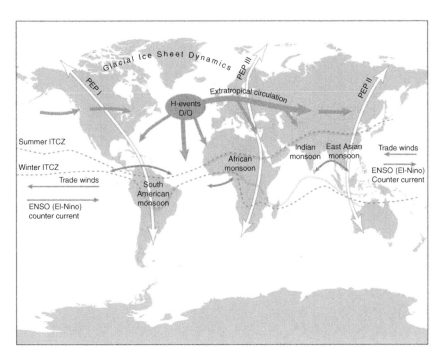

FIGURE 3.1. The pole–equator–pole transects described in this chapter. Some of the major climate events are shown, including the Heinrich and Dansgaard–Oeschger (D/O) events in the North Atlantic and the ENSO counter currents in the Southern hemisphere. Adapted from Batterbee et al. (2004).

Gasse and Stickley 2004; Dodson, Taylor, Ono et al. 2004; Markgraf 2001). Coverage varies, but two time streams provide the focus – the Holocene, and in particular the most recent 2ka, and the last two glacial cycles (200–12ka) – although attention predominantly falls on the *Last Glacial Maximum* (LGM) in Terra 3 dated to between 25ka and 18ka. In broad terms, what is being compared is a cold phase with a warm phase.

Some of the contrasts between the three transects are shown in Table 3.1. Several are an outcome of landmass and altitude that produce asymmetries in temperature gradients between southern and northern oceans and which, in the case of Asia, affect seasonal monsoon patterns.

Others such as the appearance of an east–west mammoth steppe and a Green Arabia will be looked at in more detail in Chapters 6 and 7. But the general features stemming from the higher resolution of the record concern rapid climatic fluctuations, ice-sheet advance and sea-level change.

TABLE 3.1. *The three pole–equator–pole transects and their major contrasts (see Figure 3.1)*

	P-E-P I	P-E-P II	P-E-P III
	The Americas	Africa and Europe	Australasia and Asia
Current conditions			
Land and ocean asymmetries	Antarctic seas colder than Arctic produce asymmetric temperature gradient, steepest in the south. Boreal forests extensive in the north. Temperate latitudes 4000 km wide in north, 800 km in south	Temperate and tropical latitudes separated by Arabian–Saharan desert. North–south symmetry in size of Africa to Europe.	East–west asymmetry due to Tibetan plateau. High levels of tectonic activity.
Quaternary highlights			
Glaciation	Largest continental ice sheet in North America; local ice caps in Andes	Major ice sheet in Europe and extensive permafrost	Minor but largest area of global permafrost
Low sea-level palaeocontinents	Beringia, Pacific coastal shelf, Caribbean dry archipelagos	North Sea Doggerland, South African shelf	Sunda and Sahul
Climate systems affected	Westerlies pushed towards the equator	African monsoon	Asian monsoon
Major habitat changes			
Moisture controlled	Reduction of Amazon rain forest	Alternating Green Sahara Yellow Sahara and equivalent in Arabia	Expansion of tropical grassland in Sunda and Sahul, only found today in Australia
Mammoth steppe	Expansion of arid zones Beringia	Wind-blown dust from larger deserts Eurasia	Wind blown dust from larger deserts Siberia
Sea-surface temperatures	Discharge of icebergs into Atlantic from Laurentide ice sheet	Cooling Atlantic and southward movement of polar front	Cooling of world's oceanic Warm Pool and major source of atmospheric moisture from Indonesia to New Guinea
Abrupt environmental transitions			
Cold stage	D/O interstadials; Heinrich events; Younger Dryas	D/O interstadials; Heinrich events; Younger Dryas	Lake events
Warm stage	8.2ka event	8.2ka event; Little ice age; Medieval warm period	8.2ka event

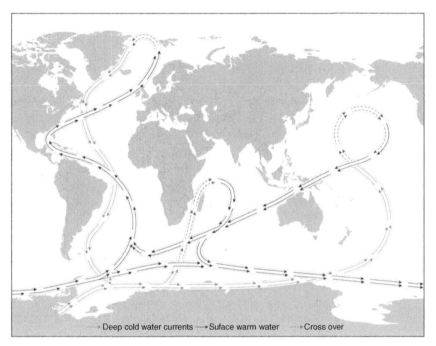

Deep cold water currents ➞ Suface warm water ➞ Cross over

FIGURE 3.2. The circulation of the ocean currents. Alterations in this conveyor belt that exchanges cold and warm waters change the sea surface temperatures and affect terrestrial climates. Adapted from Lowe and Walker (1997).

Ocean Temperatures and Abrupt Environmental Transitions

Compared to the environments and climates of Terrae 1 and 2, the main differences are a smaller role for tectonics and a greater one for changes in ocean temperatures. The looping pattern of ocean currents (Figure 3.2) influences the climate of the land system by exchanging cold deep water with warm surface water. The moderating effects of this *thermohaline circulation* are felt today in Northern Europe where warm surface water gives Britain its characteristic mild winters and allows the Norwegian port of Tromsø, which lies above the Arctic Circle, to remain ice-free in winter. The ENSO, El Nino–Southern Oscillation, in the southern oceans results in extreme weather events, such as floods and droughts, at low latitudes due to periodic changes in ocean temperatures.

Sea-surface temperature (SST), which can be estimated from deep-sea cores, provides a crucial input to modelling the effects of cold- and warm-phase climates on land. For example, it has been applied to the abundant research data from Western Europe and the last cold stage which spans

Terra 2 and 3 (118–12ka) and several Marine Isotope Stages (MIS; see Box
2.1). In particular, MIS3, dating from 60ka to 25ka, is modelled using SST
as the baseline data to generate environmental simulations relevant to
hominins; these include maps of snow cover, temperature, wind chill and
precipitation (Van Andel and Davies 2003).

Of course, thermohaline circulation occurred during Terrae 1 and 2,
but in Terra 3, it is possible to examine the fine grain of climate variability and link this into other aspects of the climate system (Bond, Broecker,
Johnsen et al. 1993; Oldfield and Thompson 2004; Vidal and Arz 2004).
Measurements of ^{18}O in organisms from deep-sea cores are now supplemented by comparable data from the highly detailed ice cores drilled in
Greenland and Antarctica. Thanks to the fine-scale resolution, climate
change can, on occasion, be seen operating at a sub-Milankovitch scale
(Figure 2.3). In practice, this means abrupt environmental events measured in centuries rather than millennia. As a result, we see that climate is
never static, neither during an interglacial nor glacial phase, while within
a single MIS, it is constantly fluctuating (Figure 3.3).

One example is the identification in the ice and deep-sea cores of short-
lived oscillations. Discovered twenty years ago in the high-resolution
Greenland cores (Dansgaard, Johnsen, Clausen et al. 1993; Johnsen, Clausen,
Dansgaard et al. 1992), these consist of extreme cold snaps, Heinrich events
and a series of warmer intervals known as Dansgaard–Oeschger (D–O) interstadials. Six Heinrich events occur between 70ka and 14ka, and show rapid
decline in SST and salinity brought on by the massive discharge of icebergs
into the Atlantic from the Laurentide ice sheet in North America (Lowe and
Walker 1997: 336). They are short lived, typically lasting less than 1000 years.
The D–O interstadials are more numerous – twenty-four occur between
110ka and 14ka – and also short lived at 500–2000 years. Interstadial is a relative term when it comes to the degree of warmth. Annual temperatures
during a D–O interstadial are 5–6°C colder than present but well above the
intervening cold stages. They begin very abruptly and decline more slowly
(Dansgaard, Johnsen, Clausen et al. 1993; Lowe and Walker 1997: 340).

Of a different magnitude and duration is the Late Glacial *Greenland
Interstadial* (GI) that can be traced across the Northern hemisphere
beginning 15ka. It has three distinctive warm peaks, each one less marked,
and ends in a return to near-glacial conditions in Greenland Stadial 1
(GS-1), better known as the Younger Dryas (Chapter 7; Figure 3.3).[3] The

---

[3] The Younger Dryas was first recognised in the pollen diagrams of changing vegetation
from Northern Europe that is characterised by the alpine-tundra flower *Dryas octopetala*,
the "edelweiss" of the Pleistocene, indicating cold conditions.

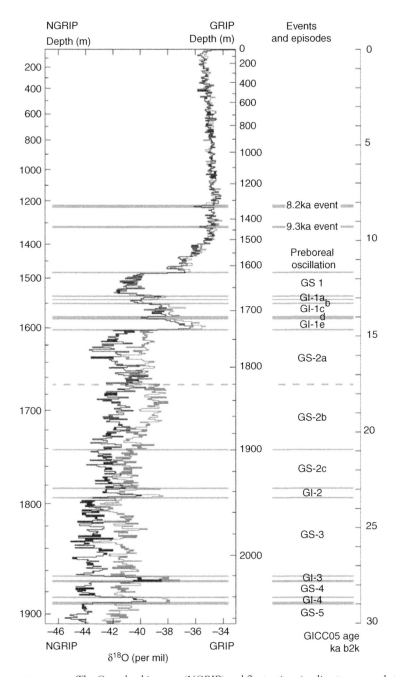

FIGURE 3.3. The Greenland ice core (NGRIP) and fluctuations in climate, as revealed by variation in the ¹⁸O record during the last 30ka. The GICC05 chronological divisions are shown. GS = Greenland Stadial, GI = Greenland Interstadial. Adapted from Lowe et al. (2008).

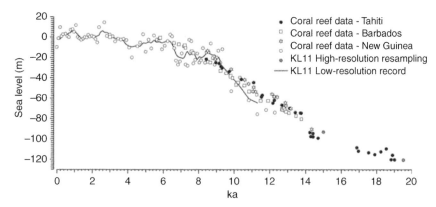

FIGURE 3.4. Changing sea levels during the last 20ka. KL11 is a core from the Red Sea. Adapted from Siddall et al. (2003).

subsequent transition to the Holocene is rapid, but once achieved, it is sustained.

The Holocene also sees several abrupt environmental transitions with global significance. At 8.2ka and 9.3ka ago, there are marked spikes in the isotope record which point to significant rapid cooling (Lowe, Rasmussen, Björck et al. 2008; Rohling and Pälike 2005). Dendrochronological data are particularly sensitive to these abrupt changes, and later spikes have been documented in the Northern hemisphere (Baillie 1995).

Ice Sheets and Sea-Level Changes

Ice advance and sea level are obviously closely linked because it is all about where moisture falls. More accurate measures of the extent of sea-level fall are available for Terra 3, as a study of the Red Sea shows (Siddall, Rohling, Almogi-Labin et al. 2003). Its narrow, shallow configuration makes it extremely sensitive to sea-level change, and this is assessed by the changing salinity values recorded in the ^{18}O archive from core KL11. At the beginning of Terra 3, 50ka, sea level stands at −70 m, falling by 50 m in the next 25ka to the LGM low of −120 m below (Figures 3.4 and 3.5). In the 4000 years from 14–10ka, sea levels rise by almost 60 m. In other parts of the world, inundation is very fast due to the topography of the revealed land. On the East China shelf, there are times when dry land disappears at a rate of 40 cm a day (Dodson, Taylor, Ono et al. 2004: 5).

The Red Sea study points to abrupt changes of the order of 35 m in sea level coinciding with abrupt changes in climate. These falls correspond to

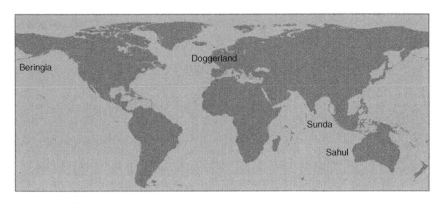

FIGURE 3.5. The shape of Terra 3 at maximum ice advance and sea level at −100 m. An additional twenty million km² of land was revealed but not all of that was inhabitable. The major palaeocontinents are shown. Map created by Fiona Coward.

TABLE 3.2. *The effect of different falls in sea level on the palaeocontinents of Sunda and Sahul (Figure 3.5).*

Region	Global	Sunda and Sahul	Sahul only	Sunda only
Modern land area	150,215,941	14,308,427	9,751,168	4,557,259
Additional land area revealed when sea level falls by				
−20 m	8,029,385	2,875,620	1,546,150	1,329,470
−50 m	14,330,962	5,183,012	2,621,932	2,561,080
−100 m	21,117,563	6,768,410	3,468,844	3,299,566
−130 m	22,968,715	7,008,185	3,588,038	3,420,147

Data compiled from GRASS by Fiona Coward.

more than twice the volume of the present Greenland and West Antarctic ice sheets, and means that during those rapid glaciation and deglaciation phases, sea level rises and falls at about the same remarkable rate – 2 cm a year (Siddall, Rohling, Almogi-Labin et al. 2003: 857).

The importance for hominins of the exposure of the Sunda shelf has already been noted in Chapter 2. In Terra 3, the gains from revealed land are even more significant due to the dispersal of humans into North America and Australia (Table 3.2). Beringia is the palaeocontinent that emerges on the continental shelf surrounding Alaska and Siberia. It adds a further 1.6M km² of unglaciated territory for settlement. With sea level at −100 m, the palaeocontinent of Sahul that links Tasmania, Australia, and New Guinea adds a further 2.4M km² to the current landmass of 9.7M km². Significant gains are also revealed in the permafrost latitudes of the Western European continental shelf and the unglaciated areas of the East Siberian and Laptev Seas. The maximum extent of the continental ice sheets is shown in Figure 3.5 where it is apparent that moisture builds ice primarily around the North Atlantic, attaining thicknesses of 2 km in Europe and 3 km in North America (Lowe and Walker 1997: figs. 2.13 and 2.14).[4]

Veneer Two: Ecology

Trophic Ecology and Effective Temperature

The second veneer is ecology: how living systems function and how exploiting them affects patterns of human social behaviour. Since diet and nutrition are the keys to reproductive success, the ecology of edible resources has formed a major focus of archaeological research. Drawing on the insights of behavioural ecology, these also acquire an evolutionary dimension; for example, the adaptive radiations of carnivory and aquatic resources (Table 2.4), as well as the altered ecology that comes with domestication. In all these examples, energy is the currency of change. Whether judged by quality or quantity, the long-term trend in hominin diets is towards capturing more energy at different levels of the *trophic pyramid*.

The first move is up, from plants to meat. Carnivory is important for growing large brains because feeding the expensive tissue needs high-protein animal foods. The ecological constraint is that herbivores form a fraction of the available resources, since they depend on plant food. Carnivores who specialise exclusively on herbivores are in an even worse ecological position when it comes to increasing their numbers. Omnivores hedge their bets with more versatile diets, but their numbers still remain low. The solution for hominins is to move down the feeding pyramid to those super-abundant resources that capture the sun's energy more directly. Such a move to devour the lowly mussel and the humble grass seed allows something else to be grown – population.

In particular, the link between a peripatetic lifestyle and resources has been studied, with societies judged to subsist primarily on FGH. These

---

[4] The Fennoscandian and Laurentide ice sheets respectively. The Cordilleran ice sheet based on the Rockies does join with the Laurentide, while the Fennoscandian extends onto the revealed continental shelf and across large parts of the British Isles.

peoples are the catalysts for thinking outside the agricultural box. The sample is small (Kelly 1983, 1995). Most of these highly mobile societies have been destroyed, marginalised or incorporated into industrial networks. But those that remain are widespread, ranging from the equator to the Arctic in all three pole-to-pole transects (Figure 3.1). Diversity is their hallmark. Ecological setting, languages, genes, technology, diet and recent history are all highly variable, leading some anthropologists to conclude that no picture of what this once universal lifestyle was capable of is possible. Moreover, the stark contrast of FGH variability with the million-year-long technological stasis in Terra 2 compounds this perception.

One archaeologist who did not accept this assessment was Lewis Binford (2001). His concern was to look beneath the Holocene veneer to examine that most basic of human capacities – mobility – to see how it varies as populations adjust to the ecological circumstances they face. His other main concern was the density of these populations because as they increase, so the options to move, and solve, a resource problem diminish.

Binford set out to compile a massive FGH data set. He greatly expanded existing global surveys that tabulated many aspects of their lifestyles, including the proportions of their diet obtained by fishing, gathering and hunting. His sample, not evenly distributed across the world, has two tiers. The full sample consists of 399 cases, and from this he selected a second tier of 142 cases on the basis of the detail and reliability of the ethnography. These come mostly from the Arctic and Australia. Moreover, he regarded the 142 cases as relatively unaffected by contact with farmers or colonial activity, a strategy employed by other anthropologists such as James Woodburn (1980) but open to dispute (Wilmsen 1989). The variability shown by these FGH peoples is then compared with modern environmental data. By understanding these relationships in the present, Binford argued, there is a framework for investigating very different adaptations in the past.

The reconstruction of vegetation habitats, so dependent on the prevailing ecology, is a first step, but what is needed is an index of their potential for settlement. This is provided by estimating the productivity of the world's habitats based on a single parameter – temperature – since this controls the length of the growing season and shows a strong relation with latitude away from the equator. This index is *Effective Temperature* (ET) and has a scale from 8°C to 26°C (H. P. Bailey 1960).[5] Seven broad divisions are shown in Figure 3.6.

[5] ET was constructed by H. P. Bailey in 1960, and is calculated as follows: $ET = 18W – 10C/W – C + 8$, where W = average for the warmest month (July) and C = coldest (January).

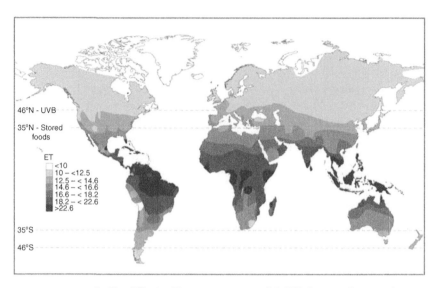

FIGURE 3.6. The Effective Temperature zones (°C ET) from modern weather sta-
tions. The habitats are described in Table 3.4. The latitudes are shown where storage is
required (>35°N and S: Table 3.6) and the thresholds above which changes in diet are
required to counter UVB deficiency (>46°N and S). Adapted from Binford (2001: 4.12)
and Jablonski and Chaplin (2012).

In his first use of ET, Binford (1980) showed how the frequency with
which people moved their residential camps and employed food storage as
a tactic to combat seasonality varies with this productivity index. Surprising
to many was the demonstration that FGH in low-ET settings, principally
the Arctic, were more sedentary when it came to living in one place than
the "nomads" of the high-ET tropical forests who moved camp frequently.
With the 399 FGH sample, he was able to look at more aspects of mobility,
such as household size and annual gathering size (Binford 2001: 150–151),
and the changing proportions of fishing, gathering and hunting activities.

From these data on subsistence, Binford (2007) highlights three critical ET thresholds. The lower is at ET 9.5°C (Table 3.3). Below these values, and associated with polar climates in the Arctic, fishing and hunting
marine mammals are always the dominant subsistence activities. Between
ET 9.6°C and 11.75°C, fishing and terrestrial hunting are the principal
activities, with occasional use of plant food. The third threshold occurs
at ET 12.75°C, when the first cases of gathering with values of fifty per
cent or more are seen. Above this threshold, fishing declines, and the ET
index in Table 3.3 points to the importance of gathering as growing seasons

TABLE 3.3. *The changing proportions of the use of resources by FGH at Binford's three Effective Temperature °C thresholds*

	ET <9.5		ET 9.6–11.75		ET 11.76–12.75		ET >12.75	
	Mean %	SD	Mean %	SD	Mean %	SD	Mean %	SD
Fishing	80	10.17	47	26.61	43	25.93	29	25.3
Gathering	0.1	0.38	5	5.86	22	13.05	35	13.00
Hunting	20	10.00	48	23.78	35	20.97	36	15.88
Sample size	7		78		55		22	

A small sample only is shown above ET12.75°C to indicate the decline of fishing and the rise of plant foods. Adapted from Binford (2001: tables 4.01 and 5.01).

TABLE 3.4. *An ordinal habitat scale based on Effective Temperature °C and corresponding projections for population growth*

Climate habitat	Key	Effective Temperature	Population growth
Polar	1	<10	Low
Boreal	2	10.1–12.5	
Cold temperate	3	12.6–14.6	Optimal
Warm temperate	4	14.7–16.6	
Subtropical	5	16.7–18.2	
Tropical	6	18.3–22.6	Low
Equatorial	7	>22.6	

Adapted from Binford (2001: table 4.02 and population growth expectations 20: 441). The key refers to Figure 3.6.

lengthen. The balance between gathering and hunting now varies due to a range of other ecological variables, among them rainfall, evapotranspiration, continental seasonality and altitude.

The ET 9.5°C, 11.75°C and 12.75°C thresholds are significant from a global settlement perspective because they point to constraints on human settlement at the margins. In order to settle regions with low ET values, an adaptive radiation into fishing is required. Similarly, occupation of ET environments below 11.75°C will need carnivory as a staple. As Figure 3.6 shows, this threshold falls in the Boreal – a zone notorious for its low conversion of energy into foods usable by humans (Tables 3.4 and 3.5). The boundary today lies at a latitude of approximately 49°N, the border between Canada and the United States, and to the north of the Caspian Sea in

TABLE 3.5. *Where to live*

Habitat	Primary (gm/m²/yr) production	Primary (g/m²) biomass	Secondary (g/m²) biomass	Plant accessibility Primary production/ Primary biomass	Animal accessibility Secondary production/ Primary biomass (×10⁻³)
Tundra	140	600	0.4	0.23	0.70
Boreal forest	800	20,000	5	0.04	0.20
Deciduous forest	1200	30,000	16	0.04	0.50
Lake and stream	250	20	5	12.50	250.00
Swamp and marsh	2000	1500	10	1.33	6.60
Desert and semi-desert	90	700	0.5	0.13	0.7
Grassland	600	1600	7	0.38	4.30
Savannah	900	4000	15	0.23	3.80
Rainforest	2200	45,000	19	0.05	0.40

Adapted from Kelly (1983, 1995). The higher the figure for the accessibility of plant and animal food indicates the relative ease or difficulty of each habitat for those living by fishing, gathering and hunting. Low-latitude savannahs and grasslands stand out as the most accessible habitats. Also emphasised are the local resource hotspots of lakes, rivers and marsh habitats, all of which can occur within the major vegetation habitats.

the Old World.[6] Only the tip of the southern cone, comprising Chile and Argentina, falls below this threshold, reinforcing the asymmetry in productive land between the Northern and Southern hemispheres.

ET can also identify the extent to which FGH depend on stored foods. Storage is an important tactic in combating seasonal variation in resources and solving issues of availability and mobility. It is a difficult aspect of FGH life to measure quantitatively, and Binford offers an ordinal scale ranging from none to massive (Table 3.6). The threshold of ET 15.25°C that falls in warm-temperate habitats (Table 3.4) emerges as an important one. At lower ETs, stored foods become increasingly important for FGH.

Cultural Ecology and Diversity

Human cultural diversity has an ecological basis. But how can these Holocene patterns be extrapolated back into the earlier Terrae? What is certain is that

---

[6] This boundary marks a northern growing season of no more than four to five months (Binford 2001: figure 4.09).

TABLE 3.6. *The investment in food storage by Effective Temperature °C and latitude*

Latitude	Below 35°N and S	35–90°N and S
	ET >15.25	ET <15.25
Investment in storage	%	%
None or minor	91	2
Moderate	5	8
Major	4	76
Massive	0	14
Number of cases	123	214

Adapted from Binford (2001: fig. 8.04).

much more cultural diversity exists in the last 10,000 years than in the preceding two million. That diversity is something to explain but also a veneer when it comes to examining hominins in Terrae 1 and 2. Recent human diversity, as pointed out by Foley and Lahr (2011: 1082), takes two forms. Genetically and phenotypically, variation is high within populations and low between them. The reverse is the case with human cultural diversity. I will examine this structure here with languages, cultures and technology. The currency of information, critical to survival, unites the approach.

Languages and Cultures

Many ecological markers have been put forward to account for patterns in human cultures, and none more so than languages. For example, in a study of world languages, anthropologist John Whiting identified the 10°C isotherm for mean temperature during the coldest month as a barrier to the dispersal of farmers (Whiting, Sodergren and Stigler 1982: fig. 7). The 10°C threshold establishes a direction for their dispersal from warmer conditions, where almost two-thirds of the languages are found, to colder.

The important point from Whiting's study is not that temperature alone acts as a dispersal barrier, but rather that languages can be treated as units of historical analysis. The same is the case with human cultures, a vague term variously defined, and where spoken language forms one element in a package alongside technology, social organisation, religious beliefs and many other facets. The process at work is adaptation to the environment and in particular the ability to form inclusive social boundaries. The proposition to test is that the extreme cultural diversity found in the Holocene arises from a need for boundedness on a scale previously not seen.

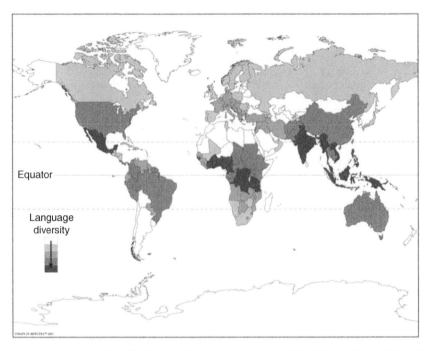

FIGURE 3.7. The distribution of languages by country. The highest diversity is found between the Tropics. Adapted from Nettle (2007).

The diversity of languages provides a starting point. Today, there are 6500 languages spoken by vastly different numbers of people. Rather than using a single isotherm to differentiate them into significant groups, anthropologist Daniel Nettle (1998) plots their geographical occurrence (Figure 3.7). He finds two trends: language diversity decreases away from the equator, and is very low in arid environments. As Figure 3.7 shows, there is exceptional diversity throughout the tropics, which Nettle explains as populations attaining an ecological equilibrium with resources. The key variable is the length of the growing season, which increases in the tropics and leads to greater reliability in food production. And so, under conditions of local self-sufficiency with high population densities, boundaries are set up between groups, and local languages proliferate. In areas away from the tropics, where climate variability is greater, languages tend to cover larger areas because the size of the social network that is needed to ensure reliable subsistence is that much greater.

In another study, Ian Collard and Robert Foley (2002; see also Foley and Lahr 2011) examine the ecological patterning of 3814 human cultures.

Once again, these are predominantly agricultural societies, and the density of cultures correlates strongly with increasing rainfall and moisture. Their explanation for this strong patterning is similar to Nettle's in that the formation of boundaries is promoted by the reliability and concentration of resources. When reliability is based on agriculture and horticulture, with stores and defence a practicable option, then this principle appears to hold.

However, it is at this point that the Holocene veneer starts to matter, and we have to ask how representative such patterns are for older Terrae and within early Terra 3 before farming. Nettle (1998: 369) argues that before agriculture, language diversity would have been even greater in the tropics and by extension throughout Terra 3 wherever subsistence security could be achieved without recourse to wide social networks. This suggestion rehearses a long-running debate concerning the openness of FGH adaptations and where one side argues that ecological unreliability promotes links between social groups rather than closure (Dyson-Hudson and Smith 1978; K. R. Hill, Walker, Božičević et al. 2011; Lee and DeVore 1976; Yellen and Harpending 1972). An open rather than closed ethic to others acts as a social insurance policy when resources fail for one group. Mobility, the option to find and adjust population to resources, remains the key local strategy, but now the ability to extend beyond the local group, as in Barnard's notion of universal kinship (Chapter 1), represents an equally important factor that allows unfettered short-term dispersal.

Technology can also act to reduce unreliability and with it the risk of dietary failure. In a comparative analysis of subsistence technologies, anthropologist Wendell Oswalt (1973, 1976) assessed the relative complexity of ethnographic technologies. He did this by counting the number of components, or *technounits*, that go into making an artefact. On his scale, a digging stick would be one technounit, and a seal harpoon with several elements – haft, barbs, glue, twine, buoyancy sac – would be counted as five. Oswalt initially compared the complexity of technology to the amount of hunting practiced by that group. This was refined by Robin Torrence (1983, 1989) who asks why some hunting technologies are more complex than others. In particular, the most complex are the marine mammal hunters of the Arctic, and she argues that the small windows of opportunity for hunting seals, walrus and whales provides a time pressure that selects for greater artefact complexity. In this instance, artefacts are designed to reduce hunting failure rather than signal social boundaries.

These interpretations are reviewed and revised by anthropologists Mark Collard, Michael Kemery and Samantha Banks (2005). They use information gathered from twenty FGH technologies to test four explanations for why toolkits vary: character of the food resources, risk of dietary failure, residential mobility and population size. These are then tested against a series of ecological variables that include ET and above-ground productivity (M. Collard, Kemery and Banks 2005: table 3). They then examined the relationship between toolkits and ecology with a regression analysis. This suggested that the best explanation of the technological variability was the risk of not meeting dietary needs, combined with the costs that follow from such a failure (Torrence 2000: 77).

Technological diversity can be plotted against Binford's ET thresholds. Figure 3.8 shows the technounit counts from twenty-eight cases among Binford's 399 FGH. As expected, a cluster of higher values occurs at temperatures below 12.75°C, the plant exploitation threshold. An exception is the Wulumba–Murngin peoples of the Northern Territory who live in a high-ET environment, and despite this still have a complex technounit score. As noted by Collard, for other cases that did not conform to their general findings, there may be alternative, local explanations for the variability. Wulumba–Murngin technology is geared to taking small, difficult-to-capture prey, especially birds (Satterthwait 1980), while sixty-six per cent of all their technounits are designed to catch aquatic prey (Satterthwait 1979: table 9.5). This suggests that Oswalt's original interpretation, the nature of the prey, also needs to be considered.

Veneer Three: Population

There are five elements to population: size, density, growth, distance and thinking. The last addresses the evolving exchange of information.

Estimates of population size and density start with contemporary FGH societies and extrapolate back to the past (Bocquet-Appel 2008; Hassan 1975). Growth of population is usually presented as a hockey-stick curve showing exponential increases in numbers following farming, urbanisation in Terra 4 and finally the industrial societies of Terra 5. However, there is another route to investigate the handle of the hockey stick when no growth seems to be the case. These growth rates come from the analysis of molecular data that contain information on the geographic dispersal of humans in Terra 3 (Box 3.1). I will briefly look at migration distance and its consequences for genetic variation during dispersal. Finally, these estimates are reviewed through a population thinking approach where variation in culture is linked to the selection forces of different population sizes.

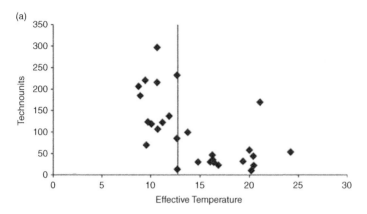

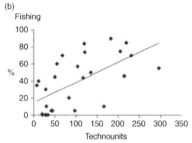

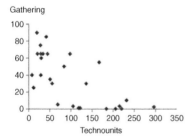

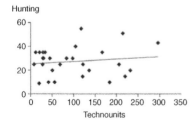

FIGURE 3.8. Technological diversity and environment. (a) The number of technounits, a measure of complexity, plotted against °C ET. This shows that the most complex technologies occur below the 12.75°C ET threshold. (b) Technological complexity increases as fishing assumes a greater role in the dietary mix and decreases as plant foods become dominant. The relationship between technological complexity and land hunting is less clear. Adapted from Collard et al. (2005).

TABLE 3.7. *Estimates for global population in deep history.*

		Population in millions			
		Deevey (1960)	Birdsell (1972)	Hassan (1981)	Binford (2001)
T2	Lower Palaeolithic	0.125	0.4	0.6	
T2	Middle Palaeolithic	1	1	1.2	
T3	Upper Palaeolithic	3.34	2.2	6	7
T3	Mesolithic			8.63	

Adapted from Binford (2001: table 5.07).

Estimating Population Size, Density and Growth

Today, according to Binford (2001: 453), 573,224 people live by FGH. As a guide to how many people might live in a world peopled only by FGH, Binford extrapolated the population densities in each of the major habitats to those areas now occupied by farmers (Binford 2001: table 5.06). The result is a world population of 7,032,402 FGH with a mean density of 0.0527 persons per km². Binford suggested this was the population of Terra 3 some 11–12ka ago, at the beginning of the Holocene just before agriculture appears.

The figure of seven million is one of the larger estimates shown in Table 3.7. These range from 2.2 million to 8.6 million for the Holocene in Terra 3. By contrast, world population at the LGM some 22ka is estimated at two million (Cavalli-Sforza, Menozzi and Piazza 1994; Rohde, Olson and Chang 2004). This should be considered a minimum because it depends on the settlement, or not, of the Americas. In the same way, estimates for earlier Terrae are fraught with difficulty and depend on how much of the world was settled and the extent of population packing. However, some estimates using Binford's figures are presented in Table 3.8.

When it comes to world population at the start of Terra 4, an estimate of twenty-five million is suggested by Biraben (1980; see also Cavalli-Sforza, Menozzi and Piazza 1994: table 2.1.2) which would represent a global population density of one person per 5.6 km² (Table 3.8). The estimate for the start of Terra 5 is between 437 and 497 million (Maddison 2001; Rohde, Olson and Chang 2004: supp. table 1) at a density of three persons per km². Today that density is forty-seven per km² and rising.

Binford (2001) used his FGH data set to look at the critical issue of the effect of population density on the hominin strategy of mobility. From the

TABLE 3.8. *(a) Population estimates in millions for Terrae 1–3 using Binford's (2001) estimates from modern FGH societies at three different densities, and (b) global population for Terrae 4 and 5 from Maddison (2001) and Rhode, Olson and Chang (2004).*

(a)	Terra 1	Terra 2	Terra 3
Area km^2	36,096,914	65,439,004	139,616,380
Density per 100 km^2			
Low 1.57	0.6	1.03	2.2
Average 5.27	1.9	3.4	7
High 9.1	3.3	6	12.7

(b)	Terra 4	Terra 5
Area km^2	141,207,100	150,215,941
1 AD	25	
1400 AD		437
Present		7000+

data, he identified two recurring densities at 1.6 persons per 100 km^2 and a higher value of 9.1 per 100 km^2. In broad outline, FGH with the lower density always solve the problem of what to eat by mobility, fission, fusion and sometimes the storage of one season's food for use in another. The option of mobility is not available to groups living at the higher densities, and here we see a greater degree of sedentism and the use of aquatic and plant foods, as well as stores of food and resource territories that are defended. This loss of mobility is further reflected in the fact that, according to Binford, none of these groups depends on hunting land animals as their primary staple. He accounted for this situation as a change to the way social units are *packed* into a region. This packing is a result of a regional history of population increase (Binford 2001: 442). Accordingly, the big changes in local group sizes, mobility and technology cannot be explained by differences in the quality of the environment but by the selection forces stemming from population packing (Binford 2001: 438).

Binford also proposed that in very dry and very cold environments, the rates of FGH population growth are primarily limited by food. A different set of conditions faces those in warm and moist environments because of the way disease and food limitations interact. The result is that in high-biomass conditions such as the tropical forests and equatorial climates (Tables 3.4 and 3.5), rates of population growth will be relatively low. Consequently,

TABLE 3.9. *Population growth rates from a study of mt*DNA *lineages using coalescent theory.*

Region	Population	ka molecular years	Key events
Sub-Saharan Africa	Slow growth	193–143	Mitochondrial 'Eve' starts the human lineage. 86–61ka major expansion of L3 lineage within Africa
Eurasia	Rapid expansion	70–50	First non-African mtDNA lineages
Southern Asia	Fast regional growth	~52	Between 45ka and 20ka, more than half the global population lived on the Indian subcontinent and Sunda. Peaked at 60%, 38ka
Northern and Central Asia		~49	
Australia		~48	
Europe 1		~42	Expansion from the Levant
Middle East and North Africa		~40	45–40ka into Europe and North Africa
New Guinea		~39	
The Americas		~18	
Europe 2		10–15	Recolonisation of Northern Europe with deglaciation

The table shows the estimated ages (ka molecular years ago) when new geographical lineages began to expand (see Figure 3.9; Atkinson, Gray and Drummond 2007, 2009).

the optimal zones for FGH population growth are the cool subtropical and warm temperate regions (Binford 2001: 441, proposition 12.10).

While population estimates for FGH in Terra 3 are complex, the study of molecular variation can shed light on regional growth rates. What is of interest here are the rates arrived at from the analysis of mtDNA data using *coalescent theory* (see Chapter 6, Figure 6.3). Central to this method is the notion of a *population bottleneck* where, for whatever reason, a constriction on the size of the gene pool occurs. Such bottlenecks make it possible to estimate the size of the *effective population*, defined as the number of breeding females. The results (Table 3.9, Figure 3.9) take the form of estimates of the growth of effective population sizes, and these, as expected, show

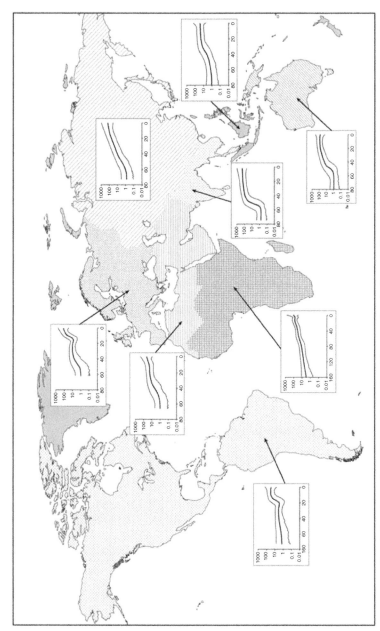

FIGURE 3.9. Population size and growth in eight regions (shown as hatched areas). The graphs show the results of a coalescent analysis using mtDNA data (Figure 6.3). In each graph, the thick line represents the median values, and the thinner lines show the 95% confidence limits. Age in ka molecular years is shown on the horizontal axes and effective population size in '000s on the vertical. The graphs point to early, high growth rates in South Asia as compared to other regions. Adapted from Atkinson et al. (2007).

97

different timings away from the source in Africa. Coalescent theory does not give us population size, but it does, through the study of the regional history of genetic lineages, indicate relative rates of growth.

Population growth begins in Africa with an mtDNA lineage known as L3 between 68ka and 61ka molecular years ago. This is some 8–12ka molecular years older than the first modern mtDNA lineages found outside Africa, suggesting major population dispersal and growth took place within sub-Saharan Africa (Atkinson, Gray and Drummond 2009). Each of the regions shows a different growth trajectory (Atkinson, Gray and Drummond 2007), with India and Sunda proving the population engine once people had arrived there. By 38ka molecular years ago, this region of Terra 3 contained sixty per cent of the global population. Growth then declines across all settled areas of Terra 3, and in Europe, effective population size declines, as shown by the dip in the graph (Figure 3.9).

When dispersal and population growth occurred across Terra 3, global temperatures and ET values were lower in MIS3 and 4. It remains to be seen if Binford's proposition (Table 3.4) that the cool temperate to subtropical ET zones might be net exporters of population to the higher-ET environments which acted as a *population sink*. Such a model is favoured for both the Saharan and Australian deserts that acted as *population pumps* exporting people to higher moisture areas where they replenished those populations that were more densely packed but subject to higher disease levels (Sutton 1990).

Migration Distance

A factor that emerges in Terrae 3–5 is the role of distance as humans settled the Earth. As anthropologist Alan Fix (1999) describes it, distance is often seen as the primary determinant in the amount of movement between populations. The only exception is seafaring between islands. Until the invention of the jumbo jet, the dispersal history of most populations was extremely *philopatric*,[7] involving only short distances for one partner after marriage. Leaving aside the diasporic migrations of Terra 5 (Mascie-Taylor and Lasker 1988), deep-history dispersals, as a rule, involve close kin moving small distances in small numbers.

The point Fix (1999: 79) makes is that the scale of migration can affect the structure of migration. If dispersal involves unrelated individuals, like

---

[7] Philopatry, or *love of place*, marks the return of a seasonally migrating animal to its nesting site.

TABLE 3.10. *Distance and kin dispersal (Fix 1999: 86).*

	Dispersal distance	
	Low	High
Group and individual dispersal	Not kin selected	Kin selected with high fission–fusion

many of the sailors in Columbus' fleet, then they might be drawn randomly from the host population, and a representative sample of the ancestral gene pool is carried into new territory. But with the population levels envisaged in Terra 3 (Tables 3.7 and 3.8), it is much more likely that dispersal was by small closely related groups. In such instances, dispersal may be kin structured, with the result that it represents a highly selected, non-random sample of individuals and their genes from the parent population. The extent of kin-selected dispersal will vary, and two scenarios are probable (Table 3.10).

Distance, which here implies separation, from the starting gate is another way to look at it, and the reconstructed charts of small genetic changes form a phylogeography of human dispersal (Box 3.1). These phylogeographies are possible because we are studying the kin-selected dispersal of a single hominin species, ourselves, through the genetic archives of anyone living today. What differentiates us are adaptations by our phenotypes such as skin and eye colour, body form and disease resistance that vary according to environmental selection, a consequence of our dispersal history.

Box 3.1. Phylogeography and archaeogenetics

We are our own deep history: a personal archive bound up in blood, bone and brain. At the threshold of Terra 3, these personal archives are already ancient. Skeletons and teeth contain information on our primate ancestry, as well as the innovations of upright walking and big brains. This much has been known since Thomas Huxley published his influential *Man's Place in Nature* in 1863. What has happened since is the discovery of deep-history archives in human genes. These take two forms. There are a few highly provocative studies of ancient DNA where the genetic code of fossil hominins has been directly accessed. Then there are many investigations, mostly conducted in the last thirty

(*continued*)

Box 3.1. *(continued)*

years, that chart the geographical history of all living people from their molecular structure. These personal geographies are drawn from the four nucleic acid bases, ACGT, in the DNA sequence and their multifarious combinations, deletions, substitutions, loss, coalescence and mutations that arise from the mating opportunities made possible by dispersal, displacement and diaspora. A phylogeographic approach to human history combines evolutionary relatedness as established genetically with geographical location.

Phylogeography began by using the classic markers such as blood groups (Cavalli-Sforza and Cavalli-Sforza 1995; Cavalli-Sforza, Menozzi and Piazza 1994). It then migrated to the study of *mitochondria* in DNA cells (mtDNA) and the male-specific region of the Y *chromosome* (MSY; Oppenheimer 2003, 2006). The choice is deliberate, since mtDNA is only inherited through the female line and therefore provides a deep history of female dispersal, while the MSY chromosome provides the other side of the story.

A classic study by Rebecca Cann, Mark Stoneking and Allan Wilson (1987) used mtDNA to demonstrate what had been suspected from fossil crania – that all people alive today have a recent African origin (Figure Box.3.1). The reason we know that the dispersal started somewhere in Africa, and the diversity of FGH genome data in that continent suggests a southern location (Henn, Gignoux, Jobin et al. 2011), is that its people are genetically more diverse. In other words, Africa is where these lineages first arose, and the length of time is reflected in the higher variability due to small mutations (Chapter 6).

More recently, the genetics of the HLA (Human Leucocyte Antigen) immune system molecules have been examined to construct comparable phylogeographies based in some instances on the study of disease. Drawn from medical science, these are based on very large samples. They have the added advantage of recovering more subtle geographic signatures of dispersal because of the importance of the immune system to health and survival (Chapter 8).

The pattern of kin-selected dispersal (Table 3.10) involving small groups travelling considerable distances is the underlying principle that unlocks our personal genetic archives for a deep history of human dispersal. By budding off and dispersing first within late Terra 2 and then outside it into Terrae 3–5, these small groups left behind a trail of genetic footprints that are non-random and which vary due to the elapse of time from where they started.

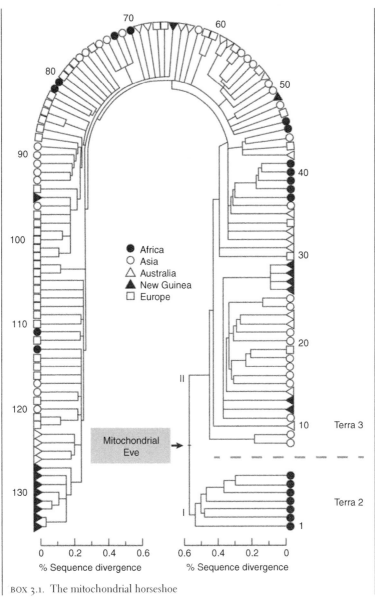

BOX 3.1. The mitochondrial horseshoe

(*continued*)

Box 3.1. *(continued)*

Box 3.1 The study by Cann, Stoneking and Wilson (1987) of the mtDNA from 134 women living in four geographical locations in Terra 5. The cases from Africa, at the bottom right of the horseshoe, show the greatest diversity and hence are the oldest. The position of the common ancestor to all these genetic lineages, the Mitochondrial Eve, is indicated. She was alive in Terra 2. The mtDNA lineages that she gave rise to left Africa at the end of Terra 2 60ka, first towards Asia and Australia and then into Europe (Table 3.9). The pattern of Africa-first has been reproduced in many other studies and with larger samples and is corroborated by MSY studies.

The genetic surprise for some anthropologists has been that during the global human dispersal in Terra 3, there is only limited evidence for genetic exchange as local populations were displaced. The sequencing of the Neanderthal genome shows that we share only four per cent of genes with these Eurasian hominins that we encountered after 50ka (Green, Krause, Briggs et al. 2010).

Contrast this very low figure with the diasporas of Terra 5 when Europeans freely mated with the Terrae 3 and 4 populations during the great human reunion, displacing many of them in a short space of time. However, we know that mating between Neanderthals and ourselves did occur, as the exchange of head lice and other souvenir parasites indicative of close contact shows (Araujo, Reinhard, Ferreira et al. 2008; Reed, Smith, Hammond et al. 2004).

Population Thinking

The final aspect of population concerns the transmission of information, both genetic and cultural. The importance of population has recently been highlighted by the study of social learning and the transmission of culture. These are treated as a Darwinian process with natural selection applied not to genes but to aspects of material culture. The key concept is *population thinking* that regards changes in biological and cultural systems as similar because they are both subject to the process that governs reproductive fitness. This process, as Darwin argued, is natural selection working at the level of the population, constantly testing which variants contribute to reproductive success and discarding those that do not. The evolutionary currency is information viewed either as genetic code or cultural variation.[8]

[8] Richard Dawkins called bits of cultural information *memes* and treated them as transmitted and inherited in the same way as genes. But whereas genes can be understood in terms of

TABLE 3.11. *Predictions for the impact of environment on the modes of cultural selection (Richerson and Boyd 2005: 131).*

	Rate of environmental change		
	Too slow	Just right	Too fast
Selection will favour	Organic evolution to track the changes	Social learning to help the accumulation and transmission of information	Individual learning with no transmission of information will suffice

As an example of population thinking, anthropologists Peter Richerson and Robert Boyd (2005: 5) define culture as information, acquired from others, that is capable of affecting an individual's behaviour. In this context, information can be as varied as marriage systems and the innovation of new items of technology. They suggest that social learning develops as a response to climate variability because it is most advantageous as a survival strategy when there are big differences in environments in time and space. Moreover, the responses can be predicted depending on the speed of environmental change (Table 3.11).

What remains unclear, however, is what constitutes "just right" (Table 3.11) when it comes to the pace and scale of environmental change. Richerson and Boyd's assessment of changes in the Milankovitch cycles is of the warm–cold variety I criticised at the beginning of Chapter 2. The influence of the Holocene veneer is also apparent with their assumption that this recent climatic period is representative for all Terrae. As a result, the model they propose has not been independently tested.

In the same way, reading the climate curve as a proxy for population size, as proposed by archaeologist Stephen Shennan (2000, 2001), has similar procedural difficulties. His argument is that population goes up and down as temperature fluctuates from warm to cold conditions. Population thinking in genetics shows that small populations are more affected by genetic drift than large ones (Nettle 2007). The upshot is that natural selection is less efficient at removing mildly deleterious mutations. As argued by Shennan, any innovation in the cultural sphere is less likely to have a harmful effect

chromosomes and the ACGT bases that form DNA, memes cannot. For example, is each technounit in a well-made arrow a meme or is the entire implement? Is it possible to regard the belief system of the Catholic Church as a super meme? Trying to reduce culture to bits of information is to miss the point of its agency in human activity.

the larger the population. The problem in small populations is that innovations which do not contribute significantly to reproductive success, and
that are less attractive to imitate, can still be retained rather than selected
out of the cultural repertoire (Shennan 2001: 12). This led archaeologist
Ben Cullen (2000) to invoke the metaphor of "too few trees in the forest". There were not enough individuals, or minds, to either innovate or fix
new cultural items. For innovations to become fixed through social learning and transmitted to the next generation, populations must cross a size
threshold (Table 3.8). But what the size might be remains unclear. Rather,
it is assumed that when archaeologists find evidence for innovations, the
threshold has been exceeded. So these thresholds, when there *are* enough
trees in the forest, depend on what archaeologists regard as innovations –
new stone technologies, art, burials and other items (Powell, Shennan and
Thomas 2009). New items are abundant in Eurasia after 40ka but not in
South Asia. However, following dispersal from Africa, sixty per cent of Terra
3's population is found in Asia at this time (Figure 3.9). The lack of artefacts
regarded as innovations would therefore seem to provide a test case against
their model. It suggests we should expand the concept of novelty. In the
same way, M. Collard, Kemery and Banks' (2005: 16) study of variation in
FGH toolkits finds little statistical support for population size having an
effect on the transmission of technological information and hence giving
rise to variation. That a relationship between population and the transmission of culture exists is highly plausible. However, it needs to be carefully
articulated with the archaeological evidence for change so as to avoid committing another instance of ethnography with a shovel.

What Was Novel in the Holocene?

Throughout this chapter, I have concentrated on the outcomes for hominins and humans of being mobile and living in small populations. During
Terra 3, and typically in the warming climates of the Holocene, both these
ancestral strategies changed. In those places, humans settled down, and
their populations burgeoned. The domestication of plants and animals, the
rise of villages, towns and cities and the many social and political changes
dependent on these new economies and demographics have all been put
forward to explain these fundamental developments.

But underlying them all are the themes of encephalisation and global
settlement. The latter preceded these social and economic changes across
all the continents of Terra 3, while domestication proved critical in settling
the islands and archipelagos of Terra 4. Only in one continent, Australia,

did the change to large, settled populations never happen. As a result, we are accustomed, as Joseph Conrad wrote, to view our world as a shackled monster conquered by industry and farming. For deep history, the shackles are the three veneers of climate, ecology and population that I have examined in this chapter. I have done this principally from the perspective that FGH lifestyles provide on mobility as a means to adapt to variable conditions and as a source to fuel dispersal.

Mobility emerges as a hominin's best means for coping with ecological conditions such as variable productivity, useable resources and seasonality. But it only works as a strategy if the social group can be fragmented and then reunited with no ill effects. Sedentism is not exactly the enemy of FGH because reducing mobility does allow more frequent and constant interaction between social partners. This may be seen as an evolutionary benefit. Packing more demographic units into a region because of population growth has consequences for intensification and diet breadth. It is a trade-off, and one which does not exist until Terra 3.

Agriculture was a definite Holocene novelty. It was necessary in order to build the first civilisations and send us on our way in shallow history. It was (Chapter 8) essential to get us to Easter Island and complete our global settlement begun in deep history. It is this second strand that I concentrate on and which determines the following highlighted novelties: the imaginative thinking behind defending resources and extending ourselves across time and space.

Storage and Defence

The loss of mobility rather than the beginnings of settled agriculture is one of the key questions for a global deep history to address. It is very much a Holocene question but not exclusively. Much flows from this development besides the appearance of villages, towns and other aspects of high-density living. One consequence in particular changes the character of hominin socioecology, when males begin to control resources. This brings to the fore two other responses available to human groups: *storage* and *defence*.

The socioecological structure of primates is clearly laid out by primatologist Richard Wrangham (1980). The starting principle is that females bear more of the reproductive costs than males (Chapter 1). This asymmetry results in the classic cascade seen for all primates (Figure 3.10). Here, the distribution of resources determines where the females will be located and only then where the males will be found as cooperative partners. Wrangham also establishes the ecological conditions for bonding between females. His

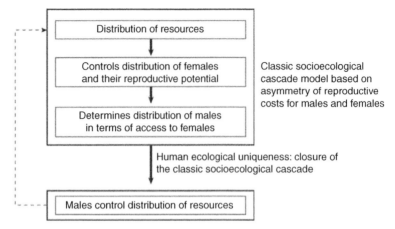

FIGURE 3.10. The importance of resources for the socioecology of primates and homi-nins (Chapter 7). The human pattern where males control access to resources breaks with this ancestral pattern. Adapted from Foley and Gamble (2009).

model is strongly seasonal with growth and subsistence diets found at dif-ferent times (Figure 3.11). The ones that matter most, and which bring females together, are the growth diets eaten during periods of abundance. Subsistence diets are the resort of times with food scarcity. When growth diets come in a limited number of high-quality patches, then there is a pos-itive benefit for females to group together and cooperate. The opposite is the case with continuously distributed subsistence diets.

The spatial density of growth diets can lead to the defence of the territo-ries which contain the food. Here, males can play a role, but too many of them means that the territory has to get bigger to feed the extra mouths and, as a result, is more difficult to defend. Hence, a female-bonded group with one male is expected. In a non-territorial system, still focused on growth diets, the female-bonded group cooperates with multi-male groups, as this aids in competitive interactions with neighbouring groups. This is what is meant by a socioecology where males follow females.

But this classic primate socioecology is not the human pattern. At some point in deep history, which I investigate in Chapter 7, males start to con-trol resources and hence female reproduction (Figure 3.11). Here, we see another veneer arising from Holocene socioecology. It takes the familiar form of patterns of social organisation such as the male ownership of flocks, paying bride price and dowry at marriage and the rules surrounding the inheritance of capital through the male line. I will not go into this further

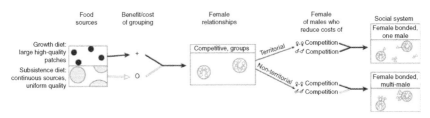

FIGURE 3.11. Growth and subsistence diets and their implication for primate socio-ecology. Adapted from Wrangham (1980).

here except to say that such control does not depend on an agricultural economy. Instead, I would stress again those two elements – storage and defence – that make it possible and which change the costs of male cooperation. Certainly, the costs are changed by the intensive use of resources and a move down the trophic pyramid to those more abundant food resources. Granaries are always more defensible than fields of undomesticated grass seeds, and they feed their protectors. They are a good example of the social practices of accumulation and consumption and, through these, the enchainment of people in relationships that I described in Chapter 1.

Kinship and Extension

And this is the issue of Terrae 3–5 and deep history. How many of these aspects go back beyond the three Holocene veneers of population, climate and ecology? How many were innovations that set humans on the journey of global settlement and coincidentally settled life based on the world's domesticates? We saw in Chapter 1 that anthropologist Alan Barnard regards modern FGH and in particular their universal kinship as extending back long before Terra 3. A study led by Kim Hill (2011) discovered that FGH have a unique residence pattern where people who live together are genetically unrelated. This pattern is not found among the primates. This finding raises the question of when this first occurs. Does it relate to that same ability to extend social life in time and space so that acting it out in front of another social partner is no longer necessary? The human ability to extend in this way, to form working relationships that are not kin-based, to use these building blocks to create social units the size of Metropolises and today's nation states is a triumph of that imaginative quality we possess and which I now investigate with the evidence.

CHAPTER 4

Walking and running down the tectonic trail: Terra 0, 10–3.3Ma, and Terra 1, 3.3–1.8Ma

I don't really think, I just walk.

Paris Hilton, 2007

Trails and Rhythms

Terra 0 is a tentative hominin world. The fossil evidence is sparse and especially fragmentary. Not until its last days is any technology found and then only through the proxies of cut marks on bones rather than tools. It is, as we saw in Chapter 2, a changing Terra where tectonic activity played a major role in forming potent evolutionary landscapes, and climate progressively became cooler and drier.

By contrast, Terra 1 seems positively sunny – much richer in hominin fossils and archaeological evidence for stone technology and diet change. But drawing up the limits to this Terra is not easy. A burst of climatic variability marks its opening, while it ends with changes to the circulation patterns that drive the low-latitude monsoons. This end point coincides with the current evidence for settlement in Asia 1.8Ma.

Terra 0 was a bigger world than Terra 1 (Figure 4.1a and b). Due to higher temperatures and precipitation, the ecologically productive low latitudes extended further north, providing conditions for the dispersal of apes and monkeys. Terra 0 belonged to the Miocene apes who radiated throughout the expanded arboreal habitats. But, beginning in Terra 0, and exacerbated in subsequent Terrae, the primates saw their ranges shrink due to environmental changes in temperature and moisture. This trend has resulted in today's distribution of apes and monkeys that are mostly restricted to a tropical refuge zone, a pattern which also holds true in the New World. At the

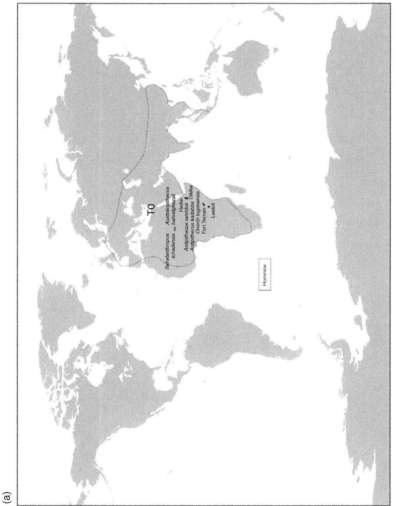

(a)

To

Sahelanthropus
tchadensis ■ *Au. bahrelghazali*
Hadar
Australopithecus
Ardipithecus ramidus ■ Dikika
Ardipithecus kadabba
Orrorin tugenensis
Fort Ternan ✷
Laetoli

Hominins

FIGURE 4.1 (a) Terra 0 and (b) Terra 1 with key sites, regions and hominins.

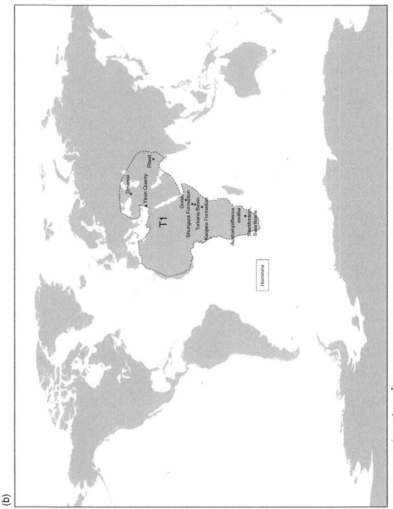

FIGURE 4.1. (continued)

end of this chapter, I will examine the most northerly primates, the Asian macaques, to establish the limits to these Terrae.

It was in this shrinking, refugial world for the zoological order of primates that the first hominins appeared. With hindsight, their mission was to reverse the trend of contraction, as seen during Terrae 0 and 1, by evolving new ways to disperse and displace competitors. The principal responses, already indicated in Chapter 1 and examined in more detail here, were bipedalism, technology and a change of diet. The dispersal success of these adaptations is best seen in Terra 2 when hominins became widespread throughout the Old World. But there was more to Terrae 0 and 1 than just setting the stage for the entrance of later, cleverer hominins. There were dispersals within these two Terrae, while the limits to greater geographical expansion were tested.

My boundaries to Terra 1 are greater than Africa where currently all the evidence comes from. Within Terra 1, I include Arabia and east to Pakistan – regions that were at times, like the Sahara, green lands with standing lakes. And there is evidence for the interconnectedness of these regions. Elephants, bovids, lions and hyenas dispersed eastwards from an African centre within Terra 1 in the period 2.7–2.5Ma and then into Asia, beyond the limits drawn in Figure 4.1b (Bobe, Behresmeyer and Chapman 2002; van der Made 2011). At the same time, *Equus* moved the other way. None of these major faunal exchanges was accompanied by hominins (O'Regan, Turner, Bishop et al. 2011). But the possibility remains strong that both their fossils and artefacts will be found in the non-African areas of Terra 1.

In Terrae 0 and 1, we see the major drivers of hominin evolution at work. These were the *tectonic trail* (Figure 2.6) that promoted both dispersal and speciation by vicariance, and the *long-term climate rhythms* (Figure 2.1) that, like stop lights, turned the northern deserts alternately green and yellow and filled the lake basins along the Wall of Africa. These twin mechanisms, as I will show in this chapter, set the conditions for a history of hominin evolution through dispersal and where the main requirement was for a bio-tidal zone, of whatever size and scale, into which population expanded from homeland areas. What then happened to them is the stuff of deep history. Over the long term, the outcome of hominin dispersal was to increase, through a combination of geographical happenstance and cultural innovation the size of those bio-tidal regions. But these geographical gains were not achieved according to some grand plan, an unfettered expansion into *terra nullius* by cleverer, technologically savvy ancestors. Rather, this grand evolutionary design was played out at the local level and at the human tempo of generational replacement. And at this local scale, it was the individual's home range, that area habitually traversed for food and mates as well as comfort and protection afforded by shelter, which formed the dominant relationship in the history of dispersal.

The Hominin *Bauplan*

In Terrae 0 and 1, we see major changes to the hominin *bauplan* – the body plan on which selection produced the evolutionary outcomes that link us to our ancestors. The components that concern us here are brains, guts, teeth, body size and locomotion. Change in one aspect of the *bauplan*, as we saw with the expensive tissue hypothesis (Figure 2.10), has consequences for all the others. The changes between Terra 0 hominids and Terra 1 hominins, including the appearance of our genus *Homo*, are shown in Table 4.1. These are presented as the outcomes of an environmental trend and climatic variability.

Brains take the lead in organising the evidence. In terms of their size, Terrae 0 and 1 were inhabited by hominids and hominins with primate and small-sized brains. This distinction is shown in Table 4.2 by two notional thresholds: the 400 cm^3 and the 900 cm^3 brain. Small-brained hominins fall between these values, and a representative range of species is shown in the table. Brain volume is comparatively easy to measure from complete fossil crania, while advances in computed tomography (CT) scanning now make it possible to quantify fragmentary materials. Brain volume then allows demographic and spatial estimates to be made, and these form the basis for my comparisons between species.

Of course, all of these estimates come with a health warning. As shown in Table 4.2, the number of measureable crania remains very small for most fossils, and the number of whole, or nearly complete, skeletons from Terrae 0 and 1 is even smaller. Such sample sizes require caution when estimating mean values and seeking trends (Robson and Wood 2008).[1]

Palaeoanthropologists Wood and Lonergan (2008) provide such an overview for the major species and the three main hominin genera:

---

[1] The fragmentary character of the data makes normal statistical assessments difficult, and a biologist would despair. However, these are the data we have. Sample size becomes important when the goal is to assess variability within populations as, for example, in estimates of body size. Robson and Wood (2008) list at least six methods that are used to estimate body mass from fossil data. Among these are orbit height and femoral head diameter. These methods can be cross-checked, but it is rare for the same method to underpin values of body size and further implications for the degree of sexual dimorphism in a population.

TABLE 4.1. *The co-evolving hominin* bauplan

Terra 0 hominin *bauplan*	Challenges	Met by adaptive and behavioural plasticity	Resulting in amplified changes to		Terra 1 *Homo bauplan*
			Genotype	Phenotype	
Brains	*Environmental trend*	Diets	Body and brain size		Large brains
Guts	Declining primary productivity leads to a different spatial pattern of resources	Technological innovation		Personal network size	Small guts
Teeth			Dentition		Small teeth
	Climate variability				
Body size	Greater variation in the frequency and amplitude of habitat transitions	Pattern of land use adjusted through fission and fusion of the group	Locomotion Walking, running		Large bodies
Locomotion				Home range size	Long legs

The table lists the main, interrelated components and indicates in general terms how these changed over the course of Terra 0 and Terra 1. Attention is paid to the amplified outcomes that take the form of phenotypic and genotypic changes. The outcomes are the hominin grades in Table 4.3. Adapted from Antón, Leonard and Robertson (2002).

Australopithecus, Paranthropus and *Homo.* In particular, Table 4.3 contrasts taxonomic approaches that either split or lump the evidence. As a result, seventeen species assigned to the three main genera are lumped into seven species. Furthermore, Wood and Lonergan describe the variation in terms of six hominin *grades*, a term in evolutionary taxonomy that refers to the outcome of evolutionary history as opposed to *clade* that refers to the process. These outcomes sort hominins into the broad functional categories shown in Table 4.3. I have also added Foley's adaptive radiations from Table 2.4.[2] Bipedalism is also presented as a three-stage process,

---

[2] Two points need to be noted about Wood and Lonergan's classification. In the first place, their grade system brings in the early hominins/hominids from T0 which, apart from *Ardipithecus ramidus*, are extremely fragmentary. Second, *Australopithecus garhi* from Chad cross-cuts two genera, *Paranthropus* and *Australopithecus*, is lumped into *A. africanus* and therefore raises questions about some of the functional distinction between the grades Archaic and Megadont. Such blurring is to be expected with small and often fragmentary samples of fossil material. Other palaeoanthropologists will cut the cake differently.

TABLE 4.2. A sample of hominin and hominid fossils organised according to their encephalisation.

	Terra	Age (Ma)	Mean cranial capacity (cm³)	Sample size	EQ	Neocortex ratio	Personal network size	Grooming time (% daytime)	Mean height (m)	Mean adult body weight (kg)	Sexual dimorphism	Individual Home range (Ha) Ape (Ha)	Individual Home range (Ha) Human (Ha)	Group Home range (Ha) Ape (km²)	Group Home range (Ha) Human (km²)	Density (km²)
Large-brained hominins and humans																
Homo sapiens (modern)	5	extant	1352		6.04	4	136	38	1.85	49	1.16	58	360	79	490	1.7
Homo sapiens (Pleistocene)	2&3	0.19–0.01	1478	66	5.38	4.07	144	40	1.85	66	1.19	83	518	120	746	1.3
Homo neanderthalensis	2&3	0.2–0.028	1426	23	4.75	4.04	141	39	1.6	72	1.17	98	608	138	857	1.2
Homo heidelbergensis	2	0.6–0.1	1204	17	4.07	3.9	126	35	1.8	71	1.08	96	596	121	751	1.2
Homo erectus	2	1.8–0.2	1003	36	3.97	3.8	112	31	1.7	61	1.14	73	453	82	507	1.4
The 900 cm³ hominin			900			3.7	104	29								
Small-brained hominins																
Homo ergaster	1&2	1.9–1.5	764	6	2.82	3.6	93	25	1.85	64	1.26	83	518	77	482	1.3
Paranthropus robustus	1&2	2–1.5	563	2	3.25	3.4	76	20	1.2	36	1.25	38	236	29	179	2.2
Homo habilis	1&2	2.4–1.4	609	6	3.74	3.4	80	21	1.15	33	1.16	34	210	27	168	2.4
Homo rudolfensis	1&2	2.4–1.6	726	3	3.01	3.5	90	24	1.55	55	1.18	68	421	61	379	1.5
Australopithecus africanus	1	3–2.4	464	8	2.81	3.2	67	16	1.4	34	1.36	35	219	23	147	2.4
Australopithecus afarensis	0&1	4–3	458	4	2.55	3.2	66	16	1.28	39	1.53	41	254	27	168	2.1
The 400 cm³ hominin			400			3.1	60.4	13								
Primate-size brains																
Pan troglodytes (chimpanzee)	5	extant	367		1.94	3.1	57	12	0.81	41	1.31	45	282	26	161	2
Gorilla sp.	5	extant	500		1.1	3.3	70	17	1.6	128	1.68	214	1329	150	930	0.7
Ardipithecus ramidus	0	4.5–4.3	325	1	1.46	3	53	10	1.2	40	?	44	273	23	145	2
Sahelanthropus tchadensis	0	7.6	365	1		3.1	57	12								

The hominin sample is organised by brain size rather than the more familiar chronological and geographical variations in skull and dental morphology. The 400 cm³ and 900 cm³ hominin brains are notional thresholds in the evolution of large brains. Adapted from Aiello and Dunbar (1993), Leonard and Robertson (2000), Robson and Wood (2008) and Wood and Lonergan (2008).

TABLE 4.3. *The classification of hominins using grades and adaptive radiations. A lumping and splitting taxonomy is also shown, as well as the five technological modes*

Splitting species	Age (Ma)	Lumping species	Technological modes				Grades	Adaptive radiations	Terra
			4	3	2	1			
All species sensu stricto		All species sensu lato							
Homo									
sapiens	0.19–present	*Homo sapiens*	X	X			Anatomically modern *Homo*	Aquatic	2–5
neanderthalensis	0.4–0.028	*Homo erectus*		X			Pre-modern *Homo*	Projectiles	2&3
floresiensis	0.095–0.012			X					2&3
heidelbergensis	0.6–0.1			X				Fire	2
antecessor	1.2–0.5				X				2
erectus	1.8–0.2				X				2
ergaster	1.9–1.5				X	X		Bipedalism Step 3	1&2
rudolfensis	2.4–1.6	*Homo habilis*				X	Transitional hominins	Endurance running	1&2
habilis	2.4–1.4					X		Carnivory	1&2
Paranthropus									
robustus	2–1.5	*Paranthropus robustus*				X	Megadont Archaic hominins	Megadonty	1&2
boisei	2.3–1.3	*Paranthropus boisei*				X			1&2
aethiopicus	2.5–2.3					?			1
garhi	2.5	*Australopithecus africanus*				?			1
Australopithecus									
sediba	2–1.8					?	Archaic hominins		1
africanus	3–2.4	*Australopithecus afarensis*				?		Bidepalism Step 2	
bahrelghazali	3.5–3.3					?		Walking	o&1
afarensis	3.5–3.3							in the open	o&1
platyops	4–3							some arboreal	o
anamensis	4.5–3.9								o
Ardipithecus									
kadabba	5.8–5.2	*Ardipithecus ramidus*					Possible and probable early hominins		o
ramidus	4.5–4.3							Bipedalism Step 1	o
tugenensis	6.6–5.7							four hands	o
tchadensis	7–6							trees and ground	o

Adapted from Foley (2002) and Wood and Lonergan (2008).

as explained below. What emerges when these various schemes are cross-referred is a broad consensus over the major groupings, and a basis for their assessment by functional and adaptive category, that I will use in this chapter (Wood 2010).

What distinguishes the primate brain from the small hominin brain is its encephalisation quotient (EQ). Gorillas have brains larger than 400 cm³, but when scaled against their massive size, they have an EQ, like all primate brains, of less than two (Table 4.2). By contrast, all the small-brained hominins have an EQ greater than two.

The consequences for the *bauplan* are instructive. These larger hominin brains had implications for the capabilities of hominins to disperse. In particular, they affected personal network size that in turn recast the dietary requirements that arose from body size and the extent of an individual's and group's home range. Then there was the issue of how to get around these larger areas. For a versatile hominin, a change in locomotion provided one solution, but required remodelling of the genotype (Table 4.1). Technology provided another behavioural answer, as did flexible demographic strategies based on fission and fusion.

The contrast between the *bauplan* and geography of hominins and a great ape such as the chimpanzee is marked. Currently, the only fossil finds of the small-brained quadrapedal *Pan* come from Kapthurin in the Kenyan Rift of the tectonic trail (McBrearty and Jablonski 2005). They are dated to about 545ka in the Middle Pleistocene of Terra 2. No chimpanzees live in that area today, and although the finds point to a former enlarged distribution, their discovery confirms the tropical distribution of this primate.

The contrast with the australopithecines, *Archaic Hominins* (Table 4.3), is dramatic. The distribution of *afarensis* and *africanus* stretched from the plateaux of South Africa, through the African Rift to Ethiopia. Between 3.5Ma and 2.5Ma, *Archaic Hominins* such as *bahrelghzali* and *garhi* occupied a Green Sahara in present-day Chad. By comparison, the earliest examples of Wood and Lonergan's *Transitional hominins*, *Homo* at 2.4Ma, have a smaller distribution restricted to the tectonic trail, but still much larger than for the living African great apes.

The possession of a 400-cm³-sized brain and an EQ greater than two do not by themselves explain these geographical differences. Instead, there was an evolution of the hominin *bauplan* that involved aspects other than encephalisation, and some of these are set out in Table 4.1. Following Antón's lead (Antón, Leonard and Robertson 2002), it was larger home ranges, arising from changes to several components of the hominin *bauplan*, that formed the building block for extending geographical ranges and eventually the size of the settled Terrae. Hominin evolution did not have to go in that direction, but the outcome shows that it did.

Bauplan: *Personal Network Size*

The 400 cm³ brain is informative about the cognitive thresholds to personal network size and how time acts as a constraint for a social species. Table 4.2 shows the predicted values, derived from brain volume, for the size of personal networks and the amount of time needed to maintain them by fingertip grooming. These estimates are based on Aiello and Dunbar's formulae (Chapter 2) and where predictions for the fossil hominins are extrapolated from data on a wide range of apes and monkeys.[3]

The predicted values for a 400 cm³ hominin brain are as follows:

- Neocortex ratio: 3.1
- Personal network size: 60.4
- Time spent grooming during daylight hours: 13.2%

The gorilla is again informative when it comes to evaluating these values. Because of its large brain, its predicted grooming time and personal network sizes exceed these values, and yet field studies show that both are much lower. The discrepancy between predicted and observed values is best explained by body weight and its implications for diet. The gorilla's mean body weight is by far the largest of any of the taxa in Table 4.2. Such a large body requires a great deal of food and time spent locating, eating and digesting it. Gorillas are vegetarians, and the quality of their diets is lower than that of the chimpanzees who also eat fruits and have, on occasion, been observed killing monkeys and other small animals.[4]

What stands out from Table 4.2 is that the 400 cm³ brain marks a threshold above which personal network sizes regularly exceed sixty other individuals, and upwards of fifteen per cent of a hominin's day would have been spent maintaining them by grooming.

---

[3] The formulae are calculated as follows (Aiello and Dunbar 1993): neocortex ratio = −0.618 + 0.200 LOG₁₀(brain volume); personal network size = 0.093 + 3.389 LOG₁₀(neocortex ratio); daytime grooming = −0.772 + 0.287(mean group size).

[4] The Asian orang-utan sheds further light on this relationship between body size and diet. *Pongo pygmaeus* is the most sexually dimorphic of all the great apes with a value of 2.12. Yet its average body size is only half the gorilla's, and their diet quality is higher (Antón, Leonard and Robertson 2002). Orang-utan brain size is 380 cm³ and predicted group size fifty-eight, with 12.3 per cent of their day spent grooming.

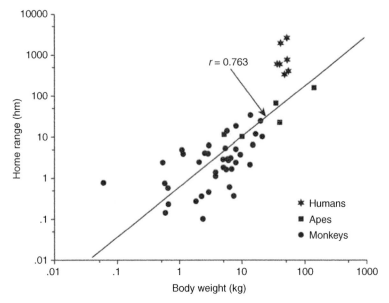

FIGURE 4.2. Body weight and increasing home range size in primates and humans. Adapted from Antón et al. (2002) and Antón and Swisher (2004).

Bauplan: *Body Size and Home Ranges*

This threshold in brain size also coincided with a reduction in body weight for some hominins (Table 4.2). The importance of body weight, as we have seen with the gorilla, is that it relates directly to diet and especially diet quality. What is striking in Table 4.2 is the spatial aspect of diet, the area that is needed to sustain an individual, referred to as a home range, and from which food is extracted on a daily basis. The size of an individual's home range varies enormously depending on the species' dietary niche. For example, the difference between a plant-food and animal-protein diet largely accounts for the differences between the sizes of ape and human home ranges. This is discussed by anthropologists Antón, Leonard and Robertson (2002) in terms of diet quality for a wide range of living primates (Figure 4.2). In their analysis, they found that body weight and the quality of the diet accounts for up to eighty per cent of the variation in home range size (Antón, Leonard and Robertson 2002: 779 and table 2).

By comparing two of the small-brained hominins of Terra 1, *Homo ergaster* and *Australopithecus africanus*, some interesting possibilities arise. For example, if the small-bodied *africanus* had a predominantly vegetarian diet, then using the ape home range figures, each individual would utilise some 35 ha. The much larger *ergaster*, who as we shall see in Terra 2 is a

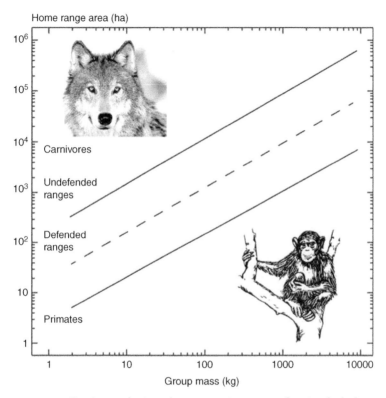

FIGURE 4.3. Carnivore and primate home range sizes measured against the body mass of the group. The limited possibility of defending larger ranges is indicated. Adapted from Gamble and Steele (1999).

candidate for making the shift towards a significant use of meat, and hence a higher-quality diet, would have a home range of 83 ha – more than twice as large. Add to this the larger personal networks, estimated at sixty-seven and ninety-three respectively, and we begin to see one of the major paths of travel in hominin evolution. Brains have always been an expensive tissue demanding large amounts of energy in the form of food. When available, higher-quality foods such as animal protein will be utilised. But as we saw in Chapter 2 (Figure 2.10), larger brains result in smaller stomachs to process the food. Moreover, any move to higher-quality foods will also mean larger home ranges (Gamble and Steele 1999: 397). For example, this increase is seen in the shift from foliage to fruits, and reflects the more dispersed, patchy and seasonal distribution of ripe fruits compared with leaves. For many carnivores, the situation is even more marked. Figure 4.3 shows the relationship between the group mass of carnivores and primates and the size of the home range they need to inhabit to obtain their food.

There were several adaptive choices facing the hominins (Table 4.1). Improving the quality of the diet and employing a basic stone technology to extract the most from food sources were two options. Technology, in the form of fire for roasting meat, would have provided another by acting as an external stomach to break down animal protein before it was eaten – a digestive problem that arose from the ratio of smaller guts and bigger brains (Chapter 2).

Group dynamics in the form of fission and fusion also provided flexible solutions to seasonal availability of food. But greater fission across the landscape would have come at the expense of daily face-to-face interaction as individuals and subgroups now lost contact with each other, albeit for short periods. Under such circumstances, the time available for social interaction started to acquire a premium. Such quality time for Wood and Lonergan's *Archaic Hominins* fostered an amplification of the methods by which social bonds have always been created and reinforced. We saw in the social brain route map (Figure 1.2) how the two resources to make those all-important bonds – hominin emotions and their response to the aesthetic appeal of materials – were available for such augmentation.

Three Steps to Walking and Running

The significance of locomotion at the start of global settlement now becomes clear. Locomotion affects the size of the home range an animal can cover. Furthermore, the ability to cover ground more quickly addresses the issues surrounding the quality time available for social interaction as well as finding higher-quality foods.

Bipedalism was the adaptive response, and there are three steps in its development. Step 1 (Table 4.3) saw the shift from four feet to two feet. However, to swap brachiating for walking also involved a move from vertically stacked food resources in the forest to less concentrated patches of food on the grasslands. Consequently, greater distances needed to be covered. As we shall see, Step 1 hominins hedged their bets, and while they walked, they also climbed and used the trees.

The pay-off for making a more fundamental change to locomotion would come if food, when found, satisfied a growth rather than a subsistence diet (Figure 3.11). Walking was one solution to finding such foods over larger areas. Step 2 hominins (Table 4.3) now adopted upright walking as their primary but not exclusive form of locomotion. The move from four to two legs had the added advantage of reducing heat stress by exposing less surface area to the tropical sun (Wheeler 1984, 1988).[5]

But as brains increased in size along with the demands for higher-quality diets, so too did the needs for even larger home ranges. Step 3 hominins evolved a novel solution: endurance running.[6] As argued by Bramble and Lieberman (2004), the human ability to run over long distances is exceptional compared to non-human primates.[7] The hominin record shows that the essential adaptation for endurance running – long legs relative to body mass and the spring-like function of the long arch of the foot – are present in *Homo* by the end of Terra 1 and the beginning of Terra 2. It is possible that such adaptations extend back as far as the earliest *Homo* at 2.4Ma (Table 4.3), but the evidence is not secure. The australopithecines were not adapted for endurance running, since they lacked the effective spring in the plantar arch of their foot bones (Bramble and Lieberman 2004: 347). Furthermore, they did not have the larger joint surfaces seen in *Homo* and which acted to lower joint stress while running.

Bramble and Lieberman (2004: 351) suggest that endurance running evolved in early *Homo* to make them effective scavengers and opportunistic hunters in open, semi-arid environments and even, perhaps, to compete better with other carnivores. The reward was a diet rich in fats and animal protein that fuelled the unique hominin *bauplan*: large bodies, long legs, small guts, big brains and small teeth (Table 4.1).[8]

Terra 0: Walking the Evolutionary Spine

Miocene Apes and Earliest Hominins

The limits of Terra 0 are set by the distribution of Miocene and Pliocene apes. They range in time from 23Ma to 5Ma, and their distribution covered

---

[5] Evolved sweat glands and hair on the head and shoulders also act to reduce heat stress. Wheeler also suggests that this would open up a noon-day niche for hominins at the time when most carnivores were resting.

[6] Defined by Bramble and Lieberman (2004: 345) as the ability to run over many kilometres over extended time periods using aerobic metabolism.

[7] Humans regularly run 10 km, about the same distance travelled in a day by African hunting dogs. Wolves and hyenas do better at 14–19 km. Bipedal running is, however, more costly than quadrapedal. In that respect, we are more like kangaroos in our ability to vary running speeds without a change of gait. This is unlike horses that move from trot to cantor to gallop (Bramble and Lieberman 2004: 346).

[8] Bramble and Lieberman (2004: 351). The importance of bipedalism was discussed in a classic paper by Lovejoy (1981) where he posited it as part of the package along with monogamy.

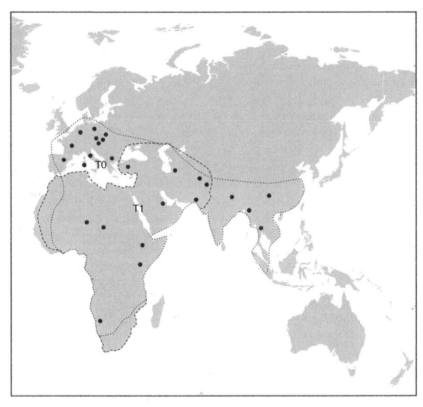

FIGURE 4.4. Distribution of Miocene apes across Terra 0. The smaller distribution of hominins in Terra 1 is also shown. Adapted from Senut (2010).

Africa, Europe and Asia (Figure 4.4; Andrews 2007; Folinsbee and Brooks 2007; Harrison 2010; Senut 2010). They formed a highly diverse group of small-bodied, arboreal primates with a variety of ape-like dentitions. Their distribution reflected the expansion of the tropics during the warmer and moister Early Miocene (23Ma–16Ma), a situation that started to change after 9.5Ma (Chapter 2), at the beginning of Terra 0. This saw the gradual trend towards colder and drier conditions and the expansion of C_4 grasses (see below) after 5Ma (Harrison 2010).[9]

The early ancestry of the hominids is linked to these widespread Miocene apes. Molecular studies of the Asian orang-utan indicate that they shared

[9] Two factors were at work. At 9.6Ma in the Middle Miocene, there was a dramatic turnover among mammals which included the anthropoids. This continued with the greater Asian monsoons driven by the uplift of the Tibetan plateau 7–8Ma.

a last common ancestor with their African counterparts 10Ma at the beginning of Terra 0. The other Southeast Asian great ape, the smaller and supremely arboreal gibbon, shared a last common ancestor some 12Ma.

The evolution from anthropoid (Miocene apes) to hominid (living great apes) and then to hominins is difficult to trace from the fossil evidence. The outcome is measured in terms of teeth, locomotion and, where possible, brain volume. In particular, three recent finds in Wood and Lonergan's *Possible and Probable Early Hominins Grade* (Table 4.3) are significant for the deep history of encephalisation and dispersal in Terrae 0 and 1.

The oldest is *Sahelanthropus tchadensis* dated to between 6Ma and 7Ma from Chad in Central Africa. The evidence takes the form of a single contorted skull that shares a series of features with hominids and later hominins. It is more of a hominin-like ape than a hominin, and is seen as distinct from any chimpanzee clade (Wood and Lonergan 2008: 356).

Orrorin tugenensis found in 1974 in the Tugen Hills at Baringo in Kenya is slightly younger, dated to the late Miocene. Thirteen pieces have been found from four localities, and include fragmentary teeth and mandibles described as ape-like. The partial femur divides opinion. Its neck has been interpreted by some as indicating habitual bipedal locomotion, while for others there is a hint of a bipedal and non-bipedal mix.

But by far the most important fossils from the *Possible and Probable* grade come from Aramis in the Middle Awash drainage basin in Ethiopia. These were found in 1993 and are the remains of *Ardipithecus ramidus*, among which is a nearly complete skeleton of a female dated to 4.3–4.5Ma ago. Two features stand out. The first is the pelvis, which confidently sexes the fossil, and the lower limbs show that *Ardipithecus* walked upright. Yet at the same time, the length of her arms and her big toe, that worked more like a thumb, show that she was adapted to climbing trees. The second feature is her canine. This is reduced in size from that expected for a chimpanzee but is much larger than the later early *Homo* – a possible indication of the transitional nature of the *Ardipithecus* fossils.

The current lack of male fossils makes it difficult to assess how variable the species might have been. *Ardi*'s cranium was found in pieces and is small at 325 cm³. This allows us to estimate a personal network size of fifty-three, with only ten per cent of the daytime devoted to grooming. She was 120 cm tall and weighed 40 kg (Table 4.2). Her home range size on an ape-quality diet was 44 ha, which makes it equivalent to the chimpanzee's. The sediments which contained her bones also yielded palaeoenvironmental evidence. As might be expected, these data revealed a very different environment to the present arid, treeless landscape. Her niche was open woodland, and within it she was an omnivore feeding in and below the trees on a range of plant foods.

The big question about *Ardipithecus*, and the older fossils (Table 4.3) from Kenya's Tugen Hills (*tugenensis*) and elsewhere in Ethiopia's Middle Awash (*kadabba*), is whether they were ancestral to the later australopithecines that appeared in Terra 0 and flourished in Terra 1. Three hypotheses have been put forward by the *Ardi* team (Suwa, Asfaw, Kono et al. 2009):

1. The transition occurred over the entire African range of *Ardipithecus*.
2. It was a local evolution, centred on Ethiopia, during Terra 0.
3. The outcome was due to geographic isolation.

Currently, it is not possible to choose confidently between them. However, the combination in Ethiopia, and East Africa generally, of high biodiversity (Figure 2.5), an extremely active stretch of the tectonic trail (Figure 2.6), and the conditions for local lake basins and woodland make a combination of hypotheses two and three the most likely.

The Versatile Ape

What *Ardipithecus* highlights is a general point about hominin and human dispersal made by palaeoanthropologists Wells and Stock (2007: 214): hominins colonised ecological niches rather than expanded into territories. They dispersed into the ecologically productive, broken topography of the tectonic trail (Figure 2.6) rather than into the wide-open spaces of Terra 0 or Terra 1. Furthermore, once in a new niche, hominins have always fitted existing anatomy and physiology to the conditions they find. *Ardipithecus*, who could walk upright yet still moved easily in the trees, was exhibiting that strategy, moving away from a specialist adaptation to one better suited to a generalist.

Wells and Stock make the key point that this trend, what they call plasticity, freed hominins from adaptations based on long-term genetic strategies. Hominins, they argue, were characterised by their refusal to commit to such strategies. The evolutionary card they held was the plasticity of their phenotype rather than the rules of the genotype. As a result, they could twist on behaviour and stick on anatomy and physiology. Of course, the latter did change. At some point, hominins evolved with larger brains, shorter arms and proper big toes. Four hands became two hands and two feet. But what the Terra 0 hominins achieved was to radiate into more variable niches, and this radiation, say Wells and Stock, initiated versatility by selecting for phenotypic plasticity.

It is for these reasons that dispersal matters in hominin evolution. It was the mechanism by which hominins sought, under natural selection, to improve their environmental conditions in terms of food supplies and access to mates and to lower the risk of predation (Fix 1999; Wells and Stock 2007). What is of interest is the impact that climatic variability had on the selection of these versatile hominins, an approach I examined in Chapter 2. There, I noted a distinct pulse of variability 3.3Ma ago – a pulse that coincided with some of the best-known grade of fossils in Terra o, the *Archaic Hominins* (Table 4.3). Among these are *Australopithecus afarensis*, first found in 1974 at Laetoli in Tanzania, and then in the Hadar region of Ethiopia with the discovery of a partial skeleton of an adult female, AL-288, better known as Lucy and dated to 3.3Ma. Both discoveries lie firmly on the tectonic trail and are close to contemporary bio-hotspots (Figures 2.5 and 2.6). There are outliers. *Bahrelghazali* comes from Chad, replicating the discovery of the much-older *tchadensis* from the same country.

The *Archaic Hominins*, as represented by *afarensis*, were markedly sexually dimorphic. They were upright walking, but above the waist were still adapted for climbing, as shown by their elongated fingers and specialised shoulder blades. The Terra o evidence for bipedal locomotion is complemented by the Laetoli footprint trail preserved soon after three hominins walked across fresh volcanic ash that then solidified. This occurred 3.6Ma ago. The stride length falls within the range of modern humans', and although the gait was rolling and so not quite modern in all its aspects, the speeds were fast.[10] The Lucy skeleton confirms this anatomical development for walking, but the clearest evidence now comes from a find of the same age from Dikika in Ethiopia where the skeleton of a three-year-old girl was found (Alemseged, Spoor, Kimbel et al. 2006). Enough of the skeleton survived to show that, below the waist, she was a bipedal hominin, while above it, she had the body of an ape: shoulder, arms and long grasping fingers. Furthermore, she had an ape-like hyoid bone that anchors the tongue and assists the production of sounds from the larynx.

These *afarensis* skeletons from Terra o draw together the threads of diet, anatomy and encephalisation in early hominin evolution. With a brain size well above ape values, *afarensis* emerges as a hominin with a mosaic of features. Its brain of 458 cm³ predicts a personal network size of sixty-six,

---

[10] The walking posture for Lucy has been much studied, and there is no overall consensus. For a recent review, see Raichlen, Pontzer and Sockol (2008).

which needed sixteen per cent of the daytime to be spent servicing it by fingertip grooming (Table 4.2). The small body weight of 39 kg, very similar to *Australopithecus africanus*, the other taxon in the *Archaic Hominin* grade (Table 4.3), points to a small home range of 41 ha on an ape-quality diet. This would rise to 254 ha per individual if diet quality were enhanced (Table 4.2). The relatively small encephalisation is matched by a modest reduction in gut size, and a predominantly ape-quality diet of leaves and fruits is strongly suggested. In support of their expensive tissue hypothesis, Aiello and Wheeler (1995) pointed out that the Lucy skeleton had the flared ribcage that is seen in the small-brained, large-gut primates, chimpanzee and gorilla.

The Hominin Niche

The question then arises of into what sort of niches these hominins radiated. An array of palaeoenvironmental evidence exists from the best-studied localities in tropical Africa during the Miocene and Pliocene such as Fort Ternan and Lake Turkana in Kenya (Behrensmeyer 2006). The findings have been summarised by Kingston (2007). What emerges is not a simple dichotomy between savannah or woodland environments, but a mosaic of intersecting habitats combining major vegetation types that varied according to the geographical scale of analysis. Kingston (2007: 43) summarises the results of the palaeoenvironmental studies as an expression of habitat heterogeneity that, in the long term, was dependent on the rhythms of orbital forcing.

But as Kingston (2007: 44) points out, simply invoking the concept of heterogeneity explains nothing in hominin evolution. The tectonic trail and the Milankovitch cycles produced fragmented, heterogeneous environments. These in turn channelled climate trends into specific local outcomes during the Late Miocene and Pliocene. Looked at with hindsight, these were very likely the necessary conditions for radiation and evolutionary change. But they were not sufficient to make change in this direction an inevitability among a small zoological group such as the hominins. The local scale also needs to be considered.

Versatility and Dispersal Thresholds

Viewed through the lens of variability selection (Chapter 2), the shifting sands of local environments are another means to examine the interplay of those three hominin strategies: specialist, generalist and versatilist. The

Miocene apes who dispersed during Terra 0 from Africa to Asia and back again appear to have been generalists at best and more often than not specialists (Folinsbee and Brooks 2007; Harrison 2010). It is possible that the difference between the two strategies can be summed up by differences in dispersal thresholds as an adaptive response to changing local environments. If this was the case, then the versatilist raised the threshold by taking phenotypic plasticity to a new level.

A more detailed aspect of dispersal thresholds is examined by Kingston (2007: 48) when species were faced with the appearance and disappearance of local niches. He describes this as a *shifting heterogeneity model* that weaves together local, regional and continental scales of habitat change. It was not the shift in major habitat types from lake to plain or from woodland to grassland that counted. Rather, it was the shifts in heterogeneity of those local environments that impacted on hominins through their dispersal capabilities. Could they follow their preferred habitats when the only way to do this required leapfrogging over intervening barriers (Figure 2.9)? Or did they instead need a continuous stretch of the same conditions in order to disperse?

In the case of the Miocene apes, it seems that their dispersal thresholds were closely controlled by the replication of ecological heterogeneity in forest environments, even though those forests differed in their regional and latitudinal composition, hence their geographical contraction during Terra 0 and the hominin response in Terra 1.

The appearance of the grade *Possible and Probable Early Hominins* (Table 4.3) in Terra 0 might therefore be an example of versatilists outcompeting generalists and specialists through an adaptive radiation. This involved a change in behaviour relating to diet, and then in locomotion and encephalisation. If so, this was an instance of behavioural plasticity in response to common conditions of habitat heterogeneity. This was then followed by a later adaptation, expressed anatomically and cognitively through bipedalism and larger brains. Tracing the causal sequence in such an evolutionary journey is not easy, but irrespective of the steps, the end point was the far-flung representatives of the *Archaic Hominins* across Africa in Terra 0.

Brain Size and Diet Quality

The appearance in Terra 0 of the 400 cm^3 hominin was significant for these dispersal thresholds. Network size and grooming time increased considerably. But the evidence from body size does not currently suggest a corresponding increase in home range. However, as Table 4.1 shows, home range would also have increased significantly if the quality of the diet changed, heralding a further adaptive radiation based on carnivory.

For the moment, however, let us assume an ape-quality diet of fruits and plant foods and compare two hominid taxa above and below the 400 cm³ threshold: *afarensis* and *Pan*, the living chimpanzee. They have comparable body weights (Table 4.2), but due to encephalisation, *afarensis* has a predicted personal network size of sixty-six as opposed to the chimpanzee's fifty-seven. When these network sizes are multiplied according to the group's home range, based on combined body mass, the figures are similar: 27 km² for *afarensis* and 25 km² for the chimpanzee (Table 4.2).

But what happens if diet quality is increased? On the upside, a versatilist moving into that niche might outcompete other hominins with a specialist or generalist strategy. However, the downside is that 27 km² becomes 168 km² for that same network of sixty-six closely interacting individuals, a sixfold increase. Social interaction now has a strong spatial constraint because of the need for fission and fusion over a larger home range. This can be countered in two ways: either select higher-quality growth foods in larger package sizes that bring people together and allow them to linger longer over their social interactions, or up the tempo of mobility by changing the pattern of locomotion. If both coincide then, potentially, a versatilist is born.

Locomotion, Technology and Female Strategies

There must, however, be sufficient reason to overhaul hominid locomotion so profoundly. One possibility returns us to the importance of growth and subsistence diets in determining reproductive success (Figure 3.11). As discussed in Chapter 3, the female strategy drives evolution because of the costs of reproduction that fall on them in the form of child bearing and rearing.

Therefore, mobility for a versatilist is driven by female priorities – getting to those growth foods before others. When group home ranges are as small as 27 km² (equivalent to a circle with a radius of 3 km), then growth foods must be locally abundant to keep the costs of travel and social interaction low. When the sizes of home ranges rise because of better-quality diets and larger body size, then the *bauplan* needs to change if local dispersal is to occur. That is the genotype route (Table 4.2).

The behavioural, phenotypic route involved technology, and an indication from Terra 0 of an interest in higher-quality diets comes from Dikika in Ethiopia. In levels below the child skeleton, and dated to 3.41Ma, a small series of bovid bones were found. These carry the telltale traces of cut marks caused by stone tools. But there are no stone tools in these deposits, and currently the oldest come from Ethiopia dated to 2.5Ma. However, it is unlikely that the oldest stone tools have yet been found, and the Dikika evidence suggests that an antiquity of another one million years, at least, is to be expected.

The evidence for cutting flesh off carcasses and possibly breaking the bones for the energy-rich fats and marrow they contain fits well with an evolutionary story driven by the selection pressure on females. Gaining access to higher-value growth foods such as animal protein marks one strand in a developing plasticity of behaviour. Technology and mobility go together, and in so doing open a pathway to brain expansion and an extension of home ranges in Terra 0.

Terra 1: Running down the Tectonic Trail

If Terra 0 was a world of primate possibilities, then Terra 1 was the first hominin geography. The *bauplan* was now well established: brains larger than 400 cm^3, smaller teeth and guts compared to the hominids and anthropoids of Terra 0, Step 2 walking and, for *Homo* at least, Step 3 running that assisted radiation into heterogeneous niches. However, there were other, contemporary, evolutionary pathways. For example, the *Megadonts* retained large teeth and not all of the *Archaic Hominins* achieved Step 2 bipedalism (Table 4.3). The heterogeneity of these hominins is marked, and further discoveries will only increase the variety, as is the case with the 2Ma fossil *Australopithecus sediba* from Malapa in South Africa (Pickering, Dirks, Jinnah et al. 2011) that shows a mixture of *Archaic* and *Transitional* features (Table 4.3). However, at 2Ma years old, it is unlikely, as claimed, to be a precursor to *Homo* that first appears as the species *habilis* and *rudolfensis* 2.4Ma at several localities in East Africa (Spoor 2011; Wood and Lonergan 2008).[11]

Stone Technology

Part of this hominin variety extended to stone tools and technology generally. Which species made the tools remains unclear. However, following

---

[11] *Sediba* is described by Spoor (2011: 45) as a late australopithecine with several intriguing *Homo*-like features. Two of these features are the shapes of the pelvis and ankle joint.

the discovery of the Dikika cut marks, it is likely that Mode 1 artefacts (Box 2.3), consisting of stone cores, hammerstones and sharp-edged flakes, whose edges were sometimes trimmed, were made by several hominin grades (Table 4.3).

The variety of chimpanzee technologies, what some even regard as evidence for distinctive regional cultures, has shattered the idea that one size fitted all when it came to the earliest technology (Davidson and McGrew 2005; Gowlett 2000). Their artefacts consist almost exclusively of instruments with few convincing containers (Gamble 2007; McGrew 1992: table 7.2). Termite probes and a variety of other tools that "fish" for foods by extending the reach of the arm, as well as anvils and hammerstones to crack open nuts, are testament to chimpanzee diversification, while their deliberate percussive technology now has an archaeology extending back 4.3ka (Mercader, Barton, Gillespie et al. 2007). Nut-cracking today takes place in the context of mother–child dyads, and often up to eight years is needed to pass on this skill. The nutritious nuts are a growth food only available through the application of technology.

But the important point about chimpanzee technology is that it never led to geographical expansion. Instead, as their preferred habitats fluctuated, their technology allowed them to stay put and become more efficient specialists.

The oldest stone tools occur in Terra 1. They come from Gona in the Afar region of Ethiopia and are dated to 2.5Ma. A detailed study of the raw materials has shown that there was deliberate selection from stone outcrops a short distance from the locale (Stout, Quade, Semaw et al. 2005). The cobbles available to the Gona hominins varied according to four criteria: rock type, phenocryst percentage, average phenocryst size and groundmass texture. Rather than just using the nearest to hand, the Gona hominins appreciated the flaking qualities of different stones. Such an appreciation of the relative merits and properties of stone was partly on the basis of practical knowledge and partly an aesthetic judgement.

The earliest stone tools of Terra 1 currently form a cluster in East Africa (Figure 4.5; de la Torre 2011). Among these, the Omo River in Ethiopia has provided a large series of stone tools from members F and E in the Shungura formation, dated to between 2.32Ma and 2.4Ma. Comparable to the artefacts from Gona, as well as material from the Turkana Basin in Kenya, fresh analyses of the Omo material have reversed the view that Mode 1 assemblages were expedient and procedurally simple. Instead, as archaeologist de la Torre (2004) shows, the methods of production and stone knapping were far removed from simple rock bashing to produce sharp-

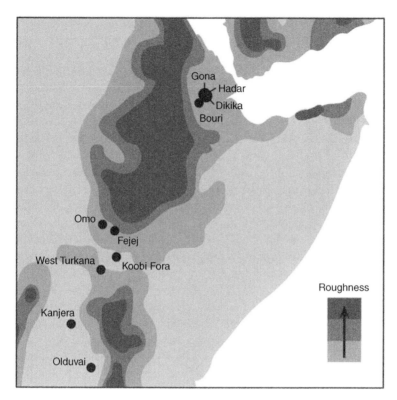

FIGURE 4.5. The earliest stone tools in East Africa and the tectonic trail (see Figure 2.6). Adapted from de la Torre (2011).

edged flakes and, in the process, reduce a stone nodule down to a core that might, in some circumstances, have seen service as a hammerstone. There was no careful preparation or later flaking designed to rejuvenate these cores to knap more flakes. Yet the standardised shape of the flakes shows that the hominins doing the knapping appreciated volume, while the knapping surfaces were worked sequentially rather than randomly. In de la Torre's (2004: 455) opinion, these were rational makers of stone technology. They selected the stones to produce the results they desired and then systematically produced flakes in an efficient manner.

Terra 1 Hominins Isotope Diets and Territories

The study of isotopes in the bones of fossil hominins represents a revolution in archaeological science. The traditional route to reconstructing diets rests on the morphology of teeth and a chain of inferences drawn from animal and plant remains. Now, direct measurements of $\delta^{13}C$ from the teeth of fossils shorten those chains of inference. They do not tell us what species of plants and animals they ate, but they do estimate the relative proportions of two photosynthetic pathways: C_3 and C_4. When combined with evidence from cut marks on animal bones, a clearer picture emerges of the dietary composition of Terra 1 hominins.

There are two main routes by which CO_2 (carbon dioxide) is bonded with H_2O (water) to produce sugar and oxygen through the process of plant photosynthesis. C_3 and C_4 pathways are named after the number of carbon compounds and are particularly important in understanding the evolution of low-latitude vegetation. Most plants follow the C_3 pathway leading plant chemists to conclude that C_4 is more recent (Ambrose 2006; Lee-Thorp and Sponheimer 2006).

In the tropics, most trees, bushes, shrubs and herbaceous forbs use the C_3 pathway, while grasses and sedges follow C_4 (Sponheimer, Passey, De Ruiter et al. 2006: 980). $\delta^{13}C$ can be measured in animal teeth and also in soil nodules (Plummer, Ditchfield, Bishop et al. 2009),[12] and combining the evidence from the stratified sequence at Kanjera in south-western Kenya identifies when a shift to C_4 grasslands took place (Plummer, Ditchfield, Bishop et al. 2009).[13] The Kanjera sequence falls firmly in Terra 1 with the earliest sediments (KS-1 to KS-3) dated to c. 2.3–1.95Ma. The isotopic evidence points to a predominance of C_4 grasses in this period, and the trend started earlier in Terra 1 associated with cooler and drier temperatures (Figure 2.1). In the 2Ma-year-old grasslands of Kanjera (KS-2), archaeologists excavated almost 2500 stone tools from an area of 169 m². Such a high density of artefacts is clear evidence that, by this time, either *Archaic* or *Transitional* hominins (Table 4.3) were living in these novel habitats along with other C_4 herbivores (Plummer, Ditchfield, Bishop et al. 2009: 3).

The isotopic analysis of $\delta^{13}C$ in the teeth of fossil hominins can also reveal the C_3 to C_4 ratio (Lee-Thorp and Sponheimer 2006: 139; Plummer, Ditchfield, Bishop et al. 2009). When applied to Terra 1 hominins from South Africa, Lee-Thorp and Sponheimer (2006: fig. 5) found a component of C_4 plants in *Australopithecus africanus*, *Paranthropus robustus* and early *Homo*. While clearly distinguished in their analysis from the herbivores which grazed exclusively on C_4 grasses, the three hominins were

---

[12] These are measurements of palaeosol carbonates taken on the pedogenic nodules forming in C_3- and C_4-dominated environments.

[13] A grassland environment is defined as having more than seventy-five per cent C_4 grasses (Plummer, Ditchfield, Bishop et al. 2009: 1).

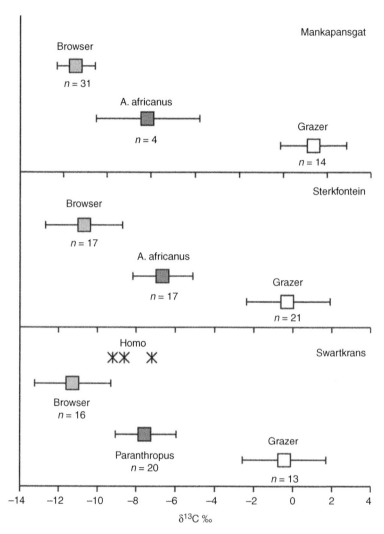

FIGURE 4.6. Hominin diets, as revealed by stable isotopes from three South African fossil sites. The graph shows the variation in a carbon isotope. This suggests a more versatile diet for the australopithecines as well as early *Homo*. Adapted from Lee-Thorp and Sponheimer (2006) and Sponheimer et al. (2006).

also sufficiently different from the C_3 browsing herbivores (Figure 4.6). In fact, the two *Archaic Hominin* genera, *Australopithecus* and *Paranthropus*, obtained almost thirty per cent of their carbon from C_4 sources (Lee-Thorp and Sponheimer 2006: 138).

The question then becomes how they acquired this component. Were they eating small grass seeds or eating the animals that had fed on C_4 grasses, and thereby ingesting $\delta^{13}C$? Seeds are highly productive resources, but their tiny size makes them labour intensive to harvest and process. The same energy can be obtained from animals at a fraction of the processing cost. But finding and capturing animal resources can be time-consuming, sometimes dangerous and hence energetically expensive. However, the returns in the form of a higher-quality diet are considerable and, as I have been arguing, necessary for any 400 cm³+ hominin.

More work is needed, but what we can say is that the carbon intake of these *Archaic* and *Transitional* hominins indicates a different dietary strategy to modern tropical great apes who are almost exclusively C_3 feeders (Lee-Thorp and Sponheimer 2006: 139). Furthermore, the shift to C_4 grasslands did not drive hominins down the meat-eating–seed-eating pathway, but it did reward the versatilist who was radiating into new niches (Braun, Harris, Levin et al. 2010).

The direct isotope techniques are also evolving. Laser ablation techniques allow the sampling of incremental growth in teeth, and the $\delta^{13}C$ they contain (Ambrose 2006). When applied to the enamel of four teeth of *Paranthropus robustus* from South Africa, dated to 1.8Ma ago, Sponheimer, Passey, De Ruiter et al. (2006) found considerable seasonal variability over the lifetime of the individuals they had sampled. The average seasonal variation was 3.4‰ while for the herbivore species used as a control sample the same technique only produced 0.7‰. Moreover, besides revealing seasonal differences, laser ablation also pointed to significant interannual variation in the same teeth.

Two suggestions to explain this finding have been made: first, that they reflect differences in rainfall that impacted on the availability of food, and second, that the hominins were migrating between habitats that were more open and more wooded (Sponheimer, Passey, De Ruiter et al. 2006: 981). Comparisons with two primates, chimpanzees and baboons (*Papio* sp), are instructive. Similar studies have shown no seasonal variation among the C_3 chimpanzee feeders. By contrast, savannah-living baboons who eat considerable quantities of C_4 plants in the form of seeds and roots do have variable $\delta^{13}C$ values.

These findings, when combined with microwear studies of teeth to determine the abrasive quality of the foods being eaten, point to some major shifts in diet among the *Archaic Hominins* of Terra 1. Sponheimer, Passey, De Ruiter et al. (2006: 981) argue that after 3Ma, the diets of *A. africanus* were more variable than those of the older *A. afarensis* (Figure 4.6).

Therefore, *Homo* was not unique in making the dietary shift, although we still need more information on the components of the diet: plant and animal. Furthermore, the idea that the *Megadonts* were highly specialised hominin herbivores, as indicated by their big teeth, has had to be revised. As revealed by their isotope diets, they were more versatile than that.

The Scale of Landscape Use

Another isotope, strontium (Sr), now points to the scale of landscape use among *Archaic Hominins* (Copeland, Sponheimer, De Ruiter et al. 2011). Strontium isotopes, taken up when drinking water, become trapped in teeth as they grow. Their analysis provides a means to compare the geology of where they were found with the geology represented in the teeth. The geographical divergence between the two sets of data indicates the scale of landscape use and shows where they travelled with their mothers.

The study was based on the nearby cave sites of Sterkfontein and Swartkrans in South Africa, and involved analysing the $^{87}Sr/^{86}Sr$ ratio in the teeth of nineteen hominins ascribed either to A. *africanus* (Sterkfontein 2.2Ma; eight individuals) or P. *robustus* (Swartkrans 1.8Ma; eleven individuals). These ratios were then compared to those in the surrounding geology.

The results showed different Sr values for the teeth from the smallest and largest individuals, a size distinction that Copeland, Sponheimer, De Ruiter et al. (2011) interpret as males and females. The females' Sr was more varied and non-local (seventy-five per cent of the sample) to the valley in which the caves are found. By contrast, the large, probably male, teeth have predominantly local (eighty-three per cent of the sample) Sr counts. These clear differences suggest that when females reached reproductive age, they moved away from their natal group, while the males never strayed far from the dolomite where they were born. The Sterkfontein valley where the caves are located forms a roughly 10-km-wide band that runs for some 70 km (Copeland, Sponheimer, De Ruiter et al. 2011: fig. 1). Since the males would only have had to move 2–6 km to reach a different geological stratum, it seems they were confined to an area of only some 30 km^2 (Schoeninger 2011). Young females matured elsewhere and then moved into the males' area.

The geological sources of the stone tools provide another piece of evidence for the scale of land use in Terra 1. At Gona, the stone tools came from no farther than 3 km away from where they were dropped and then incorporated into sediments. This pattern is widespread and continues into

TABLE 4.4. *Group home range (HR) sizes among selected small-brained hominins in Terra 1*

	Mean adult body weight (kgs)	HR Ape diet (ha)	HR human diet (ha)	Personal network size	Group HR (km²) Ape–Human diet
Paranthropus robustus	36	38	236	76	29–179
Australopithecus africanus	34	35	219	67	23–147
Homo rudolfensis	55	68	421	90	61–379

Data from Table 4.2.

the better-documented Terra 2 where raw materials are rarely found more than 10 km from their geological source and invariably much closer.

Such a small area for these hominins fits best with a home range using an ape-quality diet (Table 4.4), suggesting that seeds rather than animals might explain those C_4 values. Included in the table are the body-size estimates for the much larger Terra 1 hominin *Homo rudolfensis* who required a home range almost three times as large on an ape-quality diet and at least twice as large on a human-quality diet. Schoeninger (2011) makes the point that the Sterkfontein evidence fits better to a gorilla than a chimpanzee pattern; groups of the former occupy 25 km², while the latter roam over 600 km². The key issue is protection against predators. Gorillas do this through their size. The small-brained hominins who occupied a similar-sized area did it through their numbers and, in that respect, resemble more closely modern baboons who live on the open grasslands. Here is an instance where predation pressure (Figure 2.10) provides a selective force for group size, and, I would argue, the necessity for encephalisation in order to cope with the additional cognitive load of a larger social life.

When the Sr data, the stone sources and the body-size data are drawn together, the conclusion is overwhelming that Terra 1 hominins operated in small spatial areas. Their lives were local. In addition, there is the hint from the dispersal evidence that the female strategy based on access to growth foods was, as expected, setting the evolutionary direction.

The Limits to Terra 1

The boundaries to Terra 1 are imprecise, emerging piece by piece like the early charts of the coast of Terra Australis to European explorers. That it is smaller than Terra 0, with its widespread Miocene apes and its restricted Pliocene hominins, is clear. Also apparent is the importance of the tectonic trail for creating environments to settle and conditions for evolution to occur. We now expect high levels of hominin diversity along this trail, connecting biodiversity hotspots in Africa with those in Asia.

So what are the limits to Terra 1? Terra 1 hominins live at altitudes between 1000 and 2500 m in the high plateaux of South and East Africa. They do not appear to live on the coast, but at these timescales, preservation is poor for such environments. The rare finds in the Sahara point to dispersals within Terra 1 that are driven by changes in rainfall and the creation of lakes and streams, as described in the model of pulsed variability (Chapter 2; Maslin and Christensen 2007). These opportunities, currently poorly documented, indicate at this early stage in hominin evolution the geographical principle of recurrent, bio-tidal dispersal.

Given this range, which defies the tropical disease belts, it is expected that future research will extend the diversity of *Possible and Probable Early Hominins* (Table 4.3) throughout the north-eastern extension that I have drawn for Terra 1. These limits, and indeed the importance of the tectonic trail, are hypotheses that only future fieldwork will test.

But what underlies these limits? We know that the great apes, African and Asian, are restricted by body size and diet to the tropics where resources are sufficient to support them in small home ranges (Table 4.2). But other primates, and many omnivores, are settled well outside the tropics and particularly in the more northerly latitudes of Asia. Moreover, animals as different as pigs and macaque monkeys achieve these large distributions without recourse to carnivory, where animal protein is the growth food of the north.

Macaques have the most northerly distribution of any primate in either the Old or New World (Abegg and Thierry 2002; Thierry, Iwaniuk and Pellis 2000). Asian in origin, they consist of several regional species that subsequently expanded into Europe and North Africa (Fooden 2007). Their current distribution is extremely vicariant due to human disturbance imposing geographical barriers, with a widely separated western population and several island populations in Japan and throughout Indonesia (Figure 4.7).

Macaques are small bodied, ranging from 5 to 8 kg, and small brained, 63 cm³, with an EQ of 1.7–1.2.[14] Their personal network size is forty, and

---

[14] These figures, supplied by Robin Dunbar, are for *Macaca mulatta* found today throughout South Asia; neocortex volume = 63.4 cc, neocortex ratio = 2.6, mean group size = 39.6.

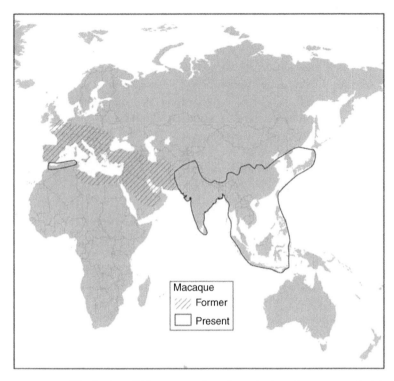

FIGURE 4.7. Distribution of Macaque monkeys. Several subspecies are recognised in Asia and note their extension into Northern Europe during the Pleistocene. Adapted from Abegg and Thierry (2002), Delson (1980) and Fooden (2007).

their individual home ranges are 1.8–5 ha each, giving a group home range of between 0.7 and 2 km². The three species listed by Antón, Leonard and Robertson (2002: table 2) have a mean diet quality of 196.[15] This is considerably higher than for the gorilla with a diet quality of 114, and superior to the chimpanzee (178) and orang-utan (183). Macaques are not meat eaters, so their higher diet quality results from a greater use of the reproductive parts of plants, seeds and fruits, rather than the fibre from the plant stems that forms the gorilla's staple fare. Macaques have been noted for their innovations in behaviour, most notably in Japan where they colonised hot springs and learned to wash rice in the sea, a capacity that was transmitted to the next generation.

[15] The range of diet quality is from 100 (a diet of all foliage) to 350 (a diet of all animal food). The quality is calculated from the relative contribution of three components: (1) structural plant parts, (2) reproductive plant parts, and (3) animal material (Antón, Leonard and Robertson 2002: 779).

Here, then, is an example of the dispersal success of a small-brained anthropoid. What underpinned the macaque's success during their adaptive radiations was their small body size and higher-quality diet. Their tiny home ranges when compared to the great apes and the *Archaic Hominins* made it possible to radiate into a variety of Eurasian habitats and, in Terra 2, up to a latitude of 51°N in England (Schreve 2001). Further north, diet quality declined, and they could not compensate either by moving to animal foods or by increasing home range size. As Antón, Leonard and Robertson (2002) point out, the difference between monkeys such as macaques and the great apes such as the chimpanzee is the difference between an *r* and K selected species (see Chapter 1). Macaque dispersal is fuelled by shorter lifespans, greater reproductive rates and reduced periods of infant dependency. As such, they present another primate dispersal pattern; one that differs from that followed by the big bodies and large home ranges of the hominins.

Other non-primate species (Figure 4.8) have had similar success in colonising within and beyond the limits of Terrae 0 and 1. These include the omnivores, pigs and bears, as well as large carnivores such as hyena, wolf and lion. The carnivores have, of course, upped the quality of the diet to be almost exclusively animal protein but without going down the route of encephalisation. When combined with efficient four-footed locomotion, they can sustain the larger home ranges they need in order to find enough food (Gamble and Steele 1999). Alternatively, pigs have specialised digestive systems that can extract nutrition from otherwise toxic, high-energy seeds and nuts, most notably acorns in northern deciduous forests. Finally, hibernation is a tactic bears use to overcome prolonged seasonality in northern latitudes, only emerging when growth foods are plentiful in spring and summer. This ability to store food in the body, and so avoid the penalty of high altitudes and northern winters, is not an option for hominids or hominins.

These anthropoids, omnivores and carnivores all display specialist diets to which their physiology and anatomy are supremely well adapted. Many of them are also highly social and cooperative. But to achieve these impressive distributions, they invest heavily in the genotype (Table 4.1). This emphasises Wells and Stock's (2007) point that hominins are freed up from following this route by the variable nature of their behaviour – that extreme adaptive plasticity. What limits the macaques is not their sociability or their inventiveness, but the corporal and spatial scale at which they operate. Small, low-EQ brains and small bodies do not need a change in diet. Macaque settlement is therefore bio-tidal, shifting with the availability

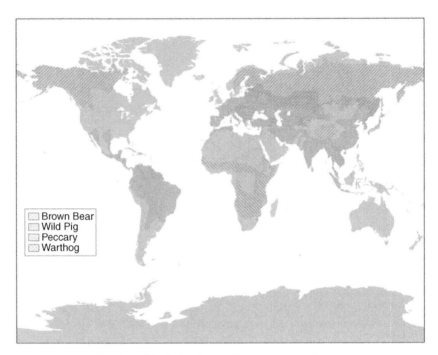

FIGURE 4.8. The worldwide distribution of some major omnivores.

of food in the environments to which they are adapted. Large, high-EQ brains and large bodies need bigger territories and, to settle beyond Terra 1, a change in diet to include those prized northern growth foods – animals. It is those behavioural, or phenotypic (Table 4.1), changes that have to be made before settlement beyond Terra 1 is possible.

The bonanza, as Dennell (2009) argues, for any hominin who gets beyond Terra 1 is the mid-latitude C_4 grasslands because the food they possess is highly accessible (Table 3.5). This is the geographical target for a versatile, tropical-born species, who has solved that co-evolutionary puzzle of how to link up diet change and environmental knowledge with cooperation (Gowlett 2010). These grasslands include and extend beyond the tectonic trail. They demand the stomachs and cooperation of the social carnivores and the group size and encephalisation of the macaques. Then both elements need to be amplified to overcome the limitations of either. It is unsurprising that hominins lived within Terra 1 for so long. How they transcended its boundaries and started the first moves to global settlement now needs our attention.

CHAPTER 5

Three strides across a bio-tidal world: Terra 2, 1.8Ma–50ka

> *It is one thing to allow that a given migration is possible and another to admit there is good reason to believe it has really taken place.*
> Thomas Huxley, *Man's Place in Nature*, 1863

Hominins on the Move

Terra 2 is a world of expansion and contraction (Figure 5.1). Major geographical gains occur with large areas of Eurasia now settled for the first time. But the boundaries to further dispersal are rigid. No hominin crosses the comparatively short ocean distance from Indonesia to Australia, and elsewhere there is no significant expansion above 55°N. Indeed, the northern distribution of Terra 2 hominins looks very similar to the Pleistocene distribution of macaque monkeys (Figure 4.7).

Terra 2 sees a step change in the quantity and diversity of evidence. The varied hominins who inhabit and settle Terra 2 left behind an archaeology that is increasingly rich in quantity and variety. When scrutinised by archaeologists, it reveals there were technological changes to the stone tools, the novel use of materials for aesthetic enchantment, fire, ochre and shell, as well as evidence for new concepts such as containers and composite tools. By contrast, the fossil evidence remains patchy for much of Terra 2, its classification and interpretation often disputed. But this situation changes towards the end of this Terra with more abundant fossil data from Europe and Indonesia.

Much happens during Terra 2. Hominins increase in body and brain size. They become top predators. They evolve language and display cognitive abilities such as theory of mind. They change the way they live in landscapes by fragmenting, accumulating and consuming materials to create special places that take the form of "super sites". On the social front, their

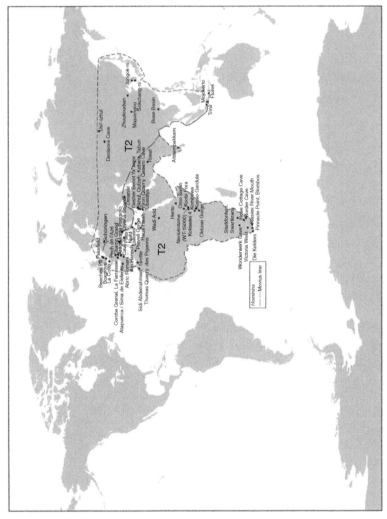

FIGURE 5.1. Terra 2 with key sites, regions and hominins. The Movius line in Asia is shown.

personal networks grow in size, as indicated by greater encephalisation. And, as they settle further north, they have to tackle the demands of more pronounced fission and fusion and a degree of separation. They respond by amplifying, through memories, music and dance, the emotional basis by which social bonds are forged. This made the bonds stronger and better able to manage the cognitive demands of monitoring more people now scattered widely across larger home and regional ranges.

The tectonic trail remains important for dispersal, but the hominins in Terra 2 now depart from it by expanding into areas of low tectonic activity such as Northern Europe and Southern India and more widely across the Sahara. Instead, it is the long-term climate rhythms that have a greater shaping power on settlement (Figure 2.1, Box 2.1). Changes driven by the Milankovitch cycles extend the duration of each warm–cold cycle, accentuating the maximum and minimum conditions. One of the major outcomes is the creation of five great bio-tidal zones in Terra 2 – regions which appeared and then disappeared for hominin settlement. These five zones of contraction–expansion are: glaciated Europe, the green deserts of North Africa and Arabia, the rainforests of Central Africa, the Sunda shelf and Moviusland, the northern boreal boundary across Eurasia. These bio-tidal zones set the machinery in motion for population dispersal.

Three Strides Across Terra 2

The deep history of Terra 2 is covered in three large strides (Table 5.1). It begins with dispersal beyond the limits of Terra 1 by *Homo erectus*. This phase lasts for one million years (1.8–0.8Ma) during which time the boundaries of the Terra are established. Large-brained hominins from the *Homo* lineage now exceed the second threshold of 900 cm³ (Table 4.2). Carnivory is a common dietary niche. Technology changes with the widespread appearance of Mode 2 Large Cutting Tools (LCT), comprising picks, cleavers and bifaces/hand axes. But encephalisation and the timing of technological change do not show a simple connection.

The second stride (800–200ka) sees hominins with even larger brains, an augmentation of stone technology with the earliest Mode 3 projectiles, composites of wood and stone, and an ability to cope with greater environmental changes. Diets are improved as new skills, unique among large predators, ensure the successful capture of animals in their prime. It is during this stride that language develops to meet the cognitive demands of larger networks. Music and dance are further mechanisms that amplify the strength of social bonds through group activities. It is also a time when

TABLE 5.1. *Three chronological strides in Terra 2 associated with encephalisation in the Homo lineage*

Terra 2	Stride 1 1.8–0.8Ma	Stride 2 0.8–0.2Ma	Stride 3 200–50ka
Direction of dispersal	East	West	East
Milankovitch dominant cycle	Obliquity 41ka	Eccentricity 100ka	Eccentricity 100ka
Climate outcomes	Small Northern hemisphere glaciation; Monsoon pattern	Sunda shelf and Doggerland Middle Pleistocene 'revolution'	Green desert phases
Brain size	Above 900 cm³	Above 1200 cm³	Up to 1600 cm³
Technology	Mode 1 and Mode 2 Large Cutting Tools, PCT*, Karari cores/ scrapers large flakes	Mode 2 LCT and evidence for hafting and composite tools, PCT, Kombewa, Victoria West	Mode 3 and evidence for hafting and composite tools, PCT, Levallois
Fire	Possible evidence	Hearths and control	Hearths and control
Language	No	Yes	Yes
Theory of mind	Level 2	Level 3	Level 4 and above
Levels of intention	Level 3?	Level 4	
Emotions	Mood, Primary, Social?	Mood, Primary and Social	Mood, Primary and Social
Imagination on display	No evidence	Limited evidence, possible burials	Shells, ochre and bone items, Burials

*PCT = Prepared Core Technology.
Adapted from McNabb (2001) and Barham and Mitchell (2008: 194).

hominins redefine their relationship with the land they dwell in by creating special places – super sites – which consume and accumulate vast sets of artefacts and materials; environmental knowledge now has a basis in long-term memories. These hominins show an advanced theory of mind – the ability to second-guess someone else's intentions.[1] Theory of mind represents an imaginative leap for hominins. It creates social emotions, such as guilt, to underpin codes of social behaviour. It opens up the way to concepts of "going-beyond" that will prove essential during the settlement of Terra 3.

[1] This is also referred to as mentalising (Gamble, Gowlett and Dunbar 2011).

The final stride (200–50ka) sees the pace of cultural change quicken. Hominin bodies are now wrapped in cultural materials that include simple sets of beads made from shells, while other evidence for technologies that use the concept of containment, such as hearths, is forthcoming. There are also shifts in the breadth of diets that now include the abundance of seashore resources.

Throughout Terra 2, speciation remains dynamic. *Archaic Hominins* such as *Paranthropus* still settled parts of Africa during the first stride. But above all, Terra 2 is the stamping ground for the several species of *Homo*: *Transitional*, *Pre-modern* and *Modern* (Table 4.3). And it is during the final stride that our direct ancestors, *Homo sapiens*, evolve in East Africa, a small regional population among many other hominin populations. What begins as a routine process in hominin evolution develops into a species with immense ecological versatility; a potential that is realised in the extraordinary geographical expansion we shall see in Terra 3 (Chapters 6–7).

Large Brains and Bauplan

Brains larger than 900 cm³ first appeared during Terra 2, and all of them are classified as *Homo*. However, during the first stride, several small-brained hominins of the genera *Homo* and *Paranthropus* (Table 5.2) were present, and both saw brain growth (Elton, Bishop and Wood 2001: fig. 7).

In the case of *Paranthropus*, the cranial volumes showed a long-term trend for encephalisation from 2.4Ma in Terra 1 to 1.2Ma in Terra 2. Brain sizes in Terra 1 for these robust australopithecines were between 440 and 500 cm³ rising to 545 cm³ in a small sample from Terra 2 (Elton, Bishop and Wood 2001: table 7), an increase of almost a quarter in 1.2 million years. By contrast, those fossils classified as *Homo* from early Terra 2 (1.9–0.75Ma) range from an average of 614 cm³ for *Homo habilis* to 1067 cm³ for the *Homo erectus* skull from Olduvai Gorge, an increase of almost three-quarters in 1.2 million years (Elton, Bishop and Wood 2001: table 7).

A 900 cm³ brain predicts a personal network size of 104, much higher than any observed among living primates (Table 4.2). These numbers also suggest that almost thirty per cent of daylight hours had to be spent fingertip grooming if that was the only means by which social bonds were negotiated and confirmed.

An important fossil from Terra 2's first stride was found in 1984 in the West Turkana region of Kenya and dated to 1.53Ma (Walker and Leakey 1993). The Nariokotome skeleton (WT-15,000) was an adolescent male, eight to twelve years old, who most likely died of septicaemia from an infected

TABLE 5.2. *Terra 2 hominins (a) encephalisation and bauplan data for hominin species. The figures for a 900 cm³ hominin provide a baseline. Terra 2 hominins (b) individual fossil skulls, large and small brain sizes, grouped according to the grades in Table 4.3*

	Terrae	Age (Ma)	Mean cranial capacity (cm³)	Sample size	EQ	Neocortex ratio	Personal network size	Grooming time (% daytime)	Mean height (m)	Mean adult body weight (kg)	Sexual dimorphism	Individual Home range (Ha Ape) (ha)	Individual Home range (Ha Human) (ha)	Group Home range (Ha Ape) (km²)	Group Home range (Ha Human) (km²)
(a)															
Terra 2 Large-brained hominins and humans															
Homo sapiens (modern)	5	extant	1352		6.04	4	136	38	1.85	49	1.16	58	360	79	490
Homo sapiens (Pleistocene)	2&3	0.19–0.01	1478	66	5.38	4.07	144	40	1.85	66	1.19	83	518	120	746
Homo neanderthalensis	2&3	0.2–0.028	1426	23	4.75	4.04	141	39	1.6	72	1.17	98	608	138	857
Homo heidelbergensis	2	0.6–0.1	1204	17	4.07	3.9	126	35	1.8	71	1.08	96	596	121	751
Homo erectus	2	1.8–0.2	1003	36	3.97	3.8	112	31	1.7	61	1.14	73	453	82	507
The 900 cm³ hominin			900		3.7	3.7	104	29							
(b)															
Terra 2 Pre-modern Homo large brained															
Homo heidelbergensis															
Dali	Asia	0.2	1085	1	5.3	3.8	118	33		46		53	331	63	391
Jinniushan	Asia	0.28	1255	1	5.1	3.9	130	36		59		75	464	98	603
Sima de los Huesos 5	Europe	0.4	1125	1	5.9	3.9	121	34		40		44	273	53	330
Arago	Europe	0.45	1128	1	6.8	3.9	121	34		35		37	228	45	276
Bodo	Africa	0.6	1208	1	3.7	3.9	127	35		84		121	749	154	951
Petralona	Europe	0.4–0.25	1189	1	5.3	3.9	125	35		52		63	390	79	488
Kabwe (Broken Hill)	Africa	0.4–0.7	1236	1	3.8	3.9	128	36		84		121	750	155	960
Steinheim	Europe	0.4–3	1066	1	6.4	3.8	116	32		35		37	228	43	264

Homo erectus

Zhoukoudian XII	Asia	0.45	1000	1	4.4	3.8	112	31	52	63	391	71	438
Zhoukoudian XI	Asia	0.45	986	1	4.8	3.8	110	31	46	53	331	58	364
Trinil	Asia	1	940	1		3.7	107	30					
Daka (Bouri)	Africa	1	995	1		3.8	111	31					
Olduvai 9	Africa	1.25	1067	1		3.8	116	33					
Sangiran 17	Asia	1.3	975	1	2.8	3.7	110	31	94	141	874	155	961
KNM-WT 15000 (Nariokotome) large estimate	Africa	1.5	909	1	3.7	3.7	105	29	68	104	643	109	675
KNM-WT 15000 (Nariokotome) small estimate	Africa	1.5	857	1	3.5	3.7	101	28	56	70	432	71	436
Terra 2 Archaic *Homo* small brained													
Homo erectus/georgicus/ergaster													
KNM-ER 3883	Africa	1.55	785	1	3.2	3.6	95	26	59	75	464	71	441
Dmanisi 2280	Asia	1.77	775	1	2.9	3.6	94	26	49	58	360	55	338
Dmanisi 2282	Asia	1.77	660	1		3.5	84	23					
Dmanisi 2700/2735	Asia	1.77	600	1	3.1	3.4	79	21	40	44	273	35	216
KNM-ER 3733	Africa	1.8	850	1	3.7	3.6	98	27	52	63	391	62	383

Data and equations from Aiello and Dunbar (1993); Asfaw et al. (2002); Lordkipanidze et al. (2007); Rightmire (2004); Rightmire, Lordkipanidze and Vekua (2006); and Wood and Lonergan (2008).

tooth. He has been variously described as *Homo ergaster* and *Homo erectus*, with the latter now commanding majority support. He had a modern body form, as judged by leg-to-body length, while the arms and the shape of his ribcage are both of modern shape. His hands and feet were not found.

What first impressed was his body size. This pre-teen was already tall (F. Brown, Harris, Leakey et al. 1985; MacLarnon and Hewitt 1999). Allowing for a later growth spurt, it was thought that his adult height could have been as much as 1.8 m and his weight a hefty 68 kg. However, this figure has now been revised downwards based on evidence that *erectus* matured faster than we do (Gibbons 2010b). Alternative estimates place his height at 1.63 m and his adult weight at 56 kg. This still makes him a large hominin, although considerably smaller than the 75 kg adult weight that some still claim (Gibbons 2010b). The two body-size estimates (68 and 56 kg) allow us to predict (Table 5.2) that he had an individual home range of between 432 and 643 ha and a group range of 436–675 km^2. Given the size of this range, it is unsurprising that even without his feet, he is regarded as a candidate for endurance running (Bramble and Lieberman 2004).

The size of his juvenile brain was between 857 and 880 cm^3 and would, it is calculated, have reached 909 cm^3 on maturity (Rightmire 2004; Wood and Lonergan 2008), predicting personal network sizes of 101–105 (Table 5.2). The costs of interaction in these large social networks were therefore high, and a new more rapid form of grooming, such as language, might be expected.

But in one important respect, his body was not modern. A study of Nariokotome's hypoglossal canal (MacLarnon and Hewitt 1999), preserved in his thoracic vertebrae, shows that it was smaller than in modern humans. The significance of this finding is that the nerve which controls tongue movements passes through this canal, and the conclusion drawn is that Nariokotome lacked the fine-muscle control needed to make human speech. MacLarnon and Hewitt (1999: 359; 2004) conclude from this evidence that the hominins who first settled beyond Terra 1 did so without the developed breath control necessary for modern human speech. Nariokotome could make sounds but he could not control them as human speech. He was not able to produce long phrases from a single breath and punctuate these with very rapid breaths, which is how we break up the pattern of speech and make it meaningful. This ability came later during Terra 2's second stride (MacLarnon and Hewitt 1999: table 5).

Homo erectus was long lived and highly variable. They extended across Terra 2, and Rightmire (2004: 118) assigns thirty fossil crania to this taxon that range in age from 1.8Ma to 0.04Ma (Rightmire 2004: table 1). During this long time period, brain volumes increased (Table 5.3, Box 5.1).

Box 5.1. Pathways in hominin evolution during Terra 2

The evidence points to at least three pathways for hominin evolution in Terra 2:

1. Small brains–small bodies (*Paranthropus*);
2. Small brains–larger bodies (*Homo ergaster*, *Homo rudolfensis*); and
3. Large brains–larger bodies (*Homo erectus*).

All three pathways were successful. All of them could have made Mode 1 technologies. Only *Homo erectus* dispersed outside Terra 1. All of them existed side by side in Africa where the evidence is richest. From the rich fossil hunting ground of the Koobi Fora formation east of Lake Turkana came two skulls found in situ and dated to 1.8Ma, the beginning of Terra 2 (Figure Box 5.1; Elton, Bishop and Wood 2001; Leakey and Walker 1976).

	1.8Ma KNM-ER3733	1.7Ma KNM-ER 406
	Homo erectus	*Paranthropus*
Brain volume cm³	850	510
Estimated body size, kg	52	36
Personal network size	98	71
Individual home range, ha	381	237
Group range, km²	383	168

The adult cranium KNM-ER 3733 (Kenyan National Museum East Rudolf, now known as Lake Turkana) is a particularly well-preserved *Homo erectus* skull with a brain volume of 850 cm³. Contemporary with it was an equally well-preserved skull of *Paranthropus*, KNM-ER 406. This has a sagittal crest to anchor its large jaw muscles. A comparison of the degree of postorbital constriction vividly shows how brain growth in *Homo* changed the architecture of the skull. KNM-ER 406 has a brain size of 510 cm³, sixty per cent of KNM-ER 3733. As we saw in Chapter 4, there is evidence from the South African paranthropines that they had broadened their diets (Figure 4.7) and were by no means dependent on plant foods alone. Furthermore, they cannot be discounted as toolmakers and users, since much older australopithecines in Terra 1 had this capacity. However, the combination of body and brain size points to hominins who lived at different spatial scales when it came to getting resources, interacting with others and coping with competitors.

(*continued*)

Box 5.1. *(continued)*

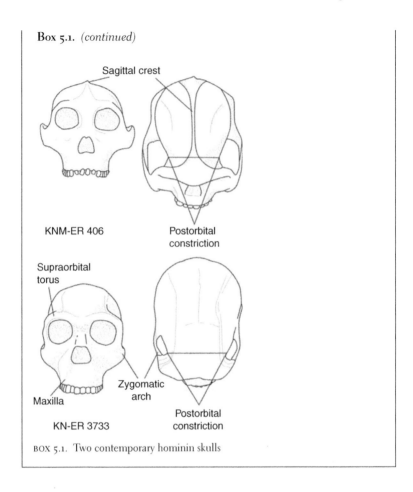

BOX 5.1. Two contemporary hominin skulls

The start of the second stride in Terra 2 was marked by a significant shift in brain size among large-bodied hominins, particularly after 600ka (Figure 1.3). Ruff, Trinkaus and Holliday (1997: 1740) show that in the period 1.8Ma to 0.6Ma, *Homo* was about one third less encephalised than recent humans. Moreover, there was no increase in encephalisation quotients (EQ) during this long period. The spurt in brain growth between 600ka and 200ka raised EQ values to within ten per cent of those seen subsequently, and is associated with the widespread *Homo heidelbergensis* (Table 5.3). Their large bodies and brains resulted in greater personal networks, 126 as compared with 112 for *Homo erectus*, and group ranges of 751 km² rather than 507 km² (Table 5.1).

TABLE 5.3. *Increases in mean brain volume during Terra 2 (Aiello and Dunbar 1993, Rightmire 2004).*

	Stride 1 1.8–0.8Ma	Stride 2 0.8–0.2Ma	Stride 3 0.2–0.05Ma
Homo erectus	906 cm³	984 cm³	1151 cm³
Sample size	15	10	5
Homo heidelbergensis		1206 cm³	
Sample size		10	
Homo neanderthalensis			1426 cm³
Sample size			23
Homo sapiens			1518 cm³
Sample size			6

Late *Homo erectus* (Ngandong, Indonesia). *Homo sapiens* (Herto, Skhul ×3, Omo and Qafzeh).

These larger ranges would only have been possible with enhanced carnivory that assured access to high-value animal foods on a regular basis. Large ranges also meant that the resources they contained could no longer be defended against other hominins (Figure 4.3) – factors of particular importance during Terra 2 as higher latitudes were settled.

It was also during the second stride that the hypoglossal canal probably reached modern size, although well-dated, definitive osteological evidence is still awaited (MacLarnon and Hewitt 1999: table 2, 2004). This was a necessary development for those complex sounds which produce speech.

Homo heidelbergensis was strongly built and robust. Not only were the skulls of these large-brained hominins extremely thick walled with heavy brow ridges, but their long bones were also massive. A cross-section of the 500ka-year-old tibia from Boxgrove in southern England (M. B. Roberts, Stringer and Parfitt 1994) reveals a thick-walled bone that, if compared to a modern human tibia, emphasises how lightly built or gracile we have become.

Robustness characterised the *bauplan* of the large-brained hominins during the final stride of Terra 2 (200–50ka). Neanderthals, the descendants of *Homo heidelbergensis* outside Africa, had a robust frame with a crural index[2] that emphasised their short leg lengths and long bodies. The

[2] The crural index is the ratio of the length of the tibia to the length of the femur and is correlated with temperature. Populations living in warm climates tend to have high crural indices, and populations in cold climates low ones. The Neanderthal crural index indicates short legs to torso, and is similar to people who today live above the Arctic Circle. This adaptation retains body heat in cold temperatures. The opposite is the case among equatorial populations where long legs and short torsos are the norm, and crural indices are high.

body form of these robustly built hominins reflected their adaptation to the environmental stresses of cold temperatures in the last stride of Terra 2. By contrast, the much older, robustly built Nariokotome boy had an African body shape adapted to lose heat through long legs and short torso.

The Push–Pull of a Bio-tidal Terra

During Terra 2, environmental changes driven by increased variation in the Milankovitch cycles came to play a major role in dispersal (Chapter 2). Tectonics remained important in the first stride, but subsequently dispersal was shaped by the dramatic exposure of the continental shelves when, 800ka, continental ice sheets began to increase in thickness and extent. This followed the Middle Pleistocene revolution – a variability packet that lasted from 1.2Ma to 0.8Ma (Table 2.2).

These lower sea levels produced, on a regular but fluctuating basis, two major landmasses at either end of Eurasia. In the east was Sunda (Table 3.2) that added an additional 3.4 million km^2 between latitudes 10°S and 15°N (Sathiamurthy and Voris 2006; Table 3.2; Figure 3.5).[3] A further large exposure occurred on the shallow shelf of the East China Sea between latitudes 20°N and 40°N.

The exposure of Sunda coincided with low temperatures and ice formation at high latitudes, a pattern that took on extra significance in the second stride (800–200ka). Therefore, while this low-latitude continent lay within the zone of highest solar productivity, the amount of energy it received was less than during the interglacials. A reconstruction of the vegetation and river patterns shows a reduced area of rainforest and increased belts of grassland and savannah (Figure 6.7) – a landscape attractive to hominins.

The Sunda landscape was fragmented by several major rivers swollen at some times of the year by the seasonal melt water from ice caps and glaciers on the ramparts of Asia to the north. In the warm phase of the climate cycle, habitat fragmentation also occurred as the islands of Indonesia were reinstated. Beyond Sunda lay several large islands which were never joined to this palaeocontinent, among them Flores.

At the other end of Eurasia, the process was similar, but the outcome different. Here, low sea level revealed Doggerland that greatly expanded the size of the bio-tidal zone to the west of the continental divide (Coles 1998;

---

[3] This is at maximum exposure when sea level was −116 m below present levels. At −50 m there was an additional 1.5M km^2. See http://www.eeb.ucla.edu/Faculty/Barber/SundaSeaLevels.htm for a visualisation of the changing land mass.

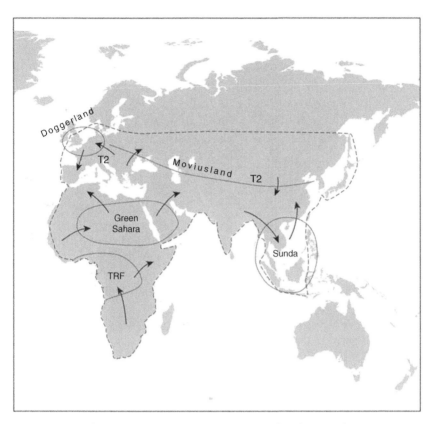

FIGURE 5.2. Five bio-tidal regions in Terra 2. The push–pull is shown by the arrows where the continual import and export of population depended on the climate cycle and sea level (Tables 5.4 and 5.7).

Gamble 2009). The average depth of this continental shelf is shallow, adding as much as 0.5 million km² of additional land south of the ice sheets. Geophysical prospection of the seabed on a vast scale has now revealed a complex pattern of topography and river drainage across the North Sea. Dredging and fishing with drag nets has recovered a wealth of Pleistocene animals, as well as some Mode 2 and Mode 3 artefacts (Hublin, Weston, Gunz et al. 2009; Mol, Post, Reumer et al. 2006). However, because Doggerland lay between 45°N and 55°N, it was a much less productive environment than Sunda. Moreover, it was fringed to the north by the expanded ice sheets that covered Ireland and Scandinavia and much of Britain.

These landmasses revealed by climate change presented opportunities for population expansion (Figure 5.2). The last eight cycles of 100ka duration saw their greatest exposure. When available for settlement, they exerted a major pull on any dispersing population that was versatile enough to take the opportunity. This pull was reflected in population growth. But as global ice volumes shrank, the process reversed, and Sunda in particular pushed population back into Terra 2. In most cases, the push took the form of local extinction rather than population movement.

The pull–push dynamic was initiated during the second stride of Terra 2. It led, as described in Table 5.4, to a regular pattern of regional population growth and decline. Furthermore, the disparity in productivity between Sunda and Doggerland established a dominant pattern for hominin dispersal throughout Terra 2; an initial strong pull to the east with a subsequent weaker pull to the west.

Sunda and Doggerland are the two most conspicuous and cyclical examples of bio-tidal zones during Terra 2. More difficult to measure in both extent and timing are the green and yellow phases of Arabia and the Sahara. As shown in Figure 5.3, the appearance–disappearance of megalakes and river systems at these latitudes acted as a pump, sucking population in during a green phase and pushing it out during a yellow. The wealth of Mode 2 and Mode 3 artefacts from across these regions, little of which has been systematically collected or quantified, points to that potential. For example, the aptly named Wadi Arid, 200 km east of Lake Nasser in Egypt, is today devoid of human settlement, and no rainfall has ever been recorded. However, Mode 2 LCT in the form of Acheulean bifaces have been found in deposits dating to 141ka and 212ka, indicating times when this part of the Sahara was green and drew in population (Szabo, McHugh, Schaber et al. 1989).

During wet phases, the savannah grasslands expanded into the southern margins of what today is the Sahara. Conversely, during a decline in precipitation across Africa, those same habitats extended into the rainforest to the south, thereby increasing the size of those environments with both the potential for optimum population growth (Table 3.4) and the most accessible resources (Table 3.5). These suited hominins with both generalist and versatile adaptations. By contrast, specialist forest primates such as gorillas and chimpanzees followed the shrinking rainforest into its refuge areas of West Africa and pockets along the equator.

The final major bio-tidal zone lay along the northern boreal margin of Terra 2 (Figure 5.2). During a high sea-level phase, such as the MIS11 interglacial 400ka, settlement in the east was north of the Tibetan plateau and reached up to 55°N in southern Siberia. A similar latitude was achieved in the west (Figure 5.1; Dennell 2009: fig. 11.5). By contrast, during a major

TABLE 5.4. (a) The bio-tidal regions of Terra 2 and their reaction to the climate cycle; (b) a model of the outcomes for population pull and push in the five bio-tidal regions (Figure 5.2).

(a)

| Climate | West | | | | East |
	Doggerland	Moviusland	Sahara-Arabia	African rainforest	Sunda
Cold–dry	Ice sheets expand onto the continental shelf, exposed area up to 0.5 million km² tundra and steppe conditions predominate; polar front migrates south	Contraction of settlement by 10–15° latitude across the northern boundary of Terra 2	Arid phases with very little standing or flowing water; expanded deserts	Refuges in West and Central Africa; expansion of Sahel grasslands southwards	Up to 3.4 million km² of continental shelf with major grassland habitat at low latitudes
Warm–moist	Inundation of continental shelf and a northwards movement of the polar front that contributes to marine productivity	Expansion of settlement by 10–15° latitude across the northern boundary of Terra 2	Megalakes, fans and watercourses; expansion of Sahel grasslands northwards	Expansion of rainforest sometimes beyond historic limits	Inundation of continental shelf; isolation of fauna and hominins on islands

TABLE 5.4. (continued)

(b)

Climate	West				East
	Doggerland	Moviusland	Sahara-Arabia	African rainforest	Sunda
All in phase population pull	Ice sheets expand onto the continental shelf, exposed area up to 0.5 million km² tundra and steppe conditions predominate; polar front migrates south	Expansion of settlement by 10–15° latitude across the northern boundary of Terra 2	Megalakes, fans and watercourses; expansion of Sahel grasslands northwards	Refuges in West and Central Africa; expansion of Sahel grasslands southwards	Up to 3.4 million km² of continental shelf with major grassland habitat at low latitudes
Outcome	Dispersal opportunity but with low population growth	Dispersal but with low population growth	Green phase population dispersal and growth	Population growth in savannah habitats	Population growth in savannah habitats
All in phase population push	Inundation of continental shelf and a northwards movement of the polar front that contributes to marine productivity	Contraction of settlement by 10–15° latitude across the northern boundary of Terra 2	Arid phases with very little standing or flowing water; expanded deserts	Expansion of rainforest sometimes beyond historic limits	Inundation of continental shelf; isolation of fauna and hominins on islands
Outcome	Local extinction but with population growth elsewhere due to interglacial conditions	Local extinction	Yellow phase local extinction	Lower population growth in continuous rainforest habitat	Lower population sizes on islands and in expanded rainforest

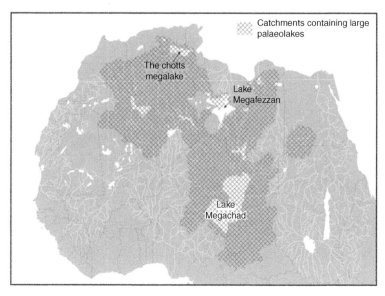

FIGURE 5.3. The megalakes and drainage system of the Green Sahara. Adapted from Drake et al. (2011).

continental glaciation and low sea levels such as MIS6 160ka, settlement contracted to about latitude 40°N, and in Europe to 45°N (Dennell 2009: fig. 11.6). For reasons I shall discuss, this vast area of expanding and contracting hominin settlement is known as Moviusland.

Faunal Exchanges and the Limits Of Terra 1

The dispersal of animal faunas during Terra 2 was powered by the pull–push forces, as Milankovitch cycles were translated into geographical opportunities – the bio-tidal model. Hominins were once thought to be "fellow travellers", hitching a ride as African animals moved into Eurasia in a succession of faunal waves. However, such scenarios are no longer supported by the evidence (O'Regan, Turner, Bishop et al. 2011). The pattern of faunal exchanges was rather modest and uncoordinated. Animals dispersed singly rather than in groups. When Terrae 1 and 2 are taken together, we see (Table 5.5) that from 3Ma to 0.5Ma, thirteen genera of indisputable African origin dispersed outside the continent, while only four entered (O'Regan, Turner, Bishop et al. 2011: 1347).[4]

[4] O'Regan, Turner, Bishop et al. (2011: 1347) list the four taxa entering Africa as *Equus*, *Nyctereutes*, *Lycaon* and *Antilope*. The dispersal histories of the last are difficult to assess and do not appear in Table 5.5.

TABLE 5.5. *Terrae 1 and 2 faunal exchanges between Africa, Asia and Europe (O'Regan et al. 2011; van der Made 2011).*

Genera		First appearance (Ma)			
		Terra 1		Terra 2	
		From Africa into Asia	Into Africa from Asia	From Africa into Asia	Into Europe from Asia or Africa
Theropithecus	Large gelada baboon			0.6	1
Hippopotamus	Hippo			1	~1.3
Palaeoloxodon	Straight-tusked elephant			1.4	0.9
Pelerovis	Extinct buffalo			1.5	
Pachycrocuta	Large short-faced hyena			1.66	1.5
Megantereon	Sabre tooth			1.7	1.5
Homo	Various hominins			1.7	1.2
Lycaon	Hunting dog		~1.8		
Equus	Horse		2.3		
Crocuta	Spotted hyena	<2.5			0.8
Panthera	Lion and leopard	<2.5			1.9
Damalops	Extinct antelope	<2.5			
Potamocheros	Bushpig	<2.5			1.8
Nyctereutes	Raccoon dog		2.5		
Hippotragus	Antelope	>2.5			
Oryx	Large antelope	3.4–3			

The ages, Ma years ago, are the first appearance of these animals outside their area of speciation. Africa was a major exporter with only three species coming into the continent.

When studying dispersal, Africa and Asia are portrayed as distinct biogeographical provinces that oscillated between donating and receiving species from each other. But basing the boundary on current distributions creates problems. A traditional biogeographical approach would count any African species found in Israel and the Levant as an example of dispersal. As Table 5.5 shows, these would extend major faunal exchanges back to 2.5Ma. But if different boundaries are drawn, as I have done with Terra 1, then we see dispersal taking place within a single biogeographical province rather than exchanges of fauna between them.

These biogeographical issues are well illustrated by two exceptional sites in Western Asia: Dmanisi in Georgia dated to 1.77Ma, and 'Ubeidiya in Israel where a long sequence of fauna and artefacts has been dated to between 1.6Ma and 1.2Ma. The fauna of both sites is predominantly

Eurasian. There are a few African, or more precisely Ethiopian, elements, but the majority of species fit with comparable-age faunas in Europe and Western Asia (Agusti and Lordkipanidze 2011). At the younger site of 'Ubeidiya, the African elements are represented by a few large herbivores. As a result, Bar-Yosef and Belmaker (2011: 1330) argue that the Caucasus was isolated from East Africa at the time of Dmanisi and only later became a dispersal corridor.

Agusti and Lordkipanidze (2011: 1340) use these data to review the dispersal history of the early Terra 2 hominins. Like many others, they reject the model that a dispersal wave of other animals swept hominins along. Species did not travel together, and the palaeontological record overwhelmingly shows isolated cases of dispersal; for example, the hippopotamus dispersed into Asia some 400ka *after* a large hyena had left Africa (Table 5.5). These sporadic rather than coordinated dispersals imply that hominins could have left at any suitable time.

This raises for Augusti and Lordkipanidze the distinct possibility that Dmanisi will be superseded one day as the current candidate for the earliest hominin occurrence outside of Africa. They suggest that the appearance of Mode 1 tools at least 2.5Ma in Terra 1 (Chapter 4) may prove a more reliable benchmark against which to assess future discoveries. I agree, and in light of that possibility, I set the limits of Terra 1 as larger than contemporary Africa, both politically and biogeographically, and therefore greater than the present well-dated distribution of archaeology and fossil hominins. As Agusti and Lordkipanidze (2011: 1340) argue, hominins were already in Western Asia during Terra 1, and the evidence is the 2Ma-year-old artefact site of Yiron in Israel (Tchernov, Horowitz, Ronen et al. 1994).

Furthermore, the Dmanisi evidence highlights an obvious yet salient feature of Terra 1 – that it was not a suite of coterminous environments and uniform habitats. Instead, it represented the extension of the African Rift into Southwest Asia and the Caucasus in what Augusti and Lodkipanidze describe as their expanded African home model – what I call Terra 1. This model relocates the biogeographical border for Africa at the level of the Taurus and Zagros mountains, well to the north of where it is placed today. With the maps redrawn, there is no point in talking of a "migration from Africa" by hominins, what is often referred to as Out of Africa 1. Instead, there was a circulation of hominins and fauna along the tectonic trail that ran for 4000 km from Olduvai Gorge to the Jordan Valley, terminating in the Caucasus. Moreover, on these timescales, the fauna along this track were constantly subject to vicariant forces that fragmented their distributions, whether from tectonic activity or environmental variability. As a result, there must have been several centres of speciation, and dispersal from a single source was not the dominant pattern.

Terra 2: The First Stride 1.8Ma–0.8Ma

The familiar rhetoric of an early Out of Africa dispersal needs to be tempered. In the first place, they never left "Africa", since Terra 1 was larger than this continent, and second, as Agusti and Lordkipanidze (2011) point out, the appearance of large brains and stone technology does not explain why dispersal took place.

Dmanisi, located in Terra 1, provides the evidence that questions the Out of Africa model. Three skulls and extensive postcranial remains are now classified as *Homo georgicus*.[5] They were all small-brained hominins (Table 5.2) ranging from 600 to 775 cm^3 (Rightmire, Lordkipanidze and Vekua 2006). Body size was large at 40–50 kg, so these fossils score low for EQ, between 2.9 and 3.1 (Lordkipanidze, Jashashvili, Vekua et al. 2007). Brain and body size suggest a personal network size of between seventy-nine and ninety-four contacts, and group range estimates of 216–338 km^2 (Table 5.2), well above those achieved by *Australopithecus* (Table 4.2). Associated with *Homo georgicus* is an assemblage of Mode 1 stone tools – simple cores and flakes made on stone local to the site.

The Out of Africa 1 model has also been questioned by Dennell and Roebroeks (2005). They draw attention to the spread of grasslands after 2.5Ma which, as we saw in Chapter 4, was a significant development for hominins. They call this expanded habitat *Savannahstan* that united Asia and Africa by a common habitat and which later formed the heartland of Terra 2. Moreover, they argue there is no a priori reason why hominins were not more widely distributed throughout it.

The Savannahstan model raises the possibility that *Homo* might have originated anywhere in this grassland habitat, and if this happened to be in Asia, then they would have dispersed from there into Africa, but all within the boundaries of Terra 1. Evidence from outside Africa is poor and often open to question in terms of dating. The Yiron Quarry is a candidate with an age of 2Ma, as are the few artefacts from Riwat in Pakistan (Dennell and Roebroeks 2005). As Figure 5.4 shows, plenty of ecological space existed in Asia at the beginning of Terra 2 to accommodate more hominin species

---

[5] The crania have variously been described as *Homo ergaster* and *erectus*. Their size and morphology clearly place them in the genus *Homo*, but there are sufficient differences to warrant a separate species.

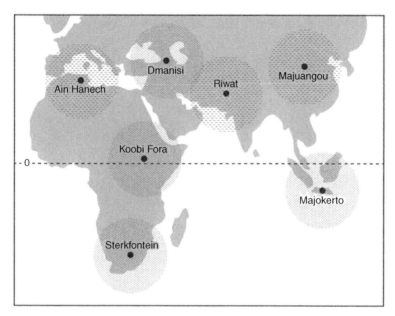

FIGURE 5.4. Terra 2 and the Asian Savannahstan which provided ecological room for hominin evolution. Representative archaeological and fossil localities are shown. Adapted from Dennell and Roebroeks (2005).

than have, so far, been discovered. Out of Africa 1 is a convenient model to explain the current disparity in the evidence base and where Africa dominates Asia (Dennell and Roebroeks 2005: 1103), and we must expect this imbalance to change.

Technology, Dispersal and Diet

This dispersal into Terra 2 was not facilitated by the appearance of Mode 2 LCT at c. 1.6Ma. The earliest archaeological finds (Table 5.6) both east and west were solidly Mode 1; for example, at Majuangou sites I–IV in the Nihewan Basin in North China at 1.7Ma (Dennell 2009: 174) and at Kuldaro in Central Asia dated to 0.96–0.88Ma (Dennell 2009). In the west, the Sima del Elefante locale (TE9) at Atapuerca in Spain is securely dated to 1.2Ma (Carbonell, Bermudez de Castro, Pares et al. 2008), while Pirro Nord in Italy is possibly older. At both European locales, the number of artefacts is very small: three cores and six flakes from Pirro Nord (Arzarello, Marcolini, Pavia et al. 2007) and thirty-two artefacts from Atapuerca TE-9 (Carbonell, Bermudez de Castro, Pares et al. 2008: 466). The outputs are

TABLE 5.6. *Terrae 1 and 2 stone tool chronology Modes 1 and 2*

Mode 1 South	Ma	Mode 1 East	Ma	Mode 1 West	Ma	Mode 2 South	Ma	Mode 2 East	Ma	Mode 2 West	Ma
Terra 1											
Dikika	3.4										
Gona	2.5										
Lokalalei sites 1 and 2C	2.3	Yiron Quarry	2								
		Riwat	~1.9								
Terra 2											
		Dmanisi	1.77			Karari and Kokiselei 4	1.7–1.4				
		Nihewan Basin Majuangou	1.66–1.32	Pirro Nord	1.6–1.3	*Olduvai Bed II above Tuff IIB*	1.5	Attirampakkam	1.51		
		Wole Sege	1	*Sima del Elefante Atapuerca TE9*	1.2–1.1	Sterkfontein Acheulean breccia	1.5	*Ubeidiya*	1.4		
		Mata Menge	0.88–0.8	Fuente Nueva-3	1.2	Konso-Gardula	1.4	Isampur	1.2		
				Barranco Leon	1.3–1.2			Bose Basin	0.8	Estrecho del Quipar	0.9
				Pont-de-Lavaud	1.1			*Gesher Benot Ya'aqov*	0.78	Solano del Zamborino	0.76
				Happisburgh Site 3	0.94–0.81					Happisburgh Site 1	0.7
				Monte Poggiolo	~0.85					Waverley Wood	0.6
				Gran Dolina Atapuerca TD4	>0.85					*Boxgrove*	0.5
				Gran Dolina Atapuerca TD6	0.85–0.78						
				Pakefield	~0.7						

Italics = hominin remains present. Data from Carbonell et al. (2008) and Muttoni et al. (2011).

broadly Mode 1 with a manufacturing concept comparable to the finds from the much older Terra 1 locales such as Lokalalei and Peninj (de la Torre 2011; Chapter 4).

The oldest Mode 2 stone technologies with their distinctive picks, cleavers and bifaces/hand axes are currently 1.76Ma years old. The evidence comes from West Turkana at the Kokiselei 4 site (Lepre, Roche, Kent et al. 2011) where bifaces were made by flaking river cobbles of phonolite. Subsequently, the evidence in Africa comes from Bed II in Olduvai Gorge (M. D. Leakey 1971) and from the Acheulean breccia in the Sterkfontein Cave in South Africa (Kuman 1998; Kuman, Field and McNabb 2005). One of the earliest finds of Mode 2 comes from Tamil Nadu in south-east India where, in the deeply stratified locale of Attirampakkam dated to 1.51Ma, a large collection of Mode 2 artefacts has been excavated (Pappu, Gunnell, Akhilesh et al. 2011).[6] These were made from local cobbles of fine- and coarse-grained quartzites. Elsewhere, at 'Ubeidiya in Israel in levels above assemblages of older Mode 1 stone tools, there are bifaces dated to 1.4Ma (Bar-Yosef and Belmaker 2011). And at Konso-Gardula in the Ethiopian Rift, LCT bifaces have been found above and below a volcanic tuff dated to 1.34–1.38Ma, indicating an age of at least 1.4Ma (Asfaw, Beyene, Suwa et al. 1992: 734). The first hand axes in the west of Terra 2 were much younger, the earliest occurrence at c. 600ka in both Spain and Britain (Ashton, Lewis and Stringer 2011; Jiménez-Arenas, Santonja, Botella et al. 2011).

Taken together, we see a familiar geographical pattern (Table 5.6). The earliest appearance in Terra 2 of either Mode 1 or Mode 2 was first in the east and then subsequently in the west (Europe; Patnaik and Chauhan 2009). The time lag for Mode 1 was 600ka, while for Mode 2 it was up to 1Ma. The exact ages are fiercely contested, and this has led to two rival timetables: the short and long chronologies (Box 5.2). The ages in Table 5.6 indicate my support for the shorter version of these two timetables.

What is evident are the significant advances in stone technology from simply flaking nodules to knapping flakes from which LCT were then fashioned. We saw in Chapter 4 that the oldest stone technologies were more sophisticated than once thought. However, beginning 1.7Ma in the Koobi Fora region of East Africa, there was a step change in the conceptualisation of stone working. At sites along the Karari escarpment, hominins started to strike large flakes directly from boulders found at outcrops of basalt (Isaac 1997). Rather than selecting and then flaking cobbles, as was the practice

---

[6] The collection consists of 3528 artefacts of which seventy-seven are LCT, and of these hand axes are the largest category. They were found in excavations seven metres below the surface in alternating sands and silty clays.

Box 5.2. Long and short chronologies

Dating the earliest sites is not easy, and there is no single scientific method. The ages in Table 5.6 are based on isotope decay methods such as ^{39}Ar/^{38}Ar, the palaeomagnetic signal from the sediments that can be tied into a worldwide stratigraphy and biostratigraphy where correlations are made on the basis of key animal taxa.

In Europe, the long chronology for settlement was questioned by Roebroeks and van Kolfschoten (1994, 1995). They pointed out that the ages of most of the earliest sites were aspirational claims rather than grounded in science-based methods. And if the dating did not impress, many of the archaeological specimens were unconvincing as hominin artefacts, and there were very few of them. After their house cleaning, they proposed that Europe was first settled c. 500ka.

They raised the bar in terms of the tests that evidence for a long chronology had to pass before being accepted. But soon well-supported claims from Spain at Barranco León and Fuente Nueva in the Orce Basin (Gibert, Gibert, Iglesias et al. 1998) and Atapuerca TD6 (Carbonell, Bermudez de Castro, Arsuaga et al. 1995) and then Pakefield in Northern Europe (Parfitt, Barendregt, Breda et al. 2005) showed that their figure was an underestimate (Carbonell, Mosquera, Rodriguez et al. 1996). The first occupation is now regarded as the Sima del Elefante site at Atapuerca (Carbonell, Bermudez de Castro, Pares et al. 2008). Here, level TE-9 is dated 1.1–1.2Ma by combining evidence from biostratigraphy, palaeomagnetism and cosmogenic nuclides. It has a few Mode 1 tools made from local cherts and a hominin mandible (ATE9-1) provisionally assigned to *Homo antecessor* known from another Atapuerca locality (TD6).

However, the long–short chronology controversy continues. Recently, Muttoni, Scardia, Kent et al. (2011) redated the Italian Mode 1 site of Monte Poggiolo to c. 0.85Ma and in a critical review of the evidence for other localities, such as Pirro Nord and the Spanish sites, put forward the case for a short chronology. They claim that the time window c. 0.94–0.87 marks the earliest evidence for the occupation of Europe in western Terra 2 and that this occurred when hominins were swept up in a faunal exchange triggered by significant climate changes 850ka – what is known as the Middle Pleistocene Revolution (Table 2.2).

Interest in long and short chronologies is not confined to Europe. Twenty years ago, absolute dating of fossil remains of *Homo erectus* from Java at Mojokerto (Antón and Swisher 2004; Swisher, Curtis, Jacob et al. 1994) gave them an age of 1.81Ma – much older than previously thought. The technique involved dating single crystals of hornblende grains from volcanic pumice and marked a major breakthrough in science-based dating. The results were matched between the geological deposits where the skull was thought to have been found and sediment inside the skull.

However, subsequent archival work combined with a reappraisal of the sites through new fieldwork has questioned the stratigraphic position of the dated fossil skull, and a revised date of 1.49Ma is now widely accepted (Dennell 2009: 155). Larick, Ciochon, Zaim et al. (2001) established that the ages of the Terra 2 hominins from the Sangiran dome in Java, where so many fossils have been recovered, are between 1.3Ma and 1.1Ma years old. The provenance of the Trinil skull, also from Java, is much better known and is of the order of 0.9–1Ma years old (Dennell 2009). The erratic collection history of the Modjokerto and Sangiran fossils is set out by Dennell (2009: table 5.1).

in Mode 1 (Chapter 4) and at the earliest Acheulean sites such as Kokiselei, they were now literally knapping the landscape. What this approach to stone working produced were large flakes often of predictable size due to the fracture patterns in the boulders and the skills of the hominins. This led to two technological pathways. At Karari, these flakes became cores, and small, secondary, flakes were then knapped from around their edges. These flakes met the criteria of well-planned knapping, since they were consistent in size (20–40 mm in length), and method of production (Barham and Mitchell 2008: 131). The second pathway used the initial large flakes as blanks for making the LCT trinity: picks, cleavers and bifaces/hand axes (Barham and Mitchell 2008: fig. 4.8). Both pathways can be described as examples of prepared core technologies (PCT) which, as Barham and Mitchell (2008: 131) point out, produced intended end products as a result of a systematic, planned process of reducing stone nodules to serviceable stone tools.

Terra 2: The Second Stride 0.8Ma–0.2Ma

The Middle Pleistocene revolution (Table 2.2) that preceded the second stride saw significant changes to climate and environments that impacted on landscapes. But for all the upheavals associated with this variability packet, not that much in terms of settlement and technology appears to have happened. On the side of the status quo, the boundaries of Terra 2 continue to be respected rather than challenged, and the flakes of Mode

1 and the LCT of Mode 2 continue to be made. There are novel ways by which large flakes were manufactured from boulders and prepared cores. These have been named after Kombewa and Victoria West where they were first recognised (Barham and Mitchell 2008). In essence, they continue the tradition of making stone blanks for small flakes or LCT that first appeared at Karari in the Koobi Fora region of Kenya. For example, the inhabitants of Gesher Benot Ya'aqov in Israel dated to 0.78Ma fashioned basalt bifaces and cleavers using the Kombewa technique (Goren-Inbar, Feibel, Verosub et al. 2000).

There is a further development in prepared core technology (PCT) with the appearance of the Levallois technique that is one method of stone flaking that underpinned Mode 3 technologies throughout Terra 2 and indeed beyond (Foley and Lahr 1997). For skilful knappers, the Levallois technique is not inhibited by size and quality of raw materials. Its use points to a volumetric appreciation of stone nodules to produce flakes of regular and repeated dimensions.

Ranged against the status quo are the larger brain sizes of *Homo heidelbergensis* (Table 5.3), a widespread Terra 2 hominin. The evidence for carnivory is now clear-cut at locales such as Boxgrove and Schöningen dated to 500ka and 400ka respectively. Abundant butchered bone at the former (M. B. Roberts and Parfitt 1999) and the presence of well-made spruce javelins and hafted tools at the latter (Thieme 2005) make this point unequivocally. Meat eating, carnivory, as we saw in Chapter 4, is an old strategy and a necessary adaptive radiation to make dispersal into Terra 2 possible (Table 2.4). The novelty in the second stride is the focus on prime-aged animals (Stiner 2002). Other predators hunt the old, the sick and the young, avoiding the prime because they are best able to escape and defend themselves. However, animals in their prime offer the richest resources, the growth diet (Figure 3.11) of meat, marrow and fat for big-bodied hominins with large, energetically expensive brains and extensive group ranges (Table 5.2). By 400ka at Qesem Cave in Israel, there is good evidence for fire, cooperative hunting and sharing the meat of fallow deer (Stiner, Barkai and Gopher 2009).

The average group range size for *Homo heidelbergensis* (Table 5.2) is 751 km², which places them firmly on the carnivore line (Figure 4.3) with the inference that they could not defend the resources in such large territories. These extensive ranges resulted from two factors: a sharp rise in encephalisation, and greater body size after 600ka (Ruff, Trinkaus and Holliday 1997). Taken together, these led to an increase of almost forty-eight per cent in group home range. As a result, increased evidence for carnivory is to be expected. Archaeological evidence points to larger open sites and the inference that group size had also increased (Grove 2010).

Hominins showed their versatility in what seem small ways. Landscapes in Europe generally lacked the basalt outcrops that were flaked by African hominins. Quartzite cobbles were common in many rivers, but the big difference lay in the abundance in many northern areas of fine-grained rocks, particularly cherts and flint. Such resources occurred either in river gravels or as seams of large nodules. There is no evidence that mining for these ever took place in Terra 2, but at Boxgrove, these raw materials were abundantly available, as they eroded out of a collapsing sea cliff (M. Pope and Roberts 2005). The result was a different form of manufacture to the large flakes found at Gesher Benot Ya'aqov and much closer to the flaked cobbles from Kokiselei. Bifaces were made by *façonnage* – a French term where the shape of the tool is revealed by a process of nodule reduction. The point to note is that the abundance of fine-grained stone in those parts of Terra 2 that were settled during the western dispersal did not result in a change of artefact form. Settlers continued making either Mode 1 or Mode 2.

Movius Line, Moviusland and Population Sizes

The Movius line (Figure 5.1; Table 5.4) has been a focus for archaeologists ever since Hallam Movius described a major geographical distribution between flake and simple core stone tools (Mode 1) and hand axes/bifaces (Mode 2). The interpretation he offered was that east of the line "were monotonous and unimaginative assemblages" (Movius 1948: 411). Here, in his view, was a province of cultural stagnation. To the west lay the innovative Mode 2 and above all else its bifaces.

For sixty years, the line has held. It was expanded by McBurney (1950) to include the non-hand-axe province of Europe that lay to the east of the Rhine. There have been claims for the occasional breach, although all have been contested on age and technological criteria. These include Mode 2 hand axes from the Bose Basin of China (Hou Yamei, Potts, Baoyin et al. 2000) and Sokchang-ni and Jongok-ni in South Korea (Yi and Clark 1983). These all date to the second stride.

Not surprisingly, Movius' negative opinion has been replaced (Lycett and Bae 2010). The geographical division between Mode 1 and Mode 2 has been put down to the availability of bamboo in China and throughout Southeast Asia – a versatile raw material from which knives and containers could have been fashioned (G. Pope 1989). The inference is that effort went into these perishable technologies rather than the stone tools.

Bamboo, however, does not explain the non-Mode 2 province in Central Asia and Eastern Europe.

Lycett and Norton (2010) explain the line by examining the role of population size in determining how cultural traits are transmitted. They propose that the Mode 1 assemblages to the east of the Movius line are a proxy for smaller populations. Under such conditions, the opportunities for innovation are reduced, as explained in earlier chapters. Consequently, they see larger population sizes and greater innovation rates in those regions of Terra 2 where Mode 2 technologies are found. The case is plausible but lacks an independent means of assessing population levels and so testing the model.

The geographical division identified by Movius remains significant. However, in the context of global settlement, it is better to think instead of a bio-tidal zone of continental dimensions: Moviusland. This land lies well to the north of the line Movius originally drew, and represents the furthest extent of settlement in Terra 2 – about 10–15° of latitude stretching from Europe's North Sea to the China Sea (Figure 5.2).

The limits of northern settlement in Europe have been obliterated by repeated glaciation and may have exceeded 55°N, as shown by the British data. In the centre of Moviusland, settlement was controlled by climate. Archaeological evidence for Mode 1 tools from the huge loess deposits of Central Asia are found only during interglacials (Dennell 2009: 331), indicating an ebb and flow to settlement. These occur between latitudes 38°N and 50°N. Settlement ebb and flow was probably the case in southern Siberia where the site of Ust'-Izhul' located at 55°N on the upper Yenisei River has a last interglacial age of 130ka (Chlachula, Drozdov and Ovodov 2003).

The significance of Moviusland is clearest in the east where the history of settlement is intimately connected to the rise and fall of oceans on the Sunda shelf to the south and the East China Sea. As Table 5.7 predicts, it was during times of low sea level in the second stride that the Sunda grasslands were most productive, while the lands to the north were less so because of lower temperatures. Conversely, when Sunda was drowned, the tropical rainforest returned to the region and presented poorer environments for hominins who would now be pulled to the north.

All the regions of Terra 2 in Table 5.7 are characterised by Mode 1 technologies which, according to Lycett and Bae (2010), indicates universally low populations. However, within this vast province, we can begin to see highly variable levels of population density that changed on a regional basis according to the rhythms of climate. While it is still not possible to

TABLE 5.7. *The changing size of regional populations in eastern Moviusland. These result from the bio-tidal effect of climate on settlement*

High sea level Interglacial	Low sea level Glacial		East
Relative population size			
			55–50°N
Lower	None	Moviusland	
			40° N
Higher	Lower		
			15° N
Lower	Higher	Sunda	Equator
Less land and islands	More land no islands		
			10° S

provide absolute numbers, there is every reason to expect that those zones in Table 5.7 where relatively higher populations are predicted were also those which supported optimal habitats for population growth (Table 3.4).

Population size does not provide the answer for the Movius line, and the search for an explanation goes on. But what we do see is strong continuity either side of it. In the east, the earliest occupation of the island of Flores in Indonesia is represented by significant Mode 1 assemblages excavated at Wole Sege and Mata Menge, dated respectively to 1Ma and 0.8Ma (Brumm, Aziz, van den Bergh et al. 2006; Brumm, Jensen, van den Bergh et al. 2010; Moore and Brumm 2007; Table 5.6). This stone technology was then stable for more than 800ka, as shown by the Terra 3 age artefacts from Liang-Bua Cave on the same island (Morwood, Soejono, Roberts et al. 2004).

In Europe, at the other end of Terra 2, there is continuity over at least 400ka in both the Mode 1 and 2 technologies that are found to the east and west of the Movius line (Gamble 1999). In the centre and west of Moviusland, hominins settled the high-latitude grassland habitats of Savannahstan. But irrespective of when this settlement occurred, either during a cold or warm climate phase, there were always severe seasonal constraints on productivity and resources – a combination of higher latitudes and the effects of continentality and altitude. The settlement of Moviusland needed either highly productive conditions or an innovation such as food storage to combat seasonal effects. There is no evidence of the latter in Terra 2. Instead, the precariousness of life at the settled margins of western Moviusland is indicated by the changing frequencies of Mode 2 artefacts in the British Lower Palaeolithic located in the European bio-tidal zone. A census of the artefacts, dating mostly to three interglacial–glacial cycles between 450ka and 130ka, shows a decline during Terra 2 from sixty bifaces per km^2 and seventy-two per 100ka in MIS11–10 to four and three in MIS7–6 (Ashton, Lewis and Hosfield 2011).

What Changed in the Second Stride?

This brief review shows there were adaptive changes in stride two at a time of environmental upheaval and hominin encephalisation. But given that the changes in hominin brains and range size were only possible at considerable cost, the case for the disconnect, discussed in Chapter 1, between archaeological and cognitive evidence remains. Put simply, why didn't the archaeological record change fundamentally?

Hafting

The answer is that there are changes, but they lack the scale and wow factor of an Upper Palaeolithic or Neolithic revolution when the pattern of human culture alters dramatically. So what are they? The first development was an adaptive radiation based on projectile technology and enhanced carnivory with prime-age prey the target (Table 2.4). The evidence consists of those wooden projectiles, and more broadly, Barham (2002, 2010) makes the case for composite tools during stride 2 (Table 5.8). This combination led to more continuous settlement in the west of Terra 2, as indicated by a major change in the quality and quantity of the archaeological evidence after MIS13, 500ka ago (Gamble 1999: 119–125) – evidence that an adaptive radiation has occurred (Box 5.2).

Super Sites

A second change found throughout Terra 2 is the move from a horizontal to vertical concept of place. As Stiner (2002: 40) puts it, by 250ka, there is, for the first time, a well-established pattern of sites in the landscape. These sites are recognised by archaeologists through the repeated accumulation and consumption of materials in one place and which, over the long term, results in massive deposits of stone, bone, shell and fire debris. For archaeologists, they offer a marked contrast to the scattered localities

TABLE 5.8. *The super sites of Terra 2*

Super sites Terra 2	Caves		
	South	East	West
800–200ka	Border Cave, Wonderwerk	Zhoukoudian, Qesem, Tabun	Caune de l'Arago, La Cotte
200–50ka	Klasies River Mouth, Pinnacle Point, Blombos, Rose Cottage Cave, Die Kelders, Haua Fteah	Kebara, Skhul, Qafzeh	Combe Grenal, La Ferrassie, Abric Romani, Pech de l'Azé, Crvena Stijena, Vindija

To qualify, the site must have accumulated large quantities of material in one place over at least two marine isotope stages. This favours caves and rockshelters as archaeological containers.

found previously. It is during the second stride that such Palaeolithic super sites appear; super in the sense of superimposed levels of habitation that led to vast archives of material often in a deep stratigraphy that spans more than one MIS. These super sites are normally protected locales such as caves and fissures (Table 5.8). But where they differ from older examples such as the Terra 1 and early Terra 2 caves of Swartkrans and Sterkfontein is the sheer quantity of cultural and artefact remains they contain. The history of erosion and accumulation always needs to be considered but the super-site phenomenon is so widespread and cross-cuts so many environmental and latitudinal factors that the pattern is robust (Roebroeks and van Kolfschoten 1994).

The interpretation of super sites as something other than handy artefact quarries for archaeologists is just beginning. Hominins used and returned to them because they added security to a mobile, carnivorous lifestyle. Due to the local topography, resources were predictable, and opportunities for ambush and disabling herd animals presented themselves. But as cultural places in the landscape, they also afforded more. They marked a shift in hominin imagination from conceiving the world in a horizontal manner to stacking it vertically – a representation of accumulated time. They were places built on individual and group memory distributed over larger ranges and greater numbers of people (Table 5.2). Those memories concerned detailed landscape knowledge and social collaboration. Once established, the super-site niche set the stage for thinking differently about places. They now formed part of the hominins' distributed cognition.

Fire

A third development was fire, in particular, evidence for its managed use. Gowlett (2010) discusses the evidence for hearths where fire was both kindled and conserved. Such managed fire contrasts with the occurrences in Terra 1 of an opportunistic use of this material resource. During the second stride of Terra 2, archaeological evidence for managed fire is widespread at locales such as Beeches Pit in England, Schöningen in Germany and Qesem Cave in Israel, and is exemplified by the excavations at Gesher Benot Ya'aqov (Table 5.9; Alperson-Afil and Goren-Inbar 2010).[7]

As Gowlett (2010) points out, managed fire, in the form of hearths, is a game changer. It extends the hominin day for social interaction, thereby revising the time constraint imposed by the daylight hours (Table 5.2). At the same time, a fire focus assists a move to greater carnivory because roasting breaks down the enzymes in meat, making them more easily digested (Wrangham, Jones, Laden et al. 1999). Fire acts as an external stomach, a handy technology for hominins who had traded gut for brain size. As a result, hearths are a social technology that re-creates the experience of containment and the embodiment of food through cooking. Fire drew people into the circle and provided a space for emotional amplification through warmth and the enchantment of flickering light. Fire protected – not only precious food resources from other scavengers but also through the bodily and psychological comfort of materials. Fire was a facilitator, an amplifying social form (Figure 1.2), in the eternal triangle of hominin evolution – the relationship between diet change, detailed environmental knowledge and social collaboration (Gowlett 2010).

Language, Theory of Mind and Imagination

Archaeological evidence exists for these three developments that led to the amplification of material and, by inference, emotional resources (Figure 1.2). And along with such amplification came language. The anatomy of modern speech control was achieved sometime during the second stride (MacLarnon and Hewitt 2004). Furthermore, neuroimaging studies of modern stone knappers have revealed that the difference between making Mode 1 and Mode 2 artefacts is linked to those areas of

---

[7] The evidence has been drawn together by Villa ("Foreword" in Alperson-Afil and Goren-Inbar 2010). Of particular interest for the study of hearths is Alperson-Afil and Goren-Inbar's (2010) discussion of "phantom hearths" most readily traced through the spatial position of burnt micro-debitage – very small stone chips.

TABLE 5.9. *Terra 2 and the archaeological evidence for fire*

Ma	Region	Site	1	2	3	4	5	6
0.8–0.2	East Levant	Revadim Quarry	X					
	East Levant	Misiliya Cave	X					
	East Levant	Qesem Cave	X	X		X		
	East Levant	Berez Cave	X	X		X		
	East Levant	Tabun Cave	X			X		
	Asia	Zhoukoudian	X	X				X
	West Europe	Bilzingsleben	X	X		X		X
	West Europe	Terra Amata	X	X		X	X	X
	West Europe	Torralba			X			X
	West Europe	Bolomor Cave	X	X		X		X
	West Europe	La Cotte	X	X		X		X
	West Europe	Vértesszöllös	X					X
	West Europe	Schöningen	X					X
	West Europe	Beeches Pit	X	X		X	X	X
	West Europe	Menez Dregan	X	X		X		X
	West Europe	Prezletice	X	X		X		X
1.8–0.8	South Africa	Kalambo Falls			X			
	South Africa	Cave of Hearths	X			X		
	South Africa	Wonderwerk Cave		X		X		
	South Africa	Gadeb				X		
	South Africa	Middle Awash				X		
	South Africa	Chesowanja				X		
	South Africa	Koobi Fora	X			X		
	South Africa	Swartkrans		X				
	East Levant	Latamne	X					
	East Levant	Gesher Benot Ya'aqov	X	X	X			X
	East Levant	Bizat Ruhama	X					X
	East Levant	Ubeidiya	X					X
	Asia	Yuonmou		X				X
	Asia	Trinil					X	
	Asia	Gongwangling		X				X
	Asia	Xihoudu		X				

Key : 1 = burned stones, 2 = burned bones, 3 = burned wood, 4 = burned sediments, 5 = burned shells, 6 = charcoal. Adapted from Alperson-Afil and Goren-Inbar (2010).

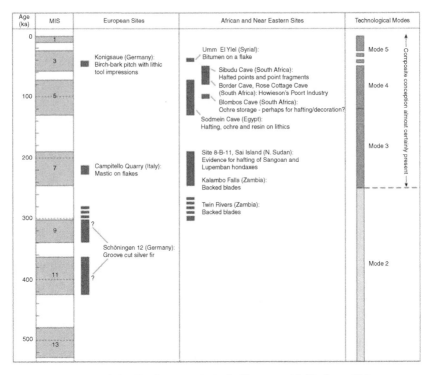

FIGURE 5.5. A timeline for composite tools. Figure provided by James Cole.

the brain most closely associated with language (Faisal, Stout, Apel et al. 2010).[8]

Barham (2002, 2010: 383) infers language from the composite technologies that appear in strides 2 and 3 (Figure 5.5). These are tools which do not exist in nature and so represent an example of hierarchically organised cognition. Hafting, he claims, is a creative act underpinned by an imaginative capacity. By making associations between different materials, it involves comparable forms of recursive analogical reasoning that underpins the capacity for complex language (Barham 2010; Bickerton 2007).

These data support Aiello and Dunbar's (1993) proposition that larger personal network size would, at some time, have selected for more rapid means of communication than fingertip grooming. In their model,

[8] The experimental study by Faisal, Stout, Apel et al. (2010: fig. 1) showed that making an Acheulean biface, as opposed to a Mode 1 flake and simple core, involved higher-level cognitive organisation, as shown by MRI scans, rather than differences in manipulative dexterity.

language first augmented primate grooming routines, and then came to replace them, as group size increased above 120 persons.

Dunbar (2003) argues further from brain sizes that these large-brained hominins also possessed theory of mind, and not only that, but an advanced theory of mind with higher levels of intentionality which indicate the awareness of what someone else plans to do. Intentionality is the skill of projecting outside yourself and into the intentions of another. Level 1 intentionality is a matter of being self-aware, and great apes, elephants and dolphins are capable of this. The higher levels of intentionality are the preserve of hominins and humans. Those hominins who exceeded the 400 cm³ threshold for brain size had level 2 intentionality – that ability to recognise another mind and adjust social reasoning accordingly. Most of the hominins in Terra 2 had brains larger than 900 cm³ and were capable of level 3 intentionality. Here, the complex narrative chain of belief about other people's intentions results in social manipulation to make others do what you think (Table 1.3). Level 4 intentionality takes social reasoning to new heights by weaving together the agency of materials and emotions to spin myths and beliefs that owe everything to relational systems of cognition and increasingly little to rational ones. It is difficult to be precise about which hominins scaled these heights. But those with language, material metaphors and large personal networks must be candidates. Certainly, the focus for these abilities should be on any hominin with a brain equal to or greater than 1400 cm³; in other words, not just ourselves, *Homo sapiens*, but other hominins in Terra 2 (Tables 5.2 and 5.10).

An advanced theory of mind and higher-level intentionality are the cognitive devices that allow us to make a distinction between primary and social emotions (Table 1.4; Damasio 2000; Turner 2000). Primary emotions are common to all social animals: fear, anger, surprise and happiness. They assist survival when novel situations or dangerous predators are encountered. They also form the basis for nurturing that precious bundle of reproductive investment. By contrast, social emotions require a theory of mind and the ability to ascribe intentions to others (Figure 1.2). No other animal, unless it has been domesticated like the family dog to "feel" that way, experiences guilt or shame or questions the concept of trust and the bond of love. A social emotion, or conscience, is the inner voice that warns you somebody may be looking even if they are not present.[9] Guilt and shame act as emotional rules that govern, not always successfully it has to be said, our behaviour out of sight of our intimate and other personal network partners (Table 2.9).

---

[9] I am paraphrasing the writer H. L. Mencken and his observation on conscience.

TABLE 5.10. *A map of emotions, material culture and intentionality among hominins*

Intentionality	Hominin	Age	Community size	Emotions	Amplifying mechanisms	Material metaphors
Level 4 and greater	*Homo sapiens/ neanderthalensis*	Terra 2 Stride 3	150		Religion, Myth, Symbols	Containers/ instruments
Level 3	*Homo erectus/ heidelbergensis*	Terra 2 Stride 2	120	Social emotions	Language, Ceremony	—
Level 2	Early *Homo habilis/ergaster*	Terra 2 Stride 1	100		Dance, Music Crying, Laughter, Focussed-gaze	—
Level 1	Australopithecines	Terra 1	70	Primary emotions	Satisfaction, assertion Aversion, disappointment	Instruments/ containers

Social crying and laughter are unique to humans and, by inference, any hominin that achieved a theory of mind and level 2 intentionality. Adapted from Gamble (2010).

In this stride of Terra 2, the social world of hominins had now become one of imagination layered with interpretations and codes of conduct that were not so dependent on being in each other's eyeline but at a distance. In short, the first steps in a technology of separation, the ability to live apart for prolonged periods, had begun (Gamble 2010b).

Building those chains of understanding was complicated; an imaginative exercise in both time and space that depended on the hominin ability for metaphorical thinking (Gamble 2007). It is important, however, to realise that metaphor is not just a linguistic ability, as in the phrase "the eyes are windows to the soul". At a basic level, objects are material, or solid, metaphors, translating that embodied understanding we have of ourselves and the world that surrounds us. Furthermore, they have been doing that since the oldest stone tools in Terra 1 and long before language amplified the ability by making "windows of the eyes" (Gamble 2007). A well-made hearth, with logs burning and people sitting around it talking, is an expression of that feeling of containment. Living in houses, wearing clothes, putting on a necklace, getting a tattoo, applying hair gel – these are all examples of how we wrap ourselves in the material world and why the process acquires significance through the metaphor of containment (Gamble, Gowlett and Dunbar 2011).

It was during the second stride that significant material changes appeared in the form of hafting, fire and super sites. Rather than a disconnect between growing encephalisation and limited material evidence, the second stride in Terra 2 witnessed emotional amplification, assisted by materials. It was through their senses and emotions that hominins coped with the greater cognitive loads that were the consequence of larger personal network sizes and group ranges. Therefore, I would expect to see the appearance at this time of laughter, crying and many of the other rituals which we have brought to the evolutionary party – the ceremonies that make the social gathering *effervesce*. The purpose of these basic social forms is to amplify further the means by which our social lives cohere as they become ever more complicated by the number of others, and more extended in space and time.

Terra 2: The Third Stride 200ka–50ka

The judgement that not much happened in the second stride, even though brains showed significant increases, is contradicted by the evidence. Hominins entered the third stride with a suite of versatile skills that are the basis of our modern distributed cognition and extended minds. These include language, composite technologies, super sites as places in the landscape and complicated social lives that routinely made decisions on the basis of predicting the intentions of others.

Turning up the Volume: Music and Dance

Amplification is a dominant theme throughout Terra 2. But rather than making technology more complex and able to do additional things, the innovation of Terra 2 hominins was to amplify the emotional basis of social life. The outcome was an ability to manage larger personal networks and forge stronger social bonds. These made it possible to cope with larger gatherings and increased fission and fusion as settlement took place in strongly seasonal environments such as Moviusland. The contribution of music and dance to these enhanced social performances was critical.

However, I am well aware that the suggestion of an amplified emotional life in Terra 2 is unsupported by artefacts. There are no archaeological data, such as musical instruments and sequins, to shore up my inference that social forms such as music and dance acted to amplify social interaction (Figure 1.2). My conclusion stems instead from the evidence of brain size and settlement expansion during this Terra. But there is a fundamental artefact, the hominin body, which was always present. The body is the ultimate musical instrument able to produce a wide range of sounds, rhythms, gestures and steps without the assistance of technology (Blacking 1973). When musical instruments such as bone flutes finally appear in Terra 3 (Chapter 7), they serve to amplify further the *effervescent* experiences of social gatherings, their excitement and enchantment, which had existed for some time (Gamble 2012).

Hominins danced their way into the third stride. The focus is on the African evidence because the process of co-amplification using materials alongside emotions started here. This slow development is not necessarily a pointer to the appearance of people with abilities like ourselves, *Homo sapiens*, although we do make an anatomical entrance during the third stride. In fact, their impact is equivocal. Currently, in Terra 2, Sapiens has not been found beyond the margins of Southwest Asia. As a result, the distribution of humans at this time looks very similar to the settlement history of hominins in the older Terra 1, tucked into the north-east pocket of an ancestral hominin geography.

Hominin Creative Skills

Ancient DNA extracted from a number of Neanderthal skeletons has shown that Sapiens diverged from the common ancestor we shared with

Neanderthals some 400–270ka (Briggs, Good, Green et al. 2009; Green, Krause, Briggs et al. 2010). In the third stride, brain sizes reached maximum volumes (Table 5.2). There was also an increase among the small-brained descendants of *Homo erectus* (Table 5.3), as represented by the Ngandong sample from Indonesia (Dennell 2005; Rightmire 2004).

In Europe, the descendants of *Homo heidelbergensis*, the Neanderthals, had brains that on average were eighteen per cent larger than their ancestors, while in Africa and Southwest Asia, the *Homo sapiens* lineage added a further twenty-six per cent. The eight per cent does not indicate great differences. Sample size is small and highly variable (Table 5.3). Both Sapiens and Neanderthal inherited the *bauplan* of large body sizes from *Homo heidelbergensis*. Big bodies and big brains produce group home ranges for the southern Sapiens and northern Neanderthals of 746 km^2 and 857 km^2 respectively (Table 4.2). It is therefore no surprise that isotopic studies of Neanderthal diets, contained in their bones, confirms their position as top predators almost exclusively dependent on meat (Richards, Pettitt, Trinkaus et al. 2000; Richards and Trinkaus 2009). They hunted prime-aged herd animals, reindeer, mountain thar, bison, aurochs, horse and mammoth, and often these were killed in considerable numbers (Adler, Bar-Oz, Belfer-Cohen et al. 2006; Gaudzinski 1995, 1996; Gaudzinski and Roebroeks 2000; Jaubert, Lorblanchet, Laville et al. 1990; Schreve 2006; see also Gamble 1999: table 5.12).

North or south, the hominins of the third stride were large and robustly built. The earliest examples of Sapiens are dated to 195ka in the Omo Valley of Ethiopia and to 160ka in the Herto Bouri region of the same country. No artefacts were found with the Omo skulls, but at Herto, there were Mode 2 bifaces with the two adult skulls and one juvenile skull. At the super site of Mt Carmel near Haifa in Israel, excavations at Skhul Cave yielded three robust early Sapiens dated to between 135ka and 90ka (Barham 2010: 371), while at Qafzeh, another cave in Israel, a Sapiens skeleton is similarly dated between 120ka and 90ka (Stringer 2011: 44). Intriguingly, at the nearby Kebara Cave, a Neanderthal skeleton, widely accepted as an intentional burial, is dated to 60ka (Bar-Yosef, Vandermeersch, Arensburg et al. 1992) – an example of the pattern of dispersal by different hominins into and out of this region. At these super sites, the technology is largely Mode 3, irrespective of hominin, as it is at another such site, Klasies River Mouth in South Africa. However, instances of Mode 4 based on a prepared core technique producing long, parallel-sided stone blades rather than flakes is known across the southern and western parts of Terra 2 (Boyle, Gamble and Bar-Yosef 2010).

The major technical advance was the widespread use of composite tools. This skill can be traced back into the second stride to locales such as

TABLE 5.11. *Instruments and containers as social technology.*

Instrument: Hunting spear	Materials and senses	Container: Clothing, coat and hat
Wood, stone, mastic, sinew	*Combines different materials and aesthetic properties*	Fibre, skin, fur, feathers
Animals, trees, rock outcrops and humans	*Establishes significant relationships by creating associations*	Plants, animals and humans
Touch, sound, sight, smell	*Brings sensory experience to the business of making*	Touch, sound, sight, smell
Haft, projectile, glue, binding	*Transforms materials into composite artefacts*	Textiles, leather, trim, highlight
Extension of the hand and arm; strength, leverage, power, speed	*Produces amplified sensory and emotional outcomes*	Enveloped and wrapped body; warmth, softness, protection, comfort, well-being
Changing the shape of the arm	*Imaginative possibilities*	Altering the surface of the body

The two examples of spears and clothing show how materials and senses are transformed and the metaphorical consequences of composite tools realised.

Schöningen in Germany and is implicit in the earliest Mode 3 technologies 300ka. The skill in making composite artefacts is to integrate materials with different properties, wood and stone, into a single tool. Such technical compositions are a good example of an evolving hominin imagination that made associations between materials such as wood, stone, mastic and sinew brought them together and realised something novel (Table 5.11). Composite tools such as stone-tipped wooden spears or knives with handles were hand-held instruments. At one level, they contributed to the top-predator status of the hominins that wielded them. But the imagination that underpinned their creation was social because, by bringing things together, they made relationships out of different materials (Gamble 1999, 2007).

The skill of making associations was particularly developed in the southern regions of Terra 2. Here, new materials were regularly used, and often on a substantial scale, as revealed by the super sites Pinnacle Point, Klasies River Mouth, Die Kelders and Blombos. The importance attached to the first appearance of shell beads, engraved ochre, microliths and shellfishing is the interpretation that they represented the capacity to base behaviour on symbols, referred to by some as behavioural modernity (Conard and Bolus

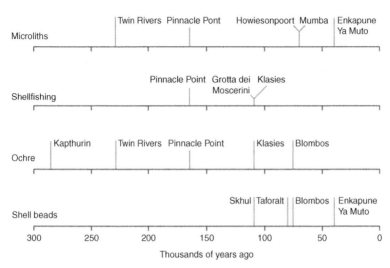

FIGURE 5.6. A staggered timeline for objects regarded as marking the appearance of modernity. Adapted from McBrearty and Stringer (2007).

2003; Wadley 2001; Zilhão 2007). Figure 5.6 shows how long this process took to become commonplace.

But what difference did these new objects, small stone tools, molluscs, ochre and shell beads make for hominins? Nothing in terms of expanding beyond Terra 2. Those sets of tiny blade-based tools, microliths, that made more complex, Mode 4, composite artefacts were for local consumption rather than international export. In the case of adding shellfish to the diet, Stiner (2002) has shown how the use of such highly abundant, r selected resources marked the entry of hominins into a broader dietary niche. This dietary expansion represents a logical amplification of the carnivory pathway hominins had embarked on long before. But the time lag from Pinnacle Point where shellfish appear 160ka ago to the dispersal of Sapiens into Terra 3, 50ka ago, militates against a simple cause and effect.

The third stride of Terra 2 sees a good deal of regional experimentation. Super sites such as the coastal caves of South Africa display one trajectory, and the Mt Carmel caves in Israel another. On occasion, there are linkages across such enormous distances, as with the use of *Nassarius kraussianus* shells to make simple bead necklaces. These have been dated to 80ka at the Grotte des Pigeons at Taforalt in Morocco and are of comparable age at Blombos 8400 km to the south. These simple shell beads, when worn, are another example of a composite technology that now, by circling and wrapping the body, acts as a container. Throughout the third stride, experimentation with materials was the name of the game, a delight-ful bricolage of fitting things together to make a relational point rather than rational sense. For example, at Herto in Ethiopia there is a combination of Mode 2 technology with bifaces and Sapiens skulls that had been scraped and polished after death (J. D. Clark, Beyenne, WoldeGabriel et al. 2003) – a case of archaic technology greeting behavioural modernity.

The use of ochres, lumps of red and yellow iron oxide, to transform appearance shows what is aesthetically possible. When rubbed on a surface such as skin, ochre changes the appearance of someone or something by altering its colour and texture. The timeline (Figure 5.6) for these crea-tive skills indicates an age of at least 280ka. Ochres may indicate symbolic behaviour, but more to the point, they demonstrate an aesthetic under-standing of materials and resources.

Distance Learning

During the third stride, there are innovations outside Africa. The discov-ery of Mode 2 quartz artefacts at Preveli on the south coast of the island of Crete (Strasser, Panagopoulou, Runnels et al. 2010; Strasser, Runnels, Wegmann et al. 2011) indicates an ability to cross oceans.[10] But this skill was already ancient, as the finds on Flores show. In both instances, they predate the appearance of Sapiens outside Africa.

Still in Europe, the super site of Abric Romani in Spain (Table 5.8; Carbonell 1992) has evidence for the repeated construction of hearths that underlines its significance as a place of accumulation and consumption. Such deeply stratified behaviour stems from repetitive visits over many mil-lennia and where memories of place, that crystallise detailed landscape knowledge in a locale, are combined with recollections of social collabo-ration. Both Abric Romani and the super site of La Cotte on the island of Jersey (Callow and Cornford 1986) provided Neanderthals with opportu-nities for hunting, socialising and social performances of varied sorts. But what also accumulated in the sediments were sets of hearths, bones and hundreds of thousands of stone tools. In the case of La Cotte, these accu-mulations vividly record the deep history of the landscape as the coastal shelf surrounding the granite headland came and went as the oceans rose and fell.

---

[10] The age of the Preveli artefacts is difficult to pinpoint, but their position within the terrace stratigraphy suggests an age of at least 130ka sometime in MIS6.

Bringing local raw materials into La Cotte was the rule (Callow 1986). Rising sea levels cut off supplies of flint and chert – rocks that do not occur on the island. Neanderthals adjusted to these changes by knapping quartzites and other stone. What they did not do was import fine-grained rocks from far afield, something they could have done either by visiting the source as a special trip or obtaining raw materials through exchange.

Throughout Terra 2, the majority of distances over which stones were transported from their source remained a two-day walking radius. But in the third stride, longer distances up to several hundred kilometres for the transfer of raw materials are known both from Africa and Europe (Féblot-Augustins 1997; Marwick 2003; McBrearty and Brooks 2000; Merrick and Brown 1984). However, these are invariably a tiny proportion of the artefact set and almost always appear as retouched pieces rather than nodules or initial knapping flakes (Gamble 1999). The 250 km over which stone was transferred to the Neanderthal site of Champ Grand in France (Slimak and Giraud 2007) is interesting because it points to an amplification of landscape use. But the small quantities involved also indicate the rarity of the behaviour. Strontium-isotope evidence obtained from a Neanderthal tooth excavated at the site of Lakonis in Greece has been interpreted as a lifetime range of 20 km for that individual (Richards, Harvati, Grimes et al. 2008), a range of 1270 km² if that distance is regarded as a radius.

Local patterns also dominate in South Africa. The rich layers of Mode 3, Middle Stone Age artefacts at Klasies River Mouth were interrupted between 80ka and 60ka by a Mode 4 type assemblage known as Howieson's Poort.[11] The MSA levels used quartzites that were picked up a short distance from the mouth of the cave. The Howieson's Poort levels changed this pattern. Here, a quarter of the 120,000 stone tools were silcretes from the Cape Folded Mountains located 15 km inland (McBrearty and Brooks 2000: 516), further away but no great distance. At Blombos Cave, the large set of engraved ochre pieces came from between 15 and 32 km away (Henshilwood, D'Errico, Marean et al. 2001: 433), all within a one- or two-day walk-in or round trip.

The Limits to Terra 2

The boundaries to Terra 2 can be drawn more precisely. Hominins are widespread throughout the Old World, but they do not go ocean voyaging

---

[11] This B-List entity (Table 2.7) is known for its large crescent-shaped pieces, one edge of which is blunted, presumably to aid hafting in a composite tool.

or store food. As a result, the limits to this Terra are set by oceans, latitude and altitude. There are some intriguing exceptions: the Mode 1 finds on the island of Flores, and the Mode 2 artefacts from Crete. But these developments did not lead to the peopling of Australia or indeed many other islands near the coasts of Terra 2; for example, Madagascar and the Comoros Islands, its stepping stones, remained uninhabited.

The northern limits are also well defined. There have been claims for early Terra 2 occupation in Yakutia, north-eastern Siberia above the Arctic Circle (Mochanov 1977; Mochanov, Fedoseeva and Alexeev 1983). But in the thirty years following the discovery of Diring-Ur'akh, where Mode 1 tools were claimed, the evidence has not stood up to closer scrutiny.

The northern boundary, which I call Moviusland, is an example of the bio-tidal model. Approximately 15° of latitude was regularly settled and then abandoned as the Milankovitch cycles rhythmically drove changes of climate. This bio-tidal engine means that repeated dispersals within Terra 2 were the norm. Neither were population numbers ever static. They may have been higher in more productive latitudes (Table 3.4) and where food was more accessible (Table 3.5). But the location of these population centres changed with climate, and none more so than the Sunda region (Table 5.7).

The success of Terra 2 hominins lay in solving some of the problems of being large brained and big bodied. This entailed amplifying the diet shift that had its roots in the much older Terra 1. In the north, they were now obligate carnivores who became top predators assisted by technology and supported by larger social collaborations. In particular, fire and projectiles which involved novel compositions with different materials mitigated the impact of much larger home ranges.

These ranges varied in size across Terra 2, reflecting ecological circumstances. Evidence comes from Moutsiou's (2011) study of obsidian, a black volcanic glass found in East Africa and Europe, and the technological uses it was put to. Not all volcanoes produce obsidian. It is found in clusters and isolated pockets along the tectonic trail that starts in East Africa and runs through Greece, Turkey and the Caucasus, ending in Hungary. Some obsidian is on small islands such as Melos in the Mediterranean, while others in Armenia and Turkey are at high altitude and so inaccessible in Terra 2.

The sources of obsidian were fixed points in the landscape of hominins. The distances over which such material was then moved to other places in the landscape can be determined. Moutsiou's (2011) results show that these distances are responsive to latitude and hence to the productivity of

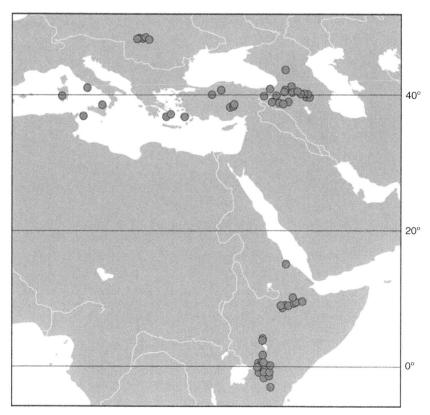

FIGURE 5.7. Obsidian sources in mid-latitude Europe and low-latitude East Africa. The scale of exchange of this volcanic glass is conditioned by the productivity and ecology of these two regions (Tables 5.12 and 5.13). Data provided by Theodora Moutsiou and reproduced with permission.

resources (Tables 5.12 and 5.13 and Figure 5.7). The distribution of sources contrasts the tropics, with high ETs, and hence productivity with Europe and Southwest Asia where ET was lower. Moutsiou (2011) calculates the notional size of territories as indicated by the minimum and maximum distances that obsidian is found from the source (Figure 5.6), and this supports the prediction that the higher the ET, the smaller the size of home ranges (Chapter 3). When the distances are examined by period, we find there are no examples of obsidian use in the north during the second stride. Furthermore, the distances in the south between the A-List Earlier and Middle Stone Ages were consistent. The major contrast is between the

TABLE 5.12. *The distances over which obsidian was moved from its source during Terra 2*

	Terra 2 Second stride (800–200ka)	Terra 2 Third stride (200–50ka)	Terra 3 (50–10ka)
West			
Europe and Near East	No obsidian use	Mode 3: Middle	Mode 4: Upper
Distances km		Palaeolithic	Palaeolithic
Mean		97	200
Median		76	210
STDEV		51	164
South			
Africa	Mode 2: Earlier	Mode 3: Middle	Mode 4: Later
Distances km	Stone Age	Stone Age	Stone Age
Mean	45	41	78
Median	21	22	43
STDEV	60	50	69

Medians and standard deviations provide further comparisons, emphasising the consistent differences between low (south) and high (north) latitudes and the trend to greater distances over time. Data from Moutsiou (2011).

distances in the Middle Palaeolithic and Middle Stone Age (north and south respectively) where a doubling of distance is apparent.

These responses point to versatile Terra 2 hominins adapting to new niches as their population expanded. But ultimately, what set the limits were the problems of going beyond. As the obsidian evidence shows, this was not the issue in Terra 3 when distance moves to a new order of magnitude (Table 5.12). What they had not yet solved in Terra 2 was the business of living apart yet staying together. Coping with separation was not yet part of their versatility.

But this does not make them uninteresting hominins. They had a range of advanced cognitive skills, as enumerated by Wynn and Coolidge (2012) for Neanderthals. Terra 2 hominins had theory of mind and social emotions such as guilt and pride, which allowed them to make moral judgements based on a code of socially correct behaviour. In addition, I have argued in this chapter for the amplifying mechanisms of music and dance, among other social forms (Figure 1.2), that created stronger bonds to cope with a degree of separation. In short, Terra 2 hominins had an imaginative capacity that drew on linguistic and material metaphors to make sense of the world in a social and cultural manner that we can relate to.

TABLE 5.13. *Obsidian home ranges calculated using the distance from source as a radius*

	South	West
	Africa	Europe and Near East
Effective temperature range °C	25–16	16–10
Minimum obsidian territory km^2	13	50
Maximum obsidian territory km^2	123,101	750,840

The differences in these notional ranges meet the expectation that declining productivity, indicated here by ET, will impact on hominins through greater mobility. Data from Moutsiou (2011).

But in two ways, I believe they differed. It is unlikely that they had universal kinship, that passport to go anywhere and you will find either a long-lost relative or make a new one, even if genetically the person in question is no such thing. It is also the case that their socioecology was still the time-honoured primate pattern driven by the reproductive costs of females (Figure 3.10). In order to break out of Terra 2 and find the wide worlds of Terra 3, it seems our ancestors had to review the moral sense they now had, decide who their friends were and begin to control resources in a way that would fundamentally determine the sort of globe-settling primate we became.

CHAPTER 6

Going beyond, keeping in touch: Terra 3, 50–4ka

What country, friends, is this?
Viola, *Twelfth Night*, Act 1, Scene 2

Brave New Worlds

Terra 3 is a riot of human rather than hominin imagination. In a short span, the boundaries of Terra 2 are far exceeded as, for the first time, hominins cross oceans and settle arid continental interiors. And in the process, there is archaeological evidence for innovation in technology, imaginative geographies of the living and the dead and the increased reach of social networks. Dispersal in Terra 3 is also charted by archaeogenetic data that indicate when regional populations arose and where from. Broad patterns at a continental scale come from the study of modern DNA, while a small sample of ancient genomes is beginning to add colour and complexity to the geographical patterns of population dispersal.

In terms of the hominin *bauplan*, there is little to add (Table 5.2). Maximum body and brain sizes were achieved during the third stride in Terra 2. However, it is during Terra 3 that the Sapiens dispersals occur into the continents of Australia, North and South America and throughout Siberia and the Arctic. These indicate a remarkably versatile approach to environments that fluctuated from full ice age to interglacial. And this plasticity brings significant biological developments among *Homo sapiens* who become ever more gracile in their skeletal build. This gracilisation is especially the case with the onset of the Holocene warming. Now regional diversity in human body shape and cranial architecture adapt sensitively to temperature and precipitation. Other phenotypic differences represent further regional adaptations: skin colour to low UVB levels, variation in the immune system to waterborne disease and adaptations to altitude and the effects of hypoxia (Table 2.6). But the human diversity that confronts the bio-anthropologist studying living populations eludes the palaeoanthropologist working with older samples. Regional variation across Terra 3 in skin colour and variation in hair type will have to wait for more ancient DNA work rather than a larger sample of fossil skulls.

This chapter will look at some of that ancient regional data (Figure 6.1). I begin by setting out what had to change when humans pushed beyond the boundaries of Terra 2 and rapidly settled more than fifty per cent of the Earth's surface (Table 1.1). Their initial course, however, followed the well-established pattern of hominin geographical expansion which we saw in the bio-tidal world of Terra 2 – a move east followed at a later date by a surge west. In this chapter, I will examine the southern dispersal route that humans took through Terra 2 and then across the Wallace line to Terra 3 Australia. As in previous chapters, the accent is on the amplification of social and cultural forms which include technology and kinship (Figure 1.2). Within the boundaries of Terra 2, humans encountered other hominins: *erectus* in Asia, *floresiensis* in Indonesia, Neanderthals in western Asia and Europe and the Denisovans of southern Siberia.

Extinction is a feature of the Terra 3 expansion. It applies to hominins as well as large animals. At some time during Terra 3, and for the first time in our evolution, there was a single hominin species, *Homo sapiens*. In addition, the large mammals of the new lands, Australia and the Americas, decline dramatically. The human settlement of Northern Asia, an area that previously was a bio-tidal reservoir for animals such as the woolly mammoth and woolly rhino, now has repercussions for these species' survival, particularly as the climate warmed 11,000 years ago. And during Terra 3, the domestication of animals and plants is added to this mix – a process that amplifies productive resources but at the same time simplifies ecosystems in the interests of supporting larger human populations.

What Had to Change?

Humans approach Terra 3 well equipped. They have language and use varied materials, some of them in complex, composite ways (Table 5.11). They have a theory of mind that allows social reasoning and good working memories to build and sustain relationships between things and people. The surprise is that they do not exit Terra 2 much earlier and initiate the process that leads to global settlement.

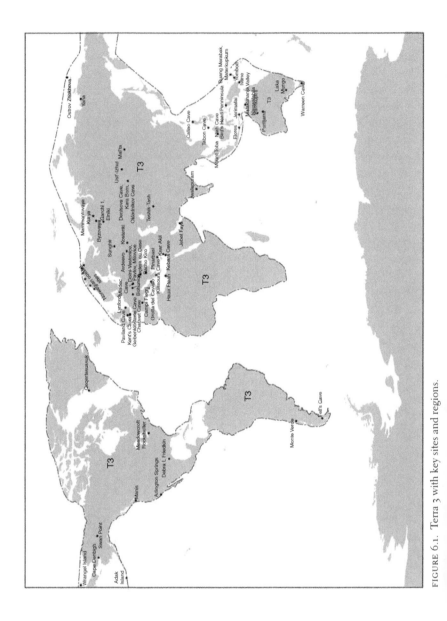

FIGURE 6.1. Terra 3 with key sites and regions.

As a result, this is one of those deep-history disconnects between our expectations and the evidence (Chapter 1). Archaeogenetic data (Box 3.1) indicate that the modern lineages of mtDNA (female inheritance) and MSY chromosome (male inheritance) arose in East Africa between 80ka and 60ka molecular years ago, and soon after spread throughout Terra 2. At this juncture, there is nothing remarkable about *Homo sapiens*, another African species in a world with several other hominin species following a time-worn direction of eastwards travel. Their expansion is assisted by Mode 3 technologies and little in the way of other cultural items such as beads and body ornaments. The population movement witnesses some dramatic events such as the super eruption of the Toba volcano on Sumatra 71ka. This poured out 2800 km³ of ash and created a crater lake 100 × 30 km (C. Oppenheimer 2011). Ambrose (1998) argues that this event set in train a long-lasting volcanic winter that decimated Asian populations, making it possible for humans to disperse, largely unopposed, Out of Africa.

However, spectacular as the Toba eruption must have been over wide areas of Terra 2, a more dramatic moment in deep human history came when humans crossed the short ocean distance to the palaeocontinent of Sahul – New Guinea, Australia and Tasmania combined by low sea level. This dispersal event occurred soon after 50ka and marks the start of Terra 3. What we call modern behaviour may, however, be older (Box 6.1), emphasising that there were alternatives to dispersal. Humans could have carried on as a Terra 2 species as they did between 200ka and 50ka. The fact that during this time *Homo sapiens* are found in the African region of Terra 2 only highlights their parochialism. Getting out of Africa was neither novel nor unexpected for a large body-brain hominin. Humans were not the first to do this, as we saw in Chapters 4 and 5. The expansion of humans between 80ka and 50ka seems fast because we have more precisely dated evidence backed up by estimates derived from molecular clock models. Currently, we cannot estimate the expansion rates of *Homo erectus* or *Homo heidelbergensis*. We must remember that it is a common assumption, one of those veneers covering deep history (Chapter 3), that everything speeds up as we approach the present day.

Therefore, if the initial expansion of *Homo sapiens* across Terra 2 was neither novel nor unexpected, and possibly no faster than any earlier hominin dispersal, what structural limitation in the ancestral *bauplan* (Chapters 4 and 5) had to change to allow the settlement of Terra 3? And what solutions, those amplified and novel cultural techniques (Figure 1.2), were on hand?

Box 6.1. Modern humans and behavioural modernity

The deep-history events that took place between 80ka and 50ka are seen by many palaeoanthropologists as critical to understanding our origins. Soon after the discovery of three Terra 2 age skulls at Omo Kibish in 1967, the initial description of them as a "very early representative of *Homo sapiens*" (Leakey, Butzer and Day 1969: 1132) was revised to read "anatomically modern *Homo sapiens*" (Brose and Wolpoff 1971: 1183). Subsequently, palaeoanthropologists often qualify "*Homo sapiens*" and "human" with the adjective "modern". The trend to qualification has continued so that the literature now contains many references to "fully modern humans" with the implication that an "anatomically modern human" such as Omo Kibish looked the part but didn't cut the mustard (Gamble 2010).

The transition to fully modern human has received much attention, best described as a quest for the origins of behavioural modernity (Henshilwood, D'Errico, Yates et al. 2002; D'Errico, Henshilwood, Lawson et al. 2003; Henshilwood and Marean 2003; Klein 2008; Mellars 1973; Mellars, Bar-Yosef, Stringer et al. 2007; Mellars and Stringer 1989). For example, in an important paper that wrenched the focus of such concerns away from Europe and towards the African evidence, McBrearty and Brooks (2000) identified the archaeological evidence for four key cognitive skills that in their opinion warrant the tag "modern" (Table Box 6.1). Others have supplemented this list by stressing working memory (Belfer-Cohen and Hovers 2010; Wynn and Coolidge 2012).

What behavioural modernity boils down to is that humans are regarded as better planners as well as more culturally adept than other hominins. Why this was the case is put down to increased brain power (Henshilwood and Marean 2003), an advantageous neural mutation (Klein 2008) and a dramatic volcanic event producing a population bottleneck accompanied by cultural advance (Ambrose 1998).

But the quest in deep time for behavioural modernity is, as Shea (2011) points out, an outdated project. It only works if humans and hominins are imagined as possessing different sets of innate or essential qualities such as those in Table Box 6.1. Moreover, it restricts the qualities listed to those that can be directly matched by material evidence for elements such as symbolism and planning depth. This traditionally excludes many aspects of human behaviour – the emotions, moral judgements and psychological desires – because apparently there are no Palaeolithic artefacts symbolising honesty or trust. Elsewhere (Gamble 2007: ch. 3), I have criticised behavioural modernity in a similar manner when it is

TABLE BOX 6.1. *A view of behavioural modernity and supporting archaeological evidence (after McBrearty and Brooks 2000: 492–493)*

Cognitive skills	Definition	Cultural capabilities	Archaeological evidence
Planning depth	The ability to formulate strategies based on past experience and to act upon them in a group context	Technological	Evidence reveals human inventiveness and capacity for logical thinking
Symbolic	The ability to represent objects, people and abstract concepts with arbitrary symbols, vocal or visual, and to reify such symbols in cultural practice	Symbolic	Features of the record demonstrate a capacity to imbue aspects of experience with meaning, to communicate abstract concepts and to manipulate symbols as a part of everyday life
Abstract thinking	The ability to act with reference to abstract concepts not limited in time and space	Ecological	Aspects of the record reflect human abilities to colonise new environments, which require both innovation and planning depth
Innovation	Behavioural, economic and technological	Economic and social	Features show human abilities to draw models from individual and group experience, to develop and apply systematic plans, to conceptualise and predict the future and to construct formalised relationships among individuals and groups

cast in the familiar terms of a human, or Upper Palaeolithic, revolution. In brief, modernity when qualified as behavioural, political or artistic is best left to shallow history to investigate (Proctor 2003). When applied to the deep past, it applies too thick a veneer to the issues under investigation (Thomas 2004). Instead, Shea makes the case that the issues that need investigation are the changes in hominin behavioural variability that arose from social and environmental selection. In the same way, none of the adaptive radiations that led to dispersal (Table 2.4) needed, or indeed indicate, "modern" behaviour.

The Hominin Rule of Local Interaction

The recurring structural limitation for a dispersing large-brained hominin is the relationship between diet, home range size and the number of social partners (Table 5.2). The estimates from body-mass equations and social-brain estimates for group size point to home ranges for Pleistocene humans of 746 km². The larger Neanderthal hominins push this estimate up to 857 km². These home ranges approximate to circles with a radius of between 15 and 18 km. As discussed in Chapter 4, when resources, and especially animals, are abundant and predictable, then such home ranges can be efficiently covered by a bipedal carnivore. Within these structural constraints, as we saw in Chapter 5, amplification can occur to accommodate more social partners; for example, by hunting prime-aged animals and using topographical locations to increase predictability – the so-called super sites that appear in Terra 2 stride 2.

However, what these estimates point to is the importance of the local food supply. Once resources decline, as they did during the Pleistocene climate cycles so that the group can only sustain itself in quadrapedal carnivore-size home ranges (Figure 4.3), there are three options: either innovate by amplifying the social core of senses and materials further (Figure 1.2); relocate to areas that allow a rebalancing of the equation between dietary needs and home range; or become locally extinct. The last two solutions were the hominid and hominin defaults throughout Terrae 0–2. Innovation did occur, as with the adaptive radiations based on fire and composite tools including projectiles (Table 2.4) and the evolution of language as a time-efficient alternative to fingertip grooming (Chapter 5). These adaptive shifts allowed larger numbers of social partners while keeping the balance between population, diet and home range. In this way, the increasing climatic variability of the Pleistocene selected for versatile solutions among Terra 2 hominins.

Terra 3 humans went further. To go either north of Moviusland or populate, after an ocean crossing, an arid continent such as Australia represents more than a rebalancing. Growing seasons, as indicated by ET (Figure 3.6), decline with latitude away from the equator, and when net primary productivity is lowered, it impacts on the secondary biomass, which takes the form of animals (Table 3.5). However, these animals have now become the required staple to meet the high-energy requirements of large-brained hominins. And at the same time, the predictable decline in animal resources that is not matched by corresponding increases in edible plant foods starts to thin out the human population, and the rule of local interaction – to stay in touch – becomes stretched as the frequency of interaction between social partners declines because people are looking for food over larger areas and in smaller units.

Living Apart and Staying in Touch

I have identified the structural limitation in the ancestral *bauplan*. What about the Terra 3 solutions? Some fission and fusion of groups must always have characterised hominins due to their large body size and dietary needs. In the same way, there must always have been a degree of relocation to adjust to the seasonal abundance of resources. The home ranges in Table 5.2 were not fixed, annual absolutes, with hominins tethered like a goat to a patch of land. People could move to take advantage of predictable changes in the density and availability of prey elsewhere in the region. The constraint on their movement was competition from other groups. Such short-term migratory adjustments (Table 2.3) took two principal forms: relocating the home range by moving short distances, as in the string-of-pearls model (Figure 2.9), or breaking the chain by leapfrogging greater distances between patches of resources. Either way, hominin mobility makes it possible to rebalance the equation between space, time and people (Chapter 3).

But staying in touch, a consequence of the local rule of hominin social interaction, raises a further structural weakness: how to live apart. How is knowledge of the social environment updated and transferred between individuals, and at what point does interaction break down due to social separation by distance? One indication might be the scarcity of evidence for crossing water. The suggestions from Crete and Flores are the only indication prior to Sahul being settled (Chapter 5). Overwatering the minimum of 69 km from the island of Sulawesi off the eastern coast of Sunda (J. Allen and O'Connell 2008) to the western shore of Sahul serves as an indication of the constraint on expansion arising from the negative impact of social separation. A strong motive was needed to break the rule of local interaction and set out. But what provided the assurance that a return would be happy and reintegration follow?

These structural limitations for hominin dispersal were solved by innovation in four social forms (Figure 1.2):

1. Relational kinship categories (Read 2010) that enshrine rights and obligations, such as hospitality, and which extend through the capacity of kinshipping (Barnard 2011; Shryock, Trautmann and Gamble 2011) to non-genetic kin (Chapter 1);

2. The storage of foods and materials;
3. The male control of those resources (Foley and Gamble 2009);
4. The domestication and intensification of those resources.

All four solutions build on that core of the senses and materials to amplify stronger social bonds, their strength tested by the rule of local interaction and where living apart and staying in touch become possible even though people are often distant.

Kinship is a diverse branch of human culture (N. J. Allen, Callan, Dunbar et al. 2008; Fox 1967). But whatever categories are used, these systems exist to relate and bind people to each other. Kinship provides a medium to roll the generations forward and transfer rights and obligations, often in the form of who you can marry and how property is inherited. They are, above all, as James (2003: 159–160) states, about recruitment to a group through marriage and alliance. Kinship sets boundaries that take the form of social obligations such as hospitality. And in the process, a container-based logic is revealed. N. J. Allen's (1998) model of tetradic kinship illustrates this well (Figure 6.2). His scheme combines the human generation, along the horizontal axis, with the principle of descent, on the vertical. From this arrangement, four kinship boxes appear governed by a simple rule. Someone in Box C can only marry someone from Box D. In their parents' generation, the same rule applied, but this time marriage was only possible between Boxes A and B.

Kinship alone does not create stronger bonds. These are amplified within the box, the group. Ceremony and ritual, as we have seen in Chapter 5, are available to heighten social gatherings through social forms such as dance, singing and music that play on the senses and produce that *effervescence*, the spirit of the gathering that lingers long after the participants have dispersed. What kinship does is to concentrate those emotions in the interests of building stronger bonds.

At the same time, kinship allows people a greater social reach, thinking outside the box. This is Barnard's (2010, 2011) concept of universal kinship which he argues is very ancient. It allowed people to make kinship rapidly with non-kin and aided survival in habitats where access to alternative resources was a vital prerequisite. This concept has been extended to consider kinshipping as a general principle which allows people to move (Shryock, Trautmann and Gamble 2011). Kinshipping is an imaginative exercise that binds people to ancestors, gods, materials and things, as much as to the living.

Kinship may keep you in touch, but it does not keep you afloat. Another container, the boat, is needed to make that voyage to Sahul. When

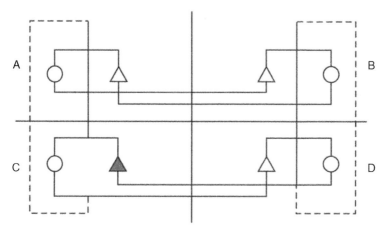

FIGURE 6.2. Tetradic kin structure. For purposes of illustration, Ego is represented by the black triangle. All Ego's sibs (circles are sisters and female cousins; triangles are brothers and male cousins) are also in the box, C, with Ego, and the rule is they all marry with the people in D. Their father's generation is in A (uncles and aunts) and their mother's (aunts and uncles) is in B. The dotted lines show how the offspring of one generation is recruited into the next culturally recognised generation. I have added the heavy lines to emphasise the compartmentalised, container-like structure. Tetradic kinship structures are commonly known as section systems and found throughout Australia and many other parts of the world. Adapted from N. J. Allen (2008: fig. 4.3) and Gamble (2007).

combined, these two containers, conceptual and material, form a powerful social technology. One allows the physical transportation of bodies, while the other relates them to the group. If dispersal is anything more than chance, it requires both to be successful (Gamble 2008).

Storage is a form of keeping (Chapter 1) – a basic human skill that far outstrips the ability of animals to accumulate foods for later consumption. Like kinship, storage is based on making relationships rather than hoarding calories and arresting their decay by drying, freezing and preserving (Ingold 1983). The ability to store depends on the four FACEs of human involvement with materials (Chapter 1). A store often involves *fragmenting* something, such as threshing the seeds from plants, that is then *accumulated*. When filled, it exists for *consumption* and making links, *enchaining*, between the people who set up the store and share its products with others through redistribution and exchange. By controlling time, storage becomes power.

In Chapter 5, I concluded there was little or no evidence for the storage of food in Terra 2. Accumulations of stone artefacts have been described as intentional caches (Gamble 1999, 2007). However, there is no evidence, as Kuhn (1992: 206; 1995) remarks, that Neanderthals and other hominins provisioned places with raw materials for future use. Furthermore, the complex activities seen in ethnographic examples of food storage among FGH are absent (Binford 1978; Gamble and Gaudzinski 2005).

Storage affects human mobility by altering when consumption takes place. By storing what passes *through* your home range, as Binford (1978) showed in his classic study of Nunamiut caribou hunters living in the Anaktuvak Pass of the Brooks Range, Alaska, you no longer have to follow it. The same principle applies to the coastal and riverine communities of the northern Pacific who harvest in great quantities the salmon that migrate up the rivers to spawn (Oberg 1973). In both cases, storage rebalances the diet–people–home-range equation. Space becomes an interception point in the landscape, and time loses its seasonal rhythm. For the Nunamiut, the all-important hunt lasts a few weeks of the year, while among the Tlingit people of the north-west coast of North America, many thousands of fish are harvested and stored in a month. These brief intervals of plenty are then spread through the rest of the year.

But in both cases, storage does not necessarily bring certainty. Will the caribou come through the Anaktuvak Pass this year or choose one of the other routes to move between their winter and summer feeding grounds? How many fish will come up the river? Storage may solve the immediate limitations on settlement imposed by having to solve the time–space–people equation, but at the risk, in those environments at the threshold to Terra 3, of becoming isolated. The solution to the uncertainty of such resources is to build geographically wide alliances, friendships and networks. These act as a conduit for information about the regions' resources and, in the event of failure, offer a safety net by calling in favours from those who have had a good year.

It is in this context that materials and their latent emotional impact come into play. Items such as non-local raw materials, ivory and shell beads and the surfaces of objects altered by colouration and engraving are examples of enchaining people and objects over space and time, one consequence of which is to go beyond the sufficiency of the local group. Such objects are a material rendition of kinshipping indicating, by their late appearance in human social technology (Figure 5.6), that a universal kinship was not a feature of all hominin organisation.

Male control of resources marks a departure from the hominid pattern of socioecology (Figure 3.10). The prime evolutionary directive is that because females bear more of the costs of reproduction than males, they, and their offspring, must have preferential access to those all-important growth foods (Figure 3.11). However, once stored in fixed locations, these foods can be defended and controlled by male coalitions, and the prime directive is overturned. This is obviously the case with domesticated foods produced by horticulture and agriculture. Here, the opportunity for settled communities to defend their food supply is an outcome of the shrinkage of the diet–home-range–population equation. Attack and warfare, the antonyms of defence, appear simultaneously.

But while this change in hominid socioecology certainly takes place with the advent of farming, it has a deeper ancestry. I can see two routes for this male strategy (Gamble and Boismier 2012: 293):

1. Granary route: the accumulation of food resources as a store so that access can be controlled and, if necessary, defended.
2. Treasury route: the investment in, and accumulation of, aesthetic materials and artefacts that enable males to control access to the ceremonies and rituals of social reproduction where they are used, and from which they derive their significance.

Human storage is distinguished by the harvesting of resources at one time and place and their transport and disbursement at another. This is the classic *granary* model of stored foods where a surplus in one season is accumulated and controlled for future use. And just as granary storage is constituted by social relations so is the social storage of aesthetic items and tokens. In the equally classic *treasury* model, social relationships are accumulated and enchained. The treasury route is not so much a hoard of valuables but a bank of obligations, the responsibilities enshrined in tokens, such as shell bead necklaces, which are available for fragmentation, accumulation, consumption and enchainment.

Both models recognise a delay to the cycle of return, whether in the form of food or social obligations. The point is that even in an economy where storage of food is a minor component, as today in indigenous FGH societies in Australia and the Kalahari, the treasury route is still open to male control (Bender 1978; McBryde 1988; Wiessner 1982; Woodburn 1980).

Domestication completes the range of solutions to the structural limitations that curtailed hominin expansion until Terra 3. A domesticated animal is itself a store. It eats the grass and converts surplus produce into protein. Its slaughter and consumption can be delayed while its renewable products of milk, hair and wool are materials that can be amplified into novel artefacts, especially clothing, which can then be accumulated and controlled. When traction is added, then an innovative composite container–artefact is created: a rider on a horse dragging a travois, a reindeer-drawn sleigh, an ox cart and a dog team pulling a sledge. The result is that the limitations imposed by distance on human settlement change again. Fresh opportunities are opened to overcome the local rule of interaction, accumulation moves to another level while the options of defence and attack take on a new aspect.

Domesticated plants present comparable opportunities for amplification. Yields per plant increase under cultivation, as well as their combined value as a crop grown under high density. Realising the latent productivity of these small-sized resources by managing an *r* selected ecology (Chapter 3) changed patterns of human mobility, their involvement with land and released the population valve. Domestication assisted population growth. But it also had a fundamental role to play in global settlement, especially during Terra 4 and *before* such demographic growth began to dominate world history, as is the case in Terra 5.

The Route East 80–50ka

The models of when and in what direction humans dispersed from a centre in Africa are currently driven by archaeogenetic studies based on living populations (Cavalli-Sforza and Cavalli-Sforza 1995; S. Oppenheimer 2004b: 43). Archaeological data are few during the period 80–50ka (Mellars 2006a, 2006c) but are needed to test the relative merits of the proposed routes and to provide a firm chronology. The interest lies in three areas: (1) the direction of dispersal; (2) the timing and frequency of dispersals; and (3) the tempo of these dispersals. In addition there is considerable interest in why population expanded and whether this is a signature of modern behaviour (Box 6.1). But since the dispersal of humans keeps to the confines of Terra 2 in the period 80–50ka, I will treat it as the latest in a well-established pattern of hominin geographical radiations. There is no reason to see this dispersal as driven by a different agenda, modern behaviour, until Terra 3 is reached sometime after 50ka. To do otherwise is to play teleology with deep history.

The ancient geography of human dispersal takes the form of genealogical trees based on the mutations that mark particular branching points (Figure 6.3). These vary according to their distance in both time and space from the original source population, conceptualised as the Most Common Recent Ancestor (MCRA). mtDNA trees are currently more comprehensive than those from MSY (Box 3.1) and have now been reconstructed for all the major living populations using full genomes (Macaulay and

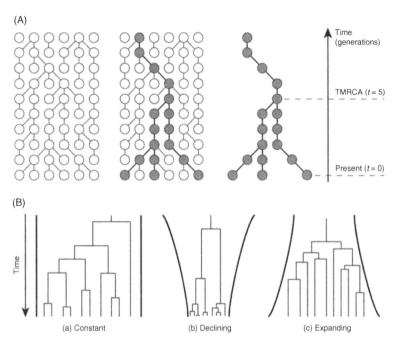

FIGURE 6.3. Coalescence models of population size from genetic data. (A) The tree structure that underlies phylogeographic history is shown here for three individuals in the present. These can be traced back to the most recent common ancestor (TMRCA) five generations previously. (B) The impact of changes in population size on the shape of the tree structure or genealogy. This is what coalescent theory addresses. The difference between a constant population size (a) and those which are either declining (b) or expanding (c) is apparent in the length of the branches. There are longer internal branches when population declines and longer external ones when it expands. Adapted from Young (2012).

Richards 2008). Furthermore, the age estimates of the branching points when new haplogroups, groups of genetic types sharing a common ancestor (S. Oppenheimer 2004b), are for a number of procedural reasons better understood for mtDNA (Soares, Ermini, Thomson et al. 2009). My emphasis will be on the dispersal history of females (mtDNA) rather than that of males (MSY) and is driven by the available data. Archaeogenetics is a burgeoning field, and this imbalance in the evidence will change.

Underpinning these phylogeographies is the principle of coalescence that looks for *historical relationships* between haplogroups. For example, a coalescence study will determine the number of steps to the time of the last common ancestor (TMRCA), as shown in Figure 6.3. There is an alternative approach that makes *predictions* about the structure of populations and then tests them with the genetic data (Nielsen and Beaumont 2009).

TABLE 6.1. *Some molecular clock timings for the likely arrival of humans in target regions.*

Phylogeography of haplogroups based on	mtDNA	MSY	mtDNA	mtDNA	mtDNA and MSY	Whole genomes
	ka molecular age estimates					
Regional targets						
Western Eurasia	<50	45–40	38–25			40–31
Australia	<50		50		70–50	
South Asia	80	50	75–62	84–60		64–38
	Oppenheimer (2009)	Underhill et al. (2001)	Rasmussen (2011)	Macaulay et al. (2005)	Hudjashov et al. (2007)	Gronau et al. (2011)

These are estimates based on assumptions concerning mutation and selection rates and should not be treated in the same way as science-based dating techniques such as radiocarbon and OSL. The variation in the ages reflects the different assumptions in the molecular age models, as well as the genetic system being studied. All of these age estimates have very large standard errors which indicates the uncertainty surrounding the methods.

However, the majority of mtDNA and MSY studies have so far followed the historical route (Underhill, Passarino, Lin et al. 2001). This introduces some weaknesses in interpretation, but where large-scale models are the goal, these can be overlooked.

Molecular Clocks

The mtDNA phylogeographic trees depend for their dating on assumptions concerning mutation rates traced back to a known reference point. The latter is usually set as the divergence between hominins and chimpanzees which is estimated to have occurred 6.5Ma (S. Oppenheimer 2004b: 43). With these assumptions, it is possible to make estimates of when the major founding haplogroups appeared in those target regions for human dispersal (Table 6.1). The methods of calculation are varied and the confidence limits necessary broad. These are not ages in the sense of science-based dating techniques used by archaeologists. This is why I refer to them as "ka molecular" ages. Moreover, the error estimates on these "ages" can be extremely large – a factor reflecting the uncertainty of the methods used to calculate them. As a result, molecular "ages" generally represent maximum ages for the appearance of branches in the phylogeographic tree. Correspondence with archaeological dates is not necessarily expected, since these measure the results of population expansion rather than its genetic origin.

The value of these molecular age estimates is that they provide archaeologists with a model of dispersal to test with more conventional dating methods such as radiocarbon and optically stimulated luminescence (OSL). The period 80–50ka is mostly beyond the range of the former technique, and OSL is comparatively new but has great potential. We can be confident that within the next twenty years, we will have a robust archaeological chronology based on stratigraphy and science-based dating.

African Diversity

The estimated age from the molecular clock of the woman, the Mitochondrial Eve, from whom all today's mtDNA lineages are derived, is 192ka molecular years ago (Table 6.2). Other estimates vary according to the assumptions they employ but are in broad agreement (Ho and Larson 2006: table 1).

From this starting point, four haplogroups evolved – L0–L3 – all within sub-Saharan Africa (Table 6.2). Of these, the most important for Terra 3 is L3 that arose about 72ka molecular years ago. The significance of this founding haplogroup is that it is the only branch of haplogroup L whose descendants are found outside Africa. We have already seen (Figure 3.9) that growth in effective population size for L3 was marked during the period 86–61ka molecular. This growth is not matched by any other L haplogroup at this time, and represents a demographic expansion within Africa that resulted in L3 haplotypes becoming the most frequent in East Africa (Atkinson, Gray and Drummond 2009: 371). Not only is this region a biodiversity hotspot (Figure 2.5) but also the most genetically diverse region for humans (Soares, Alshamali, Pereira et al. 2012; Torroni, Achilli, Macaulay et al. 2006).

The oldest non-African descendants of L3 are haplogroups M, N and R. M and N are two founding groups with rather different geographies. N and its subgroup R are widely spread across Terra 2 and are found subsequently in the western Eurasian part of Terra 3, a region that includes another biodiversity hotspot, Turkey–Iran (Figures 2.5 and 2.6), and then Europe (S. Oppenheimer 2009: 8). M has a southern and eastern distribution in Asia and is not found in the west of Terra 3. These three haplogroups are the foundation points for all subsequent phylogeography throughout Terra 3. For example, U, which is an important haplogroup for Europe and the Near East, diverged from R some 54ka molecular years ago (Table 6.2).

TABLE 6.2. *The molecular age estimates for the founding of selected haplogroups in human phylogeography.*

mtDNA haplogroup	East Africa (ka)	West Africa (ka)	North Africa (ka)	West Eurasia (ka)	South Asia (ka)	East Asia (ka)	Australia and NG (ka)	Europe (ka)	Mongolia (ka)	Americas (ka)
Mitochondrial Eve	192.4									
L0	149.7									
L1	140.6									
L2	89.3									
L3	71.6									
L3bd		60–50								
L3e		56–36								
L3k			40–30							
N				61.9	71.2	58.2	53.2			
R				59.1	66.6	54.3	58.4			
U				54				55		
U5								36		
U6				45–40						
U8								50		
M					49.4	60.5	53.4			
M1				45–40						
M7						55				
M7a						27.5				
P							51.7			
Q							32			
S							25.4			
H								18.6		
V								13.6		
A									35.5	
B1									40.5	
B2									33.5	
D									44.5	
F									42	
A, B, C, D										20–15

The standard errors are not shown, but these are often very large and should be taken into account before accepting these ages as anything other than range-finding estimates of the age when haplogroups were founded. Data from Forster (2004), Hudjashov et al. (2007), Kivisild (2007), Soares et al. (2009), Soares et al. (2010), Soares et al. (2011) and Soares et al. (2012).

The Direction of Dispersal

One way to break down the complexities of phylogeography is to consider source and target regions for each Terra. M and N only appear in the mtDNA genome once populations have left Africa, but initially are still within the old geography of Terra 2. East Asia, and in particular Sunda, was the target area 80–50ka molecular years ago in Terra 2 where M, N and R are found. The first Terra 3 target is Australia and where M is one of the founding haplogroups linking it firmly with those source regions in South Asia that face the Indian Ocean (S. Oppenheimer 2004b: 43). The second Terra 3 target is Beringia and the mammoth steppe north of Moviusland and from there to the Americas (Chapter 7). By contrast, the dispersal into Europe is a traditional Terra 2 target.

The estimates from the molecular clock (Table 6.2) show the relative age of each haplogroup. They also indicate that the direction of expansion, those geographical targets, was primarily towards South and East Asia. A much clearer pattern emerges from mtDNA mismatch analysis that measures the frequency of genetic differences between pairs of individuals in European, Asian and African populations (Harpending, Sherry, Rogers et al. 1993). What these distributions show is the pattern of dispersal within the old geography of Terra 2 with that familiar expansion east followed later by a move west. The molecular clock ages placed on these three population expansions are c. 80ka, 60ka and 40ka (Mellars 2006: fig. 1).

On this point, there is general agreement, and the archaeological evidence broadly supports the model. But when it comes to the details of this expansion, opinions differ. The first issue is the route out of Africa. Voyaging across the Indian Ocean is considered unlikely, which leaves a northern and a southern gateway (Figure 6.4). The former, the desert route, exits Africa across the Sinai Peninsula and into the Levant. This route was almost certainly taken previously when *Homo sapiens* reached the Near East, as the skeletons in the Skuhl and Qafzeh Caves of Israel indicate (Chapter 5). This occurred 135–90ka, mostly during the last interglacial warm period, MIS5. The latter, the channel route, crosses into Arabia across the narrow Bab-al-Mandab straits at the mouth of the Red Sea. This southern route did not need elaborate overwatering skills (Lambeck, Purcell, Flemming et al. 2011; Siddall, Rohling, Almogi-Labin et al. 2003). There was never a land connection, but whenever sea level fell below −50 m, the crossing shrank to 4 km and was dotted with stepping-stone islands. This has been a regular occurrence in the last 120ka, and it is interesting to note that between 70ka

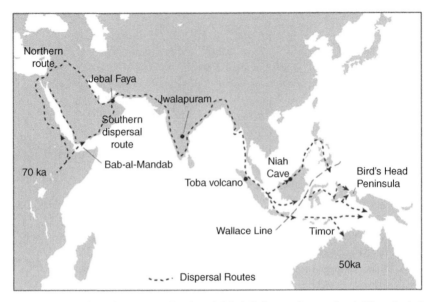

FIGURE 6.4. The routes to Sunda and Sahul (Balme et al. 2009: fig. 2). The principal routes are shown for humans leaving Africa and a coastal route to reach Sunda. The Wallace line marks the division between Asian and Australian animals, mammals and marsupials – the world of elephants from the realm of kangaroos. The Wallace line lies immediately east of Sunda. A northern and southern sea crossing to Sahul are also shown.

and 60ka, this narrow passage existed during MIS4 (Lambeck, Purcell, Flemming et al. 2011: fig. 24).

Many species, as we saw in Chapter 5, have passed through these African exits and entrances. An mtDNA study of hamadryas baboons (Fernandes 2012; Winney, Hammond, Macasero et al. 2004), an African species found either side of the Bab-al-Mandab straits, reveals they made the crossing, unassisted by humans, more than 10ka. Moreover, the phylogeography of the African and Arabian hamadryas populations argues against them taking the northern route (Winney, Hammond, Macasero et al. 2004). Instead, the genetic connections are strongest between the most southerly populations either side of the straits. Needless to say, these baboons did not need watercraft.

The choice of route is important. A northern route moves population towards the diversity hotspot of Turkey–Iran, a familiar part of the tectonic trail (Figure 2.6). From there, population could disperse west into the European peninsula either via the Mediterranean coast or into southern

Russia and the Ukraine. Alternatively, they could follow a higher latitude and go east into Central Asia flanking the Tibetan plateau (Kingdon 1993). The southern route lands them on the coast of Arabia rather than the Mediterranean. One favoured model is that they kept to this coastal environment with its rich marine resources (Field, Petraglia and Lahr 2007; Sauer 1967) and followed it, in S. Oppenheimer's (2009) phrase, across a great arc of dispersal to the target regions of India and Indonesia. This route then acted as the source region for New Guinea and Australia in Terra 3.

The Pull and Push of Green Arabia and Sunda

Two environments at either end of this southern dispersal are critical. In the west are the deserts of Arabia and the Sahara, while to the east is the target region of Sunda. The status of Arabia as either green or yellow depending on the moisture cycle presented a very different set of possibilities for an expanding population (Armitage, Jasim, Marks et al. 2011). A series of environmental records (Figure 6.5) has identified two humid and wetter phases when lakes were present and monsoon activity greater (Parker 2012). These were 135–120ka, which covers the last interglacial when those early *Homo sapiens* fossils have been found in Israel, and 82–78ka. There is also evidence for a Green Sahara at 125ka during the last interglacial when both watercourses and lakes were present (Drake, Blench, Armitage et al. 2010; Drake, ElHawat, Turner et al. 2008) and across which a humid corridor extended to the Mediterranean coast of Libya (Osborne, Vance, Rohling et al. 2008). In tropical southern Africa, the picture was reversed. Lake Malawi experienced repeated extreme aridity in the same MIS5 warm period between 135ka and 70ka (A. S. Cohen, Stone, Beuning et al. 2007).

A Green Arabia and Sahara could have acted as a pull on population during these wet phases. If this coincided with aridity elsewhere in Africa, it is possible that major rebalancing of population occurred between regions. Equally, the arid phase that existed in Arabia between 70ka and 60ka (Armitage, Jasim, Marks et al. 2011: fig. 3), when dunes were forming (Figure 6.5), was a period when population would be pushed out rather than pulled in. Rose (2010: fig. 1) argues for a refuge area, the Gulf Oasis centred on the United Arab Emirates, during this period into which population in Arabia retreated and persisted through arid MIS4. This refuge suggests that dispersal during such a dry phase might necessitate keeping to coastal areas, as these represented the best area for fresh water and a higher density of foods (Field, Petraglia and Lahr 2007). Then, following the

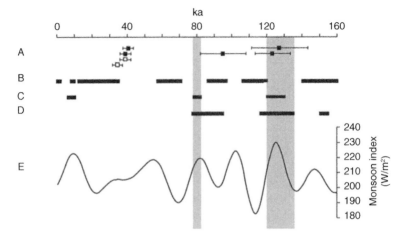

FIGURE 6.5. The timing for a Green Arabia. The following data are brought together to determine when the region was moist and humid, as shown by the vertical grey bars. (A) The OSL dates from Jebel Faya in the UAE. (B) Arid phases when aeolian dunes formed in the Wahiba Sands, Oman. (C) Wet phases recorded in speleotherms from caves in Oman. (D) Appearance of lakes in Mudawwara, Jordan. (E) The monsoon index from Indian Ocean cores. Adapted from Armitage et al. (2011: fig. 3).

human dispersal into Arabia, later variants of L3 (Table 6.2) had dispersed between 60ka and 30ka molecular from a source in East Africa to targets in North and West Africa (Soares, Alshamali, Pereira et al. 2012: fig. 5).

A green and brown Arabia has to be put into a wider context to understand human dispersal. Aridity in Arabia and the Sahara during MIS4 was, by contrast, a time of opportunity as lower sea levels uncovered more of Sunda (Chapter 3). Between 70ka and 60ka, sea levels fell from −80 m to −96 m, rising in the next 10ka to −60 m, only to fall back, with some rapid variation, to −85 m (Figure 6.6; Siddall, Rohling, Almogi-Labin et al. 2003).

What this meant in terms of additional land area is impressive. A fall from −50 to −80 m produced an extra 744,000 km² (Sathiamurthy and Voris 2006: table 1), representing almost a quarter of the total exposed shelf (Table 3.2). Moreover, as described in Chapter 3, much of the exposed shelf supported savannah and grassland rather than tropical rainforest (Figure 2.2; Balme, Davidson, McDonald et al. 2009: fig. 4), thereby raising its productivity and useable resources for human settlement (Table 3.5). More detailed environmental reconstructions reveal a broad savannah corridor (Figure 6.7) that divided the tropical rainforest (Bird, Taylor and Hunt 2005).

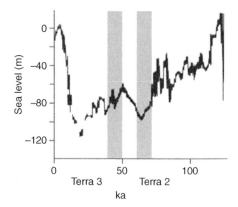

FIGURE 6.6. Changing sea levels during the last cold stage. The times of maximum exposure of the Sunda shelf are shaded. Adapted from Siddall et al. (2003).

In terms of continuing land gains, the best time to arrive in Sunda was during sea-level fall at the beginning of the global cold stage MIS4 between 70ka and 60ka (Figure 6.6). This does not mean that humans arrived here at this time, but if they did, it might help explain the exceptional growth rates in population that resulted in fifty per cent of MIS3 humans living in South Asia (Figure 3.9).

What Went with Them

The low-latitude disease belts have been suggested as a barrier to dispersal (Bar-Yosef and Belfer-Cohen 2001). However, archaeogenetic studies now show that the parasite *Plasmodium falciparum*, which today accounts for 230 million cases of malaria a year, left Africa with one of the human dispersals during the Pleistocene (Tanabe, Mita, Jombart et al. 2010). The evidence is based on geography and where more than ninety-five per cent of the genetic diversity of this parasite is accounted for by the distance away from its source in tropical central Africa (Tanabe, Mita, Jombart et al. 2010: fig. 1). This means that humans were infected with the malaria parasite before they dispersed from Africa, and the inference is that this would have been during the first departure.

However, the subsequent history of human demography had a role to play in making malaria such a devastating disease. Much larger populations in the Holocene, particularly after the appearance of agriculture, provided enhanced breeding conditions for the *Anopheles* mosquito that transmits the parasite. The disease belts existed but were not a barrier to

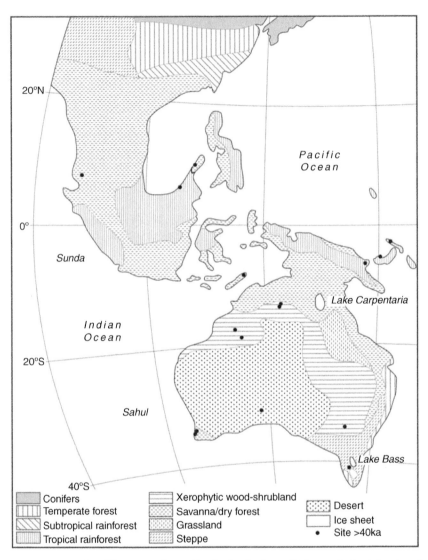

FIGURE 6.7. The savannah corridor in Sunda that split the tropical rainforest and opened up a land route through Sunda to Sahul. Adapted from Balme et al. (2009: fig. 4) and Bird et al. (2005).

dispersal because population numbers were small (Chapter 3). Rather, it was through zoonosis, the transmission of diseases from domestic animals to humans, and usually as a result of close contact and overcrowding, that people infected themselves. This was the case with bovine tuberculosis as food production was intensified. Domestication and the settled life had consequences for health that did not apply to mobile populations living by FGH.

The Timing and Frequency of Dispersals

Molecular estimates for early dispersals in Terra 3 are set out in Table 6.1, and a two-stage model is believed to make the best sense of the patterns (Forster 2004; S. Oppenheimer 2009). The oldest saw humans expand from the source of Arabia to the target of South Asia–Sunda along a southern route (Figure 6.4). The younger witnessed a second expansion to the same target area but along a more northerly route closer to the Himalayas, while at the same time, a western expansion from Southwest Asia also took place (Rasmussen 2011: fig. 2). Molecular estimates separate these two events by as much as 30ka (Table 6.1).

The Southern Dispersal

The oldest, southern dispersal at 84ka molecular years ago has a source in Southwest Asia and the target of reaching South Asia and Sunda. In a coalescent study of whole genome sequences, the effective population size of this founding population, and from which everyone alive today is descended, has been variously estimated as between c. 9000 (Gronau, Hubisz, Gulko et al. 2011) and c. 100–620 females (Macaulay, Hill, Achilli et al. 2005: supporting online material page 5). This expansion is remarkable for having a single founder haplotype unlike all later major regional dispersals which have multiple founders (S. Oppenheimer 2009: 8). One archaeogenetic lacuna, however, is that due to much later population replacements, the likely source area in the Arabian Peninsula lacks these early ancient mtDNA lineages. This suggests that people either did not linger long in Arabia or that they soon became extinct (Macaulay and Richards 2008: 3).

The single founder haplogroup and the absence of ancient lineages in the source area both point to the L3 founding event as separate and distinct from what came later. Subsequently, there were dispersals with Sahul as the target from the source area of South Asia–Sunda and a further two targets from the Southwest Asian source area 50–40ka molecular years ago – a more northerly route into Asia and a westwards track into Europe (Rasmussen 2011: fig. 2).

The archaeological evidence for the earliest, southern dispersal is sparse (Petraglia, Haslam, Fuller et al. 2010). Artefacts from open sites are plentiful but largely undated. And without reliable dates, it is difficult to identify the cultural signature of these early dispersals among a mass of Mode 3 artefacts, many of which could have been made by older populations.

Three sites emerge as important for the archaeological evidence they contain. The earliest is the UAE rockshelter site of Jebel Faya on the Persian Gulf dated to 125ka by OSL (Armitage, Jasim, Marks et al. 2011). In assemblage C, archaeologists found Mode 3 artefacts consisting of small bifaces and other leaf-shaped tools. These have affinities with material excavated in East Africa rather than the nearby Levant, and are regarded by the excavators as evidence for humans exiting Africa.

The second archaeological site on the southern dispersal confirms the Jebel Faya pattern. The open-air site of Jwalapuram locality 3 in south-central India has levels with stone tools immediately above and below 2.5 m of Toba ash which fell here 71ka, 2600 km from the volcanic crater in Sumatra. The 215 artefacts so far excavated are described as Mode 3, Middle Palaeolithic, and were found with a single piece of red ochre that shows striations due to use (Petraglia, Haslam, Fuller et al. 2010; Petraglia, Korisettar, Boivin et al. 2007: fig. 2). Petraglia, Korisettar, Boivin et al. (2007) have argued that they represent evidence for the ancient southern dispersal – a dispersal that does not appear to have been made possible, or interrupted for long, by the Toba super eruption (C. Oppenheimer 2011: 201–207).

The third site is Niah Cave in the heart of Sunda on the island of Borneo. This rich archaeological locale has the added bonus of a human skull, known as the Deep Skull because of its stratigraphic position. After many years of uncertainty, it is now reliably dated to between 44ka and 40ka (Barker, Barton, Bird et al. 2007). In addition, archaeological evidence extends back in the site to at least 46ka. This evidence consists of the remnants of hearths, faunal remains with cut marks and botanical evidence, while the stone tools at Niah Cave, better known from levels much younger than the Deep Skull, are Mode 1 – stone tools to make other tools in perishable materials such as bamboo (Barker, Barton, Bird et al. 2007: 255). At the moment, the Niah Deep Skull is the only *Homo sapiens* skull along the southern route and the oldest in South Asia, although by the archaeogenetic timescale (Table 6.2) rather late. One test of the archaeogenetic model will be palaeoanthropologists' ability to find older *Homo sapiens* material.

Further human material is known from the Philippines. A small collection of human remains from Tabon Cave on Palawan range in age from 16.5ka to possibly 47ka (Détroit, Dizon, Falguères et al. 2004), while at Callao Cave on Luzon, which was never joined to Sunda, a single foot bone has a U-series age of 67ka (Mijares, Détroit, Piper et al. 2010). Which species of human this metatarsal belongs to is unclear, but these data do point to the possibility of many more discoveries of fossil material that may shed light on the earliest dispersal of humans into Southeast Asia.

The Woman in Siberia

When these skulls are found, they may not provide a source for ancient DNA studies, since genetic material contained in bones is poorly preserved in tropical environments. However, this is not the case in the southern Siberian cave of Denisova located at 51°N in Terra 2 (Krause, Fu, Good et al. 2010; Reich, Green, Kircher et al. 2010). Ancient autosomal DNA (Box 3.1) has been successfully extracted from a female finger bone and a tooth. And in so doing, more questions than answers about human dispersal are raised. The genomes from these individuals are sufficiently different from any other fossil hominin so far studied that they are referred to as the Denisovans. The ages of the bone and tooth are unclear, dated to sometime between 50ka and 30ka. The archaeogenetic study reveals they were far removed from the immediate ancestors of Neanderthals and humans with whom the Denisovan female shared an MRCA 1Ma molecular years ago (T. Brown 2010). By comparison, the MRCA of humans and Neanderthals lived between 440ka and 270ka molecular years ago (Green, Krause, Briggs et al. 2010). Perhaps the Denisovans were an Terra 2 dispersal from Africa into Asia (Krause, Fu, Good et al. 2010), although an alternative has been proposed – that they were simply a dispersal within Asia (Martinon-Torres, Dennell and Bermudez de Castro 2010). Either way, they were a widely dispersed hominin within Terra 2. The significance of the female from Denisova Cave is either that her ancestors had moved into southern Siberia during Terra 2 or she had dispersed there in Terra 3 (see Chapter 7).

However, instead of recognising her dispersing capabilities, interest in the Denisovan woman has focussed on the small proportion of genes, five per cent, that point phylogeographically to Southeast Asia and to living populations in Malaysia (Reich, Green, Kircher et al. 2010). One possible scenario is that as humans dispersed, they interbred with indigenous populations such as the ancestors of the Denisovan woman. This did not occur in Siberia but instead implies the Denisovans were formerly widespread in South Asia and that Denisova Cave is simply a sampling point for that earlier distribution (Stringer 2011: 196). But which human dispersal that might be, the early one at 75–62ka molecular, the later at 38–25ka molecular (Rasmussen 2011), or both, is unclear partly because the bones which yielded the ancient DNA are so poorly dated.

The Archaeological Signature of Dispersal

The archaeogenetics of Denisova Cave raises many intriguing possibilities that will only multiply as the revolution in ancient DNA gathers pace. Data on dispersals will increase, and the patterns in ten years time will be much more complex than those we currently have. Multiple dispersals are to be expected, as Foley and Lahr (1997; Lahr and Foley 1994) proposed some time ago from fossil and archaeological evidence. Moreover, they argued that, archaeologically, these will be difficult to detect. Dispersal eastwards into Asia was not associated with a novel tool kit and large quantities of distinctive art and ornaments. This was the pattern for the later dispersal of humans into Europe and on occasion contrasted sharply with the material culture of the indigenous Neanderthals. Lahr and Foley pointed to the predominance of Mode 3 technologies (Box 2.3) in the human dispersal to the east, a pattern that continued with the settlement of Sahul. Dispersal to the west through the Levant and into Europe is marked by Mode 4, as well as by artefacts that Wobst (1990) referred to as "Arctic hysteria" – the accumulation and consumption of items such as body ornaments, figurines, engraved plaques and cave art associated with the Upper Palaeolithic of the region (Mussi and Zampetti 1997; White 1997).

The Jebel Faya artefacts alert us to the types of stone tools we might expect. Importantly, they contradict the European model of dispersal recognised by replacement. This means, archaeologically, that Mode 3 was replaced by Mode 4, the Middle by the Upper Palaeolithic and Neanderthals by *Homo sapiens*.

This European model of what a human dispersal should look like, artefactually, derives its weight from the history of archaeology but has no wider geographical significance (Box 6.2). A review of the evidence from Australia makes this point (Habgood and Franklin 2008). Those cultural items that in Europe form a signature of human dispersal are, in Sahul, poorly represented and achieve prominence in the cultural repertoires over the 30ka years following first settlement.

Box 6.2. Tracing human dispersals with archaeological evidence

The early dispersals of humans from Africa may seem clear-cut to archaeogeneticists. However, this is not the case for archaeologists. What archaeologists rely on to trace a dispersal event is one of their key propositions in the study of the past: that a link exists between a people and its products. In other words, different peoples made and accumulated things in different ways. This assumption has a long history in both archaeology and ethnology where the study of living peoples added language, customs and beliefs to the cultural mix.

There have been many proponents of the cultures-equals-peoples model in archaeology, but the most cited formulation is Gordon Childe's which defined an archaeological culture in these terms: "We find certain types of remains – pots, implements, ornaments, burial rites and house forms – constantly recurring together. Such a complex of associated traits we shall term a 'cultural group' or just a 'culture'. We assume that such a complex is the material expression of what today would be called a 'people'" (Childe 1929: v–vi).

These archaeological cultures acted as a proxy for the diffusion, or migration (Table 2.3), of peoples. Diffusion also acted as an historical explanation for cultural changes in time and space; people A replaced people B. And if people did not move, then new presumably advantageous concepts, techniques and cultural stuff diffused between populations.

When it comes to deep history, it is a species rather than a people that is expected to make things differently, the classic case being the European record of Neanderthals and humans who made, respectively, the A-List Middle and Upper Palaeolithic (Table 2.7). Packed within these classifications are the different peoples or populations who made the B-List entities such as Quina Mousterian and Mousterian of Acheulean Tradition (Middle Palaeolithic) and the Aurignacian, Gravettian and Magdalenian (Upper Palaeolithic).

Such people-culture thinking has long been challenged and, for the most part, rejected in favour of adaptive explanations for the variation found between assemblages of stone tools. But it lingers on when it comes to the study of population movements and has on occasion been adopted uncritically by archaeogeneticists. It retains adherents who seek to marry up language, phylogeography and archaeological cultures in an ethnological package (Bellwood 2005; Renfrew 1987). But since no remnants of languages older than the Neolithic and agriculture are thought to survive, much of deep history remains largely untouched by such speculations.

(continued)

Box 6.2. *(continued)*

Strong and weak signatures of dispersal and displacement

The archaeology of dispersal and displacement is marked by two signatures: weak and strong. These are primarily found among Mode 3, 4 and
5 technologies and in Terra 3 onwards where we have to be wary of the
veneer effect exacerbated in this instance by the availability of archaeogenetic data to study dispersal (Chapter 3). However, as Table Box 6.2(a)
shows, the possibilities of the two signatures present a varied picture. The
technologies draw on my discussion in Chapter 2 (see Tables 2.7–2.9),
while the qualitative assessments recognise that inclusive units rarely
exist in archaeological evidence. Instead, we expect leakage and variable attendance. This results in signatures that are polythetic rather than
monothetic (Gamble 2008: ch. 3 and fig. 3.3). This may be frustrating for
the peoples-culture model and the haplogroup-language-culture model,
but it is how the evidence presents to the archaeologist.

TABLE BOX 6.2(A)

Human remains	Weak	Strong
	None or very few	Many
Geographically and temporally distinctive stone and organic artefacts (projectile points, bifacial hand-held tools, boats, houses, ways-of-making)	None or few. Poorly defined chronological spans. Reductive technologies with an instrument focus. Some additive ways of making.	Present sometimes in quantity. Composite, additive and container-based technologies as shown by tools, dwellings and transport. Well-defined chronological spans.
Geographically and temporally distinctive display objects (body, dress ornament, materials which change surface colour and texture, e.g. ochre)	None or few. Poorly defined chronological spans.	Present, sometimes in quantity. Well-defined chronological spans.
Accumulation of distinctive artefacts	Rare and only as sets of similar objects and materials.	Common as sets of similar and diverse objects and materials.
Enchainment through materials and artefacts	Short distances and rare occurrences.	Longer distances and common occurrence.
Domestic resources (plants, animals, food and power)	None or rare.	Present and usually essential for population dispersal.

Some examples of weak and strong signatures for dispersal are given here. The strongest are those where a Terra is occupied for the first time. More often in deep history, dispersal had to fit round or go through existing populations. Sometimes these dispersals have a strong signature, but on other occasions, they do not, making it difficult to test the archaeogenetic models of population history.

TABLE BOX 6.2(B)

	Weak	Strong
Population dispersal into unoccupied land		*Homo* into Terra 2 Mode 1; Sahul
		Mode 3 Terra 3; Beringia Mode 4 Terra 3; Remote Oceania domestic resources Terra 4; Iceland domestic resources Terra 4
Population dispersal and displacement within a populated Terra	Repeated *Homo* dispersals in	Humans into Europe and southern
	Terra 2 Modes 1 and 2;	Siberia Mode 4 Terrae 2–3
	Humans from Arabia to Sunda	Thule migration from Alaska to
	Mode 3 Terra 2–3	Greenland Mode 5 Terra 4; Neolithic farmers into Europe domestic resources Terra 3 Bantu migrations within Africa domestic resources Terra 4
Transmission of cultural stuff within a populated Terra with no population movement or displacement	Acheulean biface technology Mode 2; Levallois technology Mode 3	*Nassarius* shell ornaments in South and North Africa Mode 3–4 Terra 2;
		Clovis projectile technology in North and South America Mode 4 Terra 3; Mesolithic FGH in Europe domestic resources Terra 3

But the European model has deep roots that continue to colour interpretation. Powell, Shennan and Thomas (2009) argue that the appearance of new items of technology and art reflect the pattern of social learning in larger populations and hence the ability to innovate. Indeed, they use the appearance of these items to argue that critical population thresholds had been crossed. However, this raises difficulties with those coalescent studies that see population growth in South Asia following dispersal (Atkinson, Gray and Drummond 2007). This region, if the European model is correct, should show high rates of innovation in these items. But it does not. The archaeology of the early southern dispersal shows Mode 3 technologies passing through existing Mode 3.

Instead, the model of population size and innovation rates is better served if the European signature for human dispersal is rejected. As Barker concludes for the Niah Cave evidence, while the classic markers of behavioural modernity (Box 6.1) are absent in Sunda, there are many other examples of innovation. At Niah Cave, "their subsistence practices and engagement with the landscape were of demonstrable socio-economic complexity. The levels of resource use, forward planning, and ingenuity that would have been necessary for such strategies would not only parallel many of the developments in Late Pleistocene records of Europe and Africa, but also serve to illustrate human adaptive plasticity with the emergence in Southeast Asia of strategies directed specifically towards exploiting the structure and diversity of lowland tropical environments" (Barker, Barton, Bird et al. 2007: 259).

Innovation in the exploitation of plants is a feature of the earliest settlement of Sahul. Excavations at several localities in the Ivane Valley in Highland New Guinea, at an altitude of 2000 m, have found stone axes and evidence for plant use in the form of charred *Pandanus* nutshells. These are dated to 49–44ka (Summerhayes, Leavesley, Fairbairn et al. 2010).

These dispersal events therefore took two different forms. In the east, innovation occurred in food production, although this did not lead at this early stage to domestication. No doubt the selective pressure was part of the Sunda effect where population growth was maximised in the savannah-grassland environments that occurred between 70ka and 50ka. Here were the seeds of the granary model and control over resources. Expansion to the west took a different path. Enchainment and control came through the treasury strategy where the means of social reproduction were controlled on a regional scale. Finally, which strategy was adopted within Africa varied from region to region, as might be expected given the antiquity of treasury items in northern and southern Africa but not in central and eastern parts of this vast continent.

The Tempo of These Dispersals

Two models are on offer: continuous and punctuated tempos for dispersal, as well as slow and fast rates. The former sees a continuous and rapid spread of population not only from the Arabian source area to the Sunda target but also beyond to the Terra 3 target of Sahul (Hudjashov, Kivisild, Underhill et al. 2007: 8729). The latter identifies significant pauses in the process, usually followed by rapid dispersal. As S. Oppenheimer (2009) argues from the mtDNA data, there was an African exit at 80ka molecular years ago with the South Asian target reached soon after (Figures 6.4 and 6.8). There was then a delay in the process until Sahul was settled at c. 50ka and western Eurasia at about the same time. There was then a further major delay before the move north from Central and East Asia that led to the settlement of the Americas. As a result, the process is best described as a few bursts of rapid dispersal followed by population stasis until the next, express expansion.

The rate of dispersal can be estimated, but more work still needs to be done. One study using molecular age estimates (Macaulay, Hill, Achilli et al. 2005: 1036) suggests that the 12,000-km-long southern route was settled at a rate of c. 4 km per annum. In a radiocarbon-dated study of the speed with which Northern Europe was repopulated 16ka after the retreat of the last ice sheets, archaeologists found that the rate for hunters dispersing from the southern refuge areas to the target area of Britain was much slower at c. 0.7 km per year (Housley, Gamble, Street et al. 1997). Instead of rapidly covering the 12,000 km of the southern route in 3ka molecular, under the slower rate, it would have taken 17ka. This warns us against accepting uncritically the molecular age estimates.

Terra 3 and the Sahul Target

The settlement of Sahul is the first genuine Terra 3 target. When this happened is important for the wider understanding of the mechanics of human dispersal. Currently, the best estimate comes from the radiocarbon chronology and where the excavated evidence from the Ivane Valley in eastern New Guinea is, at 49–44ka (Summerhayes, Leavesley, Fairbairn et al. 2010), the oldest throughout Sahul. Elsewhere a date of 45ka is widely accepted for first settlement (Balme, Davidson, McDonald et al. 2009; O'Connell and Allen 2004; Veth 2010).

The best candidates for the entry point into the palaeocontinent are shown in Figure 6.4, with the northern Bird's Head route emerging as the current favourite over the southern route via Timor (J. Allen and O'Connell 2008; Veth 2010; Veth, Spriggs, Jatmiko et al. 1998; Webb 2006). To get to Bird's Head on Papua New Guinea from Sulawesi took between eight and eighteen stages. These formed island stepping stones, and even at lowest sea levels, at least one of the jumps had to cross 69 km of ocean (J. Allen and O'Connell 2008: 34).

The Bird's Head is not the only route, and a more southerly one through Timor also has its supporters. Here, at the Jerimalai rockshelter, a wide range of pelagic fish, including tuna, were found in archaeological deposits dated to 42ka. These data point to a complex maritime technology capable of harvesting deep-sea fish and, by inference, crossing to Sahul. Much later in the sequence, at the same site, a shell fish hook, the first example anywhere, was recovered and dated to 16ka (O'Connor, Ono and Clarkson 2011).

Older ages of 60ka based on TL and OSL dating methods come from the rockshelters at Malakunanja and Nauwalabila in the Arnhem Land escarpment, northern Australia (R. G. Roberts, Jones and Smith 1990), and the Mungo 3 burial in New South Wales (Thorne, Grun, Mortimer et al. 1999). This long chronology has been questioned (O'Connell and Allen 1998, 2004, 2012) and is not used here. Clearly, if it was supported, the additional 10–15ka of settlement history would change the perception that Sahul was a delayed target for human dispersal.

At least thirteen sites are dated to the period 45–40ka, and these have a very wide distribution across the tropics, semi-arid and desert regions (Figure 6.7). One of them, Buang Merabak, points to further ocean crossings to the Bismarck Archipelago off the coast of Papua New Guinea (Leavesley and Chappell 2004). Two further sites in the same archipelago of 40ka-year-old age, Matenkupkum on New Ireland and Yombon on New Britain (J. Allen and Gosden 1991), confirm this early settlement of Near Oceania (Summerhayes, Leavesley, Fairbairn et al. 2010).

The Parnkupirti site at Salt Pan Creek at Lake Gregory on the edge of the Great Sandy Desert in north-west Australia has an OSL age of more than 37ka, while its stratigraphic position points to a possible age of 50–45ka (Veth, Smith, Bowler et al. 2009). This inland arid-zone site points to the dispersal soon after arrival of humans into the varied landscapes of interior Sahul (M. A. Smith 2013).

In northern Sahul, settlement, albeit seasonal, took place above 2000 m in the Ivane Valley, an area regarded today as extremely tough for human settlement (Gosden 2010b). At the other end of Sahul, in Tasmania, some 7500 km from the favoured landfall of Bird's Head, the oldest radiocarbon date from Warreen Cave on the Lancelot River is 39.9ka (Cosgrove 1999). Warreen and the other south-west Tasmania rockshelters contain long sequences with rich stone and butchered animal-bone assemblages. Today, they are found in the wet temperate rainforest (J. Allen 1996), but when they were occupied during MIS3, the environment was colder, with productive open grass and herb fields – good country for wallabies.

The earliest radiocarbon ages for Sahul suggest a dispersal rate of 1.5 km per annum from Bird's Head to Warreen. This would have entailed moving through either the hyper-arid Pleistocene interior of the continent, or taking a coastal route that has since vanished due to sea-level rise in the Holocene.

What is of interest with Sahul is the speed with which a great variety of habitats are settled. Within the interior, M. A. Smith's (1987, 1989, 2005) excavation of Puritjarra rockshelter in the Cleland Hills 300 km west of Alice Springs in central Australia has shown an early desert adaptation to severely limited water sources, plant foods and hyper-aridity. The earliest human occupation at Puritjarra layer II is 36–35ka (M. A. Smith 2009). The one environment which was settled later appears to be the tropical rainforest. Investigations in north-east Queensland show the forests contracted during MIS3 and MIS2 with human occupation at its western edge 30ka (Cosgrove, Field and Ferrier 2007). It was not until the Holocene, 8ka, that settlement is found in the forest and then at a low level. After 2ka, the evidence is more abundant.

In the case of Australia, the archaeogenetic data indicate that, once settled, the continent then became isolated for almost 40ka (Rasmussen 2011). M, N and R were all founder haplogroups, and during this isolation, new branches appeared. Haplogroup S is unique to Sahul, while Q shows dispersal between New Guinea and Australia (Table 6.2). Neither MSY nor mtDNA phylogeographies show any further significant dispersal of humans from the Sunda source into Australia. The only exception is a new mtDNA haplogroup, Austronesian B, which does appear much later on the coasts of New Guinea from a source to the east (Hudjashov, Kivisild, Underhill et al. 2007: 8728). Throughout this period, the two present landmasses of northern Sahul were joined by an extensive plain. Only when sea levels rose above −50 m, which did not occur until the early Holocene 10ka (Figure 6.6), was this reduced to a relatively narrow isthmus known as the Torres Strait Plains (J. Allen and O'Connell 2008: fig. 1).

New Guinea was separated from Australia by rising sea levels 8.3ka, and Tasmania was sundered 12ka (sahultime.monash.edu.au). At some point, pigs and dingo dogs crossed, or were transported over the Wallace line and entered the continent of marsupials. Domestic pigs came to typify the economies and rituals of much of New Guinea (Rappaport 1968), but they never dispersed into Australia, although as feral animals from European farms, they do very well. The domestic dingo which arrived in the last 5ka is found in both parts of the former Sahul but was not present in Tasmania where the marsupial wolf, the thylacine, filled this niche until it was hunted to extinction in 1930.

Explaining the Early Southern Dispersal

The dramatic explosion of Mt Toba at the MIS5/4 boundary has been put forward as a trigger for the changes that made dispersal possible (Ambrose 1998). However, doubt has been cast as to whether even this super-volcanic event could have produced the predicted volcanic winter that devastated Terra 2 populations in Asia (C. Oppenheimer 2011).

Mellars (2006a, 2006b, 2006c) favours an environmental rather than catastrophic model to explain the timing of the earliest southern dispersal. The climate which shaped the early southern dispersal is MIS4, 71–57ka (Box 2.1) – a period of major glaciations in the Northern hemisphere and low sea levels around the world. Mellars points out that the shift from MIS5 to 4 in the period 80–70ka in sub-Saharan Africa led to a fall in annual rainfall of up to fifty per cent as the climate there entered an arid phase. He regards this as the motor for change that affected populations of *Homo sapiens* in more fundamental ways than the Toba ash fall (Figure 6.8). Mellars' model provides a description of humans as an African export. They flew their continent of origin as fully fledged humans.

However, many of these cultural changes are much older, as with the discoveries at Pinnacle Point in South Africa (Figure 5.5). Neither is the question answered of why these objects, apparently so important to dispersal (Box 6.2), are so rare along the southern route. One piece of scratched ochre from Jwalapuram in India has to be placed against several thousand excavated at Blombos Cave in South Africa. And what exactly was the selective pressure for new cultural items? What adaptive advantage did they bestow? As Habgood and Franklin (2008) point out, for Sahul, this was a "revolution that didn't arrive". Items were not lost en route. There was no "package" of new things which formed a signature of dispersal for archaeologists to trace.

This is evident in South Asia where evidence for ornaments is less than 30ka years old (Balme, Davidson, McDonald et al. 2009; Perera 2010). The question then arises of whether those dispersing humans had symbolic conceptualisation, even though they did not regularly make symbolic artefacts. Balme and colleagues take the position that absence of evidence is not evidence of absence. Moreover, there is "no requirement that the emergence of propositional thought and symbolic construction of the world should

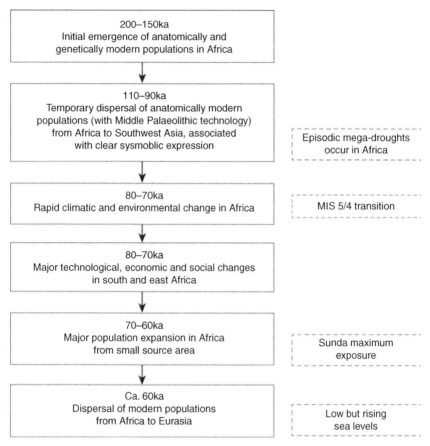

FIGURE 6.8. An environmental model supporting the southern dispersal route. Adapted from Mellars (2006).

produce a particular pattern in the archaeological record. It would have created *patterning*, but that patterning should not be the same from one population to another" (Balme, Davidson, McDonald et al. 2009: 65). In other words, expecting the European model of modern humans marked by Mode 4, art and ornaments is unfounded.

My reading of the pattern, or non-pattern, is that humans were simply the latest in a sequence of dispersals *within* Terra 2. These dispersals encountered other hominins such as the Denisovans and the small-sized, small-brained hominins, *Homo floresiensis*, who lived on the island of Flores (P. Brown, Sutikna, Morwood et al. 2004; Morwood, Soejono, Roberts et al. 2004; Box 6.3).

Box 6.3. The surprise in store on Flores

Hominin fossils come in all shapes and sizes. However, excavations in 2003 at the Liang Bua Cave on the island of Flores, Indonesia, uncovered a hominin that was off the scale. The remains of up to eight individuals from a population of tiny hominins described as *Homo floresiensis* remind us that we have only just begun to map the variation of our recent ancestry. *Floresiensis* rewrote the textbooks in four ways. First, it had a very small brain in a very small body (Table Box 6.3). Second, these fossils were recent, dated to Terra 3 sometime between 38ka and 12ka when they became extinct. Third, they were found with stone tools and charred bones. The former show continuity with 800ka-year-old material from Mata Menge on the same island (Chapter 5; Brumm, Aziz, van den Bergh et al. 2006; Moore and Brumm 2007). And finally, to get to Flores, they needed to cross water, since this island in the Indonesian archipelago was never part of Sunda.

TABLE BOX 6.3. *Comparing* Homo floresiensis *with their contemporary,* Homo sapiens. *Data from Brown, Sutikna, Morwood et al. (2004).*

	Mean cranial capacity (cm³)	EQ	Personal network size	Grooming time (% daytime)	Mean adult body weight (kg)	Home range ape individual (ha)	Home range human individual (ha)	Home range ape group (km²)	Home range human group (km²)
Homo floresiensis	401	4.3	60	13	16	13	79	8	47
Homo sapiens (Pleistocene)	1478	5.38	144	40	66	83	518	120	746

An adult *Homo floresiensis* was about 1 m in height, weighed as much as a small child, although estimates vary between 16 and 36 kg, and the first one to be described, LB1, had a small brain of 417 cm³ (Falk, Hildebolt, Smith et al. 2005). If the low estimate for body weight is accepted, then they have an EQ within the range of *Homo* but well below *Homo sapiens* (Brown, Sutikna, Morwood et al. 2004: 1060). Higher weight estimates push their EQ down to the level of the australopithecines (Table 4.2). Their personal network size was smaller than baboons. Not surprisingly, they had a home range that equated to a circle with a radius of about 4 km. This small figure reflected not only their diminutive size but also their tropical habitat.

Little *floresiensis* matched some notable achievements of much larger brained hominins and humans: overwatering skills, stone and fire technology. If these could be mastered with small brains, then the traditional impetus for encephalisation melts away. In the face of this challenge, *floresiensis* was soon described by others as a pathological human microcephalic and a pygmy adaptation, neither of which is supported by a close reading of the evidence (Falk, Hildebolt, Smith et al. 2005). The most likely explanation is island dwarfing where the release from predator pressure results in diminutive size – a trend seen in many species throughout the Pleistocene (Lahr and Foley 2004). However, it seems that island dwarfism, the biological process of size reduction, affected the brains of *floresiensis* as much as their bodies. Compared to the Pleistocene *Homo sapiens* in Table Box 6.3, their brains and body weight are about a quarter of the larger *Homo* species.

But this is a case where size might not matter. Using a CT scan of the inside of the skull of LB1, it was possible to examine the brains (Figure 1.4) as a virtual endocast (Falk, Hildebolt, Smith et al. 2005). This could then be compared with other fossil hominins and a range of great apes. The structure and organisation of the brain of LB1 is very different to *Australopithecus* with a similar encephalisation close to the 400 cm³ threshold (Table 4.2). *Floresiensis* has very large temporal lobes and highly folded and convoluted frontal lobes which control speech, hearing and planning in large-brained *Homo sapiens*. Falk and colleagues conclude from their study of the endocast that LB1 most likely represents an island dwarf endemic to Flores. Alternatively, they suggest that Asian *Homo erectus* and *Homo floresiensis* might both have shared a common ancestor that, although currently unknown to palaeoanthropologists, was both small bodied and small brained. Then evolution went in two directions: small and large. But in both instances, the brain evolved higher cognitive functions. Sadly, attempts to extract ancient DNA from the tiny hominins have so far been thwarted by its poor preservation in fossils from the tropics.

Africa did not export humans but rather just the latest version of hominins adapted to a Terra 2 environment with push–pull factors now well established by 100ka-long Milankovitch cycles (Table 5.4). What changed, and it could have been, as Dennell argues, anywhere within Terra 2, was the versatility of these humans to environmental selection. In other words, they required those four elements of kinship, storage, defence and domestication to break through into Terra 3. These four elements did not come as a package. And while there had to be an adaptive advantage for humans to expand, it could have been simply one element of four, kinship for example, that provided a competitive edge over other hominins and different dispersal centres.

These changes could be sudden; a classic case of saltation within what otherwise has the appearance of a continuously unfolding process (Renfrew and Cooke 1979). Using an ecological model of dispersal, J. Allen and O'Connell (2008: 41; O'Connell and Allen 2012) show how small changes in conditions, such as a population or competitive increase or a downturn in resources, can result in unexpectedly greater changes in the distribution of humans. Saltation, that ability to leapfrog (Figure 2.9), has always been a feature of human mobility and, as we shall now see, was instrumental in the settlement of the north.

CHAPTER 7

The call of the north: Terra 3, 50–4ka

> *The movement of humanity, arising from a countless series of*
> *actions arbitrarily performed by many individuals, is a continuous*
> *phenomenon*
>
> Leo Tolstoy, *War and Peace*, 1869

The Granary and Treasury Routes to Expansion

The model of global settlement inspired by archaeogenetic studies points
to delay. Beginning 80ka molecular years ago, humans began to disperse
throughout Africa and the South Asian part of Terra 2. A southern route to
Sunda was favoured. But then came a lengthy pause followed by a second
wave of dispersals in the same and new directions, Sahul being the first.
The human settlement of northern latitudes, the subject of this chapter,
took place at various times after 50ka (Figure 6.1).

Delay is also a feature of the archaeological evidence for later dispersals.
There were, as we saw in Chapter 5, technological and cultural changes
within Africa during Terra 2 (Figure 5.5) regarded by many archaeologists as
evidence for "behavioural modernity" (Box 6.1). But these did not become
part of a clear-cut archaeological signature indicating human dispersal outside that continent. Elsewhere in Terra 2, and particularly in South Asia,
humans using Mode 3 stone artefacts passed through older hominin populations with a similar technology. As a result, the archaeological traces of
their movements are cloaked, their earliest expansion along the southern
route unaccompanied by a trumpet blast of new things to herald the arrival
of ourselves – the modern human – onto a world stage. Indeed, as we saw
in the last chapter, the arrival of humans in Sahul was a muted affair, even
though getting there had immense significance. However, the clearest
indication that something momentous had happened in human deep history is not provided by a creative outburst of new technology and aesthetic

products of the imagination. Instead, it is signalled by the range of ecolog-ically tough habitats they settled soon after their arrival. Change, which involved an amplification of some sort, had occurred.

In Chapter 6, I listed four innovations that were needed to overcome the environmental limits to expansion set by Terra 2. First on my list was kin-ship. I argued it was highly probable that the crossing to Sahul could not have taken place without it. Why? Kinship is a unique human niche that draws its inspiration from a cognition widely distributed through people and things – an example of the culture of the extended mind. It bridges social distance, as well as linking the past and the future, recruiting and binding members to the group, and its continuation, generation by gener-ation in seamless time. The kinship niche forms a social bubble for travel and return that finally made the possibility of global expansion, which existed throughout hominin deep history, a human reality (Gamble 2008).

However, the archaeological evidence points to the next two closely related innovations on my list as central to the process of settlement: when food and materials were actively stored, and males came to control those resources (Figure 3.10; Foley and Gamble 2009). The focus on innovation in land use and plant management in Sunda and then northern Sahul addressed the requirement that the way resources were controlled had to change for expansion to proceed, and in particular this involved their defence and storage. I suggested two linked patterns of development, the granary and the treasury, that could achieve this result. On balance, the gra-nary model is more appropriate to understand the changes in land use that have been noted in the initial settlement of the tropical latitudes (Barker, Barton, Bird et al. 2007; Summerhayes, Leavesley, Fairbairn et al. 2010). But later, as the ethnography of Australia abundantly reveals, the treasury model became ubiquitous with inter-regional trade and the consumption of a wide variety of artefacts and materials commonplace (McBryde 1988; Mulvaney 1976). In addition, ritual knowledge was performed, accumulated and controlled at sacred sites by its initiated guardians (Stanner 1965).

But as our attention moves north, so the treasury model, as indicated by the archaeological evidence, seems more apt. What typified the settlement of the north in some regions was a distinctive material signature of dispersal and displacement. Archaeologists label this the Upper Palaeolithic, and regard Europe as its exemplar, albeit a contested one (Box 7.1; Bar-Yosef 2002; Boyle, Gamble and Bar-Yosef 2010; Klein 1999; Mellars 1973). At a minimum, the signature saw the first large-scale use of Mode 4 stone tech-nology (Box 2.3) and the widespread making of art and ornaments. These aesthetic objects were further amplified by the ceremonies of burial and the chains of connection that crossed continents.

My fourth innovation, domestication, was not part of the initial Sahul expansion into Terra 3 but, as we shall see, did play a role when humans moved north.

Box 7.1. Is the Upper Palaeolithic fit for purpose?

The Upper Palaeolithic of Europe has a special place in the history of human dispersal and population displacement (Box 6.2). But closer examination reveals it to be a much weaker A-List entity than often presented, and this also applies to the African Later Stone Age which followed the older European classifications (Barham and Mitchell 2008). We have already seen (Box 6.1) the weakness of the Upper Palaeolithic as an A-List indicator of modern behaviour. Now we need to consider two further problems at the B-List level (Table 2.7): when did it appear and where did it come from?

A survey of the debut of Upper Palaeolithic archaeology in different regions across Eurasia (Table Box 7.1, Figure 7.1) reveals that it made a staggered entrance (Boyle, Gamble and Bar-Yosef 2010; Brantingham, Kuhn and Kerry 2004). There were delays, and in some northern regions, it was pre-empted as a signature of human dispersal by Mode 3 technologies, just as it was in the earliest dispersals to the targets of South Asia and Sahul. In Chapter 6, I examined and rejected the claim that these delays resulted from variation in regional population growth and the increased possibility of innovation (Powell, Shennan and Thomas 2009). Mellars (2006a) has explained the delays as the loss of items away from their origin point. Hence, in his words, the Mode 3 technologies found in Australia were "heavily simplified or 'devolved' forms of Upper Palaeolithic ('Mode 4') technologies, under the influence of varying raw material effects and other purely local economic adaptations" (Mellars 2007: 598). Such a view of cultural degeneration away from its source, itself a nineteenth-century idea, has been exposed by others as an attempt to fit all Palaeolithic data into the European model (Habgood and Franklin 2008; McBrearty 2007).

The Upper Palaeolithic is not doing its job of identifying humans on the move. This is reflected in the problem of how to recognise its earliest manifestation. In Europe, this has led to the use of terms such as Pre- or Initial Upper Palaeolithic (IUP) to describe regional B-List entities such as the Uluzzian of Italy and the Bohunician of Eastern Europe. Even for a much stronger B-List entity, the Aurignacian, its earliest genesis is obscure, leading to prefixes such as Proto and Incipient. Such terms reflect the model archaeologists have of the birth-growth-decay of an

(continued)

Box 7.1. *(continued)*

TABLE BOX 7.1. *Terra 3 and the timing of the Upper Palaeolithic across Asia and Europe. The ages are from radiocarbon and OSL. Data from Bae (2010); Brantingham, Krivoshapkin, Jinzeng et al. (2001); Brantingham, Kuhn and Kerry (2004); Dolukhanov, Shukurov, Tarasov et al. (2002); Goebel, Waters and O'Rourke (2008); Hamilton and Buchanan (2010); Hoffecker (2005, 2009); Mellars (2006b); Morisaki (2012); Pavlov, Roebroeks and Svendsen (2004); Perera (2010); Petraglia, Haslam, Fuller et al. (2010); Pitulko, Nikolsky, Girya et al. (2004); and Vasil'ev, Kuzmin, Orlova et al. (2002).*

Region	Latitude °N	Age range (ka)	Mode of stone technology	Key sites	
Arctic	71	30	3	Yana	
Northwest Russia	58–68	40–35	3	Mammontovaya Kurya	Byzovaya
Northeast Siberia	60–63	30	4	Ust'-Mil 2	Ikhine 2
Southern Siberia	51–55	46–32	3 and 4	Kara Bom	Denisova Cave
European plain	52–55	45	4	Kostenki	
European uplands	49	48	4	Brno-Bohunice	
Sakhalin	52	23	4	Ogonki 5	
Mongolia	44	32–27	4	Chikhen Agui	Tsagaan Agui
Northwest China	38	25	4	Shuuidonggou	
Japan and Korea	35	35–33	4	Nogawa	Hopyeong-dong
Near East	30–33	50–45	4	Boker Tachtit	Ksar Akil
South Asia	8–19	36	4	Patne	Batadomba-lena

archaeological culture (Gamble 2008: ch. 3). These terms are not always helpful in sorting out issues of population dispersal and displacement and testing archaeogenetic models. Solutions to this problem lie, as we shall see, in improved chronologies, so that nuances in regional variation can be better understood, as well as rethinking the culture-people model (Box 6.2).

Source and Target Regions

The expansion north led first to settlement above the limits of Moviusland in southern and eastern Siberia, the source for the peopling of the Americas and the high Arctic, and second from Central Asia and North Africa to Europe. The human settlement of the north took two forms. In the west, humans dispersed into Europe with its long tradition of Terra 2 settlement and encountered a highly successful indigenous people, the Neanderthals. By contrast, Terra 3 above latitude 52°N in Asia was largely uninhabited. What unified this vast region of Eurasia was a common productive habitat known as the mammoth steppe (Guthrie 1990).

Identifying source and target areas provides a way into the complexities of the settlement of the north. Three source regions stand out for reasons of their biodiversity (Figure 2.5), their archaeogenetic information and the archaeological evidence for early settlement: (1) South Asia and Sunda; (2) the Tien Shan Mountains of Central Asia; and (3) the Southwest Asian axis of Iran and Turkey and the arc of the Caucasus.

The target areas were various, but primarily consisted of Beringia in the far north-east, Doggerland in the north-west and those unglaciated areas above the Arctic Circle. There were many smaller targets en route to these major destinations; for example, the Japanese archipelago that was united by low sea levels, the southern Siberian region centred on Lake Baikal and the north European plain.

Once Beringia was settled, the target shifted to the two American continents to the south. Then, with the rolling back of the Fennoscandinavian and Laurentide ice sheets, settlement became possible in the high latitudes of Europe, the circumpolar zone generally and high mountain regions throughout the world where hypoxia rather than ice (Table 2.6) now set the upper limit.

The process of deglaciation began about 15ka. After a brisk start, it was stalled during the ice readvance of Greenland Stadial 1 (GS-1, 12.8–11.7ka) known from the European pollen sequence as the Younger Dryas (Figure 3.3). Then, in the succeeding Holocene warming, the process was completed, the speed indicated by changes in the sea-level curves as the oceans were swelled by melting ice sheets (Figure 3.4). At the same time, the exposed shelves of Sunda, Sahul, Beringia and Doggerland were all inundated, on occasion very fast indeed (Chapter 3).

I begin with Beringia and the Americas as the two targets, and then move to the colonisation of the European peninsula by humans, completing my survey with the Arctic.

TABLE 7.1. *The northern route and Effective Temperature.*

	Tien Shan	Altai	Baikal	Lena
Latitude	39°N	51°N	52°N	62°N
Altitude metres	702	294	426	126
Mean January temperature °C	0.6	−15.4	−17.9	−38.6
Mean July temperature °C	26.2	16.8	18.2	19.5
ET °C	13.7	11.4	11.5	11.15

Moving North

The Mammoth Steppe

What faced a hominin that had spent 2Ma living mostly at low and mid-latitudes? Southern Siberia, from the Altai Mountains to Lake Baikal and then north to the Lena River, is often regarded as a harsh place to live, a view prejudiced by its extremely low winter temperatures. The region lies above 49°N that today marks the transition to the Boreal zone where productivity and the accessibility of foods for FGH decline (Table 3.5). Hunters in the Boreal zones of Siberia and North America have low population growth compared to those in more temperate climates (Table 3.4). The ET of this zone (Chapter 3) is between 10.1°C and 12.5°C. The ET of three urban centres in southern Siberia (Table 7.1) sits within this range: 11.15°C to 11.5°C. The contrast with the lower-latitude but higher-altitude city of Samarkand in the Tien Shan source area is marked.

How do FGH respond to low environmental productivity? A small number of FGH cases from Siberia (Table 7.2) live between latitudes 51°N and 73°N where ET ranges from 11.19°C to 9.23°C. Their diets are dominated by fishing and hunting. Plant gathering accounts for less than five per cent of their diet. Furthermore, such low ET leads us to expect food storage on either a major or massive scale (Table 3.6). Food storage becomes a significant tactic for FGH when ET falls below 15.25°C which approximates to latitude 35°N (Binford 2001: 257), far to the south of Siberia.

Moving into northern latitudes also carried a health warning. Above 46°N, the levels of ultraviolet radiation (UVR; Figure 3.6) become so low that diet and skin pigmentation changes are needed to combat health issues arising from a deficiency of both UVB and UVA (Jablonski and Chaplin 2010).

Finally, the impact of low productivity will be most strongly felt in the relationship between population size, mobility and home range size.

TABLE 7.2. *Effective Temperature, diet and contemporary Siberian FGH (Binford 2001: table 4.01).*

	Latitude	Longitude	ET°C	% Fishing	% Gathering	% Hunting
Nganasan	73	90	9.71	44	1	55
Yukaghir	70	145	10.29	40	5	55
Siberian Eskimo	65	170	9.23	69	1	30
Ket	62	90	11.19	50	5	45
Gilyak	51	140	11.13	85	3	12

Without stored foods, the home range size over which FGH would have to move to obtain food would be immense, as discussed in Chapter 4 (Figure 4.3).

But the growing season and UVR levels were not in themselves barriers to settlement. Elsewhere in Terra 2, hominins regularly lived above 50°N in Western Europe, notably in England where warm ocean currents would have raised ET (Figure 3.2) but not UVR. Furthermore, we saw in Chapter 5 that settlement possibly occurred as far north as 55°N in southern Siberia during MIS5e, the last interglacial 125ka (Chlachula, Drozdov and Ovodov 2003), when ET would have been comparable to modern Boreal values (Tables 3.4 and 7.2).

So did these Terra 2 hominins in England and Siberia have stored foods, and how did they cope with UVR deficiencies? Did they, for example, depend, as Siberian FGH today, on fishing? The oils that are extracted from this resource form one of the dietary responses that counter UVB deficiency by creating vitamin D through means other than solar radiation (Jablonski and Chaplin 2012).

Archaeological evidence for stored food and isotopic evidence for fish diets are so far lacking in hominins, but they are present in humans (Richards and Trinkaus 2009; Soffer 1991). We can, however, assume a phenotypic change in skin pigmentation to increase the absorption of what UVR there is at higher latitudes. So how did pale-skinned hominins such as the Neanderthals cope?

The solution rests with the productivity of the mammoth steppe. These northern environments, as Guthrie (1990) has argued, saw a rich steppe vegetation during the Middle Pleistocene, and these productive grasslands in turn supported a high secondary biomass of grazing animals. A study of ancient pollen from across northern Eurasia points to the importance of meso-philous herbs in the mammoth steppe. Their annual net primary productivity was higher during glacial periods than at present, so that even

Box 7.2. The Mammoth steppe

The mammoth steppe comes down to a simple observation by zoologist Dale Guthrie (1990: chs. 8 and 9) – that today's boreal and tundra vegetation of Beringia could not have supported the large herds of bison, horse, reindeer and above all mammoth whose bones, and sometimes carcasses, are preserved by their millions in its frozen silts. Tundra plants and boreal trees produce a toxic litter that affects the soil, leaving very little for animals to feed on. Furthermore, they act as a blanket so that the level of annual freeze–thaw is small.

The factor which changed this balance between plants and soil was the aridity of the Pleistocene. Creating the mammoth steppe depended on high evaporation and a deeper thaw in summer that released nutrients from lower down in the soil. This, according to Guthrie, broke the cycle of low soil nutrients and toxic plants. It produced a richer soil and the conditions for the abundant growth of grass. These grasses were resistant to grazing pressure, grew quickly and formed a rich mosaic of vegetation conditions, likened to the weave in a plaid, and contrasted with the stripes, or bands, of vegetation found in the warmer Holocene (Guthrie 1984: fig. 13.1). Isotope studies suggest that mammoths consumed higher quantities of dry grass than the other grazers such as reindeer, horse and woolly rhino (Bocherens 2003).

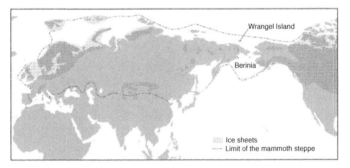

BOX 7.2. Mammoth steppe

The mammoth steppe developed across Western Europe to Beringia (Figure Box 7.2; Khalke 1994) during a major glaciation, MIS12, 500ka (Box 2.1). It supported a diverse, high-biomass animal community, compared to the present tundra and boreal forests (Khalke 1994). Besides the major herd animals – mammoths, woolly rhinos, bison, horse, red deer, reindeer, musk ox and saiga antelope – there were major carnivore guilds of lions, hyenas, wolves, leopards and foxes, and omnivores such as bears.

though these ecosystems were less productive in overall terms, the herb component which supported grazing animals showed the reverse (J. R. M. Allen, Hickler, Singarayer et al. 2010: 2616). The richness is characterised by one of Terra 3's most iconic animals: the woolly mammoth (Box 7.2).

Mammoths were exploited across Eurasia in low-ET environments, during either the last interglacial as at Ust'-Izhul', 55°N in Siberia (Chlachula, Drozdov and Ovodov 2003), or the last cold stage at the Neanderthal site of Lynford, England, at 52°N on the western edge of the mammoth steppe, 60ka in MIS3 (Boismier, Gamble and Coward 2012). Both sites are well above the critical UVR threshold of 46°N. Moreover, this settlement history was not supported by an Upper Palaeolithic bone and stone technology.

But did it require fishing and stored food as the FGH models predict? How they obtained vitamin D is not known but possibly was a combination of the animal fats and marrow, as well as eating uncooked liver, that resulted from hunting the large herbivores, mammoth included. These fats also act to metabolise protein-rich diets in the absence of plant carbohydrates (Speth 1983; Speth and Spielmann 1983). The size of the prey species also provided a successful hunt with an abundance that formed a natural seasonal store when temperatures and humidity were low. These factors are critical to storage either by drying, smoking or freezing. These methods depress and even halt the reproduction rate of the bacterium *Bacillus mycoides* which is responsible for food decaying. And even without them, rates drop dramatically between 15°C and 5°C and stop altogether at lower temperatures and humidity (Binford 1978: 91–94).

These advantageous conditions of temperature, humidity and prey abundance were not universal throughout the mammoth steppe. They would be local and regional, reflecting the mosaic structure of this complex environment (Box 7.2) and the opportunities it presented to a top predator such as the Neanderthals. However, it is not necessary in the absence of evidence to assume these early northern excursions depended either on fishing, stored foods or both. Instead, their settlement histories followed the biotidal pattern with a repeated contraction and expansion of population into and out of these areas as resources changed.

One example is provided by the apparently odd circumstance that the last interglacial MIS5e (130–120ka) has no traces of human settlement throughout the British Isles, odd because it does have evidence for a rich temperate flora and fauna, with hippopotamus found in northern England and elephants along the Thames (Sutcliffe 1985). Food was available in jumbo portions but apparently did not occur at the right density to create these natural stores. In addition, the high temperatures and humidity of this interglacial reduced the length of the keeping season following a successful kill. When combined with high sea levels, and possibly an insular phase for the British Isles (Ashton, Lewis and Stringer 2011; Stringer 2006; M. J. White and Schreve 2000), the lack of settlement is at least suggestive of an absence of stored food in the adaptive armoury of the hominins concerned.

The ebb and flow of settlement adjusted population to resources. This took place on a regional scale. The proximate factor remained that eternal hominin relationship between diet, the size of the home range and the size of the group. Well-kept, stored food allowed a reduction in mobility. Home ranges could be very large, but they did not have to be visited or known. Instead, it was like a hunter checking the traps on his trapline (Brody 1981; Nelson 1973). The track becomes his territory, his home range, although the food he harvests comes from a much wider region. Without stored foods, range contraction remained the only option in the face of deteriorating resources whether under warm or cold conditions. And as Binford (2001: generalisation 8.06) observes, storage breaks the one-to-one link between group size and the size of the consumer unit. Once stored foods become the basis of the strategy, then group size reflects the labour demands to set up those stores – what Binford calls "bulk procurement". This demand overrides the previous reason for keeping group size small which was to minimise pressure on local resources – eating yourself out of the locale where you are camped and having to move on.

It was through storage that humans could be versatile in the face of either declining or improving resources, a pattern driven by the climate cycles in predictable ways. More efficient hunting technology would raise yields and reduce the risk of famine (M. Collard, Kemery and Banks 2005). But without effective storage, the best spears and bows would make little difference to the ability to settle these regions.

And storage also has a social dimension: part of the human ability to go beyond and stay in touch. Isolation is a recurrent problem in these lands with low population density, especially if people are clustered around their stores of food. Mechanisms are needed to enchain people over large distances and to support each other when times are bad. The need for kinship, storage and the control of the means of connection are apparent in the role of the treasury model during northern settlement where selected artefacts served as tokens for social relationships built on the principles of FACE. The fourth aspect of the dispersal quartet, domestication, also comes into play. It was no coincidence that the earliest domestic dogs are found in the north during this second wave of Terra 3 dispersals (Box 7.3).

Box 7.3. Dogs, gourds and domestication

Domesticating plants and animals was a novel element of human dispersals into Terra 3. Everything is potentially a domesticate, where humans modify an animal's behaviour and development to produce larger, smaller, stronger and more abundant resources – a good example of amplification. Domestication is a process of mutualism that develops between human, plant and animal populations. It has strong selective advantages for all partners. Domestication is not the only form of mutualism, but it stands out because of the role of sustained human agency in the growth and nurture of plant and animal resources within an anthropogenic context (Zeder, Emshwiller, Smith et al. 2006: 139).

The problem is that tracing the origins of domestic plants and animals is difficult with archaeological evidence, since the changes do not necessarily alter the shape of seeds, teeth and bones. Neither do genetic data fare much better. Domestication "genes" are found in many crop species, but their presence in animals is unresolved (Zeder, Emshwiller, Smith et al. 2006: 143).

Phylogeographies of domestic animals can be reconstructed from mtDNA data and have made a notable breakthrough in the case of domestic dogs. These studies show conclusively that all the world's dogs (*Canis familiaris*) were domesticated from the wolf (*Canis lupus*) and not jackals (*Canis aureus*) or coyotes (*Canis latrans*), as was once thought possible. Moreover, mtDNA data indicate the earliest source is Southeast Asia 16ka molecular years ago (Klütsch and Savolainen 2011). Dog domestication was not a single event but, as with pigs and cattle, occurred at several times and in various places across Terra 3.

Dogs were an integral part of human dispersal. Native American dogs originated from the multiple lineages of dogs that were brought across as humans dispersed into the Western hemisphere of Terra 3. The molecular ages for these founder American dogs is between 12ka and 14ka. The Australian dingo has an age of 5ka molecular and was domesticated from dogs in island Southeast Asia before crossing the Wallace line, possibly with humans (Hiscock 2008: 146–148). Dingoes were only the second mammal to reach the continent of marsupials.

Dogs have many uses. Normally their domestication is seen as a way to increase hunting returns, but equally, in northern latitudes, the power they bring to pulling sleds and travois is just as important. Indeed, the case could be made that their domestication was selected more by the needs of human dispersal than the pressure to hunt more effectively.

(continued)

Box 7.3. *(continued)*

TABLE BOX 7.3. *Some archaeological finds of early domestic dogs*

Site	Country	ka	Remarks	Reference
Madura Cave, Nullarbor Plains	Australia	3.5	Dingo	Milham and Thompson (1976)
Koster	United States of America	8.5	Three dog finds deliberately buried in shallow pits	Morey and Wiant (1992)
Ain Mallaha (Eynan) and Hayonim terrace	Israel	11.3–12.3	Three dog finds and a puppy skeleton buried with a human	Davis and Valla (1978); Tchernov and Valla (1997)
Kniegrotte Cave	Germany	12.2–13.6	Various remains	Klütsch and Savolainen (2011); Musil (2000)
Teufelsbrücke Cave	Germany	12.3–13	Various remains	Klütsch and Savolainen (2011); Musil (2000)
Oelknitz	Germany	10.9–12.5	Various remains	Klütsch and Savolainen (2011); Musil (2000)
Bonn-Oberkassel	Germany	c. 12	Sub-adult specimen	Klütsch and Savolainen (2011); Street (2002)
Gough's Cave	Britain	12.4	Dog remains previously assigned to wolf	Currant and Jacobi (2011)
Kesslerloch Cave	Switzerland	14.1–14.6	Skull fragment	Napierala and Uerpmann (2012)
Eliseevichi 1	Russia	13–17	Dog cranium	Sablin and Khlopachev (2002)
Předmostí	Czech Republic	26–27	Three complete skulls	Germonpré, Lázničková-Galetová and Sablin (2012)
Razboinichya Cave	Russia – Siberia	29.9	Large dog	Ovodov, Crockford, Kuzmin et al. (2011)
Goyet	Belgium	31.7	A large fossil dog	Germonpré, Sablin, Stevens et al. (2009)

The archaeological picture for dog domestication is patchy but indicates an even greater ancestry (Table Box 7.3) – one which makes the dog available to assist human dispersal into the target areas of Beringia, Doggerland and the Americas below the Laurentide ice cap. The evidence consists of size changes to teeth that place Pleistocene examples with dogs rather than wolves. There are also dogs and puppies buried with humans, as at Ain Mallaha in Israel (Valla 1975) – an instance of mutual protection and keeping.

There are undoubtedly many surprises to come as the archaeogenetics of plant domestication unfolds. While early human dispersal in Terra 3 did not depend on domestic maize or wheat, it did involve other useful plants. One example is the bottle gourd, or calabash (*Lagenaria siceraria*), a tropical plant of African origin that is found, before maize agriculture, in Mexico and other parts of the Americas at least 10ka. The analysis of calabash rinds found in a number of archaeological sites shows they were domesticated rather than brought "wild" from Africa (Erickson, Smith, Clarke et al. 2005). Moreover, DNA extracted from those same specimens shows they are identical to the modern Asian reference group and so were carried from there to the Americas, via Beringia, in the Late Pleistocene (Zeder, Emshwiller, Smith et al. 2006: 150–151). Bottle gourds do not grow outdoors in northern latitudes. Seeds must have been carried in the expectation of finding warmer climates, which they did. The importance of this plant as a container for liquids and other stored foods should not be forgotten, if not an example of stored foods then one of safe keeping.

The Northern and Coastal Routes to the Western Hemisphere

The mammoth steppe counters the view that the vast territory of Siberia was resource poor and inhospitable for humans. Instead, it was a source area for the repeated repopulation of western Eurasia by cold-adapted animals that became locally extinct in regions such as Western Europe during warm interglacials (Schreve 2001). This is bio-tidal geography on the grand scale.

This east–west bio-tidal effect is complemented by a north–south refuge zone. This emerges when the radiocarbon dates for mammoth and human materials are plotted for the period 45ka to 12ka (Ugan and Byers 2007). The difference in average latitude (Figure 7.1) that persisted throughout these 30ka indicates that mammoths always had a refuge area well to the north of human settlement. The two species crossed paths

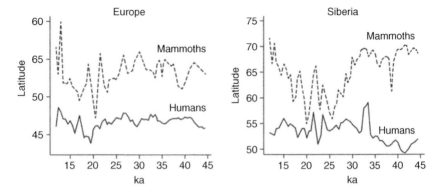

FIGURE 7.1. Mammoths and humans. The graphs show the weighted averages of radio-carbon ages on mammoth and archaeological material across Eurasia. While much variation is lost by this method, it clearly shows the northern extension of mammoths and the more southerly distribution of humans during the last cold stage. Adapted from Ugan and Byers (2007).

many times, but until the Holocene some 11ka, this refuge area for mammoths had always existed. Mammoths became extinct along an eastern transect that started in Western Europe 12ka and ended with the dwarf examples on Wrangel Island at 71°N in the East Siberian Sea dated to 3.7ka (Stuart, Kosintsev, Higham et al. 2004).

The Direction of Dispersal

One likely source area for the second wave of human dispersals was located in the region of Southwest Asia and extended to Kazakhstan in Central Asia (Goebel 2007). Today, this is a biodiversity hotspot separated from the mountain arc that extends through Iran, the Caucasus and Turkey (Figure 2.5). Within this large area, I have narrowed the focus to the Tien Shan Mountains – a decision that future research can test.

From here, there were two routes that skirted south and north of the Himalayas and Tibetan plateau. The southern route would pass through the densely, for the time, populated region of South Asia and Sunda. The northern route would proceed from the Tien Shan Mountains north to the Altai and then into the Lake Baikal region of southern Siberia. Today, this region has several major deserts, and during MIS4, these became hyper-arid. A humid corridor, indicated by present-day rainfall patterns runs from Lake Balkhash to Lake Baikal and onto the Siberian plain (Figure 7.2). This dispersal corridor flanks the high, arid Tibetan and Mongolian plateaux.

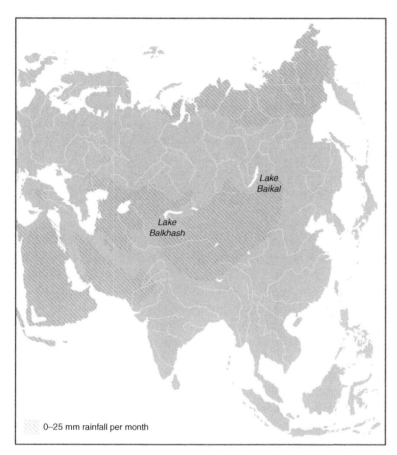

FIGURE 7.2. The humid corridor to Siberia. These modern weather data point to a route between the cold deserts that links the major lakes, Balkhash and Baikal, with the vegetation hotspot of the Altai.

The route to the Beringian target then lay across the cold desert of north-eastern Siberia where precipitation was never high enough for ice sheets to form, even though temperatures during MIS4 and MIS3 would have been extremely low.

The initial target areas were different. In the north, humans moved into regions at best sparsely populated by hominins such as the Altai (Derevianko, Shimkin and Powers 1998), Lake Baikal (Buvit, Terry, Kolosov et al. 2011) and the Yenisei River (Chlachula, Drozdov and Ovodov 2003). By contrast, the southern route through India and onto Sunda was settled by people from the earlier dispersal.

The archaeogenetics of these dispersals still has much to sort out. A division of East Asian populations has long been established by physical anthropologists based on regional phenotypic differences. Recently, a large genetic study of the HLA immune systems across this region points to a boundary at about 30°N. This north–south differentiation of Asian peoples adds support to an ancient dispersal by a southern route. But it does not rule out important contributions from more northerly dispersals (Di and Sanchez-Mazas 2011).

These routes have been discussed in detail by S. Oppenheimer (2004b: fig. 5.7). The geography of mtDNA haplogroups shows that two – C and Z – are only found above 30°N, while six – A, B, D, E, F and G – are present both north and south of this latitude, although they are regionally varied (Table 6.2).

Of these, only A, B, C and D are founder haplogroups in the Americas and come from a North Asian source area. But how exactly this regional mixture was established through dispersals is currently unclear. X is more problematic still. This is a western rather than an eastern Asian haplogroup. How it got across the Atlantic and into North America is a puzzle unresolved by any archaeological evidence.

Siberia was not the only way to reach the Beringian target. S. Oppenheimer (2004b: fig. 5.5) has drawn attention to a more southerly route that starts in the Indus Valley and then follows the Silk Road across the Tibetan plateau before dropping into northern China. He also points to a coastal route along the exposed shelf of the East China Sea that winds round the Korean Peninsula and the conjoined Japanese archipelago to reach the mouth of the Amur River at Sakhalin Island at 53°N. It is possible, he suggests, that the Lake Baikal area could have been settled from this direction by moving west down the Amur into southern Siberia and then carrying on north to Beringia.

Weak Upper Palaeolithic Signatures (Mode 3)

The question then becomes whether this route had been taken before. The Altai and Baikal regions have been investigated over many years. An important site, close to Denisova Cave (Chapter 6) in the south-western corner of the Altai Republic, is Kara Bom. This open-air locale has well-stratified Mode 3, Middle Palaeolithic artefacts of uncertain age. But over these, and again in good stratigraphic order, are several layers with the hall-mark stone blades of Mode 4 – artefact blanks that are seen as critical to the Upper Palaeolithic (Brantingham, Krivoshapkin, Jinzeng et al. 2001; Goebel, Derevianko and Petrin 1993).

The radiocarbon age for the transition at Kara Bom from Mode 3 to Mode 4 is 46.6ka (Hamilton and Buchanan 2010), although the statistical error on the date is very large, almost 2000 years, and so it must be treated with caution until confirmed by estimates with greater precision. What is clear is that the Mode 3 and Mode 4 assemblages of artefacts are separated from each other by a sterile band some 20 cm thick (Goebel, Derevianko and Petrin 1993: fig. 2). The Mode 4 artefacts at Kara Bom are not, however, particularly convincing as Upper Palaeolithic in the European and Near East sense. The site lacks any tool types such as projectile points, and there are no organic artefacts such as bone points, beads or art. At Kara Bom, stone and bone pendants along with red ochre are only found in level 5 (Kuzmin 2009: 99) that is dated between 34ka and 31ka, more than 10ka younger than the transition in levels 6–8 (Brantingham, Krivoshapkin, Jinzeng et al. 2001: fig. 2).

The problem for such transitions is that stone-knapping techniques which produced blades were never exclusive to Mode 4. They were a recurrent feature in much older Middle Palaeolithic stone-tool assemblages found in Europe (Conard 1992; Révillion and Tuffreau 1994). At Kara Bom, the making of blades certainly contrasts with the Middle Palaeolithic, Mode 3, above which it is stratified. But as one analysis concludes, that is the only substantive difference (Brantingham, Krivoshapkin, Jinzeng et al. 2001: 745). Indeed, Shunkov (2005: 73) characterises the Middle Palaeolithic of the Altai and Central Asia as possessing large numbers of blade blanks and retouched tools made on large blades. It is not surprising then that Kuzmin's (2007: fig. 2) survey of the entire Siberian Palaeolithic shows a staggered transition from Middle to Upper Palaeolithic that lasted from 43ka to 27ka across nine regions of this vast territory. If it were not for the European model of the Upper Palaeolithic as a dispersal signature for humans, and a provocative radiocarbon date that falls short of today's standards (Pettitt, Davies, Gamble et al. 2003), then I doubt a site such as Kara Bom would have attracted so much attention.

Strong Upper Palaeolithic Signatures (Mode 4)

The earliest "Upper Palaeolithic" presents a confused picture. What is not confused is the cultural change in stone and organic artefacts after 35ka across Asia (Perera 2010). What appears is a robust Mode 4 technology (Table Box 7.1). This is well illustrated by the Japanese Upper Palaeolithic that has a bipartite structure of blade and flake technology, the latter only declining after 25ka (Morisaki 2012: fig. 6). However, in contrast to the earlier Initial Upper Palaeolithic of southern Siberia, it has high counts for blades, well-shaped projectiles and other composite tools. Moreover, the Japanese sample is large. More than 14,000 Upper Palaeolithic sites have been recorded from the archipelago. During MIS3, the main islands formed a single landmass that included Sakhalin Island to the north. At its southern tip, this palaeo-peninsula was never joined to the mainland, and the earliest Upper Palaeolithic sites are 33ka years old. This matches the earliest age for the Upper Palaeolithic in Korea at c. 35ka, although the transition in this peninsula is unclear (Bae 2010: 118). What is apparent in Korea is that after 20ka, there was a reduction in the size of blades and the appearance of micro-cores.

At a similar time, 35ka, the Upper Palaeolithic fluorescence of Mode 4 is found in Sri Lanka (Perera 2010) and India (Petraglia, Haslam, Fuller et al. 2010), as well as Mongolia and Northwest China (Table Box 7.1; Brantingham, Krivoshapkin, Jinzeng et al. 2001). It is also at this time that other elements of the Upper Palaeolithic, notably beads and bone artefacts, enter the record not only as we have seen at Kara Bom but also at Denisova (Derevianko 2010) and elsewhere in the Lake Baikal region at Mal'ta (Derevianko, Shimkin and Powers 1998; Vasil'ev, Kuzmin, Orlova et al. 2002) and above the Arctic Circle. Here, at 71°N, the Yana Rhinoceros Horn Site has an assemblage of Mode 3 flake tools complemented by a few well-made horn, bone and ivory tools, among them an awl and foreshafts for composite tools, dated to 30ka (Pitulko, Nikolsky, Girya et al. 2004: fig. 6).

A strong Upper Palaeolithic signature, as shown for instance by the evidence from Korea and Japan, might be interpreted as indicating human dispersal. It is tempting to link these strong patterns in the data to archaeo-genetic models – there goes founding haplogroup C, 30ka, bedecked with beads and clutching a sheaf of Mode 4 composite tools. But some caution is needed. There are other functional reasons that might explain a shift in technology and the appearance of items of display and enchainment over such vast areas and varied environments. Population growth, rather than population movement, is one; a convergence on the solution to environmental change another. A firm chronology is vital to test the time-honoured archaeological expectation that a distinctive set of cultural materials equates to an ethnically, or in this case genetically, defined society (Box 6.2). In this regard, the peopling of the Americas serves as a paradigm.

Hitting and Sticking to the Beringian Target

What humans found when they reached Beringia sometime after 30ka was an additional 1.6Ma km² of land. Permafrost was widespread and precipitation low. The lack of evaporation across the palaeocontinent resulted in lakes, standing water and a breeding ground for mosquitoes (Elias and Crocker 2008; Hoffecker and Elias 2007). This was, however, the easternmost arm of the mammoth steppe and rich in animals (Guthrie 1990).

While much of the Alaskan part of Beringia was unglaciated, to the south and east lay two major ice sheets: one based on the tectonic spine of the North American Cordillera that continues all the way to the tip of South America, the other the largest ice sheet of MIS2, the Laurentide, centred on the Canadian Shield (Chapter 3). At times, these coalesced into a single sheet, making Alaska the cul-de-sac of Asia (Figure Box 7.2).

Archaeogenetic models suggest that humans reached Beringia at about 30ka molecular, and this was then followed by a long incubation possibly of some 15ka molecular (Balter 2011b). During this time, human genomes diversified in what had now become a source area.

The archaeological evidence supports the model of delay, but largely through gaps in the data. Yana is the oldest site above the Arctic Circle at 30ka but is 3000 km to the west of the Bering Straits. Swan Point at 14ka is currently the oldest site in central Alaska and has a Mode 4 technology based on microblades, a feature shared with similar-age sites in central Siberia (Goebel, Waters and O'Rourke 2008: 1498). Then followed a comparative wealth of evidence for human settlement centred on Alaska's Nenana River and dated between 13.8ka and 13ka (Bever 2001; Powers and Hoffecker 1989; Yesner 2001). So, if you accept Yana as an outpost of western Beringia, then a long delay, during which genetic incubation took place, seems plausible.

With Beringia now a source area, expansion south had either to wait for glacial retreat, so that a corridor between the two ice sheets appeared, or follow a deglaciated coastal passage. Exactly when these routes became ice free is much debated. However, it seems that the coastal passage was open by at least 15ka. The corridor between the ice sheets was available later, 14–13.5ka, during GI-1 (Goebel, Waters and O'Rourke 2008: 1499).

One attraction for humans of the coastal route was that it formed an extension of the tectonic trail that played such an important role in hominin dispersals during Terrae 1 and 2 (Figure 2.6). But like the southern dispersal route to Sunda (Chapter 6), archaeological evidence along this route is sparse due to rising sea levels. One indication comes from human remains found at Arlington Springs on Santa Rosa Island off the coast of California at 34°N. Dated to 13ka, the human presence here is regarded as early evidence for the use of watercraft (Goebel, Waters and O'Rourke 2008). Another pointer is provided by the tropical parasites they carried with them and which need moisture and warmth to develop (Araujo, Reinhard, Ferreira et al. 2008: 114). These requirements suggest a rapid coastal dispersal rather than the slower overland route through cold Beringia.

Once south of the ice sheet, these northern humans from the Beringian source encountered environments they had not previously experienced. They were moving towards the sun, which was good for UVB levels and ET. As a result, below 35°N, plant foods were available to broaden their diets, and storage was less important. Moreover, the animal communities of North and South America were, like those of Sahul, extremely diverse with a significant top-end of megafauna (Martin and Klein 1984). It was not until the southern cone of Patagonia was reached at 40°S that the ecology changed to something more familiar to the source area.

The Timing and Frequency of Dispersals

The incubation in Beringia had lasted long enough. Genomes had diversified, and it was time to move south. The archaeogenetic evidence points to a single dispersal during which the founding mtDNA haplogroups A, B, C and D and MSY haplogroups C and Q were established throughout the hemisphere by fewer than 5000 individuals (Goebel, Waters and O'Rourke 2008). In molecular years, this happened between 20ka and 15ka, as indicated by coalescent ages for both mtDNA and MSY lineages (Schurr 2004). A much-later expansion from Northeast Asia occurred in the Holocene and settled the Aleutian Islands (Crawford, Rubicz and Zlojutro 2010).

After many years of sometimes bitter disagreement (Adovasio and Page 2002), the timing of dispersal into the Americas has now been resolved to most archaeologists' satisfaction. The sticking point has been demonstrating that a well-defined Mode 4 entity, Clovis, is not evidence for the earliest human presence in both continents.

Clovis is prêt-à-porter for the model of a strong archaeological signature for dispersal and settlement: large, aesthetically sumptuous stone projectiles, distinctively made to a bifacial pattern and "signed off" with a final fluting flake to show prowess and skill (Meltzer 2009). On occasion, they are excavated from among the skeletons of large animals (Meltzer 2009: fig. 48). When combined with the radiocarbon dates from both continents, Clovis was interpreted as the first rapid expansion from pole to pole fuelled by a blitzkrieg on the native fauna (Martin 1967, 1973).

What has changed is the emergence of solid evidence for an earlier pre-Clovis settlement. This takes the form of a weak signature for dispersal. It includes a small group of sites that challenge the Clovis-first model, among them Monte Verde in Chile (Dillehay 1989), Meadowcroft rockshelter in Pennsylvania (Adovasio and Page 2002) and the Debra L. Friedkin site near Austin in Texas (Waters, Forman, Jennings et al. 2011). These sites, in very different settings, do not have distinctive stone tools in common that link them, like Clovis, over such large distances. Instead, their stone inventories speak to a pattern of local and regional diversity. At all three sites, there is archaeological evidence that dates them to between 15.5ka and 14.6ka. At the Debra L. Friedkin site, a level with Clovis artefacts lies above the Buttermilk Creek complex which contains some bifacial stone tools but not the elaborate projectile points seen later. A conservative assessment of the age of this artefact complex, based on OSL dating, is between 13.2ka and 15.5ka (Waters, Forman, Jennings et al. 2011: 1601). Neither was hunting large game the prerogative of Clovis-first people. At the Manis site, in Washington State, dated to 13.8ka, a projectile point made of mastodon bone has been found embedded in a rib of the same species (Waters, Stafford, McDonald et al. 2011).

So what is Clovis if it is not a strong dispersal signature for the first settlement of the Americas? Part of its strength as an archaeological, B-List, entity has always come from its short lifespan. How short has been emphasised following a careful audit of the radiocarbon evidence using well-defined criteria. What survived this much-needed cull were forty-three dates from eleven sites with Clovis artefacts (Waters and Stafford 2007). These indicate a lifespan for Clovis of as little as 200 years: 13.13–12.93ka. Allowing for uncertainties in the radiocarbon calibration curve, its maximum duration is some 450 years between 13.25ka and 12.8ka.

Previous estimates gave Clovis a lifespan of 1000 years during which it peopled both continents from a northern source (Martin 1973). To do this, it rode a powerful population diffusion wave, perhaps fuelled by concentrating on killing megafauna. Martin (1973) even suggested that the speed of this diffusion wave was so fast that Clovis people had no time to create art and make ornaments. Instead, they obtained high-quality raw materials from considerable distances (Meltzer 2009: 247–250) and fashioned them into aesthetically pleasing projectile points.

Taken at face value, the speed of dispersal is remarkable. Clovis-bearing people, if that is what they were, went from the southern margins of the ice-free corridor to Tierra del Fuego, a distance of at least 14,000 km, in a maximum of 600–1000 years, a rate of 23–14 km per annum (Waters and Stafford 2007: 1125). The rate climbs steeply to between 47 and 40 km per annum, if the minimum lifespan for Clovis of 300–350 years is accepted. Put another way, all the Americas might have been colonised in as little as fifteen generations. Even if the focus is restricted to North America, the Clovis radiocarbon dates indicate expansion rates of 7.6 km a year (Hamilton and Buchanan 2007).

Waters and Stafford (2007) are rightly suspicious of such exaggerated rates. Rather than applauding the speed of Clovis, they use its short lifespan and these high dispersal rates to argue for an older settlement of the two continents. In other words, Clovis was not a signature of humans dispersing but rather a technology and an aesthetic that was adopted, for whatever reason, by indigenous peoples. The conclusion they reach is that the extraordinary dispersal rates are evidence that supports the presence of people before Clovis. The ages are at least as early as 15.5ka, well before Clovis at 13ka, and the early artefacts bear little relationship to those later fluted points. What these early sites in both continents point to is a base population through which Clovis technology could then disperse (Waters, Forman, Jennings et al. 2011: 1602). With this pre-Clovis settlement now well established, the rate of human dispersal south of Beringia and ending at Fell's Cave, Patagonia, was of the order of 1–2 km per annum.

Artefacts and genetics are not the only dispersal signatures. The first settlers of the New World did not travel alone (Araujo, Reinhard, Ferreira et al. 2008). They brought in their intestines some Old World parasites of which hookworm was one. A computer simulation of the spread of hookworm based on its life cycle (Montenegro, Araujo, Eby et al. 2006) also raises doubts about a Clovis-first-and-only model. These simulations predict a minimum annual migration rate for hookworm of 183 km with higher yearly rates of 366 km and 975 km more likely based on the temperatures under which this parasite thrives. Such dispersal rates are incompatible with human let alone Clovis expansion. They become possible if hookworm was using an existing population as a host framework.

Languages have also been used to argue for direction and frequency of migrations. For example, S. Oppenheimer (2004b: fig. 7.2) makes the case that the number of languages found in a region is, like genetic diversity, a coarse measure of the age of the founding population. When plotted as "numbers and time", he discovered the unexpected: that South America has more languages than North America. These data, he suggested, can best be explained by a depopulation of North America after its initial settlement, so that the later Clovis advance was into unoccupied territory – a factor that might account for those exceptionally high annual dispersal rates of 7.6 km. If correct, Clovis would then regain its status as an archaeological signature of dispersal, even though the archaeogenetic models point to a single, earlier founding event for both continents (Schurr 2004: 563).

However, there is an ecological solution to the language conundrum. The pattern for the Americas closely follows Nettle's (2007) study of the ecological relationship between latitude and language diversity (Figure 3.7). High language diversity is a feature of the tropics that in the New World lie predominantly in Central and South America. The creation of social boundaries through the differentiation of languages (Chapter 3) is, in this instance, a more plausible explanation than a dispersal signature that involves linguistics. Furthermore, Hazelwood and Steele (2004) have shown how high speeds of advance in a diffusion wave can "remove" earlier evidence leading to the appearance, but not the reality, of depopulation.

The Tempo of These Dispersals

Hitting the Beringian target from the Altai source was a three-stage process. Hamilton and Buchanan (2010) compiled 516 radiocarbon dates from 143 sites in Siberia and Beringia to establish the tempo of diffusion. Their starting point was Kara Bom whose age at 46.6 + 1.8ka I have already questioned on grounds of imprecision. However, be that as it may, from this origin point, they measured the diffusion over 7000 km to Swan Point in Alaska. What emerges from their study are three phases: quick–slow–quick. The first pulse lasted between 47ka and 32ka and covered some 3300 km. It was followed by a pause, a reduction in dispersal distance from 32ka to 16ka during which humans added a further 1000 km. Then the pace quickened after 16ka when, in about 2.5ka, a further 2400 km was covered and Alaska reached. This quick–slow–quick tempo is supported by Dolukhanov, Shukurov, Tarasov et al.'s (2002) analysis of radiocarbon dates as demonstrating three stages: 40–30ka, 24–18ka and 17–11ka.

In terms of dispersal rate, Hamilton and Buchanan estimate humans proceeded at 0.16 km per annum in the first pulse and at c. 1 km per annum in the third after 16ka. The pause between these two rapid pulses represents a much slower dispersal rate of 0.08 km per annum. Overall, the distance from the Altai to Alaska was covered at an average rate of 0.22 km a year.

The tempo of dispersal within the Americas has already been examined, and a pre-Clovis rate of 1–2 km per annum seems reasonable. The higher tempo associated with Clovis points to a diffusion wave of cultural innovation rather than the movement of people. Consequently, like hookworm, it can travel much faster.

Population growth rates do not have to be exaggerated to keep pace with dispersal at 0.22 or 2 km per annum. Using a string-of-pearls model (Figure 2.9), D. G. Anderson and Gillam (2000) showed for South America (Figure 7.3) that the tempo of dispersal was quick and continuous. The first cell, or pearl, in the string starts the simulation with a population of twenty-five that doubles every 100 years (five generations) and then buds off to form a new pearl. The diameters of the pearls in their simulation varied from 25 km to 400 km, and following these simple rules, South America became "saturated" with people in either 1500 or 700 years. The indication from archaeological work in Amazonia is that this vast region was rapidly settled after 11ka by FGH (Mora and Gnecco 2003).

A two-stage process for peopling North America was identified by Kelly and Todd (1988). They argued on ecological grounds that the optimum strategy for incoming people would be to live off terrestrial animals and keep moving. With very low populations, the lack of neighbours ruled out the social safety net of calling on others when resources failed. Moreover, depending on stored food in unfamiliar landscapes could lead to problems of establishing the future availability of prey. Their second stage saw population growth and the packing of groups into well-understood resource territories. At this stage, the regional insurance policies started to work, as did major storage of foods. Previously, this latter tactic was too risky given the state of knowledge of the environment.

Kelly and Todd's (1988) model was based on a Clovis-first perspective. But while the rates of Clovis expansion might have coloured their thinking, the issue of high mobility applies equally to a pre-Clovis chronology for the initial settlement of the American continents. The model can be further formalised (Table 7.3) by exploring the two stages as the difference between populations of pioneers and residents (Gamble 1993).

The critical difference is between high exploration distances and rapid population growth. Both elements are important in the structure and interpretation of diffusion waves – the way we model population dispersal. The standard demic model assumes exploration to be the mean distance between the birth and first reproduction of an individual. Drawing on ethnographic instances, Hazelwood and Steele (2004: 677) estimate this figure to be 300 km. Therefore, at a population growth rate of between one and

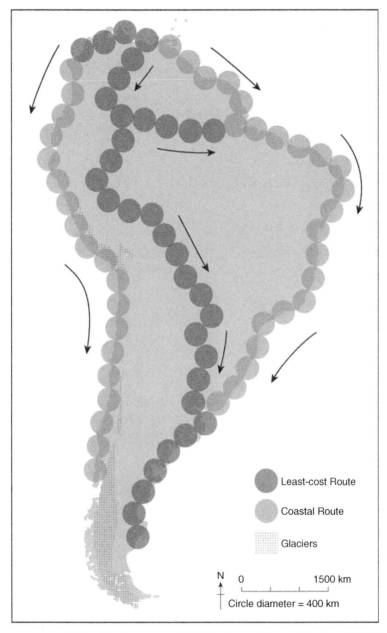

FIGURE 7.3. String of pearls as one model for the dispersal of population through South America in as little as 700 years. Adapted from Anderson and Gillam (2000).

TABLE 7.3. *A model for two contrasted styles of dispersal (Kelly and Todd 1988, Housley et al. 1997; Davies 2001).*

	Pioneer	Resident
Diffusion-wave shape	Shallow and fast	Steep and slow
Driven by	High exploratory mobility	Reproductive increase
String-of-pearls configuration	Leapfrog	Contiguous
Direction in the radiocarbon data from source to target	No	Yes
Population	Sparse	Packed
Settlement moves	Many	Fewer
Diet breadth	Narrow	Broad
Food storage	Minor	Major, Massive
Enchainment as an insurance against food failure	Rare	Frequent
'Upper Palaeolithic' signature	Weak	Strong
Archaeogenetic prediction	High diversity	Low diversity

three per cent per annum, this gives a velocity to the diffusion wave of some 6–10 km a year.

But it is also important to appreciate that the shape of the dispersal distance, rather than the demographic parameters alone, is key to understanding these tempos (Steele, Adams and Sluckin 1998; Steele, Sluckin, Denholm et al. 1996). The radiocarbon data for Clovis imply a rapid velocity based on higher rates of exploration by individuals. In such a diffusion wave, it will be difficult to see direction in the data. This is because the speeds are so high that the point of origin is washed out of the pattern. By contrast, if the wave is slow travelling and steep, then the direction is preserved in the radiocarbon data. A good example of this is the spread of Neolithic farmers into Europe (Hazelwood and Steele 2004).

Those pioneers who first entered North America had two great advantages: the continent was uninhabited, and the shape to their dispersal led south towards greater ecological productivity. The exploration ranges of individuals could indeed have been high by following the leapfrog pattern of finding and moving between the richest patches (Figure 2.9). Population was low, site numbers thin on the ground and hence little direction appears in the radiocarbon data across the continent (Steele, Adams and Sluckin 1998). The settlement process seems instantaneous. By contrast, for the residents in the second-stage population, growth and infilling had taken place.

In Chapter 3, I discussed these differences in terms of Binford's (2001) study of FGH where he recognised two density thresholds. The lower at 1.6 persons per 100 km² relied on mobility and high rates of fission and fusion to balance population to resources; the upper threshold at 9.1 persons per km² saw a shift to sedentism, defence, stored food and greater use of plant and aquatic resources. Moving south into the Americas led them into the optimal zones for human population growth (Table 3.4), exactly the opposite to the earlier dispersal towards the target of Beringia.

The move from the pioneer to resident stage resulted from three historical factors exacerbated by the change of ecology as they moved south; population became more packed, climate became less seasonal and the diversity of prey increased (Table 3.5). Under these conditions, the need for enchainment between groups and regions to cope with fluctuations in resources could explain the near-instantaneous appearance of fluted and bifacial projectile points that set the pattern for Palaeoindian America (Kelly and Todd 1988: 240). What Clovis measures is the speed of the human imagination in deep history.

Europe

The dispersal of humans into Europe has a long history of research. It began in the nineteenth century with excavations in the caves and rockshelters of south-west France. The subdivisions of the Upper Palaeolithic, those B-List entities such as the Aurignacian, Gravettian and Magdalenian, were defined from these excavated materials (Table 2.7). Then at the beginning of the twentieth century, the sensational discovery of cave art, both painted and engraved, was added to the list of other attributes that confirmed the Upper Palaeolithic as an A-List archaeological entity (Table 7.4). It is much more than simply the blade technologies of Modes 4 and 5 (Box 2.3), and over time, the Upper Palaeolithic grew to become a marker of the transition to modern behaviour and is often referred to as a revolution in human deep history (Bar-Yosef 1998, 2002; Mellars and Stringer 1989).

But this A-List entity in Europe and the Near East, as I have already shown, has less star quality in other continents such as Africa, Asia, Australia and the Americas. In these parts of Terra 3, the light of the Upper Palaeolithic has faded, if it ever shone, due to its staggered introduction across Siberia (Kuzmin 2009), its muted appearance in Australia (Habgood and Franklin 2008) and its piecemeal assembly that started throughout

TABLE 7.4. *The major changes between the Middle and Upper Palaeolithic in south-west France.*

Material technology:

A greater range and complexity of tool forms and a replacement of stability in Middle Palaeolithic tool forms with rapid change during the Upper Palaeolithic; a development in bone, ivory and antler working; the appearance of personal ornaments

Subsistence activities:

A greater emphasis on a single species (often reindeer); a broadening of the subsistence base to include small game; the possible development of large-scale cooperative hunting and a greater efficiency in hunting due to the invention of the bow and arrow; very possibly these changes were accompanied by improvements in food storage and preservation techniques

Demography and social organisation:

A substantial increase in population density and the maximum size of the co-residential group as inferred from the number of sites and the dimensions of settlements; group aggregation occurs to participate in cooperative hunting of migratory herd animals such as reindeer; increase in corporate awareness

Adapted from Mellars (1973).

Africa in Terra 2 (McBrearty and Brooks 2000; McBrearty and Stringer 2007). Fundamentally, the Upper Palaeolithic no longer looks like the unequivocal archaeological signature for either "behavioural modernity" (Shea 2011), or a robust way to trace the earliest human dispersals around Terra 3 (Chapter 6).

Neanderthals on the Move

The reason the Upper Palaeolithic came to embody these changes arose from the association in Europe of different hominins with different A-List entities. Indeed, such is the power of the Upper Palaeolithic model that it is an archaeological tenet, often uncritically adopted by other disciplines such as archaeogenetics, that Middle Palaeolithic (Mode 3) artefacts were made and used in Europe by Neanderthals and Upper Palaeolithic (Mode 4) by humans (Slimak, Svendsen, Mangerud et al. 2011; Stringer and Gamble 1993). This association holds firm for most sets of Neanderthal stone tools. But even so, it does not rule out their occasional manufacture of either Mode 4 tools or ornaments (Zilhão, Angelucci, Badal-Garcia et al. 2010) – the traditional preserve of *Homo sapiens*. But it looks decidedly shaky for the Upper Palaeolithic. Just as South Asia has only a single early human skull from Niah Cave in Borneo (Barker, Barton, Bird et al. 2007), so Europe currently has a single human skull and mandible from Peçstera cu Oase Cave in Romania (Trinkaus 2003; Zilhão, Trinkaus, Constantin et al. 2007) two milk molars from Grotta del Cavallo in Italy (Benazzi, Douka, Fornai et al. 2011), and possibly a tooth from England (Higham, Compton, Stringer et al. 2011) that are older than 40ka – slim pickings indeed for 150 years of research. And only the Italian finds are associated with Upper Palaeolithic stone tools and shell beads.

The expansion of humans into the European peninsula was comparable to the earlier dispersal to Sunda in that they passed through, or around, a long-established, indigenous, Terra 2 population. The difference in Europe is that we know a great deal about that population, the Neanderthals: first, from a rich fossil record, widely spread, and now from the ancient DNA extracted from their teeth and bones. The mtDNA evidence reveals no admixture between Neanderthals and humans. However, a remarkable study of nuclear DNA reveals a small, but significant, number of shared genes (Green, Krause, Briggs et al. 2010). This ranges from one to four per cent in the five modern genomes: two from Africa, and one each from Europe, China and Papua New Guinea, to which the Neanderthal sequence has been compared. Significantly, these shared genes are not present in the two African genomes, but they are in the other three. These shared genes answer once and for all the question of whether these two hominins met. They did, and they mated. This did not happen in Africa, and it occurred before humans headed towards Sunda as indicated by the presence of Neanderthal genes in the Chinese and Papua New Guinea genomes. The likeliest scenario is that a few Neanderthals moved into a larger group of humans whose descendants then spread rapidly (Gibbons 2010a). Where this occurred is unclear, but somewhere in Southwest Asia seems likely. When precisely it happened, and how often, is also unclear but sometime before the rapid dispersal east 60ka molecular years ago. What is clear is that humans did not move west into Europe at the same time.

The earliest fossil record for Neanderthals, *Homo neanderthalensis*, is incomparably better than that for their Pleistocene contemporaries, *Homo sapiens*. They had distinctively shaped heads and robustly built faces and skeletons. They also possessed three hidden features on their skulls: two in the ear region and a small depression at the back of the skull, the suprainiac fossa, which are not found on human skulls (Stringer and Gamble 1993: fig. 35). It is these features, invisible in a living person with a full head of hair, rather than their lack of a chin, big noses or massive brow ridges,

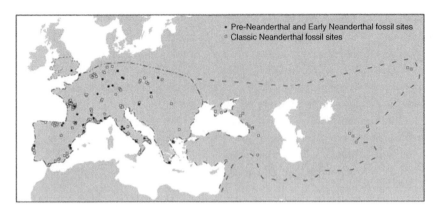

FIGURE 7.4. The Neanderthal world. The circles are fossil finds. Association of Neanderthals with Middle Palaeolithic Mode 3 technologies increases the range to include Britain and northwest Russia. Adapted from Serangeli and Bolus (2008).

features that some people today share, that distinguish them as a geographical population.

Neanderthals evolved in Europe and Southwest Asia from the earlier *Homo heidelbergensis* (Chapter 5), the same fossil ancestor for humans in Africa. Ancient DNA from Neanderthals shows that the MRCA with ourselves lived some 440–270ka molecular years ago (Green, Krause, Briggs et al. 2010).

The distribution of fossil Neanderthal remains (Figure 7.4) is extensive across the mid-latitudes with a northern limit at about 55°N. The distribution of Mode 3 artefacts would enlarge this distribution to include northwestern Russia up to a latitude of 65°N (Balter 2011a). The MIS2 ice sheet has removed the evidence from Scandinavia, while commercial dredging of the sea bed, formerly Doggerland, regularly recovers not only Pleistocene fauna but on occasion Middle Palaeolithic artefacts.

The distribution of the fossil evidence is used by Serangeli and Bolus (2008) to argue that Neanderthals were also a species that frequently dispersed. They identify the source area for these hominins as the Mediterranean and south-western France where their fossil ancestors were located. From here, they regularly dispersed, depending on the amelioration of climate, to targets such as the Near East, as at Kebara Cave in Israel (Bar-Yosef, Vandermeersch, Arensburg et al. 1992), Central Asia, as at Teshik-Tash in Uzbekistan (Movius 1953) and possibly in southern Siberia at Okladnikov Cave (Krause, Orlando, Serre et al. 2007). It is equally probable, however, that dispersals went in both directions, particularly during MIS3 57–24ka.

Dispersal histories also underpin a west–east division of Neanderthals that has emerged from their mtDNA sequences. Archaeogenetic data obtained from thirteen individuals across their range has revealed significant regional genetic variation (Dalén, Orlando, Shapiro et al. 2012). In the west, there is much lower mtDNA variation among those individuals dated to less than 48ka. Older individuals, and all those from the eastern parts of their range, have higher rates of variation. Such patterning points to population fragmentation and replacement in the west followed by expansion. This had nothing to do with the arrival of humans but rather the age-old pattern of north to south range contraction and expansion regulated by climate and the availability of resources. A trigger for this population event might have been the brief, but extremely cold, Heinrich Event 5, c. 48ka, that led to local extinction in the northern, bio-tidal, part of their range in Europe (Müller, Pross, Tzedakis et al. 2010).

Bio-tidal Settlement

Neanderthal settlement was sensitive to climate change. Western Europe provides the opportunity to examine this bio-tidal relationship in more detail (Gamble 2009). Here, the continental divide marks a division respected by the distribution of temperate-adapted animals during the Pleistocene (Figure 7.5). Hominins, such as the Neanderthals, persisted in the temperate refuge zone to the south, while the mammoth steppe to the east and north acted as a refuge for megafauna pushed out of their northern territories by the advance of ice sheets.

Just how bio-tidal this area was is shown by changing Neanderthal settlement histories at the end of Terra 2 (Chapter 5). In MIS4, between 71ka and 57ka, when the Sunda and Doggerland shelves were exposed, there is no evidence for settlement to the west of the continental divide. Neanderthals returned at the beginning of MIS3, their reappearance coinciding with a series of warmer fluctuations known as Dansgaard–Oeschger cycles (Chapter 3). We can be sure they were Neanderthals, not because they made a distinctive Mode 3 Middle Palaeolithic technology but because at 60–56ka, these sites are much older than the earliest Upper Palaeolithic with its tiny human fossil record.

Growth Diets

One such early MIS3 locality is Lynford at 52°N in eastern England (Boismier, Gamble and Coward 2012). Here, a small abandoned river channel contained the partial remains of eleven mammoths and 2700 stone tools,

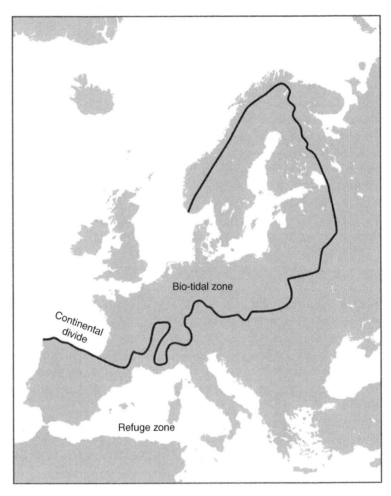

FIGURE 7.5. Bio-tidal Europe. The continental divide separates the continent into a refuge and bio-tidal area into which populations of animals and hominins expanded as conditions changed. The divide also marks the northern limits of warmth-loving fauna such as shrews and wild cattle at the Last Glacial Maximum. Adapted from Gamble (2009).

among them forty-seven distinctive flat bifaces that probably served as knives. All this material had slumped into the oxbow cut-off from the surrounding banks. But this had the advantage of preserving a rich environmental record of pollen, molluscs and beetles. These data place the occupation firmly in a warmer phase at the beginning of MIS3, 59–44ka (Van Andel and Davies

2003: table 4.3), indicating a rapid return by Neanderthals from the southern refuges once the grip of MIS4 had slackened.

Estimates of temperature at Lynford for the coldest (January) and warmest (July) months are provided by the beetle evidence, crossed-checked by pollen data. From these, an ET can be calculated of between 11.06°C and 10.86°C (Gamble and Boismier 2012: 291), a reduction of almost 4°C from today's values. As a result, MIS3 Lynford lay well below the ET threshold, where plants play a significant role in FGH diets (12.75°C) and above the 9.5°C limit when fishing predominates (Table 3.3). Hunting terrestrial animals is therefore expected, and the evidence that this occurred is present (Schreve 2012). But at these temperatures, modern FGH, as tabulated by Binford (Chapter 3), would in Lynford's environment also be expected to have major if not massive dependence on stored foods (Table 3.6). There is some evidence that Neanderthals carried away meat from the kill site, but they did not carry it far. The raw materials from which the stone bifaces were made are all local, mostly within 5 km (M. J. White 2012: 227). Neither are there any display items, beads or shells, in these lake sediments despite excellent organic preservation.

Lynford therefore provides an instance of how Neanderthals adapted to the opportunities of the mammoth steppe. The speed of Neanderthal dispersal into the bio-tidal zone, as MIS3 ushered in a warmer but far from interglacial climate, points to the availability of those all-important growth foods for their socioecology (Figure 3.11) and where their distribution determined the location of females (Figure 3.10). As Schreve and White argue, the small oxbow lake and the surrounding low-level, marshy topography allowed Neanderthals to "shepherd" the mammoths into a location where they could be disadvantaged and dispatched – a common technique among FGH when spears are the hunting instrument (Churchill 1993: 18–19). In these circumstances, Neanderthal men would have played an important role in securing the food and then defending it against other groups searching for similar growth foods in the landscape. However, these activities did not split along male–female lines. Reviewing Neanderthal settlement patterns, Burke (2011) has suggested that ranging patterns and way-finding would have been similar for both sexes. As a result, differences in spatial competence, which in humans is gendered to some extent, did not exist.

It was in these ways that the Lynford Neanderthals followed the classic pattern of primate and hominin socioecology and where the asymmetry of reproductive costs, borne by Neanderthal women, established the settlement and demographic structure. The food retrieved from the mammoths and carried elsewhere formed a natural, if short-lived, store. It was the local productivity of the mammoth steppe that tipped the scales towards settlement in the bio-tidal zone. By contrast, conditions in the earlier and climatically severe MIS4 (71–57ka) did not support Neanderthal settlement.

Neanderthal populations declined after the arrival of humans in Europe 45ka, with a small number persisting in Iberia until about 30ka (Stringer 2011: 159), and possibly in north-west Russia until 32ka (Slimak, Svendsen, Mangerud et al. 2011). Their demise coincides with a decline in temperature and ice advance during the cold phase of MIS3, 37–27ka (Van Andel and Davies 2003: table 4.3) – conditions that began to approximate to MIS4 when this part of the bio-tidal zone was uninhabited. However, human settlement persists both inside and outside the bio-tidal region. Outside, at Milovice in the Czech Republic, dated to between 22ka and 26ka and with an Upper Palaeolithic, Gravettian technology, mammoths again dominated the faunal assemblage. The eighty-six mammoth skeletons differ to the eleven from Lynford in significant ways. Limb bones are common, unlike the Neanderthal locale, while teeth, and particularly tusks, are underrepresented. This is interpreted as an intentional focus on ivory for trade either as a raw material or for the immediate production of beads (Brugère, Fontana and Oliva 2009).

Paviland Cave in the Gower Peninsula of Wales lies in the bio-tidal zone. The site was dug in 1823 when the burial of a male covered in ochre and found with ivory rods and rings was discovered (Pettitt 2011). These were possibly costume ornaments. Recent radiocarbon dating places it at 29–28ka (Jacobi and Higham 2008). This skeleton has been analysed for its dietary regime archived in the ^{13}N and ^{15}N component of its bones, and a significant marine component of fish is evident (Figure 7.6; Richards and Trinkaus 2009). Freshwater foods are also indicated by the isotope values from the much older, c. 42ka, Oase remains (Trinkaus 2003). These values contrast with those from Neanderthal skeletons analysed for the same isotopes from other parts of Europe. Here, a predominantly terrestrial diet for these top carnivores is apparent. When the locations of Lynford and Paviland are plotted against ET thresholds (Figure 7.7), it is evident that due to their different diets, the two MIS3 hominins occupied dissimilar environmental zones but at the same latitude.

Plant foods rarely survive. But some starch grains preserved in the surfaces of grinding slabs and tools at sites across Europe, and dated to 28–31ka, point to an acquaintance with seed resources (Revedin, Aranguren, Becattini et al. 2010). How significant this was in human diets is difficult to

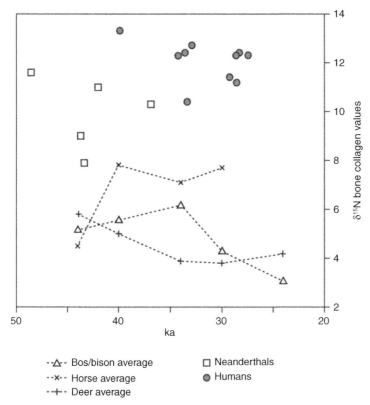

FIGURE 7.6. The measurement of nitrogen in bone collagen from European Pleistocene hominins and animals. The values separate the Neanderthal and human samples with the latter indicating mixed diets with fish and land mammals. Adapted from Richards and Trinkaus (2009).

say, but some plants were probably used as a weaning food (Mason, Hather and Hillman 1994).

Stored foods are also difficult to demonstrate even for the Upper Palaeolithic, although bones placed in pits at Kostenki (Soffer and Praslov 1993) and Pavlov (Svoboda 1994) have been interpreted as storage in the active layer, 80–110 cm, above the permafrost (Gamble 1999: 414). However, when the evidence is drawn together in terms of the treatment of growth food such as mammoth, the broadening of diets as indicated by the isotopes from human skeletons, the location of sites relative to ET thresholds and the hints of plant processing, then it is possible to see a shift from the Neanderthal pattern. Evidence that humans operated a granary model of stored food and

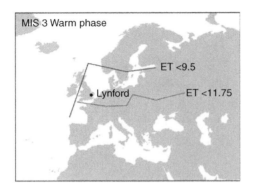

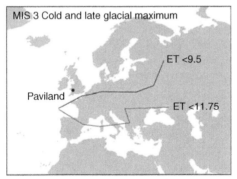

FIGURE 7.7. Effective temperature estimates during the early warm phase of MIS3 and the Last Glacial Maximum. The lines are extrapolated from January and July temperatures from palaeoclimate simulations and the boundaries of ET 9.5°C and 11.75°C that are important for predicting fishing and hunting (Table 3.3). The Lynford Neanderthal site and the human burial at Paviland Cave are found in warm and cold phases of MIS3 and lie either side of the ET line where fishing is expected. To confirm this, the Paviland skeleton had isotopic values indicating fish in the diet (Richards and Trinkaus 2009). Figure prepared by Peter Morgan.

defence remains scarce. However, it is possible that they followed the treasury route, as shown by their interest in social tokens such as ornaments. Here, special-purpose items were used to enchain others in widespread social networks. The strong hint is that a new human socioecology that linked settlement history to male control and defence of resources had begun.

The Direction of Dispersals

There were two major human dispersals in Pleistocene Europe during Terra 3. The earliest was from east to west, and saw the arrival of humans and the

Initial Upper Palaeolithic (IUP; Bar-Yosef 2007; Mellars 2006a), although the archaeological signature for this dispersal was often weak, and as a result, the archaeology is described as transitional between the Middle and Upper Palaeolithic. Most of the transitional B-List entities are regional with idio-syncratic bone and stone styles that have led to their A-List grouping as varieties of an IUP (Djindjian, Kozlowski and Otte 1999). A good example of this early regional assortment is the transitional, Mode 4 stone technology from Bohunice, an open site in the Czech Republic dated by TL and radiocarbon to 48–40ka (Richter, Tostevin and Skrdla 2008). This IUP example, the Bohunician, is a weak signature of the Upper Palaeolithic. It has no organic technology, habitation structures, burials or ornament and a small regional distribution (Jöris and Street 2008: fig. 2; Kozlowski 2010). Similarly, the presence of leaf-shaped projectile points that are highly variable in shape and manufacture links together sites in Poland, northern Germany and England in the time period 44–42ka (Jöris and Street 2008: fig. 9). These collections are small, the level of affinity between collections modest and there are no associations with human remains. The sites are interpreted as short-term hunting camps (Kozlowski 2010).

The one B-List entity that has a wider distribution, from the Near East to Doggerland, is the Aurignacian (S. W. G. Davies 2001; Hahn 1977) although it does not appear on the north European plain (Kozlowski 2010). For a century, this quintessentially French article has been seen as a strong signature for dispersal originating in the Near East (Breuil 1912; Garrod and Bate 1937). Here, sites in Lebanon, Israel and Turkey have multiple levels of IUP, including both Emiran and other Transitional assemblages from Middle to Upper Palaeolithic (50–38ka), the earliest true Upper Palaeolithic in the Levant with bone projectile points and perforated shell ornaments known as Ahmarian (38–25ka), and a Levantine version of the Aurignacian with bone points that are similar to those first found in France (36–28ka; Bar-Yosef and Belfer-Cohen 2010; Belfer-Cohen and Goring-Morris 2007; Shea 2007: table 19.1).

The chronology of the Aurignacian does not, however, follow the neat east–west direction that is usually portrayed (Mellars 2006a). For example, a small group of caves in southern Germany have bona fide Aurignacian stone and bone artefacts, as well as a regionally distinctive set of small animal and human figurines carved in ivory (Conard 2009; Hahn 1977). At the Geißenklösterle cave, the earliest Aurignacian is 43ka, much older than the Levantine Aurignacian. This small regional group is explained by the effect of the Danube corridor on east to west dispersals, providing a fast track to the centre of Europe (Conard and Bolus 2008). Elsewhere in France and

Italy, regional differences are also the norm where bone points, beads and other visual display items are concerned (R. White 1993, 2007).

So, while the IUP has a weak east to west signature of dispersal supported by some dating evidence, the Aurignacian that follows does not. This entity instead arose somewhere in Eastern Europe from the assortment of older IUP regional entities and quickly moved to the edge of the bio-tidal zone in southern Germany (Conard and Bolus 2008). It then dispersed from west to east into the Levant where it is found at super sites such as the Ksar Akil rock-shelter, north of Beirut in Lebanon (Bar-Yosef and Belfer-Cohen 2010: 93).

The second dispersal came after the LGM and is more south to north rather than east to west. Much of the bio-tidal zone was either abandoned or seldom visited in the period 24–16ka, and this extended to the northern parts of the refuge zone (Figure 7.5). Then, as the rising number of radiocarbon dates reveals (Figure 7.8), there is a strong archaeological signature of expansion northwards from the refuge areas of southern France and Cantabrian Spain (Gamble 1999; Gamble, Davies, Pettitt et al. 2004; Gamble, Davies, Richards et al. 2005). This dispersal is linked to the Magdalenian. In Eastern Europe, such dispersal is less marked due to population persisting in the refuge zone. However, in contrast to the western Magdalenian, the equally strong signature in this part of the continent is the Epi-Gravettian and where expansion onto the northern plains took place for the first time (Djindjian, Kozlowski and Otte 1999: map 282–283).

Source, Target and Trails

With Southwest Asia as the archaeogenetic source, the target zones can readily be described as bio-tidal Doggerland to the north-west and Iberia in the Western Mediterranean. The latter region has no archaeological or archaeogenetic information that it was settled across the Straits of Gibraltar from North Africa. A third target has recently emerged from archaeological evidence. This consists of sites found to the east of the Fennoscandinavian ice sheet in north-western Russia above latitude 60°N (Pavlov, Svendsen and Indrelid 2001).

The directions by which these targets were reached were various. A route north of the Black Sea is confirmed by the early ages at Kostenki on the Russian plain, and from there targets two and three could be reached. Alternatively, a more southerly route is favoured that passes through the so-called Gates of Europe in the south-east of the continent before proceeding quickly along the Danube Valley into Central Europe after which the Rhine provides a corridor north (Djindjian 1994). The Mediterranean route

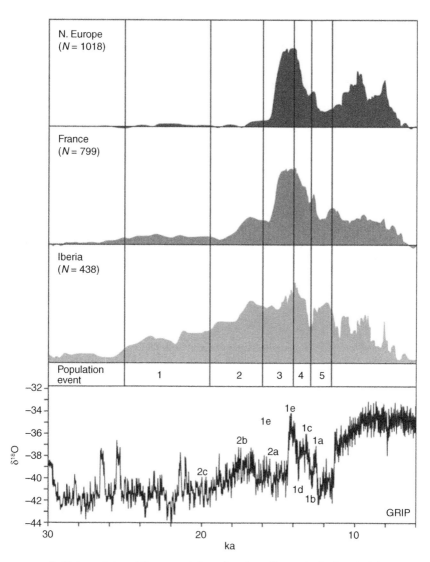

FIGURE 7.8. Dates as data and the repopulation of northern Europe in the Lateglacial (Gamble et al. 2005). The five population events are described in Table 7.8. N = number of radiocarbon dates in the data curve. Adapted from Gamble et al. (2005).

from south-east Europe is marked in Italy by Ulluzian bone artefacts and ornaments, associated at Grotta del Cavallo with the only, not entirely convincing, fossil remains of modern humans, found directly with any archaeology (Benazzi, Douka, Fornai et al. 2011: 527). This route followed a linear environment through the southern refuge zone and retraced Europe's segment of the hominin tectonic trail (Figure 2.6).

The Timing and Frequency of Dispersals

A Widespread Volcanic Marker

The timing of the earliest human dispersal into Europe is archaeologically confused and palaeontologically impoverished. What is needed is a robust chronology. However, advances in the science of radiocarbon dating lead to older age estimates of well-known sites – a constant updating that means few archaeologists are singing from the same song sheet for very long (Higham, Jacobi and Ramsey 2006; Jöris and Street 2008; Mellars 2006b).

Volcanic events where ash, tephra, is widely dispersed can provide a stratigraphic marker against which the radiocarbon evidence can be properly evaluated. In the Central Mediterranean, one such event was the major eruption known as the Campanian Ignimbrite (CI) from a volcano in the Campi Flegrei in the Bay of Naples (C. Oppenheimer 2011). This supervolcanic event ejected 300 km³ of ash in a plume that moved north-east and south-east (Figure 7.9). The chemical composition of the tephra it left as the CI footprint can be traced back to the Campi Flegrei source, where $^{40}Ar/^{39}Ar$ dating places the eruption at 40ka. This ash preserves as a visible layer in the Don River site of Kostenki in Russia, 2000 km from the Campi Flegrei. The CI tephra is also found in archaeological sites as an invisible component of the sediments, and in that way acts as a marker to date the Middle and Upper Palaeolithic transition (Fedele, Giaccio and Hajdas 2008; Lowe, Barton, Blockley et al. 2012). What is quite clear from Figure 7.9 is that the transition in Eastern Europe and North Africa from the Middle to Upper Palaeolithic took place below the CI level and so earlier than 40ka.

With this chronological marker in place, the radiocarbon record can then be scrutinised for what it tells us about the archaeology of Upper Palaeolithic dispersals. At Kostenki, there are no Middle Palaeolithic stone assemblages. The earliest Upper Palaeolithic at site 12 lies below the CI in layers III and IV with radiocarbon ages of 41.2–41.9ka (Anikovich, Sinitsyn, Hoffecker et al. 2007). Three other sites in the Kostenki complex repeat this pattern (Hoffecker 2009). The stone tools are Upper Palaeolithic and have been B-listed as Proto-Aurignacian with links to the Near East (Kostenki 1 layer III) and a regional assemblage known as the Spitsynskaya (Kostenki 17 layer II), while some bifacial tools suggest connections with the earliest Upper Palaeolithic in Hungary. The pattern below the CI is therefore

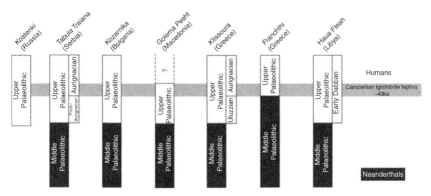

FIGURE 7.9. The transition from Middle to Upper Palaeolithic in Eastern Europe. The Campanian Ignimbrite (CI) tephra forms a chronological marker in several sites. It shows that the transition had taken place well before the eruption took place. Adapted from Lowe (2012).

varied, but in all these levels, there are artefacts made in bone, antler and ivory, as well as perforated stone ornaments. Where Middle Palaeolithic tool forms do occur, the assemblages, known as Streletskayan, use local stone and have no art or organic artefacts. They are interpreted as specialist butchering tool kits (Anikovich, Sinitsyn, Hoffecker et al. 2007: 225).

The sites at Kostenki present a strong Upper Palaeolithic signature dominated by blades. The stone raw materials used in their manufacture regularly came from 100–150 km away, while perforated shells from Kostenki 14 came from a Black Sea source more than 500 km to the south (Hoffecker, Holliday, Anikovich et al. 2008).

A strong Upper Palaeolithic signature in the form of the North African Dabban has been found below the CI at the cave of the Haua Fteah, Libya (Lowe, Barton, Blockley et al. 2012). And at Klissoura Cave, Greece, the Uluzzian, known from the Eastern Mediterranean and Italy (Benazzi, Douka, Fornai et al. 2011), is also found below the CI tephra. In both these cases, an abrupt transition is evident in the site stratigraphy from Middle to Upper Palaeolithic.

But what Figure 7.9 also shows is that trying to tie the demise of Neanderthals and the appearance of the Upper Palaeolithic to the combined devastation of the CI, and the cold Heinrich Event 4 immediately after it, does not work (Fedele, Giaccio and Hajdas 2008). Instead, the technological transition took place across Eastern Europe and North Africa long before the super-volcano erupted, prompting others to conclude that the competitive threat from an incoming population posed greater threats to the indigenous Neanderthals than a natural hazard (Lowe, Barton, Blockley et al. 2012).

The IUP Dispersal Event Before the CI Eruption

Due to the paucity of human fossils to indicate when they arrived in Europe during Terra 3, we are dependent, as we were in South Asia, on an archaeogenetic model. As seen in Chapter 6, haplogroups M, N and R were established in Southwest Asia, although subsequent depopulation means that they do not appear in modern mtDNA genomes as a record of the earliest expansions from Africa. In Europe, the oldest founder haplogroups are derived from R. These are RO, JT and U. Among these, the subclades U8 and U5 have molecular founder ages of 50ka and 37ka respectively (Table 6.2; Soares, Achilli, Semino et al. 2010), and a source in Southwest Asia is suggested. Here, U5 and U6 arose and then dispersed into Europe and North Africa respectively (Olivieri, Achilli, Pala et al. 2006). Two strong Upper Palaeolithic signatures have been linked to these dispersals, both of which are older than the CI tephra level: the Dabban in North Africa, and the Levantine earliest Upper Palaeolithic. But the idea that the Aurignacian was the first Upper Palaeolithic in Europe with a source, suggested by the archaeogenetics, in the Levant (Olivieri, Achilli, Pala et al. 2006: 1769) shows how necessary it is to retain a firm grip on the chronology of the archaeology. It also requires less faith in our ability to match the haplogroup alphabet to B-List archaeological entities.

What we do know is that, below the CI marker, there were an assortment of highly versatile regional ways of making stone tools. If there was an emphasis, it was on the knapping sequences by which nodules became cores, and where both flakes (Mode 3) and blades (Mode 4) were the outcome. This is apparent much earlier and over a wide area that spans Arabia, the Nile Valley and Nubia. For example, a number of Palaeolithic quarries for chert from which blades and flakes were produced have been excavated at Taramsa Hill in the Nile corridor (Van Peer and Vermeersch 2007). Cooperation is inferred from the large scale of the quarrying and the amount of stone blanks. A seated burial of a human child was found in Taramsa phase III, dated to 78.5ka by OSL (Van Peer and Vermeersch 2007; Vermeersch, Paulissen, Stokes et al. 1998). And in Phase IV, dated by OSL to 56.2ka in MIS3, many blades were excavated that are regarded as antecedent to the earliest Mode 4 in the Levant (Shea 2007).

The versatile skills of these stone knappers are readily evident both at Taramsa and the Negev Desert site of Boker Tachtit where the oldest level is dated by radiocarbon to 47ka. At this open site, preservation was excellent, and flakes and cores could be fitted back together to show the knapping sequences. The surprise, at least to adherents of a strict species and cultural distinction between the Middle and Upper Palaeolithic, was that both knapping strategies were used interchangeably to make the same triangular-shaped projectile known as an Emireh point. On one refitted nodule, the knapper began with a Middle Palaeolithic, flake technique and then as the nodule dwindled in size, she/he switched to an Upper Palaeolithic blade technique (Marks 1983, 1990). The end products, Emireh points, were the same – an example of equifinality in stone tool skills.

A Strong Signature After the CI Eruption

As we have seen in many other parts of Asia and Africa, a strong Upper Palaeolithic signature is frequently found after 35ka. This is the case also in Europe with the widespread Gravettian and where the contrast with the older Aurignacian is particularly marked (Gamble 1999: 287–292; Roebroeks, Mussi, Svoboda et al. 2000). Some Gravettian sites are huge, multifaceted accumulations of artefacts and animal bones, as at Kostenki site 1 layer I (Praslov and Rogachev 1982) and the Dolni-Vestonice/Pavlov/ Milovice site complexes near Brno in the Czech Republic (Svoboda, Lozek and Vleck 1996). The human-fossil record also becomes much richer after 35ka at locations such as Mladec Cave and the burials at Pavlov and Dolni-Vestonice (Gamble 1999: 387–414; Jöris and Street 2008: fig. 3).

The Lateglacial Dispersal Event After 16ka

The archaeogenetics of both mtDNA and MSY and the archaeological evidence for resettlement are very clear on the south to north direction of this dispersal in Western Europe. Indeed, such are the effects of small founder populations that a large proportion of the haplogroups in Europeans stem from this event. These relate to mtDNA haplogroups H and its sister clade V. Haplogroup H accounts for up to forty-five per cent of mtDNA in modern European genomes (Soares, Achilli, Semino et al. 2010: 177). H arose in the Near East at 18ka molecular, and the age for this founder in Europe is about 15ka molecular years ago (Achilli, Rengo, Magri et al. 2004; Richards, Macaulay, Hickey et al. 2000; Soares, Achilli, Semino et al.

TABLE 7.5. *Four major refuge areas for Europe, as identified by archaeogenetics and the major archaeological signatures of dispersal (Pala et al. 2012).*

Refuge areas	mtDNA haplogroups	Dispersal phase archaeology
Southern France and Iberia	H1, H3, V, U5b1	Badegoulian, Magdalenian, Azilian
Italy	U5b3	Epi-Gravettian
East European plain	U4, U5a	Gravettian, Epi-Gravettian
Near East	J, T	Epi-Palaeolithic complex

2010). This is in good agreement with the increase in number of radiocarbon dates (Figure 7.8).

Using mtDNA, archaeogeneticists have identified four refuge areas from which the bio-tidal zone was resettled (Table 7.5). Of these, the Near East was thought to be the source of haplogroups that were introduced to Europe by the earliest farmers. However, recent whole genome studies now identify a dispersal of haplogroups J and T from this refuge sometime between 19ka and 12ka molecular years ago (Pala, Olivieri, Achilli et al. 2012). At the Anatolian site of Pinarbai (Baird 2011), settlement occurred during the Greenland Interstadial (GI-1, 14.7–12.9ka), and artefacts indicate links to the Mediterranean coast and the Levant. This raises the possibility that expansion occurred from Turkey into Eastern Europe during the Lateglacial. It formed a part of the Epi-Gravettian expansion that eventually reached the north European plain. Here, in the same Greenland Interstadial, widespread B-List entities distinguished by distinctive projectile points proliferated (Burdukiewicz 1986; Djindjian, Kozlowski and Otte 1999).

The Tempo of the Upper Palaeolithic Dispersals

Uncertainties over dating and the lack of a strong dispersal signature make it difficult to estimate the speed of the pre-CI dispersals. These may have been fast, as the appearance of the Aurignacian in southern Germany implies (Conard and Bolus 2003). And if so, these speeds could be explained by higher exploratory distances, in the form of leapfrogging, that can characterise human dispersal. The dispersal from an IUP site such as Bacho Kiro in Bulgaria (Kozlowski 1982) to south-western France could, at a minimum, have taken 2–3ka over a distance of some 2500 km (Bar-Yosef 2007: fig. 18.1). This provides an average dispersal rate of 1.25 and 0.83 km per annum.

TABLE 7.6. *Population estimates during the refuge and expansion phases of the Lateglacial settlement of Western Europe (Bocquet-Appel and Demars 2000, Gamble et al. 2004).*

	Cantabria-Aquitaine	Rest of France	Rest of Iberia	Rest of Western Europe	Total
Expansion phase	18,875	15,271	15,271	14,860	64,277
Refuge phase	10,246	3396	3396	0	17,038

The Lateglacial population expansion from the southern refuge areas back into the bio-tidal zone is much better dated. The Western European rate of dispersal is 0.77 km per annum, as measured from Switzerland to the British Isles, a distance of 925 km (Housley, Gamble, Street et al. 1997: table 5).

While these figures must be treated with caution, it is noteworthy that the rates are comparable, even though the earlier event dispersed through an already inhabited continent while the later resettled largely unoccupied territory. Perhaps this similarity is indicative of the fragmented distribution of Neanderthals following the severe climate downturn during Heinrich Event 5, 48ka (Müller, Pross, Tzedakis et al. 2010).

Where the data are more robust is in indicating relative levels of population. The archaeogenetic data on population coalescence show that following dispersal into Europe, population levels were very low for the next 30ka (Soares, Achilli, Semino et al. 2010). This is supported by the low frequency of radiocarbon dates until the Lateglacial resettlement when, across Europe but particularly in its western part, the curves rise dramatically (Figure 7.8). Using inventories of archaeological sites, radiocarbon and population densities from FGH the population levels in the refuge areas of south-western Europe are estimated to have been 17,000 people, while resettled Western Europe had a population of 64,000 (Table 7.6; Bocquet-Appel 2008; Bocquet-Appel and Demars 2000; Bocquet-Appel, Demars, Noiret et al. 2005).

On closer examination, the dispersal events, both early and late, appear to have followed a two-stage process (Table 7.7). S. W. G. Davies (2001: 205; 2007) has divided the Aurignacian evidence into two types of archaeological assemblage: simple ones with relatively low counts of stone tools and low typological diversity, and complex occurrences with larger counts, greater typological diversity, as well as evidence for social interaction in the form of art and musical instruments. In his pioneer phase, population expanded

TABLE 7.7. *Major differences in the archaeology of two phases of dispersal: Initial Upper Palaeolithic (Aurignacian) and Lateglacial.*

	Pioneer campsite phase	Residential base phase
Early Aurignacian	46–37ka	
Later Aurignacian	37–29ka	
Lateglacial population events (Table 7.8) and ages	2–4 19.5–13.5ka	4–5 14–11.7ka
Evidence for seasons	One season	Multiple
Faunal assemblages	Small	Large
Dominant prey	Single species	Greater diet breadth and range of species
Artefact accumulation	Small, medium-sized sites	Small and large size sites
Artefact refitting	Within and between sites	Within sites
Site architecture	Rockshelters, open-air hearths and tents	House, pits, tents, fewer rockshelter occupations
Presence of art and symbols	Rare	Common
Burials	Caves, usually males	Open sites, both sexes

See text for explanation (Housley et al. 1997: table 4; Gamble et al. 2005; Davies 2007: table 22.1). This has been applied to the east–west axis of dispersal and where the Aurignacian is the example and the south–north axis found in the Lateglacial expansion of the Magdalenian.

rapidly, probably as a result of large individual exploratory ranges, but numbers were always low. Then followed a developed or residential phase during which population size grew. The character of the archaeological record between these two phases reflects these changes.

What characterises the archaeology after the CI ash at 40ka, and in particular the major change after 35ka associated with the Gravettian, is the appearance of large, open sites with rich inventories of stone, bone and art. These include the Dolni-Vestonice/Pavlov/Milovice complex near Brno in the Czech Republic (Svoboda, Lozek and Vleck 1996) and from the Russian plain Sunghir, Kostenki and Avdeevo (Soffer 1985; Soffer and Praslov 1993). Such open-air centres of accumulation and enchainment are lacking in Western Europe and particularly in the bio-tidal zone. Instead, in southwest France, large numbers of multilayered rockshelters are found while the elaboration of surfaces by painting at Chauvet Cave dates to this second phase (Chauvet, Brunel Deschamps and Hillaire 1995). This Gravettian

TABLE 7.8. *Five events in the population history of Western Europe (see Figure 7.8)* (*Gamble et al. 2005*).

Population event	Settlement pattern	Dominant settlement type	Phylogeography	GRIP stratotype	GRIP ice-core years (ka)
1. Refuge	Dispersed	Rockshelter	Low population size	LGM–GS-2c	25–19.5
2. Initial expansion	Pioneer	Rockshelter and open	Low population size	GS-2b–GS-2a	19.5–16
3. Main expansion	Residential	Rockshelter then open	Founder effect and expansion	GS-2a–GI-1e	16–14
4. Populaion stasis	Nucleation	Open sites	Founder effect and expansion	GI-1d–GI-1a	14–12.9
5. Population contraction		Open sites		GS-1	12.9–11.7

phase did not lead to growth in Europe's population, but rather a steady contraction of settlement out of the bio-tidal zone and a highly nucleated pattern of settlement in the more continental areas of Europe as MIS3 ended and the Last Glacial Maximum of MIS2 began 24ka.

The Lateglacial dispersal of Western Europe can be also divided on radiocarbon and archaeological evidence into a two-stage process – pioneer and residential – and some archaeological expectations are set out in Table 7.7 (Housley, Gamble, Street et al. 1997). In particular, the settlement pattern changed markedly during the interstadial (GI-1). During this warmer interval, rockshelters fell out of use, and large open sites in the Rhine, Paris Basin and Northern Plain become common (Figure 7.8; Table 7.8). This shift from a dispersed to nucleated settlement pattern is part of the process of settling into the territory, as predicted by Davies, and it is noticeable that during the succeeding Younger Dryas (GS1 12.9–11.7ka) when temperatures plummeted again and a limited readvance of the ice sheets took place, they did not revert to the earlier pattern. Neither, as the radiocarbon curve shows (Figure 7.8; Table 7.8) did occupation rates at sites return to the very low levels seen before population expansion took place at 16ka.

The Arctic

The settlement of the Arctic needs explorers with imagination. In 1948, Eigil Knuth led a Danish expedition to Pearyland in northern Greenland

and found rich evidence for human occupation in such a barren place where no Inuit then lived. He described what he had found, in a Conradian phrase, as a "prehistoric town so far beyond the limits of history and reason" (McGhee 1996: 31). At the same time, Louis Giddings was excavating a coastal village at Cape Denbigh in western Alaska. These two sites separated by at least 4500 km, but in real travel distance much more, established a source and a target for the study of Arctic settlement. But determining direction, timing and tempo across this immense land is not easy. Archaeological fieldwork is limited to a few summer months and requires expensive logistical support. The data are hard won but on occasion spectacular due to the quality of preservation.

Peopling the Never-glaciated Arctic

The earliest settlement of the Arctic can be divided into two regions: the unglaciated and the glaciated. The former lay between the Barents Sea ice sheet in the west, part of the Fennoscandinavian ice cap, and Alaska in the east. On the small island of Ostrov Zhokhova at 76°N in the East Siberian Sea, ET today is 8.1°C, a result of mean July temperatures reaching only 1°C. Yet this island was settled at least 7.8ka, as confirmed by excavations of a well-preserved stone, wood and bone technology that included fragments possibly from a sled (Makeyev, Pitul'ko and Kasparov 1992). Reindeer dominated the animal prey, reflecting the lower sea levels and the larger size of the island. Some remains of walrus, seal and birds were also found. To the south-west at 71°N is the Yana RHS site dated by radiocarbon to 30ka where a diverse fauna that included mammoth, horse, reindeer and bison is a reminder of the productivity of these MIS3 steppes.

In the western part of the never-glaciated zone lay a corridor that was settled between the Urals and the Fennoscandinavian ice cap. The most northerly settlement is the river bluff site of Mammontovaya Kurya on the Arctic Circle at 66.5°N. Mammoth, reindeer and horse bones have been found in sediments which contain a few stone tools and a mammoth tusk that bears cut marks, and all dated to between 34–38ka (Pavlov, Roebroeks and Svendsen 2004). The river terrace site of Byzovaya, 300 km to the south-west at 65°N, has 300 stone tools that are described as Middle Palaeolithic, leading some to suggest a late refuge area for Neanderthals between 34ka and 31ka (Slimak, Svendsen, Mangerud et al. 2011). There are no hominin fossils to support this claim. One option is to regard this corridor as a target area that was reached quickly by humans as they dispersed into Europe, moving above the limit of Neanderthal settlement at sites such as Garchi 1 and Elniki, at 59°N (Pavlov, Roebroeks and Svendsen 2004: fig. 1). In that case, the Mode 3 artefacts are an example of a weak dispersal signature. Alternatively, the Pechora Basin where the sites are found was a final northern refuge for Neanderthals exploiting the mammoth steppe as climates deteriorated towards the end of MIS3 (Slimak, Svendsen, Mangerud et al. 2011). Whichever option is confirmed by further research, it is apparent that settlement was earlier at these high latitudes to the west of the Urals than to the east (Pavlov, Roebroeks and Svendsen 2004: 14), and where Yana RHS is currently the earliest evidence. In my view, these incursions into the never-glaciated Arctic were most probably human rather than hominin dispersals.

But expect the unexpected is the story of Arctic archaeology. An ET of <9.5°C predicts for FGH a dependence on fishing and marine hunting. Complex, composite technologies with many components (Chapter 3) are also to be expected as a means to increase hunting returns. Storage is a necessity. It might even be thought that the Arctic's severe climate would select, for a limited number of adaptations, ways to survive and thrive. Yet, as these sites from the unglaciated region show, there were alternative choices for diet and technology – a pattern repeated throughout the archaeology of those areas in Europe and North America that were once under the ice caps.

Peopling the Once-glaciated Arctic

Human settlement in the circumpolar zone that was glaciated depended on rising temperatures and sea levels, as well as storage, fishing and hunting marine mammals such as seals and whales.

The retreat of the Laurentide and Fennoscandinavian ice sheets began in earnest during the Greenland ice-core Interstadial (GI-1, 14.7–12.9ka) but proceeded rapidly at the onset of the Holocene warming 11.7ka. The Laurentide ice sheet shrank quickly between 9ka and 6.8ka, and sea levels rose accordingly (Carlson, Legrande, Oppo et al. 2008). In Fennoscandinavia, the coastal zones of Norway and Finland were ice free during GI-1, as was all of southern Scandinavia. Small ice caps were still present over inland northern Scandinavia 10ka in the early Holocene (Bergman, Olofsson, Hörnberg et al. 2004: fig. 1).

The Scandinavian evidence points to a swift northwards dispersal along the coast and above the Arctic Circle. Six sites between 65°N and 70°N in Norway are dated between 10.7ka and 12.1ka (Bergman, Olofsson, Hörnberg et al. 2004: fig. 2; Nygaard 1989). The rate of dispersal was probably higher, as the older dates occur in the north, and a figure of 200–300 years has been proposed (Bergman, Olofsson, Hörnberg et al. 2004), a high rate of 3.3–5 km per annum made possible by boats. However, while a maritime adaptation is assumed, it remains untested. Rather, the archaeology is indicative of a large number of small and highly mobile groups rather than large sedentary villages living off stored marine mammals. In terms of direction, the evidence points to dispersal up the western coast and not round the top from Russia.

A maritime adaptation is, however, evident in the volcanic Aleutian Islands that, at 2000 km in length, form the world's longest archipelago (Balter 2012). This necklace of islands is not strictly Arctic, as they are found between 52°N and 58°N. But their small size and proximity to rich marine feeding grounds make them a good example of what adaptations were needed in other parts of the North American Arctic. The oldest sites in the chain are 9ka years old, but only ten of these have been found (Veltre and Smith 2010: 488). This contrasts with the more than 1000 archaeological sites known from the last 4ka of human settlement. The early sites are clustered in the eastern part of the chain (R. S. Davis and Knecht 2010: table 3), while in the middle of the chain, Adak Island has a site (ADK71) dated to 7ka with evidence for fishing (Balter 2012). These early sites have abundant blades, grindstones for pigment, stone bowls, net sinkers, oil lamps and tent-like houses (R. S. Davis and Knecht 2010). To the west of Adak Island, settlement is later, starting about 3.5ka.

The dispersal direction along the Aleutians is firmly east to west, Alaska to Kamchatka. This geographical pattern results from extensive mtDNA work, showing that the ancestors of the Aleuts crossed into Beringia about 9ka molecular years ago and then expanded westwards along the islands (Crawford, Rubicz and Zlojutro 2010) – a pattern predicted by the archaeology.

The settlement of the Canadian Arctic and Greenland proceeded rapidly after 6ka with the final retreat of the Laurentide ice cap. Rising sea levels resulted in more than 200,000 km of coastline. Western Alaska, and the Cape Denbigh site, form an archaeological source area. From here, about 4.5ka, dispersal began with the targets of central and eastern Canada and then the unglaciated margins of Greenland (Hoffecker 2005; Hood 2009). The dispersal signature is strong and can be grouped under the general A-List heading of the Arctic Small Tool tradition. In each of these target areas, B-List regional variants are described, such as Independence and Saqqaq in Greenland and Pre-Dorset in eastern and central Canada respectively (McGhee 1996: fig. 2.1). The range of technology is impressive and more so when permafrost aids preservation as at the Saqqaq-age site of Qeqertasussuk in Disko Bay, 69°N, west Greenland (Grønnow 1988, 1994). At this coastal site, occupied between 3.9ka and 3.1ka, excavations recovered forty-five animal species that were hunted, including four species of whales, as well as walrus, narwhal and seals. Land mammals were also hunted, along with an impressive range of birds and fish. The domestic dog was present. The technology consists of many wooden shafts into which large bifacial projectile points had been hafted. Spears, lances, fish leisters, toggle harpoons, atlatls and bows were found, as well as stone saws, knives and scrapers, also bifacially worked, and similarly mounted in wooden handles (Grønnow 1994). Some kayak parts were also identified. All of this evidence confirms a maritime focus with, as might be expected, a high-scoring technounit technology (Chapter 3).

Among the frozen remains at Qeqertasussuk was human hair from a person dated to 4ka. A full genome has been sequenced from this material (Rasmussen 2010). It reveals that the first people to settle Greenland entered North America 5.5ka molecular years ago. Moreover, they are genetically distinct from the ancestors of both contemporary Inuit and Native North Americans. This archaeogenetic finding that there were multiple dispersals into the Arctic following deglaciation is backed by the regional archaeological diversity of the subsequent 4ka of settlement (Hoffecker 2005; Maxwell 1985; McGhee 1996).

The routes into this area must also have been multifarious. In 1948, Knuth was interested in tracing the Musk-ox Way, along which terrestrial hunters followed these large, easy-to-kill animals across the tundra to reach Greenland (McGhee 1996). Others would have taken the coastal route as the Qeqertasussuk kayak and maritime economy indicate, while the appearance of umiaks, Inuit whaling boats, 2ka intensified exploitation (Rogers and Anichtchenko in press). Yet more dispersals took the overland route from boreal Canada and others up the coasts of Newfoundland and Maine. In the historic period, these dispersals, now called migrations, were extremely rapid. The Thule migration from Alaska to Greenland took place around 1300 AD. The 4000 km was covered in a single generation, indicating a dispersal rate of 200 km per annum (Rogers and Anichtchenko in press).

Due to preservation conditions favouring ancient DNA work, the Arctic will become the classic region for the study of small-scale population dispersals. The early indications are that the patterns will be complex. And as the varied archaeology has already shown, this region presented myriad opportunities for a versatile species, whether this was exploiting local abundance or trading with other maritime nations. This last point is a key to understanding the later settlement of the Arctic, a region that is so remote to those living in lower latitudes, it has nonetheless always been globally connected. For example, the cultural source for the Alaskan variant of the Arctic Small Tool tradition, the B-List Denbigh, was the pottery-using cultures of north-east Siberia (McGhee 1996). Here, ceramics were used 10ka (Kuzmin and Orlova 2000), and population was expanding. Although Alaska lies well above the limits for reliable agriculture, political and economic changes thousands of kilometres to the south along the Ordos and Amur rivers reverberated into the Arctic. Much later, these southern civilisations would transform aspects of the Arctic, especially through the technologies of warfare and trade (Gamble 1993: 213). Indeed, the spur to the super-fast Thule migration was not just a maritime technology and lifestyle but the drawing power of trade in metals and goods that the arrival in Greenland of Norse peoples from Scandinavia had stimulated (McGhee 2009). But that is properly a dispersal story for Terra 4, as is the limit to expansion represented by the settlement history of Iceland. Set beside the versatile approaches to the settlement of the Arctic and the maritime focus of settlement in the Aleutians, Canada and Greenland, the settlement of this large island from the east, and at a time well into Terra 4, reminds us that accurate prediction of global settlement in deep human history is still a world away.

CHAPTER 8

Eyes on the horizon: Terra 4, 4–1ka

I hate travelling and explorers.

Claude Lévi-Strauss, *Tristes Tropiques*, 1955

Farming The World

Terra 4 is a world of seascapes. The globe is rapidly settled by purposeful voyages and island hopping that now reaches into all parts of the uninhabited oceans. The remote is turned into the local, and maritime neighbourhoods are created out of materials shared over great distances. The impact of these dispersals can be traced through the Pacific and across the Indian and Atlantic oceans (Figure 8.1).

Terra 4 is also a world of complex political landscapes. In conjunction with the settlement of seascapes, Terra 4 contains evidence from human biology, genetics, linguistics, texts and artefacts for repeated population displacement throughout the lands settled in Terra 3. These displacements have been the engine driving our interest in shallow history (Box 1.1, Table 2.3). They provide an understanding of the past that both supports and challenges current national identities and universal notions of humanity. These multifarious displacements are fuelled by ever-more complex societies extracting more from the land and growing larger in size (Table 3.8b).

Dispersal rather than displacement is my focus with Terra 4. But there is a common link between the deep history of dispersal on the sea and large-scale displacement on the land. That link is farming. The domestication of plants and animals that began in Terra 3 in New Guinea, East Asia, the Near East and Central and South America was further amplified after 4ka when new domesticates are found in Africa, India and North America (Table 8.1). In some parts of the Old World, ploughs then increased yields

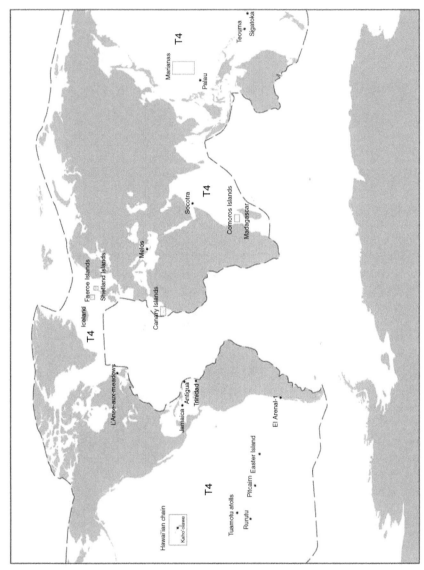

FIGURE 8.1. Terra 4 with key sites and regions.

TABLE 8.1. *Centres of plant domestication in Terra 3 that provisioned Terra 4 dispersals into less productive, island habitats (Balter 2007; Barker 2009).*

	ka		ka	
Southwest Asia	13–11.4	Rye and figs		
	10.5–10	Emmer and einkorn wheat, barley		
Central America	10–9	*Pepo* squash, maize	4	Common bean
Tropical South America	10–8	Moschata squash, arrowroot, Leren tubers, peanut, cassava	7–4.5	Potato, quinoa, yam (*Dioscorea trifidi*), cotton, chilli pepper (*Capsicum*), sweet potato (*Ipomoea batatas*), lima bean
Eastern North America			5–4	Sunflower, chenopod, marshelder
East Asia	8	Rice, broomcorn and foxtail millet, foxnut		
South India			4.5	Mung bean, horse gram bean, millets
New Guinea	7	Yam (*Dioscorea alata*) and taro, banana		
African Sahel			4–2	Sorghum, pearl millet, African rice

further, while the irrigation of mid-latitude deserts tapped into an eco-logical abundance unavailable to FGH (Sherratt 1997). Villages quickly became towns that, by Terra 4, were cities with monumental architecture designed for conversations with the gods and control of the earthbound.

Civilisation was one outcome of amplifying the use of resources, turning wolves into dogs, teosinte into maize and stones into pyramids. Society now evolved to metaphors of giving environments and growing bodies (Gamble 2007: 78). But the route domestication took was also, and we saw hints of this in Terra 3, selected by human dispersal. The link between farming, pop-ulation size and cities is so obvious, and necessary, that it has obscured this other consequence of domestication: completing global settlement. What if the primary selective force on that hominin core of materials and senses (Figure 1.2) has always been the expansion of population into new terri-tory? Then the rise of civilisation, large as it figures in our histories, is the unintended consequence of another process – global settlement – which in

Box 8.1. Island biogeography and the five anomalous giants

The biogeographical theory of island colonisation by plants and animals has been used by archaeologists to investigate the sequence and timing of first human settlement. The principles are simple. Island size is a proxy for species diversity among birds, land animals and plants. The larger the island, the greater the diversity once factors such as latitude and climate have been taken into account. The second factor, distance from source areas which can be either another island or the mainland, then addresses the historical dimension. Large islands can also be remote ones so that colonisation by new species is not as frequent as on smaller islands lying closer to large source populations. Here, configuration plays a role and the presence of stepping-stone islands can aid the process of settlement. In its classic formulation, MacArthur and Wilson (1967) used these proxies of isolation and diversity to model the rate of inflow (founding) and outflow (extinction) among island populations.

However, using present diversity without allowing for the historical veneer can be problematic. Archaeological evidence, particularly from the Pacific, shows that the diversity of bird species dropped significantly when humans arrived. Yet this is not always factored into the analysis of island biogeography. For example, it is estimated that forty-five bird species became extinct on Hawai'i after its settlement by Polynesians, and a further twenty-five followed the arrival of Europeans (Trigger 2006). This amounts to seventy species in less than 1ka.

Island biogeography has been applied in archaeological contexts to see if distance, size and configuration can also predict the pattern of first colonisation (Keegan and Diamond 1987). The results are mixed. When applied to the islands of the Mediterranean (Cherry 1990), a reasonably good fit was found with the larger islands such as Crete and Sardinia/ Corsica. However, some, such as the small obsidian-rich island of Melos in the southern Cyclades, were first visited by FGH, since flakes from it have been found in FGH levels at Francthi Cave on the mainland 10ka. Crete was first visited in Terra 2 (Chapter 5). Cyprus has no stepping stones and is therefore harder to find than Sardinia and Crete. However, it was first settled very early by FGH 12ka who, among other resources, hunted pygmy hippos at the site of Akrotiri Aetokremnos on the southernmost end of the island (Knapp 2010). In the Pacific, Keegan and Diamond (1987: 68) conclude there is a case to be made that human colonising behaviour was moulded by the pattern of islands. It was a reciprocal relationship, an example of niche construction, where the configuration of islands in the Pacific rewarded Pacific peoples more than those in other oceans with fewer islands, and so advanced maritime skills were developed. This reinforcing argument has a certain circular sense to it and does not explain the late settlement of New Zealand (Table Box 8.1).

TABLE BOX 8.1. *Size, distance and settlement of large islands in three different oceans.*

	Size (km²)	Earliest settlement (ka)	Closest continental landmass	Source area for settlement
Madagascar	587,000	2.3–0.5	Africa	Indonesia
New Zealand	256,000	0.72	Australia	Polynesia
Iceland	101,000	1.1	Greenland	Scandinavia
Las Malvinas/ Falklands	12,000	0.4	South America	Europe
Jamaica	11,000	1.4	Central America	Haiti

Island biogeography is a powerful tool for examining species diversity in maritime settings. It is less useful for predicting the timing or direction of human dispersal. Examples are provided by the three island "giants" that are settled late and in several cases from directions that do not accord with the size/distance model. I have added two smaller islands in the Atlantic – the Falklands/Las Malvinas and Jamaica – where settlement history is also complex when viewed through the prism of proximity to source areas and size.

turn depended on hominin trends in brain size and mobility. And when it came to maritime dispersal, it was food production, rather than the pattern of island geography and advances in ship science (Box 8.1), that structured the process.

The Pacific

At the start of Terra 4, there was settlement around the Pacific on the margins of the major tectonic plates. Some of this settlement was ancient, as in the case of Near Oceania with the occupation of New Ireland 40ka (Chapter 6) and Okinawa Island south of the Japanese archipelago where skeletons from the Minotogawa Cave are dated between 16.6ka and 18.3ka

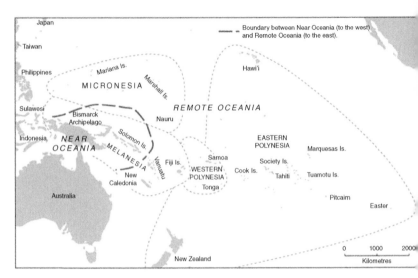

FIGURE 8.2. The target regions of the Pacific. The dashed line shows the division between Near and Remote Oceania. Adapted from Kirch (2002).

(Suzuki and Hanihara 1982). Other islands in the Pacific's fiery ring were settled more recently during Terra 3, as with the northern Aleutian Islands and the Californian Channel Islands (Chapter 7). But the rest of this vast ocean, 155 million km² in extent, was uninhabited 4ka.

It is not easy to define target areas within the Pacific. The small size of the islands in such a vast ocean makes it difficult to decide on the sequence of direction. Furthermore, the arrangement of the islands varies from those in archipelagos, such as the Hawai'ian chain and the Marianas, to distant isolates such as Pitcairn and Easter Island. Consequently, identifying islands as targets for dispersal is not appropriate. The solution is to break the ocean down into target zones. Traditionally these have been Micronesia, Melanesia and Polynesia, the small, black and many islands (Figure 8.2). Polynesia is further divided into a small western core centred on Tonga and Samoa, and a vast eastern expansion marked by the triangle of Hawai'i, Easter Island and New Zealand.

For the purposes of global settlement, this ocean geography can be simplified further into Near and Remote Oceania. The division between Near and Remote Oceania, first proposed by Roger Green, is based on archaeological evidence and the deep history of dispersal. The former wraps New Guinea together with its north-coast archipelagos and extends as far as the Solomon Islands to the east. The latter encompasses eastern Melanesia,

Micronesia and all of Polynesia.[1] Near and Remote Oceania were the targets and subsequently the source areas for Pacific dispersal. And beyond these ocean targets with their sprinkling of islands lie the continental targets of South America and, just possibly, Antarctica.

Distance and the Pacific are synonymous. The island of Manus in Near Oceania lies 4600 km from Samoa in the western part of Remote Oceania. Within the Polynesian core of Remote Oceania, we find Samoa, 1300 km from Tahiti to the east and 4100 km from Hawai'i in the north. New Zealand lies 2150 km from Australia and 1800 km from New Caledonia in Remote Oceania, while Easter Island is 1800 km distant from the nearest habitable island, Pitcairn, and 3700 km from South America.

Transported Landscapes and Making Your Niche

The distances seem daunting and the landfall returns small. But this judgement, with hindsight, is insufficient to account for the late dispersal of humans towards these various Pacific targets. Ocean-going vessels were needed (Figure 8.3). These are a prime example of a complex container fashioned as a social technology, designed to keep safe a cargo of men and women, crops and domestic animals, and launched with the purpose of geographical expansion through translocation. Drawing on the work of botanists, Kirch (2002: 109) has called this a "transported landscape". The package was varied. Not every food staple reached every island: either they were never stowed or they did not survive (Table 8.2). Furthermore, the archaeogenetics of coconuts, the fruit of the palm *Cocos nucifera*, reveals they were independently cultivated in two regions: (1) New Guinea–Sunda and (2) South India, Sri Lanka, the Maldives and the Laccadives. Furthermore, the traits, such as self-pollination, that point to earlier domestication are only found in a small subset of Pacific coconuts (Gunn, Baudouin and Olsen 2011). Fishing would have been an important activity both during a voyage and when establishing a new island community. But it would have needed the mixed economy of reef and land to ensure success, especially on the smaller islands (Valentin, Buckley, Herrscher et al. 2010).

[1] Near and Remote Oceania divides Melanesia. The main island chains in the former are the Bismarck Archipelago and the Solomon Islands. Remote Oceania comprises New Caledonia, Vanuatu, Fiji, Tonga and Samoa. Closer to Near Oceania are the Marianas, a volcanic string of fifteen islands that stretches for 750 km and is anchored in the south by Guam. These in turn lie above Palau in the Carolines and the Marshalls to the east. Together these form Micronesia (Rainbird 2004).

FIGURE 8.3. The vaka (canoe) Te-Au-O-Tonga, Mist of the South, photographed on Rarotonga in 2001. This 22-m-long double-hulled canoe was built in 1994 by Sir Tom Davis (1917–2007), former Prime Minister of the Cook Islands. He sailed it between many islands in Remote Oceania including New Zealand (Smith 2013). Te-Au-O-Tonga was badly damaged by cyclones in 2005 but has since been rebuilt by the Cook Island Voyaging Society. As Tom Davis described to me, the original Polynesian canoes were larger, up to 36 m, and could have carried 400 people. He championed the Cook Islands as the source for the settlement of New Zealand.

TABLE 8.2. *The package of major crops and animals found in the Pacific.*

Sunda and Asian domestic animals and commensals	Sunda crops	New Guinea crops	Pacific crops	South American crops
Pigs, dogs, chickens, rats	Coconut	Yams, taro, banana	Breadfruit, Polynesian chestnut, kava, sugarcane	Sweet potato, bottle gourd

The package is polythetic, membership based on some shared elements but not all elements in the set, because essential as they may seem, they do not occur throughout the Pacific. Among the animals, only the rat was introduced to New Zealand, while pigs were not widespread in the Micronesian region of Remote Oceania (Rainbird 2004:42). The polythetic nature of the package also emerges from the biogeography of species brought under cultivation. Breadfruit (*Artocarpus altilis*) is found in the wild in New Guinea and Sunda. It was domesticated in Near Oceania probably pre-Lapita, more than 3.5ka. In this region, the breadfruit have seeds, and these formed the method of their cultivation. But when this important starch staple was carried into Remote Oceania as part of the Lapita package, the mode of cultivation changed. The breadfruit became seedless relying for propagation on humans (Zerega, Ragone and Motley 2004). This change between seeds and seedless cultivation also applied to other crops, including bananas, taro, yam, sugarcane and kava.

Because the elements had to be shipped in a container, the term "transported landscape" is apt. But in the wider scheme of global settlement, it differs only in degree rather than function from those North American pioneers with their dogs and hunting skills or the arrival of humans in Europe festooned with beads and body ornaments (Chapter 7). All three are examples of the human capacity to construct niches for living in. Hominins had a similar competence, and in all cases, it stems from our distributed cognition and its capacity to create an extended mind (Chapter 1) – a feature of our evolutionary versatility (Chapter 2). As a result, the organism, in this case a human, and its environment are united rather than being separate entities. Combined, they influence the evolutionary development of each other (Odling-Smee 1993). You cannot understand the history of one without considering the other. Niche construction has been amplified by hominins and humans to cover a diverse range of environments from the savannahs to the suburbs. Transported landscapes are one example of our plasticity.

Boats, Crews, Navigation and Going Beyond

The voyaging canoes, the Polynesian vaka, were large in size and complex in construction. They were typically double hulled, of catamaran form and large enough, as reconstructions have shown, to transport people and landscapes (Figure 8.3). Their efficacy has been tested in two ways: by sailing reconstructions such as the 19-m-long Hokule'a from Hawai'i to Tahiti, and back again (Kirch 2002: 241–243), and by computer simulations that pit the canoes against currents and winds to calculate likely success and shipwreck (Irwin 1992).

As a result, all those involved in assessing Pacific seamanship are agreed that the majority of these voyages were purposeful. The motives behind them would have been various. They no doubt included pressure on land and islands closer to source, as well as a social system that rewarded discovery with prestige by founding new island polities. Keegan (2010: 18–20) identifies changes in social organisation as an essential ingredient in overcoming the increasing distance between islands in Remote Oceania. If societies in Near Oceania were matrilineal, then they faced problems in assembling the human resources needed to make long-distance settlement work. This was because men were scattered among the villages of their wives. Under such an arrangement, marriage distances had to be kept short, as men needed to keep in close contact with their clan village. But if, as they suggest, the social pattern changed to a patrilineal one, then this

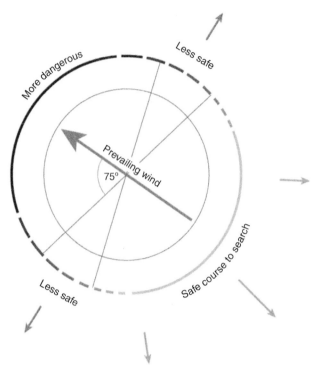

FIGURE 8.4. Strategies for sailing and returning home. Adapted from Irwin (1992: fig. 17).

scattering was resolved, and a retinue of males, who then took their wives with them, was created. Where you are allowed to live after marriage affects the possibility of dispersal (Table 3.10; Fix 1999). Recruiting a crew for long-distance voyages into Remote Oceania suddenly became easier.

The navigational skills are now well understood. In the first place, there is no longer any lingering doubt that the direction of expansion was from the west to the east. This is against the winds but makes good sense, as Irwin (1992: 56) has demonstrated, as the low-risk course of action. His survival sailing strategy is shown in Figure 8.4. In short, by sailing into the prevailing wind, the voyagers stood the best chance of returning. With a fair wind behind them, they demonstrate the intention that drove their voyaging for the simple reason that they wanted to find their way home.

Evidence for repeated voyaging after first settlement comes from a geological study of basalt adzes from nine of the Tuamotu atolls in Remote Oceania (Collerson and Weisler 2007) where such volcanic rocks are not found. Using isotope chemistry and trace element compositions, three of these can, with confidence, be sourced to the basalt-rich islands of Pitcairn and Rurutu in eastern Polynesia and Kaho'olawe in the Hawai'ian chain. Pitcairn lies 1600 km to the south-east of where its adze was found, while the Hawai'ian source is 4040 km to the north. Furthermore, the Tuamotu atolls lie at a voyaging crossroads in eastern Polynesia and were submerged until 1200 AD (Dickinson 2004: fig. 9). These stone adzes point to long-distance seafaring knowledge preserved over the long term. However, by the time of European contact in the eighteenth century, voyaging on this scale had not taken place for almost three centuries (Gamble 1993: 232.)

The second point is that they were not searching for single islands but rather for island arcs. The Marianas in the Micronesian part of Remote Oceania is a case in point. These fifteen islands are individually very small. However, when viewed as an inter-visible net of north–south-oriented volcanic peaks, spread over 750 km, the chance of hitting them as a target from a source in Near Oceania increases. The arcs of exploration suggested by Irwin (1992: 98) follow two simple rules: first, sail in the safest direction, which is into the wind (Figure 8.4); and second, previous voyages make the next one more ambitious. They went further because of what they had learned. The first rule sets an arc of safe exploration at 60°, while the second increases voyaging distance by 100 sea miles in an easterly direction. However, as Irwin (1992: fig. 39) shows, Hawai'i and New Zealand remain undiscovered by this method.

Social learning, and the transmission of that knowledge, formed a framework that fostered the skills of navigation. These have been examined more broadly as an example of our distributed cognition – the ability to reach out into the world in what has aptly been termed "cognition in the wild" (Hutchins 1995). Navigation was "taught" throughout the Pacific. It involved apprenticeships where knowledge was passed on by rote and memorised through the use of ephemeral artefacts such as star charts and stick maps.

The navigational skills were, Coward (2008) argues, first and foremost social skills. Associations between elements in the seascape were made around a framework of social relationships. The transmission of this cultural knowledge was a relational rather than a purely rational exercise of how to get from island A to island B. But its benefits were no less practical.

Most importantly, transmission of knowledge depended on that ability to go beyond which I examined in the last two chapters for expanding terrestrial settlement. In the case of the Pacific and its ocean-going vakas, we see the greatest change in hominin mobility since the development of endurance running (Chapter 4), and one matched only in Terra 4 by the domestication of the horse (Warmuth, Eriksson, Bower et al. 2012).

Going beyond is an imaginative accomplishment of the human mind. It navigates between and around relationships when people are not in face-to-face contact. It appreciates the importance of objects as signs and metaphors for governing social life. It brings the ancestors into the theatre of the living and plans a future for the unborn. The stick maps used by Pacific voyagers traced geographical relationships across a populated ocean using a social idiom. They were connected through FACE (Chapter 1), enchained by gifts such as shell armbands and obsidian that were accumulated and consumed and, on occasion, fragmented for further distribution between social partners. The outcome of these social practices that involved cultural stuff was the reproduction and maintenance of social relations at a distance. In this instance, the maps may not survive, but other evidence in the form of inter-island obsidian exchange does (Summerhayes 2009).

Direction of Dispersal

Humans dispersed into the Pacific from west to east, against the prevailing winds and currents. This long-standing archaeological pattern has been confirmed by archaeogenetics using mtDNA and MSY data to construct phylogeographies. Mitochondrial haplogroup B, and its associated sub-clades, are found throughout the Pacific, as well as in Madagascar in the Indian Ocean (Forster 2004: fig. 2). It originated in island Southeast Asia, and although haplogroup B is found throughout the Americas, it does not appear in its distinctive Polynesian motif.

The first targets comprised the islands to the east of those in Near Oceania that were settled in the Pleistocene (Chapter 6) and Micronesia in Remote Oceania. There are two candidates for a source area. The first is Taiwan where the evidence takes two forms: language and farming. Taiwan is regarded as the likely homeland where people speaking Austronesian, one of the world's major language families, arose. Austronesian is the root for the 450 distinct languages found throughout all the regions of Near and Remote Oceania (Kirch 2002: 6 and map 2), a diversity expected on the grounds of ecology (Figure 3.7) and founder effect. The second line of evidence supporting Taiwan is its archaeological data for early farming. Without farming, as Spriggs (2000) points out, there can be no sustained settlement across the Pacific. Fishing plays an important role, but the land resources are the key to settlement. On Taiwan, rice and foxtail millet are dated to 5.5–4ka in small settlements excavated around the coast of the island. These sites also contain pottery, spindle whorls and bark cloth beaters (Bellwood 2005: 134–136). The island was Austronesian speaking until Chinese settlement began in the seventeenth century. Supporters of the Taiwan source (Bellwood 2005) suggest that a farming package rapidly dispersed from here through the Philippines and then into the target of Near Oceania where, as we shall see, it was transformed into an archaeological B-List entity known as Lapita. The Taiwan source-target model also calls on mtDNA evidence in what is described as a Polynesian motif. This is associated with Austronesian-speaking populations in the Pacific and is thought to indicate rapid dispersal from Taiwan into the Pacific soon after 4ka.

However, the picture of a dispersal package that combined a common language, economic staples and material culture becomes more complicated when we add New Guinea to the mix. Here, Austronesian is not spoken, and New Guinea was a domestication centre for yam (*Dioscorea alata*), taro and banana – three food staples that, unlike millet and rice, were taken into Oceania (Table 8.2). Furthermore, the archaeogenetics of Southeast Asia are complex due to their high diversity. This stems from successive population displacements as well as many indigenous clades (Hill, Soares, Mormina et al. 2007). Complete mtDNA genomes now show that these maternal lineages were established much earlier in Near Oceania and in particular in the Bismarck Archipelago, first settled in the Pleistocene (Chapter 6). This happened more than 8ka molecular years ago (Soares, Rito, Trejaut et al. 2011) and well before early farming on Taiwan. The Polynesian genetic motif has a molecular age of more than 6ka. Rather than a made-in-Taiwan package of farming, language and people dispersing from this northern centre, the archaeogenetic data suggest that a long-term voyaging corridor existed between island Southeast Asia and Near Oceania.

This voyaging corridor can be traced through the archaeogenetics of pigs, a domesticate that is found in many areas of the Pacific as a result of human dispersal. Two clades have been recognised among modern pig populations (Figure 8.5; Larson, Cucchi, Fujita et al. 2007). The most widespread is the Pacific clade that extends into the Pacific from island Southeast Asia. The smaller area covered by East Asian haplotypes extends from mainland China across Taiwan and into Remote Oceania as far as Micronesia. On balance, the archaeogenetics of pigs supports Taiwan as a source area for the target of Micronesia and the southern voyaging corridor as the source for the target of Near and then eastern Remote Oceania. The two regions are distinguished archaeologically, and Micronesia was settled first (Rainbird 2004).

Determining direction beyond Micronesia and western Polynesia and for the rest of remote Oceania is difficult, apart from recognising a

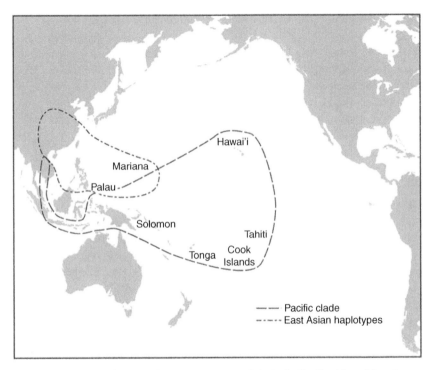

FIGURE 8.5. The two archaeogenetic groups of pigs in the Pacific. Adapted from Larson et al. (2007).

predominantly west to east orientation. There is, in addition, evidence for Polynesian voyagers who followed this direction and reached the target of South America. They then sailed back into the Pacific (Lawler 2010). It has long been recognised that contact was made in deep history since the South American sweet potato (*Ipomoea batatas*) was brought back into the Pacific where it has a wide distribution (Montenegro, Avis and Weaver 2008). The bottle gourd (*Lagenaria*), which we last encountered in Terra 3 being carried from Asia into the Americas (Chapter 7), continued its remarkable journey as it too was transported into the Pacific (Kirch 2002: 241).

This pattern has now been complemented by two archaeogenetic studies. The first concerns the discovery at the site of El Arenal-1, located 3 km inland in south-central Chile, of fifty Polynesian chicken bones that add up to at least five birds (Storey, Ramirez, Quiroz et al. 2007). One of these has been dated by radiocarbon to 0.6ka and is therefore older than the arrival of Europeans in either South America or the Pacific. Moreover, the DNA from these Chilean chickens indisputably confirms their Polynesian origin.

They compare closely with much older archaeological specimens found in Tonga and Samoa and to those from the 3ka-year-old Lapita site of Teouma excavated on Vanuatu.

Additional archaeogenetic information on humans comes from Easter Island. Previous studies of the islanders' mtDNA and MSY revealed no South American genes. However, a study of HLA genes in the immune system of the islanders does (Storey, Spriggs, Bedford et al. 2010: fig. 4). This shows that Polynesian voyaging reached the coast of South America, mating took place and some descendants returned to Easter Island. When this took place is not clear but, like the Polynesian chicken, before Europeans arrived in South America.

Finally, the direction of Polynesian voyaging may also have been in a southerly direction. Preserved in the oral histories of New Zealand is a tantalising reference to cold oceans and what might have been icebergs. If substantiated, this points to a southern voyage towards Antarctica that unsurprisingly left no archaeological evidence.

Timing and Frequency of Dispersals

What is not at issue in the settlement of the initial target beyond Near Oceania is its association with a strong archaeological signature known as Lapita. This complex meets the criteria outlined in Box 6.2. It is defined through highly decorated red pottery and where the dentate impressions are strongly related to body tattoos. This pottery is very different from earlier red-slip wares that can be traced through Southeast Asia and Taiwan. The oldest Lapita sites are found in Near Oceania 3.5–3.4ka. This pottery is then found in Remote Oceania at sites such as Sigatoka on Fiji and Teouma on Vanuatu. Along with the pottery are found some twenty-eight plant and animal species, including pigs, chickens, dogs, yams, taro and a wide range of other horticultural domesticates. These form an example of Kirch's transported landscape (Thorsby 2012). Burials are also common (Kirch 2002: 109). The importance of fishing in the Lapita, and indeed all Pacific dispersals, also needs emphasising (Petchey, Spriggs, Leach et al. 2011).

The subsequent history of Lapita is interesting. By 2.7ka, the pottery is at best minimally but mostly undecorated. Tonga and Samoa in the western Polynesia part of Remote Oceania represent the eastern limits of the Lapita dispersal. Subsequently in these islands, but not in Fiji to the west, the art of pottery making was lost 2ka, possibly as culinary techniques changed (Kirch 2002: 220–222).

TABLE 8.3. *The earliest settlement of the points of the Polynesian triangle in Remote Oceania and evidence for voyaging that reached Chile.*

	Age range of earliest settlement (ka)	Likeliest age (AD)	
Hawai'i	1.6–0.7	1000–1200	Kirch (2002)
New Zealand	1–0.45	~1280	Wilmshurst et al. (2008)
Easter Island	1.6–0.6	1200	Hunt and Lipo (2006)
Chile		1400	Storey et al. (2007)

It is, however, in this region of western Polynesia where Polynesians, as Groube (1971) argued, "became" as opposed to coming from somewhere else. Fiji–Samoa–Tonga was the source area for the later settlement of the targets of Hawai'i, New Zealand, Easter Island and South America. These three points in Remote Oceania were settled late, only 800 years ago (Table 8.3).

By contrast, the settlement of Micronesia in the western part of Remote Oceania occurred independently of Lapita and predated it (Rainbird 2004). The island of Palau and the arc of the Marianas have archaeological sites with crops and pottery that date between 4.5ka and 3.5ka. Taiwan makes a credible source area. In eastern Micronesia, the Marshall Islands formed a further target area and were settled later between 2.5ka and 2ka (Rainbird 2004). This was well ahead of the Polynesian dispersal into eastern Remote Oceania.

The Tempo of These Dispersals

Lapita set a brisk tempo for dispersal. In 200–300 years, islands over a distance of 4500 km were settled (Kirch 2002: 96). This took between fifteen and twenty-five generations, and set a dispersal rate of between 15 and 23 km per annum. This speed has been described as an express train from Taiwan to Polynesia (Diamond and Bellwood 2003). Others disagree (S. Oppenheimer 2004: 598), maintaining that some of the passengers who should have been on the train missed it. They point to a lack of concordance between the evidence from language, the age of rice agriculture and its non-association with red-slip pottery, the lack of skeletal evidence for displacement in those islands settled in Terra 3 and the fact that the domesticates transported into the Pacific came from New Guinea, Indonesia and Southeast Asia rather than China and Taiwan.

What is less in doubt is that following the Lapita expansion, there was a pause in the further settlement of Remote Oceania. This amounted to almost 1600 years, although the dating is sometimes confused as across the Marquesas (Kirch 2002: 232). Irwin (1992: 73) disagrees, writing that "the West Polynesian pause was a time trap set by latter-day theorists of culture change for the ancestors of the Polynesians, but has not held them very well". He shows that this was largely an argument constructed by linguists who wanted a long pause so that the languages could catch up and diversify before being sent into the remote Pacific. It is also the case that on many of the island groups nearer to West Polynesia, the Cooks for example, archaeological fieldwork has not proceeded at the same pace as elsewhere. It has to be remembered that before the Lapita Homeland Project in the 1980s (J. Allen and Gosden 1991), no one imagined there would be Pleistocene-aged sites in the Bismarck Archipelago or Solomon Islands (Spriggs 2000) of Near Oceania. However, while the long pause can be challenged, there still remains a shorter pause, possibly of 1ka duration and, as Table 8.3 shows, the best estimate when the points in the Pacific triangle and South America were settled is more recent still.

A purge of unreliable radiocarbon dates on Easter Island (Hunt and Lipo 2006) has narrowed the age of the first settlement to about 1200 AD, and the early evidence from Hawai'i gives comparable ages. These dates point to rapid ocean dispersal in three different directions, a rate difficult to calculate because the ages and the source areas are unknown. However, it might have been similar to the earlier Lapita dispersal.

New Zealand is a case in point. The island has been a focus for archaeological enquiry, and sites earlier than 1ka do not exist. Competing chronologies have been tested by direct dating of the commensal Pacific rat (*Rattus exulans*) that came with the first voyages (Wilmshurst, Anderson, Higham et al. 2008). This was a species that left its own archaeological record in the form of distinctively gnawed seeds. When these are dated by radiocarbon and compared with similar direct dates on rat bones, the chronology of their arrival, and by inference that of humans, becomes sharper. From these dates, it is possible to say that the rat was introduced to both the North and South Island c. 1280 AD. The impact of the rat on the moas – large flightless birds who laid their eggs on the ground – was devastating. It was matched only by human slaughter of the moas, as recorded by plentiful archaeological evidence (A. Anderson 1989). Among the larger flightless birds of New Zealand, only the kiwi survived. At least eleven moa species became extinct, their bones frequently found in moa ovens where they were cooked. Moas ranged in size from 20 to 200 kg, and the largest *Diornis giganteus* might have reached 3.5 m in height. Such devastation of Pacific Island birdlife was a feature of maritime dispersals (Flannery and White

1991; Kirch 2002: 61). On Easter Island, only one species of seabird survives from among twenty-five that lived there before humans arrived. No land birds are found today, and possibly six were originally present (Steadman, Vargas and Cristino 1994). This historical dimension needs to be taken into account in the study of island biodiversity (Box 8.1).

African Islands

The islands of Africa are found in three oceans: the Mediterranean, Indian and Atlantic. Two very different patterns emerge. In the Mediterranean, there is abundant evidence of settlement in the Late Pleistocene on Cyprus and Early Holocene visits to Melos by FGH, while much older, Terra 2 occupation on Crete has been claimed (Strasser, Panagopoulou, Runnels et al. 2010; Strasser, Runnels, Wegmann et al. 2011). The majority of settlement followed farming with a further settlement pulse during the Bronze Age of Terra 4 (Cherry 1981, 1990). The evidence points to the direction of settlement coming from the closer European shore – some support for island biogeography (Table 8.4).

By contrast, the islands of the Indian and Atlantic oceans, as reviewed by Mitchell (2004), were all settled much later during Terra 4 (Table 8.4). According to Keegan and Diamond (1987), this is because of their configuration and where maritime skills went unrewarded with significant landfall. As a result, voyaging was not encouraged. However, the limitations of applying an island biogeographic approach are apparent when we consider Madagascar. This large island lies 400 km from the coast of Africa, 300 km from the Comoros Islands which provide stepping stones to its north tip and 5600 km from the islands of Indonesia. The Madagascan flora and its distinctive fauna of lemurs, several of them giant species, and the extinct large flightless birds, *Aepyornis*, point to a very ancient isolation from Africa (Burney, Burney, Godfrey et al. 2004). However, given that Terra 2 hominins and Terra 3 humans are known from Africa, the late settlement of Madagascar, when viewed as an exercise in biogeographical distance, seems anomalous.

Claims for the earliest settlement rely on cut marks on an arm bone of the extinct sloth lemur (*Palaeopropithecus ingens*) and the appearance of *Cannabis*, an introduced species, in the pollen record. This took place 2.3ka (Burney, Burney, Godfrey et al. 2004). These two proxies do not constitute decisive proof. However, if substantiated by discovering stone artefacts alongside the megafauna bones, the likely source area is thought to

TABLE 8.4. *Terra 4 islands of Africa (Broodbank 2009; Cherry 1990; Mitchell 2004: table 1).*

	Distance from Africa (km)	Area (km²)	First settlement (ka)	Source region	Evidence
Indian Ocean					
Socotra Archipelago	100–250	3796	2.5?	Arabia	Archaeological, archaeogenetic
Comoros Archipelago (Njazidja, Mwali, Nzwani, Mayotte)	300–500	2025	1.2	Indonesia	Archaeological, linguistic
Madagascar	400	587,713	2.5? Africans 1.4–0.8 Austronesians	Africa initially but predominantly Indonesia	Archaeogenetic, linguistic, archaeological
Atlantic Ocean					
Canary Islands	90	7275	~2.5?	Africa	Archaeological, archaeogenetic
Mediterranean					
Eastern					
Cyprus	440	9251	12 FGH 10.2 Farmers	Southwest Asia	Archaeological
Crete	350	8259	130? FGH 9 Farmers	Europe	Archaeological
Malta	260	316	7.2 Farmers	Europe	Archaeological
Western					
Sardinia	220	24,090	11–10 FGH 8.9 Farmers	Europe	Archaeological
Mallorca	310	3640	7.5–6.6 Farmers	Europe	Archaeological

Only the Mediterranean islands nearest to Africa are shown. In all cases, they are closer to the shores of either Europe or Southwest Asia. All of these islands are settled in Terra 3; and evidence on Crete now suggests Terra 2 (Chapter 5). The larger Mediterranean islands were generally first settled by FGH. These may have been intermittent occupations founded on fishing and obtaining obsidian. All the African islands were first settled by farmers.

be Africa.[2] Unlike New Zealand with its moa ovens full of moa bones, Madagascar has no direct evidence for the human extirpation of its island giants. These included the elephant bird, *Aepyornis maximus*, 3 m tall, weighing an impressive 450 kg and hatched from an 11 L capacity egg (Parker-Pearson 2010). However, the last 1.8ka did witness a catastrophic extinction event that saw the demise of at least seventeen species of large lemurs, some of them the size of gorillas, flightless birds, hippos and giant tortoises (Burney, Burney, Godfrey et al. 2004: 26). The causes were multiple, and one of them was the arrival and subsequent population growth of humans.

Reliable settlement evidence has recently been excavated in the south of the island and consists of pottery known as triangular incised ware, a decorative motif found in East Africa and radiocarbon dated 1.4–1ka (Parker-Pearson 2010: 99). In the same part of the island, this settlement was then followed by another African, Swahili, enclave that lasted 300 years and ended in 1300 AD.

This archaeological evidence for an African source is, however, overwhelmed by linguistic and archaeogenetic evidence pointing to an Indonesian homeland for the Malagasy. The majority of Malagasy vocabulary can be traced to an isolated language, Ma'anyan, in south-east Borneo, while archaeogenetically the MSY and mtDNA data point to a Sunda source in island Southeast Asia. A coalescent study estimates a founding population of approximately thirty women and a molecular age of 1200 AD for settlement (Cox, Nelson, Tumonggor et al. 2012). In short, Malagasy speak an Austronesian language, and their archaeogenetics have a variant of the Polynesian motif derived from mtDNA haplogroup B (Forster 2004). Further evidence for a predominantly east–west direction of dispersal comes from studying the archaeogenetics of the coconut. This shows that the Indonesian voyagers brought their Polynesian coconuts with them (Figure 8.6). Before they reached Madagascar, these coconuts had been cross-fertilised with those from the other region where their domestication took place – Southern India and Sri Lanka (Gunn, Baudouin and Olsen 2011).

The settlement of such a large island was undoubtedly more complex than currently appreciated. I prefer the short chronology of 1.4–0.8ka with sources from both west and east, Africa and Indonesia. Whether this was purposeful voyaging, involved repeated settlement waves and was driven by maritime empires such as Srivijaya in Java, Sumatra and Malaysia is something for future research to unravel (Cox, Nelson, Tumonggor et al.

---

[2] Madagascar lacks any evidence for stone tools (Burney, Burney, Godfrey et al. 2004: 32).

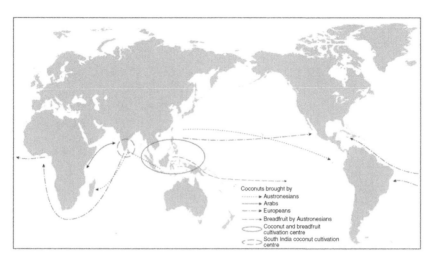

FIGURE 8.6. The movement of coconuts and breadfruit as a result of voyaging. Both these domesticates have an origin in the Sunda region, while a second, independent centre for coconut production was in South India and Sri Lanka. Adapted from Gunn et al. (2011) and Zerega et al. (2004).

2012). Additional support for a short chronology comes from the Comoros Islands which were also settled late in the eighth century AD (Table 8.4). To the east of Madagascar, the island of Mauritius, home of another distinctive flightless bird, the Dodo, was a Terra 5 settlement in 1638 AD. Its European discovery was quickly followed by those of the islands of Réunion and Rodrigues. Computer simulations of east–west voyaging tracks across the Indian Ocean (Figure 8.7) suggest a reason for such late settlement. These show that sailing with the wind has a high probability of hitting the target of northern Madagascar while missing Mauritius and Réunion (Fitzpatrick and Callaghan 2008).

Further evidence for the Terra 4 settlement of the Indian Ocean comes from Socotra, 250 km from the Horn of Africa. This large archipelogo, 3796 km², was first settled possibly 2.5ka ago, while the archaeogenetics indicates an Arabian source (Cerny, Pereira, Kujanova et al. 2008). These Arabian dispersals which led to ports of trade down the east coast of Africa did not lead to settlement on Madagascar or the Comoros.

With one exception, the islands of the Atlantic close to Africa reveal a similar late story of settlement. That exception is the Canary Islands. This archipelago is 90 km distant from Africa and was probably settled 2.5ka. The source area for this target is North Africa (Mitchell 2004). All the other African islands in the Atlantic are Terra 5 settlements (Chapter 9).

(a)
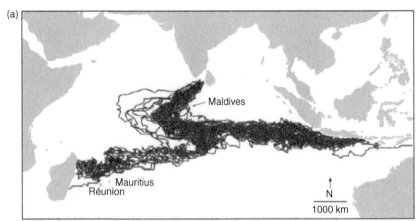

(b)
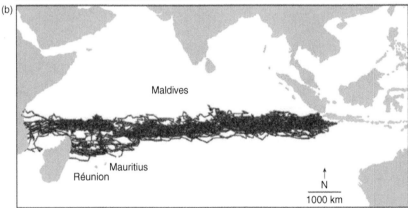

FIGURE 8.7. Computer simulations using wind and currents of the likely voyaging tracks from Indonesia across the Indian Ocean, a distance of 11,000 km. These two examples are at different times of the year and under different sailing strategies. In the top chart, the boats sail downwind, the line of least resistance. Sailing downwind, they never reached Madagascar, but did make landfall at Sri Lanka in about forty days. From here, in January, they did reach Madagascar in eighty-one days. The return was seasonally controlled. Between August and April, they were blown back to the island. In the lower chart, the voyagers were given greater skills, among them sailing to windward and with the intention of reaching Madagascar in an average of 152 days. As a result, the track is tighter, but in both simulations, the islands of Mauritius and Réunion are missed. Adapted from Fitzpatrick and Callaghan (2008: figs. 2 and 3).

The late, Terra 4, settlement of the African islands confirms the point about purposeful voyaging that was made so forcefully by the evidence from the Pacific. Around Africa, there are low-latitude islands, yet few of them were settled from this continental source, even though agriculture was available (Table 8.1). Because of the distances involved and the time available, chance discovery by ocean drifting might be expected as an example of unintentional dispersal. Instead, these islands were settled as the result of intentional voyaging either from Sunda or from Europe and as a result received a wide array of domesticates.

The Atlantic Islands

When compared to the riches of the Pacific and Indian oceans, the poverty of islands in the Atlantic is striking. There are a few volcanic islands scattered along the length of the Mid-Atlantic Ridge – the Azores, Ascencion and Tristan da Cunha – but these were all settled from Europe in Terra 5 (Chapter 9). The Terra 4 islands are confined to the Caribbean, Bahamas, Iceland, the Faeroes and the Shetlands.

Caribbean

The deep history of the Caribbean has been dominated by the idea that archaeological evidence provides a strong signal of human dispersal (Box 6.2). This is most clearly seen in the work of archaeologist Irving Rouse (1986). He divided the archaeology of the region into four A-List ages and interpreted them as evidence for successive human migrations. In ascending order, these ages were Lithic, Archaic, Ceramic and Historic (Rouse and Allaire 1978). Each age had its archaeological marker: chipped stone in the Lithic, shell and ground-stone tools such as axes in the Archaic and pots in the Ceramic. These ages were then peopled by successive series of artefacts, equivalent to B-List entities (Table 2.7), Ortoiroid, Saladoid and several more.

With the advent of detailed archaeological work on many of the Caribbean islands, and in particular a radiocarbon chronology that has overcome the challenges of accurately dating shell,[3] this scheme has been challenged. Instead, it is possible to examine the configuration of the islands and ask questions about direction, frequency and tempo of human dispersals.

Direction and Frequency of Dispersals

The long arc of volcanic Caribbean islands comprises two major targets for settlement (Figure 8.8). The first target consists of the Greater Antilles:

[3] This is because of the reservoir effect where carbon is stored in seawater and hence affects the radiocarbon age of shellfish.

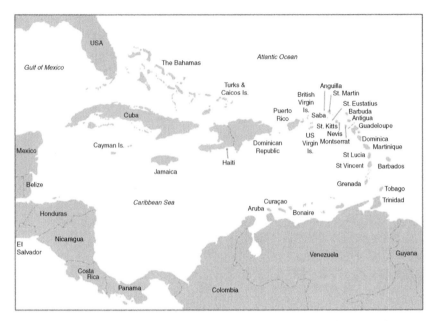

FIGURE 8.8. The target regions of the Caribbean. The line to the south of Antigua marks the Guadeloupe passage in the Lesser Antilles.

Cuba, Haiti–Dominican Republic, Puerto Rico and Jamaica. The islands in the second target are differentiated by their size and configuration in a north–south arc to the east of Puerto Rico. The Lesser Antilles begin with the Virgin Islands, and form a necklace of small inter-visible islands stretching over a distance of 1000 km. The chain is commonly divided into two groups: the northern Leeward and the southern Windward Islands. The southernmost of these, Grenada, is not visible from the South American coastal islands of Trinidad and Tobago, a distance of 150 km. Halfway along the Lesser Antillean chain is the Guadeloupe passage that lies to the north of that island and which marks a significant settlement boundary (Callaghan 2010).

Four dispersal directions are possible. The shortest distances into the target of the Greater Antilles are either from Florida in the north or the Yucatán in the west, while the shortest route into the Windwards is from South America. The long route to either the Greater or Lesser Antilles could have come from anywhere along the coast between Venezuela and Honduras (Keegan 2012: fig. 2). Anyone setting off from this coast would have made landfall somewhere on the island arc in a few days.

According to Rouse, the Greater Antilles were initially settled from west to east, with which most archaeologists agree, and the Lesser Antilles from south to north, which is disputed. In both cases, the earliest settlement was by FGH. The sites consist of small scatters of chipped stone and later some ground-stone axes, bowls and pendants, as well as adzes fashioned from shell (Keegan 1994; Wilson 2007). They are usually found in coastal locations, and the economic evidence points to the importance of fishing within the reefs and catching the large land crabs that used to live on these islands in great numbers. Sea mammals like the dugong and amphibians such as turtles were also caught. What was lacking were sufficient carbohydrate resources, roots and tubers on the smaller islands, and as a result, settlement was most probably seasonal, or intermittent, rather than permanent. Occupation stuck to the coast because the interiors had few foods, and the tropical vegetation was extremely dense. However, in a pattern reminiscent of the FGH visits to Melos in the Aegean Sea, the island of Antigua was a source of good-quality chert for making chipped stone tools. These distinctive stones are found on several other islands (Wilson 2007).

This pattern of early settlement may be an artefact of sea-level rise. At times of low sea level during the Late Pleistocene and Early Holocene, many of the islands were joined (Figure 3.4). However, there is very little evidence that any significant occupation took place before present sea levels were reached about 6ka, as recorded in the coral reefs of Barbados. It is highly probable that the pattern of itinerant coastal settlement described above has a much older antiquity and the data are simply submerged. Before 6ka, which coincides with the oldest lithic-based sites in the Greater Antilles, it was not so much a case of island hopping as beachcombing.[4] Trinidad, which at 8ka has the earliest dates for any Caribbean island, is a false island, much like Sicily in the Mediterranean, in that it was joined by lower sea levels to the South American mainland until very recently.

These lithic-evidence settlements are earliest in the Greater Antilles (Table 8.5), with the exception of Jamaica (Allsworth-Jones 2008; Callaghan 2008). The archaeological evidence points to a source from the Yucatán (Keegan 2010), while an ancient mtDNA study of FGH skeletons from Cuba indicated more than one source area (Lalueza-Fox, Gilbert, Martinez-Fuentes et al. 2003).

---

[4] Searching the raised beaches of islands such as Barbados might be one way to test this model.

TABLE 8.5. *Radiocarbon ages for the settlement of the Caribbean*

	Area (km²)	First settlement (ka)
Greater Antilles		
Cuba	110,922	6.3–5.8
Haiti–Dominican Republic	76,484	5.6
Puerto Rico	8,897	5.5–4.6
Jamaica	11,424	1.4
Lesser Antilles		
Leeward Islands		
Anguilla	88	3.6–3.2
St Martin	34	4.4–3.4
Saba	13	3.7–3.5
St Eustatius	21	2.4–2.2
St Kitts	176	4.1
Nevis	130	2.5
Montserrat	84	2.5–2.3
Barbuda	161	3.9–3.3
Antigua	280	4.2
Guadeloupe	1702	3–2
Martinique	1090	2.6
Windward Islands		
Dominica	790	3–2
St Lucia	603	
St Vincent	389	
Grenada	345	
Barbados	440	4.3
Trinidad	4828	8

There were undoubtedly frequent dispersals into both the Greater and Lesser Antilles. Sometimes these would have been continuous, while others followed the leapfrog pattern as opportunities for FGH fluctuated between the pearls on the string (Figure 2.9). One indication of this variety comes from considering the Guadeloupe passage as a settlement barrier. This approximates to the division between the Leeward and Windward Islands, as recognised by European sailors.

Sites with no ceramics, equivalent to the Lithic and Archaic ages in Rouse's scheme, are well known on all the islands to the north of this sea passage (Keegan 1994). Antigua, which has been intensively studied, has more than fifty, some of them considerable in terms of size and number. By comparison, very few sites have been found south of the Guadeloupe passage, and when they are, it tends to be a few or even a single artefact such as a shell adze made of queen conch from Barbados (Callaghan 2010: 145; Fitzpatrick 2011). These artefacts are interpreted as an FGH lifestyle with the emphasis on fishing. As discussed by Callaghan (2010), there are no particular currents or wind patterns that explain this settlement pattern, although volcanic activity was greater in the Windward Islands, and this might have led to their avoidance.

However, the direction of earliest settlement is reminiscent of the Aleutian Islands (Chapter 7) where it proceeded from east to west and paused in the middle of the chain. This suggests that settlement depended on direction and connection. The further along the chain the dispersal went, the higher the costs became to maintain regular contact with the parent population. In this case, that source was the Greater Antilles, and its satellites only extended so far down the chain. Further dispersal was not limited by boats and seamanship but by the need to make extended FGH networks work in a maritime setting with no farming and low population density.

Tempo of Dispersals

Island inter-visibility and a deep history of FGH settlement still led to pauses in later dispersals. The major change came with the introduction of horticulture. This solved the carbohydrate problem on small islands, facilitated permanent and larger settlements and led to a reduction in the dependence on the sea. The key domestic staple was the carbohydrate-rich cassava, a root crop also known as manioc, tapioca, mandioca and yuca, that was domesticated in Brazil along the southern border of the Amazon Basin (Box 8.2; Newsom and Wing 2004). Manioc was grated to produce flour and then baked on large flat ceramic griddles often more than 1 m in diameter. These are a distinctive feature of the archaeological evidence, as are the other painted white-on-red ceramics. They are known collectively by their B-List name, Saladoid. A dispersal from the Orinoco Basin up the chain of the Lesser Antilles seems the most likely direction and is confirmed by an ancient mtDNA study of skeletons from a Historic Age site in the Dominican Republic (Lalueza-Fox, Calderón, Calafell et al. 2001). This dispersal was accompanied by population displacement, as indicated by the absence of those common Central American haplogroups A and B.

Box 8.2. Caribbean farming and fishing

The simplistic equation that sites with no ceramics subsisted on fishing, gathering and hunting has to be tempered by the archaeological evidence for diet (Keegan 1994; Newsom 1993; Wing 2001). Inhabitants of Archaic sites, those with ground-stone axes and shell adzes cultivated fruit-bearing trees and some root crops. But they made their living principally from fish, shellfish and land crabs, as recorded in coastal food middens on many islands (Newsom and Wing 2004).

Native animals were scarce throughout the Caribbean. Only the extinct rice rat was found on all the islands where it was used as food (Turvey, Weksler, Morris et al. 2010). Another extinct small rodent, the hutia, and an insectivore were transported from the Greater to the northern Lesser Antilles (Wing 2001: 114). Guinea pigs (*Cavia*), a South American domesticate, were introduced probably with the appearance of cassava. Dogs are occasionally found. Cassava appears in pollen records in Belize 4.5ka and has been found in archaeological sites in Puerto Rico between 3.3ka and 2.9ka (Zeder, Emshwiller, Smith et al. 2006). It needs a specialised ceramic technology of large flat griddles to cook it.

The Saladoid package of ceramics and cassava appeared in Jamaica 1.4ka. Cassava was the most important crop followed by sweet potato, while other cultivated tubers included yam, cocoyam, arrowroot and achira, all of which are South American in origin (Allsworth-Jones 2008: 58). Squashes in the form of pumpkins were widely found, as were the legumes – peanuts, lima, jack and common beans and varieties of chilli peppers (*Capsicum*). Cereals such as maize were relatively unimportant throughout the Caribbean.

Wing (2001) has shown how the larger and more permanent island populations, which resulted from the introduction of manioc and Saladoid ceramics, led to changes in the animal faunas. The abundant land crabs, once so important for the diet, declined in size and number. In the same way, the West Indian topsnail, the most utilised mollusc, also declined. During the 1.5ka of Ceramic sites, there is also evidence for more intensive fishing. The large reef predators, groupers and snappers were susceptible to overfishing, and their size and numbers declined markedly. These were the easy pickings, as their aggressive behaviour means they take a baited hook more easily than the reef herbivores. They are also larger. The long-term result was a decline in the trophic level of fish now taken by people in the Lesser Antilles (Figure Box 8.2) and a less sustainable lifestyle.

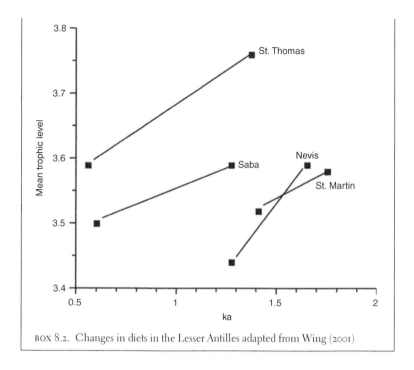

BOX 8.2. Changes in diets in the Lesser Antilles adapted from Wing (2001)

The tempo of this later, farming-led dispersal is marked by significant pauses (Keegan 2010: 17). Saladoid sites, supported by manioc, appear on Puerto Rico by 3ka and then paused for more than a millennium until horticulture passed into the next island to the west, the Dominican Republic, where it appeared 1.5ka. At the same time, Jamaica was first settled (Allsworth-Jones 2008).

This tempo for a farming dispersal challenges the demographic model of social learning and cultural transmission (Chapter 3). Put simply, the larger the population, the greater the chance of innovation in the form of new stuff and techniques (Shennan 2000). Therefore, it might be expected, given the larger populations that must have lived on the Greater Antilles, that the dispersal of horticulture would have accelerated as it approached ever-larger islands. Like a force of gravity, the larger the population, the stronger the pull and the acceptance of a new way of life. But in the Caribbean, this does not seem to have been the case. In particular, it was not the case on Jamaica that was settled later than its neighbours about 1.4ka and at a time when the Bahamas to the north-east of Cuba were also first visited (Allsworth-Jones 2008; Keegan 2012). Jamaica missed out entirely on a pre-horticulture phase, and by doing so underlines the contingent character of deep history by not conforming, when it comes to island occupation, to the predictions of biogeography (Box 8.1).

Iceland and Beyond

Terra 4 is almost complete. The final seascape to consider is the North Atlantic and the settlement of the Shetlands, Faeroes and Iceland. The first two archipelagos are 300 km apart, and there are a further 800 km between the Faeroes and Iceland to the west. Between them, they span latitudes 60–66°N.

These subarctic habitats were first settled by Norsemen coming either from Norway, Britain or Ireland. This was a farming-led dispersal which in all three instances encountered unoccupied lands. In the case of Iceland, they sailed into the wind, and there is no doubt from the sagas[5] that the voyages were purposeful. Settlement and trade were in the minds of the Vikings. They arrived just after a volcanic eruption covered much of Iceland in ash that has been precisely dated to 871 AD. Such precision is possible because the ash is found in the Greenland ice cores where the annual layers can be counted like tree rings. This "settlement ash" is overlaid by archaeological evidence for farms and fields. By 930 AD, the population of the island is estimated at between 10,000 and 20,000 people (G. Sigurdsson 2008; J. V. Sigurdsson 2008). What they brought with them were the European animals, horse, cattle, sheep, goat and pig whose secondary products of milk and blood formed a key staple, while the hides and wool were also valued. Agriculture was possible and used short growing season crops such as barley and oats, while seals, seabirds and fish were important for their diet as they were on the Faeroes (Buckland 2008).

The Greenland ice cores are also an archive of climate records contained in the ratio of different oxygen isotopes. These show that Iceland was settled during a cold phase but that the voyage in 985–986 AD by Eiríkr the Red to Greenland took place when the climate was warmer – a case of the weather report deciding the island's name. On Greenland, the Norse settlers encountered Inuit, who had arrived in Terra 3, but did not displace them. Their interest was in trade goods, walrus ivory and furs, and as we saw in Chapter 7, the arrival of the Norse triggered the rapid Inuit Thule

---

[5] There are three main sources: the Book of the Icelanders, the Book of Settlement and the sagas of Icelanders. These transcribed an oral tradition and refer to events that had taken place 400 years before.

migration from Alaska to north Greenland. In one of the first intercontinental human reunions, the sneering Norse opinion of the Inuit is recorded, characteristic of many colonial encounters to come. The sagas refer to the Inuit as *Skraelings*, weaklings wearing skins, a people to be exploited by beef-fed, wool-clad Norsemen.

The Greenland settlement amounted to no more than 400–500 people (Wallace 2008: 610). As in Iceland, marine mammals and fish were a key to survival, as well as trade and provisions from Iceland. The sagas record that "the Greenlanders did not know of bread" (Buckland 2008: 598). The Vikings continued their westerly dispersal to establish about 1ka the settlement of L'Anse-aux-Meadows on the northern tip of Newfoundland, 51°N (Clausen 1993; Wallace 2008). It lay 3000 km from the Greenland settlements. The site today has impressive earthworks that show where the Norse buildings stood. To make it work would have needed about five per cent of the Greenland population – a number that proved unsustainable on a permanent basis. L'Anse-aux-Meadows was a port of trade, a gateway, drawing in goods from a large hinterland perhaps on a seasonal basis but having little else to do with the indigenous population. The large storage rooms in the three halls bear out this interpretation (Wallace 2008: 609). In return, a wide range of traded Norse goods can be found scattered across the Eastern Arctic from Hudson Bay to Baffin Island and beyond to Ellesmere Island and north Greenland in the high Arctic (Sutherland 2008: figure 44.1.1).

The Vinland settlement of North America indicates neither dispersal nor displacement and certainly not diaspora. It existed for trade, the hallmark of Terra 5. In the subarctic of Newfoundland where the imagined abundance of Vinland met its reality, the judgement of deep history was to declare it an "impractical paradise" (Wallace 2008: 611).

CHAPTER 9

The human reunion in retrospect: Terra
5, after 1400 AD

> *And because there was nowhere to go but everywhere.*
> Jack Kerouac, *On the Road*, 1957

Colonising Prospero's Isle

Terra 5 is about many acts of reunion rather than a single age of discovery. It is a Terra of incessant colonisation with little to settle for the first time. Still uninhabited was the great polar continent, Antarctica, and several remote small islands in the South Atlantic: Ascencion, St Helena, Trindade and Tristan da Cunha. There were some also in the Pacific such as Christmas Island and Pitcairn that Europeans found empty but which archaeologists have shown to have been settled long before the ships arrived (Kirch 1984). Two uninhabited islands around Africa, the Cape Verde archipelago and Sao Tomé, were settled by Europeans in 1472 and 1486 AD. They mark a push beyond the western horizon. And before them came the settlement of the Azores, a chain of volcanic islands 1600 km to the west of Portugal, whose king, Henry the Navigator, is given credit for their settlement in 1427 AD. But despite Henry's sobriquet, there are doubts he ever sailed there, or anywhere for that matter (Fernández-Armesto 2006: 127–129). Moreover, the Azores had been visited for more than a century prior to Portuguese settlement and, along with the Canary Islands, formed the stepping stones for 1492 and Columbus' leap across the ocean.

Columbus marks a significant if unforeseen moment in the great human reunion – a colonial venture similar to the Leahy brothers' expedition into the New Guineas Highlands (Chapter 1), since both encountered unexpectedly large populations. Before Columbus, a long history of two-way trade existed between the empires of the Old World and beyond. This trade went over land and over water, leaving behind Indonesian coconuts in Africa, Roman pottery in Cambodia, Viking trinkets in Baffin Island and Islamic coins in Britain. As a result, the haplogroups of Terra 4 were already being stirred before Columbus dropped anchor in the Bahamas.

The reunion invigorated the imagination of the Terra 5 maritime powers. People were found everywhere apart from the most isolated and, to European eyes, desolate places like the volcanic Galapagos Islands that straddle the equator. Reunion is one of the themes in *The Tempest* first performed in 1611. One possible source for Shakespeare's imagined island community was the wreck of the *Sea Venture* on uninhabited Bermuda in 1609. The ship was en route to the English colony in Virginia but, in a storm, hit the reefs of this North Atlantic island. In the play, the shipwreck reunites the exiled Prospero with all his former enemies. Moreover, in a familiar scene of colonial displacement and global settlement, Prospero had previously encountered the islands' native inhabitants: Caliban, an anagram for Canibal, and Ariel, an imprisoned spirit. The reunion also provides the opportunity for his daughter Miranda to meet and marry Ferdinand, whose father the King of Naples had, together with Prospero's brother Antonio, engineered their exile. A family reunion played out on a desert island, imaginatively peopled with a deeper, "primitive" history and presenting reproductive opportunities. The history of Terra 5 in a nutshell.

Imagination often ran ahead of reality and nowhere more so than stormy Kerguelen, 49°S in the southern Indian Ocean. Kerguelen is a large island, 7215 km² in extent, and it lives up to its nickname, the Desolate Isle. In 1772, this did not stop its overenthusiastic discoverer, Yves-Joseph Kerguelen, describing to the French Court a land like southern France. Four years later, James Cook visited it on Christmas Day during his final voyage. He was unimpressed. It was also one of those rare places in his three voyages where no boats came out to greet him and no smoke rose from a shoreline settlement. But not to be outdone, the ship's artist, John Webber, captured the scene as the boats from *Resolution* and *Discovery* were drawn up on the beach and welcomed by a crowd of emperor penguins. If no humans were to be found, then another bipedal animal served as a surrogate.

The Human Imagination and Human Evolution

These islands and many others settled in Terra 4 exert a strong pull on the imagination, as with Judith Schalansky's (2010) atlas, *Fifty Islands I Have Not Visited and Never Will*. "Paradise", she writes, "is an island. So is hell". These are real places onto which we have grafted imagined geographies of pleasure and at the same time visited immense suffering. We find the isles of wonder in Shakespeare's *The Tempest*, basking in the warm ocean of our imagination, while in a cold sea of brutal historical reality, we find the British Empire's penal colony on tropical Norfolk Island.

The human capacity to imagine has been a theme throughout this book. It sums up those changes in deep history when going beyond, both socially and geographically, became a regular occurrence. This was the case in Terrae 3 and 4. But the human imagination has a longer history than that. It evolved during Terrae 1 and 2 as hominins amplified those core resources, materials and the senses (Figure 1.2) – a core that runs through all our history like a seam of black flint in white chalk.

This amplification changed simple stone tools into complex compositions that provided projections of alternative worlds. Moreover, we understand how this change happened. It was the outcome of the linked social activities of FACE. Amplification produced social technologies based on unnatural associations, binding a stone point to a wooden shaft, clothing bodies in furs and festooning them with shells. These technologies wove humans and materials ever closer together to produce the subtle stuff of an extended mind based on a distributed cognition. In an accompanying process, the sensory part of the social core, the embodied feelings and emotions of our cognition, were amplified. A sense as basic as fear was turned into an emotion as complicated as greed, the process enabled by a social cognition with a theory of mind, recognising the viewpoint of others as different to your own, and reading their emotions as if you felt them. In this way, the comfort of things was added to their practical uses. Now they were kept and treasured not for what they could do but how they made the owner feel.

The entangled sense of stuff, feelings and an imagination prepared to make the absurd natural was summed up a century ago by that distinguished philosopher, Toad of Toad Hall:

> To his horror Toad recollected that he had left both coat and waistcoat behind him in his cell, and with them his pocket-book, money, keys, watch, matches, pencil-case – all that makes life worth living, all that distinguishes the many pocketed animal, the lord of creation, from the inferior one-pocketed or no-pocketed productions that hop or trip about permissively, unequipped for the real contest. (Kenneth Grahame 1908 *The Wind in the Willows*)

The point about the evolution of our capacity for imagination is not that it produces magical islands like Prospero's or flights of fantasy like Toad Hall, but rather that it highlights the importance of our ability to relate over our need to be rational. This capacity to relate, both to other people and to stuff, things and places, is the fundamental hominin trait. Being rational may put the food on the table. But without those relational skills, we could not explain why we need a table, chairs, guests and all the other cultural accoutrements and condiments to turn food into a meal. Without coats and pockets to contain bodies and stuff, we are similarly reduced only to being rational creatures, ill-equipped in Toad's phrase for the real contest which is to engage with life.

Many other animals and birds relate in complicated ways to stuff. They make and use a wide variety of artefacts, and they are shaped by this two-way interaction with their surrounding environment. The Terra 1 hominins went further. They started to amplify the relational possibilities of stuff through FACE. This suited a versatile mind-set in a variable climate and conferred an evolutionary advantage. Ever since those earliest technologies, we have been exploring our relational imaginations, drawing together materials to fashion new associations and make complex emotions out of biological givens.

In that respect, our imagination has expressed itself through metaphors, rather than symbols, for much of our history. The embodied sense of containment, which makes a pocket a safe place to keep the keys to our identity, was a development from the instruments of wood, stone and bone that formed the oldest technologies. Engaging with the metaphorical possibilities of stuff released our imaginations long before there were words. The language threshold was crossed anatomically and culturally in Terra 2 (Chapter 5) and well before figurative art and writing appeared.

So in answer to the obvious question – why did our hominin ancestors amplify the social core of materials and senses? – the answer is that it met the demands to relate, to be social. These demands can be explained by the Darwinian imperative for enhanced reproductive success. This occurred for some individuals and groups when their social relationships became more complex, their interactions more numerous and varied. It can be accounted for by the psychology of desire, the satisfaction derived from the state of being ever-more social. Any amplification of the social had to involve the senses of the body and the stuff of life. And just as the world was settled, explored and reunited, so this core has been subject to constant scrutiny and innovation during our deep human history.

Dispersal, Displacement and Diaspora

My deep human history of global settlement has concentrated on dispersal and first arrivals. The vocabulary changes as we approach the present, and in Terra 5, it is all about displacement and diaspora (Table 2.3). These are elements of the broader historical theme of colonisation which have long been recognised. To return to *The Tempest*, Prospero displaced the residents of the island, taught them language and put them to work. With his new-found voice, Caliban speaks for the colonised and needs quoting at length:

> This island's mine, by Sycorax my mother,
> Which thou tak'st from me. When thou cam'st first,
> Thou strok'st me and made much of me, wouldst give me
> Water with berries in't, and teach me how
> To name the bigger light, and how the less,
> That burn by day and night: and then I loved thee
> And show'd thee all the qualities o' the isle,
> The fresh springs, brine-pits, barren place and fertile –
> Cursed be I that did so! All the charms
> Of Sycorax, toads, beetles, bats, light on you!
> For I am all the subjects that you have,
> Which first was mine own king: and here you sty me
> In this hard rock, whiles you do keep from me
> The rest o' the island. (*The Tempest*, Act 1, Scene 2)

The gift of speech gives Caliban a history but one that is about dispossession and displacement. It could have been delivered by one of the Wampanoag, Native Americans of Massachusetts, when they realised what their act of hospitality to the English settlers, recognised in the Thanksgiving of 1621, had led to. The massive social asymmetry of this colonial encounter, and the diaspora that drove it, was markedly different to earlier displacements between hunters and hunters (Chapter 7) or even farmers and FGH.

What is recorded in the texts of shallow history must not form a veneer over a deeper human past known through things and genes (Box 1.1). That said, texts define the history of Terra 5 and extend into some of Terra 4 to produce lopsidedness in historical accounts. The documented arrival of ships, camel caravans and wagon trains across the oceans and continental interiors created history in terms of the politics of displacement. The four centuries since *The Tempest* have seen millions of economic migrants, enforced movements of people due to war, famine, partition and slavery and resulted in countless diasporas defined by race, faith and geography. Against this backdrop, recent global history is about the constant flux and reflux of peoples and population within a finite world geography.

But this need not imply different histories for Terra 5 and the older Terrae of deep human history. Until Terra 5, the settlement of the Earth was always unfinished business. The archives available to study this history are artefacts, bodies, landscapes and more recently genetic phylogeographies and digitally constructed networks. The flux of population in the form of dispersal is a potent theme throughout Terrae 1–4. What is needed, however, is a revision of the way we trace this dynamic settlement from things – to tell big histories through small objects (E. de Waal 2010; MacGregor 2010).

The archaeological evidence, those once-strong signatures linking a people to a package of things, is coming apart (Chapters 6 and 7). This applies to world prehistories that have developed a synthesis drawn from archaeogenetics, biological anthropology, archaeology and comparative linguistics to study early farming dispersals (Bellwood 2005; Renfrew 1987). The hypothesis is a familiar one based on interpreting those strong archaeological signatures for rapid dispersal. It links a major adaptive change, farming, with people on the move, picked out by the spread of their total culture (Eliot 1948: 52). In some cases, the strong signature is undeniable, as with the dispersal of Austronesian languages and domestic resources throughout Oceania. But when displacement or diaspora are concerned, as in Europe or Africa, the signatures picked out so strongly with distinctive pottery styles all too often have feet of clay. The Clovis "dispersal" (Chapter 7), now discarded, serves as a cautionary tale. These FGH were once thought to be the pioneers of the Americas, as in Clovis First, but are now its second generation. Their archaeological signature, based on tightly dated projectile points, spread like smallpox through an indigenous population rather than scattered across two continents by fleet-footed hunters.

The rates of dispersal are beginning to emerge, as shown in Table 9.1. What is striking are the low rates for farming displacements. Bellwood (2005) draws a further distinction between *spread zones* and *friction zones* for dispersals based on agriculture. Rates are higher in the former than the latter where incoming farmers met indigenous FGH. But when measured by the number of human generations it took for farmers to cover the distances involved in both zones, they seem as slow as an expanding continental plate. Probably the rates are so low because both zones involved the displacement of well-settled FGH in agriculturally attractive landscapes. By comparison, the viral spread of Clovis is measured at between 8 and 47 km a year (Chapter 7), figures only matched by the diasporas of shallow history where political and economic asymmetries were highest.

TABLE 9.1. *The rates of dispersal and displacement in Terrae 3–5.*

	Terra	Dispersal rates (km/year)	Dispersal rates (km per generation, 20 years)	Distance (km)	Generations taken	Degrees of latitude
Dispersal by FGH						
Switzerland to Britain	3	0.77	15	925	62	6
Bulgaria to France	3	1.25–0.83	25–14	2500	100–179	2
Altai to Beringia	3	1–0.08	20–13	7000	350–538	16
Canada to Chile	3	1–2	20–40	14,000	700–350	100
New Guinea to Tasmania	3	1.5	30	7500	250	37
Displacement by farmers						
Italy to Portugal (maritime)	3–4	0.1	2	2000	1000	0
Hungary to France	3–4	0.025	0.5	1000	2000	<5
Zagros to Baluchistan	3–4	0.032	0.6	1600	2666	5
Philippines to Samoa (maritime)	4	0.085	1.7	8500	5000	0
Central Mexico to Arizona	4	0.037	0.7	1850	2642	12
Lake Victoria to Natal	4	0.043	0.9	3000	3333	30
Germany to Britain	3–4	0.004	0.08	500	6250	0
Yangzi to Hong Kong	3–4	0.004	0.08	1000	12,500	8
Baluchistan to Rajasthan	3–4	0.003	0.06	1000	16,666	0
New Britain to southern Papua (maritime)	4	0.008	0.16	1000	6250	5
Diaspora by Europeans						
North America (east to west)	5	20	400	4000	10	0
South Africa (south to north)	5	8	160	1500	9	20
Australia (south to north)	5	53	1060	4000	4	28

The archaeological evidence is dated by radiocarbon (Chapters 6–8). The FGH dispersals are generally over much greater latitudinal differences than the farming displacements. We have to wait for the colonial diasporas of Europeans in the Americas, South Africa and Australia for industrial-based agricultural societies to exceed the overland rates of FGH. Data on farmers from Bellwood (2005: table 12.1) which combines both spread and friction zone dispersal rates.

The archaeogenetic evidence has questioned the archaeological framework by proposing alternative geographical patterns, such as the southern coastal route (Chapter 6), for further investigation. However, these insights, while invaluable, cannot provide the rounded history we require. Rather, archaeogeneticists have shown how important the hard, well-dated evidence from archaeology is to independently ground-truth their genetic patterns.

Archaeologists and palaeoanthropologists need to address the issue of appropriate frameworks and fit-for-purpose terminology with some urgency. As a first step, they need to decide what sort of deep-history narratives they have and then determine the tools they need for its study. One casualty, I suspect, will be the A-List and B-List terms (Table 2.7) that are beginning to show their age when challenged by the connections now possible with the new historical archives stored genetically and retrieved digitally (Box 1.1).

Large Brains and Big Worlds

My contribution to a new framework returns to the question set out in Chapter 1: were changing brains and global settlement linked in some way, and if not why not? If social life provides the theme that unites all the Terrae, and materials and senses the core resources for our historical attention, then brains and settlement supply a measure of the direction of travel. "As we relate so we create" may be the hominins' distinguishing feature, but was it also the case that as they created relationships with people and stuff, they also expanded across the Earth?

To examine this question, I drew thresholds in the size of hominin brains – the 400 cm³ apes and hominins and the 900 cm³ and 1200 cm³ hominins and humans (Chapters 4 and 5). Brain size is not everything. The small-bodied macaques and the large-bodied omnivores show what is possible in terms of a geographical range that far exceeds the hominins' (Figures 4.7 and 4.8). Brains are just one element in the space defined by Gowlett's (2010) triangle of hominin evolution: changes in diet, detailed environmental knowledge, social collaboration. Brains cannot change without other changes in the hominin *bauplan*, such as stomachs, teeth, bipedalism, technology and the mechanisms that support social interaction (Chapter 4). And none of these elements changed independently of the environmental niche which also made up the hominin.

An essential element of a new framework for deep human history is the concept of the relational, rather than rational, mind. Hominins will never make much sense to us if we only deal with them as rational creatures interested in food and reproduction and not much else. As argued in the first three chapters, we need to abandon this concept of how the brain works if we are to be reunited with our remote ancestors. We need to replace the isolated, rational mind with one that recognises that cognition is distributed and the mind extended. These are not mental states that evolved slowly or appeared suddenly like a human revolution. They have been present in all hominins and are shared with other animals. But as a comparative study of theory of mind and intentionality shows (Chapter 5), this is a relational competence that differs markedly between the brains of a 1500 cm³ human and a 400 cm³ chimpanzee. It forms a more significant difference than that between a chimpanzee's termite probe and a Mode 1 stone tool (Box 2.3) – a difference that is not based on the efficiency or complexity of the two hand-held instruments, possibly made by hominids with similar-sized brains, but rather on the social and imaginative possibilities that higher levels of intentionality open up. It is also the case that any boundaries to brain size are arbitrary, since they tell us little about its structure and organisation. This will be another area that a new historical framework will need to explore as MRI techniques, combined with a relational rather than rational understanding of human cognition, investigate how our brains work.

In the same way, my six Terrae are put forward as opportunities to understand the changes in the relational capabilities of hominins. The outlines of the Terrae will change in detail, but the general framework, I believe, is sound. Redrawing the limits to Terra 1 or Terra 2 will depend on fresh discovery and scientific dating. But recasting the shape of a Terra must not be undertaken simply as an exercise in defining boundaries. The Movius line that separates Mode 1 and 2 technologies illustrates the limitations (Chapter 5). Instead, a change in a boundary will be the opportunity to understand the combination of factors that imposed limits to expansion. Throughout the book, I have implicitly followed the maxim that all species seek to increase their geographical range but that they lack the adaptive means to make this a global reality. Such increase is expected and can be explained by Darwinian evolution. Following Potts, I take the view that becoming versatile holds the key to understanding long-term hominin evolution (Box 2.2). Furthermore, versatility is an adaptation to variability in climate (Chapter 2). This had particular importance in Terrae 0–3 as versatile hominins did better than their specialist and generalist cousins.

Timescale is important here. The accelerated pace of dispersal in Terrae 3 and 4 compared to the older hominin worlds is significant. When the expansion to Sahul and Beringia took place in Terra 3, it was not a revolution but rather the culmination of incremental changes. These changes produced social technologies such as boats and storehouses, as well as technologies for separation; for instance, universal kinship, codes of hospitality and reciprocal gift-giving at a continental scale. They only resulted in change, measured here as settling new and uninhabited lands, when they became associated and so amplified the human capacity to create relationships. Previously in Terrae 1 and 2, hominins had regularly expanded. These dispersals followed a standard route that in Terra 2 was driven by the exposure of Sunda, the greening of the Sahara–Arabia, the expansion and contraction of the African rainforest and the climatic limits to northern settlement in what I have called Moviusland (Figure 5.2).

This bio-tidal rhythm to hominin settlement changed in Terra 3. Versatility was demonstrated by reversing the flow and expanding rather than contracting at a continental scale. Even so, further amplification in the form of domestic animals and crops was needed to continue the process in Terra 4. In Polynesia, the North Atlantic and the Indian Ocean, these dispersals show clear intention whether recorded in texts, as with the Vikings, or direction of dispersal, as with the Austronesian speakers who reached Hawai'i and Madagascar. And since intention, or motive, is a product of relating to people, stuff and circumstance, we should extend the same principle to overland dispersals such as the repopulation of Europe after the LGM, the move above the Arctic Circle in Siberia, as well as to the history of not settling nearby islands but instead leaving that to the future.

Therefore, in answer to the question about the link between larger brains and bigger worlds, it is apparent that the two are out of phase. There was nothing special about the 900 cm³ size brain that meant it needed the extra space of Terra 2 as opposed to Terra 1. Or that brains greater than 1200 cm³ led inexorably to Terra 3. But what these thresholds do point to is the hypothesis that social life drove encephalisation. Larger brains have geographical consequences. That is because they are so costly to maintain and because any change necessitates so much reorganisation to *bauplans* and evolutionary triangles; brains are indeed expensive tissues. And that co-evolutionary consequence points to the direction of travel which is more complex social interaction, requiring an amplification of the principle "relating to create", even if that is based solely on the number of partners now found in a hominin's social world. In addition, the expense does not stop with complex social life. The human brain has shown an appetite to amplify its moods through the psychotropic management of its chemical environment (Smail 2008: 163). Our brains have become addicted to exploring the possibilities of our imagination and regulating its moods. Singing and dancing first set the endorphins free (Chapter 5) and similar opioid highs result from coordinated social activity (E. E. A. Cohen, Ejsmond-Frey, Knight et al. 2010). But substances like alcohol and drugs take the process of mood control further. This amplification provides a strong motive to capture more energy, first through plant management and trade (Watson 1983) and then full-blown agriculture (Sherratt 1997) to meet this desire.

Deep Human History: A Prospect

The final part of a framework for deep human history requires overhauling the dominant metaphors for our narratives. One of these, progress, has I hope fallen by the wayside, but we have to remain vigilant. The biological direction of travel was towards gracile humans from robustly built hominins, a trend that accelerated in the Holocene with larger populations supported by farming. There is no implication of progress in this trend, although the earlier literature of physical anthropologists says otherwise.

This was also the case among archaeologists writing fifty years ago of the benefits of agriculture over fishing, hunting and gathering. We know that agriculture marks a change that is amplified by subsequent civilisations whose populations used resources on an unprecedented scale. Today, describing the process as progress is usually avoided. But standpoint remains important. If this book, for example, had been written by someone with an interest in the Neolithic rather than the Palaeolithic, I feel sure that Terra 3 would have begun 11ka and agriculture received rather more attention as a break with the hominin worlds of Terra 2 (Renfrew 2007).

However, a focus on farming as the origin point for deep human history, treating all that went before as the backstory, breaks the thread of the historical narrative. It sets up later ruptures between the methods and techniques of shallow as opposed to deep history (Box 1.1) and coats the remote past with recent veneers. The challenge has been accepted by Daniel Smail (2008) who sees the brain and its changing chemical and emotional states as the unifying theme for a truly deep history. His neurohistory offers an historical narrative freed from the concerns of the developing political organisations that scaffolded the nation state. Nonetheless, he still balances history on the Neolithic. Here, I have wedded the narrative of the brain to that of global settlement and, in so doing, avoided the need for an historical tipping point.

What is at issue, besides narratives for deep human history, are the root metaphors for its composition – what anthropologist Sherry Ortner (1973) calls key symbols. She points out that living organisms, whether human or animal, often act as a root metaphor to summarise and elaborate on experience. This is how the cultures of the world conceptualise social phenomena as with the magical growth of seeds into plants or children into adults. By contrast, industrialised nations prefer such important metaphors to be based on the machine – hence descriptions of the mind in terms of computers and the health of the heart likened to a well-oiled clock.

Elsewhere, I have employed two such root metaphors to write deep history: the giving-environment for FGH and growing-the-body for farmers (Gamble 2007). I add them to the compendium of new governing metaphors that Shryock and Smail (2011a, 2011b) propose as a framework for deep history. They argue we need to set aside ontogeny (the birth of modernity) and genesis (the inception of the human species). I would add to these the driving power of revolution in origins research, those good upheavals that got us to the present (Gamble 2007). The problem, as Shryock and Smail argue, is that these metaphors, while powerful, lead us to a history that is flattened and foreshortened. What is needed is a "revamped historical imagination that sees deep and shallow history as analytical contexts that can endlessly reshape each other once they are allowed to speak to each other" (Shryock and Smail 2011b: 20).

This has been my goal here. The brain remains central to human history, and much of it is as yet uncharted, its potential unrealised. That is the stuff of history, since the growth of the brain and the gift of the Earth are entwined metaphors with future consequences. The flow of population around the various worlds inhabited by our ancestors in both deep and shallow history provides a global history of changing competence and ability. It is a continuing journey on a planet that is creaking as she goes, the future for its seven billion travellers unsure. A finite Earth and an infinite imagination have evolved from a common core. There may be neither untouched shores to find nor new mountains to climb. But there are still fires in the night, and what unifies the two stories is the history of things.

Bibliography

Abegg, C. & Thierry, B. 2002. Macaque evolution and dispersal in insular southeast Asia. *Biological Journal of the Linnean Society*, 75, 555–576.

Achilli, A., Rengo, C., Magri, C., Battaglia, V., Olivieri, S., Scozzari, R., Cruciani, F., Zeviani, M., Briem, E., Carelli, V., Moral, P., Dugoujon, J.-M., Roostalu, U., Loogväli, E.-L., Kivisild, T., Bandelt, H.-J., Richards, M., Villems, R., Santachiara-Benerecetti, A. S., Semino, O. & Torroni, A. 2004. The molecular dissection of mtDNA haplogroup H confirms that the Franco-Cantabrian glacial refuge was a major source for the European gene pool. *American Journal of Human Genetics*, 75, 910–918.

Adler, D., Bar-Oz, G., Belfer-Cohen, A. & Bar-Yosef, O. 2006. Ahead of the game: Middle and Upper Palaeolithic hunting practices in the Southern Caucasus. *Current Anthropology*, 47, 89–118.

Adovasio, J. M. & Page, J. 2002. *The first Americans: In pursuit of archaeology's greatest mystery*. New York: Random House.

Agusti, J. & Lordkipanidze, D. 2011. How "African" was the early human dispersal out of Africa? *Quaternary Science Reviews*, 30, 1338–1342.

Aiello, L. 1998. The "expensive tissue hypothesis" and the evolution of the human adaptive niche: A study in comparative anatomy. In: J. Bayley (ed.) *Science in archaeology: An agenda for the future*. London: English Heritage.

Aiello, L. & Dunbar, R. 1993. Neocortex size, group size and the evolution of language. *Current Anthropology*, 34, 184–193.

Aiello, L. & Wheeler, P. 1995. The expensive-tissue hypothesis: The brain and the digestive system in human and primate evolution. *Current Anthropology*, 36, 199–221.

Alemseged, Z., Spoor, F., Kimbel, W. H., Bobe, R., Geraads, D., Reed, D. & Wynn, J. G. 2006. A juvenile early hominin skeleton from Dikika, Ethiopia. *Nature*, 443, 296–301.

Allaby, M. (ed.) 1991. *The concise Oxford dictionary of zoology*. Oxford: Oxford University Press.

Allen, J. (ed.) 1996. *Report of the Southern Forests archaeological project*. La Trobe: La Trobe University.

Allen, J. & Gosden, C. (eds.) 1991. *Report of the Lapita homeland project*. Canberra: Department of Prehistory, Research School of Pacific Studies, Australian National University.

Allen, J. & O'Connell, J. F. 2008. Getting from Sunda to Sahul. *Terra Australis*, 29, 31–46.

Allen, J. R. M., Hickler, T., Singarayer, J. S., Sykes, M. T., Valdes, P. J. & Huntley, B. 2010. Last glacial vegetation of northern Eurasia. *Quaternary Science Reviews*, 29, 2604–2618.

Allen, N. J. 1998. Effervescence and the origins of human society. In: N. J. Allen, W. S. F. Pickering & W. Watts Miller (eds.) *On Durkheim's elementary forms of religious life*. London: Routledge.

Allen, N. J. 2008. Tetradic theory and the origin of human kinship systems. In: N. J. Allen, H. Callan, R. Dunbar & W. James (eds.) *Kinship and evolution*. Oxford: Blackwell, pp. 96–112.

Allen, N. J., Callan, H., Dunbar, R. & James, W. (eds.) 2008. *Early human kinship: From sex to social reproduction*. Oxford: Blackwell.

Allsworth-Jones, P. 2008. *Pre-Columbian Jamaica*. Tuscaloosa: University of Alabama Press.

Alperson-Afil, N. & Goren-Inbar, N. 2010. *The Acheulian site of Gesher Benot Ya'aqov volume II: Ancient flames and controlled use of fire*. Dordrecht: Springer.

Ambrose, S. 1998. Late Pleistocene human population bottlenecks, volcanic winter, and differentiation of modern humans. *Journal of Human Evolution*, 34, 623–651.

Ambrose, S. 2006. A tool for all seasons. *Science*, 314, 930–931.

Anderson, A. 1989. *Prodigious birds: Moas and moa-hunting in prehistoric New Zealand*. Cambridge: Cambridge University Press.

Anderson, D. G. & Gillam, J. C. 2000. Paleoindian colonization of the Americas: Implications from an examination of physiography, demography, and artifact distribution. *American Antiquity*, 65, 43–66.

Andrews, P. 2007. The biogeography of hominind evolution. *Journal of Biogeography*, 34, 381–382.

Anikovich, M. V., Sinitsyn, A. A., Hoffecker, J., Holliday, V. T., Popov, V. V., Lisitsyn, S. N., Forman, S. L., Levkovskaya, G. M., Pospelova, G. A., Kuz'mina, I. E., Burova, N. D., Goldberg, P., Macphail, R. I., Giaccio, B. & Praslov, N. D. 2007. Early Upper Palaeolithic in Eastern Europe and implications for the dispersal of modern humans. *Science*, 315, 223–226.

Antón, S. C., Leonard, W. R. & Robertson, M. L. 2002. An ecomorphological model of the initial hominid dispersal from Africa. *Journal of Human Evolution*, 43, 773–785.

Antón, S. C. & Swisher, C. C. 2004. Early dispersals of Homo from Africa. *Annual Review of Anthropology*, 33, 271–296.

Araujo, A., Reinhard, K. J., Ferreira, L. F. & Gardner, S. L. 2008. Parasites as probes for prehistoric human migrations? *Cell*, 11, 112–115.

Armitage, S. J., Jasim, S. A., Marks, A. E., Parker, A. G., Usik, V. I. & Uerpmann, H.-P. 2011. The southern route "Out of Africa": Evidence for an early expansion of modern humans into Arabia. *Science*, 331, 453–456.

Arzarello, M., Marcolini, F., Pavia, G., Pavia, M., Petronio, C., Petrucci, M., Rook, L. & Sardell, R. 2007. Evidence of earliest human occurrence in Europe: The site of Pirro Nord (Southern Italy). *Naturwissenschaften*, **94**, 107–112.

Asfaw, B., Beyene, Y., Suwa, G., Walter, R. C., White, T. D., WoldeGabriel, G. & Yemane, T. 1992. The earliest Acheulean from Konso-Gardula. *Nature*, **360**, 732–735.

Asfaw, B., Gilbert, W. H., Beyene, Y., Hart, W. K., Renne, P. R., WoldeGabriel, G., Vrba, E. S. & White, T. D. 2002. Remains of *Homo erectus* from Bouri, Middle Awash, Ethiopia. *Nature*, **416**, 317–319.

Ashton, N., Lewis, S. G. & Hosfield, R. 2011. Mapping the human record: Population change in Britain during the Early Palaeolithic. *In*: N. Ashton, S. G. Lewis & C. Stringer (eds.) *The ancient human occupation of Britain*. Amsterdam: Elsevier Developments in Quaternary Science, p. 14.

Ashton, N., Lewis, S. G. & Stringer, C. (eds.) 2011. *The ancient human occupation of Britain*. Amsterdam: Elsevier Developments in Quaternary Science.

Atkinson, Q. D., Gray, R. D. & Drummond, A. J. 2007. mtDNA variation predicts population size in humans and reveals a major southern Asian chapter in human prehistory. *Molecular Biology and Evolution*, **25**, 468–474.

Atkinson, Q. D., Gray, R. D. & Drummond, A. J. 2009. Bayesian coalescent inference of major human mitochondrial DNA haplogroup expansions in Africa. *Proceedings of the Royal Society of London B*, **276**, 367–373.

Bae, K. 2010. The transition to Upper Palaeolithic industries in the Korean peninsula. *In*: K. V. Boyle, C. Gamble & O. Bar-Yosef (eds.) *The Upper Palaeolithic revolution in global perspective: Papers in honour of Sir Paul Mellars*. Cambridge: McDonald Institute.

Bailey, G. N. & King, G. C. P. 2011. Dynamic landscapes and human dispersal patterns: Tectonics, coastlines, and the reconstruction of human habitats. *Quaternary Science Reviews*, **30**, 1533–1553.

Bailey, H. P. 1960. A method of determining the warmth and temperateness of climate. *Geografiska Annaler*, **43**, 1–16.

Baillie, M. G. L. 1995. *A slice through time: Dendrochronology and precision dating*. London: Batsford.

Baird, D. 2011. Pınarbaşı: From Epipalaeolithic campsite to sedentarising village in central Anatolia. *In*: M. Ozdogan & N. Başgelen (eds.) *The Neolithic in Turkey: New excavations and new research*. Istanbul: Arkeoloji v Sanat Yayinlari.

Balme, J., Davidson, I., McDonald, J., Stern, N. & Veth, P. 2009. Symbolic behaviour and the peopling of the southern arc route to Australia. *Quaternary International*, **202**, 59–68.

Balter, M. 2007. Seeking agriculture's ancient roots. *Science*, **316**, 1830–1835.

Balter, M. 2011a. Did Neanderthals linger in Russia's far north? *Science*, **332**, 778.

Balter, M. 2011b. Tracing the paths of the first Americans. *Science*, **333**, 1692.

Balter, M. 2012. The peopling of the Aleutians. *Science*, **335**, 158–161.

Bar-Yosef, O. 1998. On the nature of transitions: The Middle to Upper Palaeolithic and the Neolithic revolution. *Cambridge Archaeological Journal*, 8, 141–163.

Bar-Yosef, O. 2002. The Upper Palaeolithic revolution. *Annual Review of Anthropology*, **31**, 363–393.

Bar-Yosef, O. 2007. The dispersal of modern humans in Eurasia: A cultural interpretation. In: P. Mellars, O. Bar-Yosef, C. Stringer & K. V. Boyle (eds.) *Rethinking the human revolution*. Cambridge: McDonald Institute.

Bar-Yosef, O. & Belfer-Cohen, A. 2001. From Africa to Eurasia. *Quaternary International*, **75**, 19–28.

Bar-Yosef, O. & Belfer-Cohen, A. 2010. The Middle to Upper Palaeolithic transition in Western Asia. In: K. V. Boyle, C. Gamble & O. Bar-Yosef (eds.) *The Upper Palaeolithic revolution in global perspective: Papers in honour of Sir Paul Mellars*. Cambridge: McDonald Institute.

Bar-Yosef, O. & Belmaker, M. 2011. Early and Middle Pleistocene faunal and hominins dispersals through Southwestern Asia. *Quaternary Science Reviews*, **30**, 1318–1337.

Bar-Yosef, O., Vandermeersch, B., Arensburg, A., Belfer-Cohen, P., Goldberg, H., Laville, L., Meignen, Y., Rak., J. D., Speth, E., Tchernov, E., Tillier, A.-M., & Weiner, S. 1992. The excavations in Kebara Cave, Mt Carmel. *Current Anthropology*, **33**, 497–550.

Barham, L. S. 2002. Backed tools in Middle Pleistocene Central Africa and their evolutionary significance. *Journal of Human Evolution*, **43**, 585–603.

Barham, L. S. 2010. A technological fix for "Dunbar's dilemma"? In: R. Dunbar, C. Gamble & J. A. J. Gowlett (eds.) *Social brains and distributed mind*. Oxford: Oxford University Press.

Barham, L. S. & Mitchell, P. 2008. *The first Africans: African archaeology from the earliest toolmakers to most recent foragers*. Cambridge: Cambridge University Press.

Barker, G. 2009. Early farming and domestication. In: B. Cunliffe, C. Gosden & R. A. Joyce (eds.) *The Oxford handbook of archaeology*. Oxford: Oxford University Press.

Barker, G., Barton, H., Bird, M., Daly, P., Datan, I., Dykes, A., Farr, L., Gilbertson, D., Harrisson, B., Hunt, C., Higham, T. F. G., Kealhofer, L. J. K., Lewis, H., McLaren, S., Paz, V., Pike, A., Piper, P., Pyatt, B., Rabett, R., Reynolds, T., Rose, J., Rushworth, G., Stephens, M., Stringer, C., Thompson, J. & Turney, C. 2007. The "human revolution" in lowland tropical Southeast Asia: The antiquity and behaviour of anatomically modern humans at Niah Cave (Sarawak, Borneo). *Journal of Human Evolution*, **52**, 243–261.

Barnard, A. 2010. When individuals do not stop at the skin. In: R. Dunbar, C. Gamble & J. A. J. Gowlett (eds.) *Social brain, distributed mind*. Oxford: Oxford University Press.

Barnard, A. 2011. *Social anthropology and human origins*. Cambridge: Cambridge University Press.

Barrett, L. & Henzi, P. 2005. The social nature of primate cognition. *Proceedings of the Royal Society of London B*, **272**, 1865–1875.

Batterbee, R. W., Gasse, F. & Stickley, C. E. (eds.) 2004. *Past climate variability through Europe and Africa*. Dordrecht: Springer.

Beall, C. M., Decker, M. J., Brittenham, G. M., Kushner, I., Gebremedhin, A. & Strohl, K. P. 2002. An Ethiopian pattern of human adaptation to high-altitude hypoxia. *Proceedings of the National Academy of Sciences of the United States of America*, **99**, 17215–17218.

Behrensmeyer, A. K. 2006. Climate change and human evolution. *Science*, 311, 476–478.

Belfer-Cohen, A. & Goring-Morris, A. N. 2007. From the beginning: Levantine Upper Palaeolithic cultural change and continuity. *In*: P. Mellars, O. Bar-Yosef, C. Stringer & K. V. Boyle (eds.) *Rethinking the human revolution*. Cambridge: McDonald Institute.

Belfer-Cohen, A. & Hovers, E. 2010. Modernity, enhanced working memory, and the Middle to Upper Paleolithic record in the Levant. *Current Anthropology*, 51, 167–175.

Bellwood, P. 2005. *First farmers: The origins of agricultural societies*. Oxford: Blackwell.

Benazzi, S., Douka, K., Fornai, C., Bauer, C. C., Kullmer, O., Svoboda, J., Pap, I., Mallegni, F., Bayle, P., Coquerelle, M., Condemi, S., Ronchitelli, A., Harvati, K. & Weber, G. W. 2011. Early dispersal of modern humans in Europe and implications for Neanderthal behaviour. *Nature*, 479, 525–529.

Bender, B. 1978. Gatherer-hunter to farmer: A social perspective. *World Archaeology*, 10, 204–222.

Bergman, I., Olofsson, A., Hörnberg, G., Zackrisson, O. & Hellberg, E. 2004. Deglaciation and colonization: Pioneer settlements in Northern Fennoscandia. *Journal of World Prehistory*, 18, 155–177.

Bever, M. R. 2001. An overview of Alaskan Late Pleistocene archaeology: Historical themes and current perspectives. *Journal of World Prehistory*, 15, 125–191.

Bickerton, D. 2007. Did syntax trigger the human revolution? *In*: P. Mellars, O. Bar-Yosef, C. Stringer & K. V. Boyle (eds.) *Rethinking the human revolution*. Cambridge: McDonald Institute.

Binford, L. R. 1978. *Nunamiut ethnoarchaeology*. New York: Academic Press.

Binford, L. R. 1980. Willow smoke and dogs tails: Hunter-gatherer settlement systems and archaeological site formation. *American Antiquity*, 45, 4–20.

Binford, L. R. 2001. *Constructing frames of reference: An analytical method for archaeological theory building using ethnographic and environmental datasets*. Berkeley: University of California Press.

Binford, L. R. 2007. The diet of early hominins: Some things we need to know before "reading" the menu from the archaeological record. *In*: W. Roebroeks (ed.) *Guts and brains: An integrative approach to the hominin record*. Leiden: Leiden University Press.

Biraben, J. N. 1980. An essay concerning mankind's demographic evolution. *Journal of Human Evolution*, 9, 655–663.

Bird, M., Taylor, D. & Hunt, C. 2005. Palaeoenvironments of insular Southeast Asia during the last glacial period: A savanna corridor in Sundaland? *Quaternary Science Reviews*, 24, 2228–2242.

Blacking, J. 1973. *How musical is man?* Seattle: University of Washington Press.

Bobe, R., Behresmeyer, A. K., & Chapman, R. E. 2002. Faunal change, environmental variability and Late Pliocene hominin evolution. *Journal of Human Evolution*, 42, 475–497.

Bocherens, H. 2003. Isotopic biogeochemistry and the palaeoecology of the mammoth steppe fauna. *DEINSEA*, 9, 57–76.

Bocquet-Appel, J.-P. 2008. *La paléodémographie: 99.99% de l'historie démographie des hommes ou la démographie de la Préhistorie.* Paris: Éditions Errance.

Bocquet-Appel, J.-P. & Demars, P.-Y. 2000. Population kinetics in the Upper Palaeolithic in Western Europe. *Journal of Archaeological Science,* 27, 551–570.

Bocquet-Appel, J.-P., Demars, P.-Y., Noiret, L. & Dobrowksy, L. 2005. Estimates of Upper Palaeolithic meta-population size in Europe from archaeological data. *Journal of Archaeological Science,* 32, 1656–1668.

Boismier, W. A., Gamble, C. S. & Coward, F. (eds.) 2012. *Neanderthals among mammoths: Excavations at Lynford Quarry, Norfolk.* London: English Heritage Monographs.

Bond, G., Broecker, W., Johnsen, S., McManus, J., Labeyrie, L. D., Jouzel, J. & Bonani, G. 1993. Correlations between climate records from North Atlantic sediments and Greenland ice. *Nature,* 365, 143–147.

Borges, J. L. 1964. *Funes the Memorious. Labyrinths: Selected stories and other writings.* New York: New Directions.

Bourdieu, P. 1977. *Outline of a theory of practice.* Cambridge: Cambridge University Press.

Boyle, K. V., Gamble, C. & Bar-Yosef, O. (eds.) 2010. *The Upper Palaeolithic revolution in global perspective: Papers in honour of Sir Paul Mellars.* Cambridge: McDonald Institute.

Brain, C. K. 1981. *The hunters or the hunted?* Chicago: University of Chicago Press.

Bramble, D. M. & Lieberman, D. E. 2004. Endurance running and the evolution of *Homo. Nature,* 432, 345–352.

Brantingham, P. J., Krivoshapkin, A. I., Jinzeng, L. & Tserendagva, Y. 2001. The initial Upper Palaeolithic in Northest Asia. *Current Anthropology,* 42, 735–749.

Brantingham, P. J., Kuhn, S. L. & Kerry, K. W. (eds.) 2004. *The early Upper Palaeolithic beyond Western Europe.* Berkeley: University of California Press.

Braun, D. R., Harris, J. W. K., Levin, N. E., McCoy, J. T., Herries, A. I. R., Bamford, M. K., Bishop, L. C., Richmond, B. G. & Kibunjia, M. 2010. Early hominin diet included diverse terrestrial and aquatic animals 1.95Ma in East Turkana, Kenya. *Proceedings of the National Academy of Sciences of the United States of America,* 107, 10002–10007.

Breuil, H. 1912. Les subdivisions du Paléolithique supérieur et leur signification. Comptes Rendus du 14e Congrès International d'Anthropologie et d'Archéologie Préhistorique, Genève, pp. 165–238.

Briggs, A. W., Good, J. M., Green, R. E., Krause, J., Maricic, T., Stenzel, U., Lalueza-Fox, C., Rudan, P., Brajkovi, D., Kuan, E., Gui, I., Schmitz, R., Doronichev, V. B., Golovanova, L. V., de la Rasilla, M., Fortea, A., Rosas, A. & Pääbo, S. 2009. Targeted retrieval and analysis of five Neandertal mtDNA genomes. *Science,* 325, 318–321.

Brody, H. 1981. *Maps and dreams.* Vancouver: Douglas and McIntyre.

Broodbank, C. 2009. The Mediterranean and its hinterland. *In:* B. Cunliffe, C. Gosden & R. A. Joyce (eds.) *The Oxford handbook of archaeology.* Oxford: Oxford University Press.

Brose, D. & Wolpoff, M. 1971. Early Upper Paleolithic man and Late Middle Palaeolithic tools. *American Anthropologist,* 73, 1156–1194.

Brown, F., Harris, J., Leakey, R. & Walker, A. 1985. Early *Homo erectus* skeleton from west Lake Turkana, Kenya. *Nature*, 316, 788–792.

Brown, P., Sutikna, T., Morwood, M. J., Soejono, R. P., Jatmiko, A., Saptomo, E. W. & Due, R. A. 2004. A new small-bodied hominin from the Late Pleistocene of Flores, Indonesia. *Nature*, 431, 1055–1061.

Brown, T. 2010. Stranger from Siberia. *Nature*, 464, 838. March online.

Brugère, A., Fontana, L. & Oliva, M. 2009. Mammoth procurement and exploitation at Milovice (Czech Republic): New data for the Moravian Gravettian. In: L. Fontana, F.-X. Chauvière & A. Bridault (eds.) *In search of total animal exploitation: Case studies from the Upper Palaeolithic and Mesolithic*. Oxford: British Archaeological Reports International Series, vol. 2040.

Brumm, A. 2004. An axe to grind: Symbolic considerations of stone axe use in ancient Australia. In: N. Boivin & M. Owoc (eds.) *Soils, stones and symbols: Cultural perceptions of the mineral world*. London: UCL Press.

Brumm, A., Aziz, F., van den Bergh, G. D., Morwood, M. J., Moore, M. W., Kurniawan, I., Hobbs, D. R. & Fullagar, R. 2006. Early stone technology on Flores and its implications for *Homo floresiensis*. *Nature*, 441, 624–628.

Brumm, A., Jensen, G. M., van den Bergh, G. D., Morwood, M. J., Kurniawan, I., Aziz, F. & Storey, M. 2010. Hominins on Flores, Indonesia, by one million years ago. *Nature*, 464, 748–752.

Buckland, P. 2008. The North Atlantic farm: An environmental view. In: S. Brink & N. S. Price (eds.) *The Viking world*. London: Routledge.

Burdukiewicz, J. M. 1986. *The Late Pleistocene shouldered point assemblages in Western Europe*. Leiden: E. J. Brill.

Burke, A. 2011. Spatial abilities, cognition and the pattern of Neanderthal and modern human dispersals. *Quaternary International*, 247, 230–235.

Burney, D. A., Burney, L. P., Godfrey, L. R., Jungers, W. L., Goodman, S. M., Wright, H. T. & Jull, A. J. T. 2004. A chronology for late prehistoric Madagascar. *Journal of Human Evolution*, 47, 25–63.

Buvit, I., Terry, K., Kolosov, V. K. & Konstantinov, M. V. 2011. The alluvial history and sedimentary record of the Priiskovoe site and its place in the Palaeolithic prehistory of Siberia. *Geoarchaeology*, 26, 616–648.

Callaghan, R. 2008. On the question of the absence of Archaic Age sites on Jamaica. *The Journal of Island and Coastal Archaeology*, 3, 54–71.

Callaghan, R. 2010. Crossing the Guadeloupe passage in the Archaic age. In: S. M. Fitzpatrick & A. H. Ross (eds.) *Island shores, distant pasts: Archaeological and biological approaches to the Pre-Columbian settlement of the Caribbean*. Gainesville: University Press of Florida.

Callow, P. 1986. Raw materials and sources. In: P. Callow & J. M. Cornford (eds.) *La Cotte de St. Brelade 1961–1978: Excavations by C. B. M. McBurney*. Norwich: Geo Books.

Callow, P. & Cornford, J. M. (eds.) 1986. *La Cotte de St. Brelade 1961–1978. Excavations by C. B. M. McBurney*. Norwich: Geo Books.

Cann, R., Stoneking, M. & Wilson, A. 1987. Mitochondrial DNA and human evolution. *Nature*, 325, 31–36.

Carbonell, E. 1992. Abric Romani nivell H: un model d'estraregia ocupacional al plistoce superior mediterrani. *ESTRAT: Revista d'arquelogia, prehistoria i historia antiga*, 5, 157–308.

Carbonell, E., Bermudez de Castro, J. M., Arsuaga, J. L., Diez, J. C., Rosas, A., Cuenca-Bescos, G., Sala, R., Mosquera, M. & Rodriguez, X. P. 1995. Lower Pleistocene hominids and artifacts from Atapuerca-TDS (Spain). *Science*, 269, 826–830.

Carbonell, E., Bermudez de Castro, J. M., Pares, J. M., Perez-Gonzalez, A., Cuenca-Bescos, G., Olle, A., Mosquera, M., Huguet, R., van der Made, J., Rosas, A., Sala, R., Vallverdu, J., Garcia, N., Granger, D. E., Martinon-Torres, M., Rodriguez, X. P., Stock, G. M., Verges, J. M., Allue, E., Burjachs, F., Caceres, I., Canals, A., Benito, A., Diez, C., Lozano, M., Mateos, A., Navazo, M., Rodriguez, J., Rosell, J. & Arsuaga, J. L. 2008. The first hominin of Europe. *Nature*, 452, 465–469.

Carbonell, E., Mosquera, M., Rodriguez, X. P. & Sala, R. 1996. The first human settlement of Europe. *Journal of Anthropological Research*, 51, 107–114.

Carlson, A. E., Legrande, A. N., Oppo, D. W., Came, R. E., Schmidt, G. A., Anslow, F. S., Licciardi, J. M. & Obbink, E. A. 2008. Rapid Early Holocene deglaciation of the Laurentide ice sheet. *Nature Geoscience*, 1, 620–624.

Carrión, J. S., Rose, J. & Stringer, C. 2011. Early human evolution in the Western Palaeoarctic: Ecological scenarios. *Quaternary Science Reviews*, 30, 1281–1295.

Cavalli-Sforza, L. L. & Cavalli-Sforza, F. 1995. *The great human diasporas: The history of diversity and evolution*. Reading, MA: Perseus Books.

Cavalli-Sforza, L. L., Menozzi, P. & Piazza, A. 1994. *The history and geography of human genes*. Princeton: Princeton University Press.

Cerny, V., Pereira, L., Kujanova, M., Vasikova, A., Hajek, M., Morris, M. & Mulligan, C. J. 2008. Out of Arabia: The settlement of island Soqotra as revealed by mitochondrial and Y chromosome genetic diversity. *American Journal of Physical Anthropology*, 138, 439–447.

Chapman, J. 2000. *Fragmentation in archaeology: People, places and broken objects in the prehistory of south-eastern Europe*. London: Routledge.

Chapman, J. & Gaydarska, B. 2007. *Parts and wholes: Fragmentation in prehistoric context*. Oxford: Oxbow Books.

Chapman, J. & Gaydarska, B. 2010. Fragmenting hominins and the presencing of Early Palaeolithic social worlds. *In*: R. Dunbar, C. Gamble & J. A. J. Gowlett (eds.) *Social brain, distributed mind*. Oxford: Oxford University Press.

Chauvet, J.-M., Brunel Deschamps, E. & Hillaire, C. 1995. *Chauvet Cave: The discovery of the world's oldest paintings*. London: Thames and Hudson.

Cherry, J. F. 1981. Pattern and process in the earliest colonization of the Mediterranean islands. *Proceedings of the Prehistoric Society*, 47, 41–68.

Cherry, J. F. 1990. The first colonization of the Mediterranean islands: A review of recent research. *Journal of Mediterranean Archaeology*, 3, 145–221.

Childe, V. G. 1929. *The Danube in prehistory*. Oxford: Oxford University Press.

Chlachula, J., Drozdov, N. I. & Ovodov, N. D. 2003. Last interglacial peopling of Siberia: The Middle Palaeolithic site Ust'-Izhul', the upper Yenisei area. *Boreas*, 32, 506–520.

Churchill, S. E. 1993. Weapon technology, prey size selection, and hunting methods in modern hunter-gatherers: Implications for hunting in the Palaeolithic and

Mesolithic. *In:* G. L. Peterkin, H. Bricker & P. A. Mellars (eds.) *Hunting and animal exploitation in the later Palaeolithic and Mesolithic of Eurasia.* Archaeological Papers of the American Anthropological Association 4.

Clark, A. 1997. *Being there: Bringing brain, body and world together again.* Cambridge, MA: MIT Press.

Clark, A. 2010. Material surrogacy and the supernatural: Reflections of the role of artefacts in "off-line" cognition. *In:* L. Malafouris & C. Renfrew (eds.) *The cognitive life of things: Recasting the boundaries of the mind.* Cambridge: McDonald Institute for Archaeological Research.

Clark, A. & Chalmers, D. A. 1998. The extended mind. *Analysis,* **58,** 7–19.

Clark, J. D., Beyenne, Y., WoldeGabriel, G., Hart, W. K., Renne, P., Gilbert, H., Defleur, A., Suwa, G., Katoh, S., Ludwig, K. R., Boisserie, J.-R., Asfaw, B. & White, T. D. 2003. Stratigraphic, chronological and behavioural contexts of plesitocene *Homo sapiens* from Middle Awash, Ethiopia. *Nature,* **423,** 747–752.

Clark, J. G. D. 1961. *World prehistory in new perspective.* Cambridge: Cambridge University Press.

Clarke, D. L. 1968. *Analytical Archaeology.* London: Methuen.

Clausen, B. L. (ed.) 1993. *Viking voyages to North America.* Roskilde: Viking Ship Museum Roskilde.

Cohen, A. S., Stone, J. R., Beuning, K. R. M., Park, L. E., Reinthal, P. N., Dettman, D., Scholz, C. A., Johnson, T. C., King, J. W., Talbot, M. R., Brown, E. T. & Ivory, S. J. 2007. Ecological consequences of early Late Pleistocene megadroughts in tropical Africa. *Proceedings of the National Academy of Sciences of the United States of America,* **104,** 16422–16427.

Cohen, E. E. A., Ejsmond-Frey, R., Knight, N. & Dunbar, R. I. M. 2010. Rowers' high: Behavioural synchrony is correlated with elevated pain thresholds. *Biology Letters,* **6,** 106–108.

Cole, J. N. 2008. Conference Poster: Identity within intentionality: Use of the body to relate the social brain to the archaeological record. *Social brain, distributed mind.* British Academy, London.

Coles, B. 1998. Doggerland: A speculative survey. *Proceedings of the Prehistoric Society,* **64,** 45–81.

Collard, I. F. & Foley, R. A. 2002. Latitudinal patterns and environmental determinants of recent human cultural diversity: Do humans follow biogeographical rules? *Evolutionary Ecology Research,* **4,** 371–383.

Collard, M., Kemery, M. & Banks, S. 2005. Causes of toolkit variation among hunter-gatherers: A test of four competing hypotheses. *Canadian Journal of Archaeology,* **29,** 1–19.

Collerson, K. D. & Weisler, M. I. 2007. Stone adze compositions and the extent of ancient Polynesian voyaging and trade. *Science,* **317,** 1907–1911.

Conard, N. J. 1992. *Tönchesberg and its position in the Palaeolithic prehistory of Northern Europe.* Bonn: Habelt.

Conard, N. J. 2009. A female figurine from the basal Aurignacian of Hohle fels Cave in southwestern Germany. *Nature,* **459,** 248–252.

Conard, N. J. & Bolus, M. 2003. Radiocarbon dating the appearance of modern humans and timing of cultural innovations in Europe: New results and new challenges. *Journal of Human Evolution,* **44,** 331–371.

Conard, N. J. & Bolus, M. 2008. Radiocarbon dating the late Middle Palaeolithic and the Aurignacian of the Swabian Jura. *Journal of Human Evolution*, **55**, 886–897.

Connolly, B. & Anderson, R. 1988. *First contact*. London: Penguin.

Copeland, S. R., Sponheimer, M., De Ruiter, D. J., Lee-Thorp, J. A., Codron, D., le Roux, P. J., Grimes, V. & Richards, M. P. 2011. Strontium isotope evidence for landscape use by early hominins. *Nature*, **474**, 76–79.

Cosgrove, R. 1999. Forty-two degrees south: The archaeology of Late Pleistocene Tasmania. *Journal of World Prehistory*, **13**, 357–402.

Cosgrove, R., Field, J. & Ferrier, A. 2007. The archaeology of Australia's tropical rainforests. *Palaeogeography, Palaeoclimatology, Palaeoecology*, **251**, 150–173.

Coward, F. 2008. Standing on the shoulders of giants. *Science*, **319**, 1493–1495.

Coward, F. & Gamble, C. 2010. Materiality and metaphor in earliest prehistory. *In:* L. Malafouris & C. Renfrew (eds.) *The cognitive life of things*. Cambridge: McDonald Institute of Archaeological Research.

Cox, M. P., Nelson, M. G., Tumonggor, M. K., Ricaut, F.-X. & Sudoyo, H. 2012. A small cohort of island Southeast Asian women founded Madagascar. *Proceedings of the Royal Society of London B*, online.

Crawford, M. H., Rubicz, R. C. & Zlojutro, M. 2010. Origins of Aleuts and the genetic structure of populations of the archipelago: Molecular and archaeological perspectives. *Human Biology*, **82**, 695–717.

Cullen, B. 2000. *Contagious ideas: On evolution, culture, archaeology, and cultural virus theory*. Oxford: Oxbow Books.

Currant, A. & Jacobi, R. 2011. The mammal faunas of the British Pleistocene. *In:* N. Ashton, S. Lewis & C. B. Stringer (eds.) *The ancient human occupation of Britain*. Amsterdam: Elsevier Developments in Quaternary Science.

Dalén, L., Orlando, L., Shapiro, B., Brandstöm-Durling, M., Quam, R., Thomas, M., Gilbert, P., Fernández-Lomana, J. C. D., Willerslev, E., Arsuaga, J. L. & Götherstöm, A. 2012. Partial genetic turnover in Neanderthals: Continuity in the east and population replacement in the west. *Molecular Biology and Evolution*, **29**, 1893–1897.

Damasio, A. 2000. *The feeling of what happens: Body, emotion and the making of consciousness*. London: Vintage.

Dansgaard, W., Johnsen, S. J., Clausen, H. B., Dahl-Jensen, D., Gundestrup, N. S., Hammer, C. U., Hvidberg, C. S., Steffensen, J. P., Sveinbjörnsdottir, A. E., Jouzel, J. & Bond, G. 1993. Evidence for general instability of past climate from a 250-kyr ice-core record. *Nature*, **364**, 218–220.

Davidson, I. & McGrew, W. C. 2005. Stone tools and the uniqueness of human culture. *Journal of the Royal Anthropological Institute*, **11**, 793–817.

Davies, S. W. G. 2001. A very model of a modern human industry: New perspectives on the origins and spread of the Aurignacian in Europe. *Proceedings of the Prehistoric Society*, **67**, 195–217.

Davies, S. W. G. 2007. Re-evaluating the Aurignacian as an expression of modern human mobility and dispersal. *In:* P. Mellars, O. Bar-Yosef, C. Stringer & K. V. Boyle (eds.) *Rethinking the human revolution*. Cambridge: McDonald Institute.

Davis, R. S. & Knecht, R. A. 2010. Continuity and change in the Eastern Aleutian archaeological sequence. *Human Biology*, **82**, 507–524.

Davis, S. J. & Valla, F. R. 1978. Evidence for domestication of the dog 12,000 years ago in the Natufian of Israel. *Nature*, **276**, 608–610.

de la Torre, I. 2004. Omo revisited. Evaluating the technological skills of Pliocene hominids *Current Anthropology*, **45**, 439–465.

de la Torre, I. 2011. The origins of stone tool technology in Africa: A historical perspective. *Philosophical Transactions of the Royal Society of London B*, **366**, 1028–1037.

D'Errico, F., Henshilwood, C. S., Lawson, G., Vanhaeren, M., Tillier, A.-M., Soressi, M., Bresson, F., Maureille, B., Nowell, A., Lakarra, J., Backwell, L. & Julien, M. 2003. Archaeological evidence for the emergence of language, symbolism, and music: An alternative multidisciplinary perspective. *Journal of World Prehistory*, **17**, 1–70.

de Waal, E. 2010. *The hare with amber eyes: A hidden inheritance.* New York: Random House.

de Waal, F. 2006. *Primates and philosophers: How morality evolved.* Princeton: Princeton University Press.

Delson, E. 1980. Fossil macaques, phyletic relationships and a scenario of deployment. *In*: D. G. Lindburg (ed.) *The macaques: Studies in ecology, behavior and evolution.* New York: Van Nostrand Reinhold.

deMenocal, P. B. 2004. African climate and faunal evolution during the Pliocene–Pleistocene. *Earth and Planetary Science Letters*, **220**, 3–24.

Dennell, R. W. 2005. The solo (Ngandong) *Homo erectus* assemblage: A taphopnomic assessment. *Archaeology in Oceania*, **40**, 81–90.

Dennell, R. W. 2009. *The Palaeolithic settlement of Asia.* Cambridge: Cambridge University Press.

Dennell, R. W. & Roebroeks, W. 2005. An Asian perspective on early human dispersal from Africa. *Nature*, **438**, 1099–1104.

Derevianko, A. P. 2010. The Middle to Upper Palaeolithic transition in southern Siberia and Mongolia. *In*: K. V. Boyle, C. Gamble & O. Bar-Yosef (eds.) *The Upper Palaeolithic revolution in global perspective: Papers in honour of Sir Paul Mellars.* Cambridge: McDonald Institute.

Derevianko, A. P., Shimkin, D. B. & Powers, W. R. (eds.) 1998. *The Palaeolithic of Siberia: New discoveries and interpretations.* Urbana: University of Illinois Press.

Détroit, F., Dizon, E., Falguères, C., Hameau, S., Ronquillo, W. & Sémah, F. 2004. Upper Pleistocene *Homo sapiens* from the Tabon Cave (Palawan, The Philippines): Decription and dating of new discoveries. *Comptes Rendus Palevol*, **3**, 705–712.

Di, D. & Sanchez-Mazas, A. 2011. Challenging views on the peopling history of East Asia: The story according to HLA markers. *American Journal of Physical Anthropology*, **145**, 81–96.

Diamond, J. & Bellwood, P. 2003. Farmers and their languages: The first expansions. *Science*, **300**, 597–603.

Dickinson, W. R. 2004. Impacts of eustasy and hydro-isostasy on the evolution and landforms of Pacific atolls. *Palaeogeography, Palaeoclimatology, Palaeoecology* **213**, 251–269.

Dillehay, T. D. (ed.) 1989. *Monte Verde: A late Pleistocene settlement in Chile, vol. 1 palaeoenvironment and site context.* Washington: Smithsonian Institution Press.

Djindjian, F. 1994. L'influence des frontières naturelles dans les déplacements des chasseurs-cueilleurs au würm récent. *Preistoria Alpina*, **28**, 7–28.

Djindjian, F., Kozlowski, J. & Otte, M. 1999. *Le Paléolithique supérieur en Europe*. Paris: Armand Colin.

Dobres, M.-A. & Robb, J. (eds.) 2000. *Agency in archaeology*. London: Routledge.

Dodson, J. R., Taylor, D., Ono, Y. & Wng, P. 2004. Climate, human, and natural systems of the PEP II transect. *Quaternary International*, 118–119, 3–12.

Dolukhanov, P. M., Shukurov, A. M., Tarasov, P. E. & Zaitseva, G. I. 2002. Colonization of Northern Eurasia by modern humans: Radiocarbon chronology and environment. *Journal of Archaeological Science*, 29, 593–606.

Dorling, D., Newman, M. & Barford, A. 2008. *The atlas of the real world: Mapping the way we live*. London: Thames and Hudson.

Drake, N. A., Blench, R. M., Armitage, S. J., Bristow, C. S., & White, K. H. 2010. Ancient watercourses and biogeography of the Sahara explain the peopling of the desert. *Proceedings of the National Academy of Sciences of the United States of America*, 108, 458–462.

Drake, N. A., ElHawat, A. S., Turner, P., Armitage, S. J., Salem, M. J., White, K. H. & McLaren, S. 2008. Palaeohydrology of the Fazzan Basin and surrounding regions: The last 7 million years. *Palaeogeography, Palaeoclimatology, Palaeoecology*, 263, 131–145.

Dunbar, R. 2003. The social brain: Mind, language, and society in evolutionary perspective. *Annual Review of Anthropology*, 32, 163–181.

Dunbar, R. 2010. Deacon's dilemma: The problem of pair-bonding in human evolution. In: R. Dunbar, C. Gamble & J. A. J. Gowlett (eds.) *Social brain, distributed mind*. Oxford: Oxford University Press, Proceedings of the British Academy 158, pp. 155–175.

Dunbar, R., Gamble, C. & Gowlett, J. A. J. (eds.) 2010a. *Social brain, distributed mind*. Oxford: Oxford University Press, Proceedings of the British Academy 158.

Dunbar, R., Gamble, C. & Gowlett, J. A. J. (eds.) 2010b. The social brain and the distributed mind. In: R. Dunbar, C. Gamble & J. A. J. Gowlett (eds). *Social brain, distributed mind*. Oxford: Oxford University Press, Proceedings of the British Academy 158, pp. 3–15.

Dunbar, R. & Shultz, S. 2007. Evolution in the social brain. *Science*, 317, 1344–1347.

Durkheim, E. 1912 (1915). *The elementary forms of the religious life*. London: George Allen and Unwin.

Dyson-Hudson, R. & Smith, E. A. 1978. Human territoriality: An ecological reassessment. *American Anthropologist*, 80, 21–41.

Earle, T., Gamble, C. & Poinard, H. 2011. Migration. In: A. Shryock & D. L. Smail (eds.) *Deep history: The architecture of past and present*. Berkeley: University of California Press.

Elias, S. & Crocker, B. 2008. The Bering land bridge: A moisture barrier to the dispersal of steppe-tundra biota? *Quaternary Science Reviews*, 27, 2473–2483.

Eliot, T. S. 1948. *Notes towards the definition of culture*. London: Faber and Faber.

Elton, S. 2008. The environmental context of human evolutionary history in Eurasia and Africa. *Journal of Anatomy*, 212, 377–393.

Elton, S., Bishop, L. C. & Wood, B. 2001. Comparative context of Plio–Pleistocene hominin brain evolution. *Journal of Human Evolution*, 41, 1–27.

Erickson, D. L., Smith, B. D., Clarke, A. C., Sandweiss, D. H. & Tuross, N. 2005. An Asian origin for a 10,000-year-old domesticated plant in the Americas. *Proceedings of the National Academy of Sciences of the United States of America*, 102, 18315–18320.

Faisal, A., Stout, D., Apel, J. & Bradley, B. 2010. The manipulative complexity of Lower Palaeolithic stone toolmaking. *PLoS ONE*, **5**, e13718.

Falk, D., Hildebolt, C., Smith, K., Morwood, M. J., Sutikna, T., Brown, P., Jatmiko, A., Saptomo, E. W., Brunsden, B. & Prior, F. 2005. The brain of LB1, *Homo floresiensis*. *Science*, **308**, 242–245.

Féblot-Augustins, J. 1997. *La circulation des matières premières au Paléolithique*. Liège: ERAUL, vol. 75.

Fedele, F. G., Giaccio, B. & Hajdas, I. 2008. Timescales and cultural process at 40,000BP in the light of the Campanian Ignimbrite eruption, western Eurasia. *Journal of Human Evolution*, **55**, 834–857.

Fernandes, C. A. 2012. Bayesian coalescent inference from mitochondrial DNA variation of the colonization time of Arabia by the Hamadryas baboon (*Papio hamadryas hamadryas*). In: M. D. Petraglia & J. I. Rose (eds.) *The evolution of human populations in Arabia: Palaeoenvironments, prehistory and genetics*. Berlin: Springer.

Fernández-Armesto, F. 2006. *Pathfinders: A global history of exploration*. Oxford: Oxford University Press.

Field, J. S., Petraglia, M. D. & Lahr, M. A. 2007. The southern dispersal hypothesis and the South Asia archaeological record: Examination of dispersal routes through GIS analysis. *Journal of Anthropological Archaeology*, **26**, 88–108.

Fitzpatrick, S. M. 2011. Verification of an Archaic age occupation on Barbados, southern Lesser Antilles. *Radiocarbon*, **53**, 595–604.

Fitzpatrick, S. M. & Callaghan, R. 2008. Seafaring simulations and the origin of prehistoric settlers to Madagascar. In: G. Clark, F. Leach & S. O'Connor (eds.) *Islands of enquiry: Colonization, seafaring and the archaeology of maritime landscapes*. Canberra: ANU Press Terra Australis, vol. 29.

Fix, A. 1999. *Migration and colonization in human microevolution*. Cambridge: Cambridge University Press.

Flannery, T. F. & White, J. P. 1991. Animal translocation. *National Geographic Research and Exploration*, **7**, 96–113.

Foley, R. 2002. Adaptive radiations and dispersals in hominin evolutionary ecology. *Evolutionary Anthropology*, **11**, 32–37.

Foley, R. & Gamble, C. 2009. The ecology of social transitions in human evolution. *Philosophical Transactions of the Royal Society of London B*, **364**, 3267–3279.

Foley, R. & Lahr, M. M. 1997. Mode 3 technologies and the evolution of modern humans. *Cambridge Archaeological Journal*, **7**, 3–36.

Foley, R. & Lahr, M. M. 2011. The evolution of the diversity of culture. *Philosophical Transactions of the Royal Society of London B*, **366**, 1080–1089.

Folinsbee, K. E. & Brooks, D. R. 2007. Miocene hominoid biogeography: Pulses of dispersal and differentiation. *Journal of Biogeography*, **34**, 383–397.

Fooden, J. 2007. Systematic review of the Barbary Macaque, *Macaca sylvanus* (Linnaeus, 1758). *Fieldiana: Zoology NS*, **113**, 1–58.

Forster, P. 2004. Ice ages and the mitochondrial DNA chronology of human dispersals: A review. *Philosophical Transactions of the Royal Society of London B*, **359**, 255–264.

Fox, R. 1967. *Kinship and marriage*. Harmondsworth: Penguin Books.

Freedberg, D. & Gallese, V. 2007. Motion, emotion and empathy in esthetic experience. *Trends in Cognitive Sciences*, **11**, 197–203.

Frith, C. 2007. *Making up the mind: How the brain creates our mental world.* Oxford: Blackwell.

Frith, U. & Frith, C. 2010. The social brain: Allowing humans to boldly go where no other species has been. *Philosophical Transactions of the Royal Society of London B*, **365**, 165–175.

Gallese, V. 2006. *Embodied simulation: From mirror neuron systems to interpersonal relations. Empathy and fairness.* Chichester: Wiley (Novartis Foundation Symposium 278).

Gamble, C. S. 1993. *Timewalkers: The prehistory of global colonization.* Cambridge, MA: Harvard University Press.

Gamble, C. S. 1998. Palaeolithic society and the release from proximity: A network approach to intimate relations. *World Archaeology*, **29**, 426–449.

Gamble, C. S. 1999. *The Palaeolithic societies of Europe.* Cambridge: Cambridge University Press.

Gamble, C. S. 2007. *Origins and revolutions: Human identity in earliest prehistory.* New York: Cambridge University Press.

Gamble, C. S. 2008. Kinship and material culture: Archaeological implications of the human global diaspora. *In:* N. J. Allen, H. Callan, R. Dunbar & W. James (eds.) *Kinship and Evolution.* Oxford: Blackwell.

Gamble, C. S. 2009. Human display and dispersal: A case study from biotidal Britain in the Middle and Upper Pleistocene. *Evolutionary Anthropology*, **18**, 144–156.

Gamble, C. S. 2010a. Thinking through the Upper Palaeolithic revolution. *In:* K. V. Boyle, C. Gamble & O. Bar-Yosef (eds.) *The Upper Palaeolithic revolution in global perspective: Papers in honour of Sir Paul Mellars.* Cambridge: McDonald Institute.

Gamble, C. S. 2010b. Technologies of separation and the evolution of social extension. *In:* R. Dunbar, C. Gamble & J. A. J. Gowlett (eds.) *Social brain, distributed mind.* Oxford: Oxford University Press, Proceedings of the British Academy 158.

Gamble, C. S. 2012. When the words dry up: Music and material metaphors half a million years ago. *In:* N. Bannan (ed.) *Music, language and human evolution.* Oxford: Oxford University Press.

Gamble, C. S. & Boismier, W. A. 2012. The Lynford Neanderthals. *In:* W. A. Boismier, C. S. Gamble & F. Coward (eds.) *Neanderthals among mammoths: Excavations at Lynford Quarry, Norfolk.* London: English Heritage Monographs.

Gamble, C. S., Davies, S. W. G., Richards, M., Pettitt, P. & Hazelwood, L. 2005. Archaeological and genetic foundations of the European population during the Lateglacial: Implications for "agricultural thinking". *Cambridge Archaeological Journal*, **15**, 55–85.

Gamble, C. S., Davies, W., Pettitt, P. & Richards, M. 2004. Climate change and evolving human diversity in Europe during the last glacial. *Philosophical Transactions of the Royal Society Biological Sciences*, **359**, 243–254.

Gamble, C. S. & Gaudzinski, S. 2005. Bones and powerful individuals: Faunal case studies from the Arctic and European Middle Palaeolithic. *In:* C. Gamble & M. Porr (eds.) *The individual hominid in context: Archaeological investigations of Lower and Middle Palaeolithic landscapes, locales and artefacts.* London: Routledge.

Gamble, C. S., Gowlett, J. A. J. & Dunbar, R. 2011. The social brain and the shape of the Palaeolithic. *Cambridge Archaeological Journal*, 21, 115–135.

Gamble, C. S. & Steele, J. 1999. Hominid ranging patterns and dietary strategies. *In*: H. Ullrich (ed.) *Hominid evolution: Lifestyles and survival strategies*. Gelsenkirchen: Edition Archaea.

Gansser, A. 1982. The morphogenic phase of mountain building. *In*: K. J. Hsü (ed.) *Mountain building processes*. London: Academic Press.

Garrod, D. A. E. & Bate, D. M. A. 1937. *The stone age of Mount Carmel*. Oxford: Clarendon Press.

Gaudzinski, S. 1995. Wallertheim revisited: A reanalysis of the fauna from the Middle Paleolithic site of the Wallertheim (Rheinhessen/Germany). *Journal of Archaeological Science*, 22, 51–66.

Gaudzinski, S. 1996. On bovid assemblages and their consequences for the knowledge of subsistence patterns in the Middle Palaeolithic. *Proceedings of the Prehistoric Society*, 62, 19–39.

Gaudzinski, S. & Roebroeks, W. 2000. Adults only. Reindeer hunting at the Middle Palaeolithic site Salzgitter Lebenstedt, Northern Germany. *Journal of Human Evolution*, 38, 497–521.

Gell, A. 1998. *Art and agency: Towards a new anthropological theory*. Oxford: Clarendon Press.

Germonpré, M., Lázničková-Galetová, M. & Sablin, M. V. 2012. Palaeolithic dog skulls at the Gravettian Předmostí site, the Czech Republic. *Journal of Archaeological Science*, 39, 184–202.

Germonpré, M., Sablin, M. V., Stevens, R. E., Hedges, R. E. M., Hofreiter, M., Stiller, M. & Després, V. R. 2009. Fossil dogs and wolves from Palaeolithic sites in Belgium, the Ukraine and Russia: Osteometry, ancient DNA and stable isotopes. *Journal of Archaeological Science*, 36, 473–490.

Gibbons, A. 2010a. Close encounters of the prehistoric kind. *Science*, 328, 680–684.

Gibbons, A. 2010b. Human ancestor caught in the midst of a makeover. *Science*, 328, 413.

Gibert, J., Gibert, L., Iglesias, A. & Maestro, E. 1998. Two "Oldowan" assemblages in the Plio–Pleistocene deposits of the Orce region, southeast Spain. *Antiquity*, 72, 17–25.

Gibson, K. R. 1986. Cognition, brain size and the extraction of embedded food resources. *In*: J. Else & P. C. Lee (eds.) *Primate ontogeny, cognition and social behaviour*. Cambridge: Cambridge University Press.

Gilbert, D. T. & Wilson, T. D. 2007. Prospection: experiencing the future. *Science*, 317, 1351–1354.

Goebel, T. 2007. The missing years for modern humans. *Science*, 315, 194–196.

Goebel, T., Derevianko, A. P. & Petrin, V. T. 1993. Dating the Middle to Upper Palaeolithic transition at Kara-Bom, Siberia. *Current Anthropology*, 34, 452–458.

Goebel, T., Waters, M. R. & O'Rourke, D. H. 2008. The Late Pleistocene dispersal of modern humans in the Americas. *Science*, 319, 1497–1502.

Goren-Inbar, N., Feibel, C., Verosub, K. L., Melamed, Y., Kislev, M. E., Tchernov, E. & Saragusti, I. 2000. Pleistocene milestones on the out-of-Africa corridor at Gesher Benet Ya'aqov, Israel. *Science*, 289, 944–947.

Gosden, C. 2010a. The death of the mind. *In*: L. Malafouris & C. Renfrew (eds.) *The cognitive life of things: Recasting the boundaries of the mind*. Cambridge: McDonald Institute for Archaeological Research.

Gosden, C. 2010b. When humans arrived in the New Guinea highlands. *Science*, **330**, 41–42.

Gould, S. J. & Eldredge, N. 1977. Punctuated equilibria: The tempo and mode of evolution reconsidered. *Paleobiology*, **3**, 115–151.

Gowlett, J. A. J. 2000. Apes, hominids and technology. *In*: C. Harcourt (ed.) *New perspectives on primate evolution and behaviour*. London: Linnean Society.

Gowlett, J. A. J. 2009. The longest transition or multiple revolutions? Curves and steps in the record of human origins. *In*: M. Camps & P. Chauhan (eds.) *A sourcebook of Palaeolithic transitions: Methods, theories and interpretations*. Berlin: Springer Verlag.

Gowlett, J. A. J. 2010. Firing up the social brain. *In*: R. Dunbar, C. Gamble & J. A. J. Gowlett (eds.) *Social brain, distributed mind*. Oxford: Oxford University Press.

Green, R. E., Krause, J., Briggs, A. W., Maricic, T., Stenzel, U., Kircher, M., Patterson, N., Li, H., Zhai, W., Hsi-Yang Fritz, M., Hansen, N. F., Durand, E. Y., Malaspinas, A.-S., Jensen, J. D., Marques-Bonet, T. M., Alkan, C., Prüfer, K., Meyer, M., Burbano, H. A., Good, J. M., Schultz, R., Aximu-Petri, Butthof, A., Höber, B., Höffner, B., Siegemund, M., Weihmann, A., Nusbaum, C., Lander, E. S., Russ, C., Novod, N., Affourtit, J., Egholm, M., Verna, C., Rudan, P., Brajkovic, D., Kucan, Z., Gusic, I., Doronichev, V. B., Golovanova, L. V., Lalueza-Fox, C., de la Rasilla, M., Fortea, J., Rosas, A., Schmitz, R. W., Johnson, P. L. F., Eichler, E. E., Falush, D., Birney, E., Mullikin, J. C., Slatkin, M., Nielsen, R., Kelso, J., Lachmann, M., Reich, D. & Pääbo, S. 2010. A draft sequence of the Neandertal genome. *Science*, **328**, 710–722.

Gronau, I., Hubisz, M. J., Gulko, B., Danko, C. G. & Siepel, A. 2011. Bayesian inference of ancient human demography from individual genome sequences. *Nature Genetics*, **43**, 1031–1035.

Grønnow, B. 1988. Prehistory in permafrost: Investigations at the Saqqaq site, Qeqertasussuk, Disco Bay, West Greenland. *Journal of Danish Archaeology*, **7**, 24–39.

Grønnow, B. 1994. Qeqertasussuk: The archaeology of a frozen Saqqaq site in Disko Bugt, West Greenland. *In*: D. Morrison & J.-L. Pilon (eds.) *Threads of Arctic prehistory: Papers in honour of William E. Taylor Jr*. Ottawa: Canadian Museum of Civilization: Archaeological Survey of Canada, vol. 149.

Groube, L. M. 1971. Tonga, Lapita pottery, and Polynesian origins. *Journal of the Polynesian Society*, **80**, 278–316.

Grove, M. 2010. The archaeology of group size. *In*: R. Dunbar, C. Gamble & J. A. J. Gowlett (eds.) *Social brain, distributed mind*. Oxford: Oxford University Press.

Grove, M. 2011a. Change and variability in Plio–Pleistocene climates: Modelling the hominin response. *Journal of Archaeological Science*, online.

Grove, M. 2011b. Speciation, diversity, and Mode 1 technologies: The impact of variability selection. *Journal of Human Evolution*, **61**, 306–319.

Grove, M. & Coward, F. 2008. From individual neurons to social brains. *Cambridge Archaeological Journal*, **18**, 387–400.

Gunn, B. F., Baudouin, L. & Olsen, K. M. 2011. Independent origins of cultivated coconut (*Cocos nucifera* L.) in the Old World tropics. *PLoS ONE*, **6**, e21143.

Guthrie, R. D. 1990. *Frozen fauna of the mammoth steppe*. Chicago: University of Chicago Press.

Habgood, P. J. & Franklin, N. R. 2008. The revolution that didn't arrive: A review of Pleistocene Sahul. *Journal of Human Evolution*, **55**, 187–222.

Hahn, J. 1977. *Aurignacian: Das altere Jungpalaolithikum in Mittel- und Osteuropa.* Koln: Fundamenta Reihe, A 9.

Hamilton, M. J. & Buchanan, B. 2007. Spatial gradients in Clovis-age radiocarbon dates across North America suggest rapid colonization from the north. *Proceedings of the National Academy of Sciences of the United States of America*, **104**, 15625–15630.

Hamilton, M. J. & Buchanan, B. 2010. Archaeological support for the three-stage expansion of modern humans across northeastern Eurasia and into the Americas. *PLoS ONE*, **5**, e12472.

Harpending, H. C., Sherry, S. T., Rogers, A. R. & Stoneking, M. 1993. The genetic structure of ancient human populations. *Current Anthropology*, **34**, 483–496.

Harrison, T. 2010. Apes among the tangled branches of human origins. *Science*, **327**, 532–534.

Hassan, F. 1975. *Demographic archaeology*. New York: Academic Press.

Hazelwood, L. & Steele, J. 2004. Spatial dynamics of human dispersals: Constraints on modelling and archaeological validation. *Journal of Archaeological Science*, **31**, 669–679.

Hendry, J. 1993. *Wrapping culture: Politeness, presentation, and power in Japan and other societies*. Oxford: Oxford University Press.

Henn, B. M., Gignoux, C. R., Granka, J. M., Macpherson, J. M., Kidd, J. M., Rodríguez-Botigué, L., Ramachandran, S., Hon, L., Brisbin, A., Lin, A. A., Underhill, P. A., Comas, D., Kidd, K. K., Norman, P. J., Parham, P., Bustamante, C. D., Mountain, J. L. & Feldman, M. W. 2011. Hunter-gatherer genomic diversity suggests a southern African origin for modern humans. *Proceedings of the National Academy of Sciences of the United States of America*, **108**, 5154–5162.

Henshilwood, C. S., D'Errico, F., Marean, C. W., Milo, R. G. & Yates, R. 2001. An early bone tool industry from the Middle Stone Age, Blombos Cave, South Africa: Implications for the origins of modern human behaviour, symbolism and language. *Journal of Human Evolution*, **41**, 631–678.

Henshilwood, C. S., D'Errico, F., Yates, R., Jacobs, Z., Tribolo, C., Duller, G., Mercier, N., Sealy, J., Valladas, H., Watts, I. & Wintle, A. G. 2002. Emergence of modern human behaviour: Middle Stone Age engravings from South Africa. *Science*, **295**, 1278–1280.

Henshilwood, C. S. & Marean, C. W. 2003. The origin of modern human behaviour: Critique of the models and their test implications. *Current Anthropology*, **44**, 627–651.

Herrmann, E., Call, J., Hernandez-Lloreda, M. V., Hare, B. & Tomasello, M. 2007. Humans have evolved specialized skills of social cognition: The cultural intelligence hypothesis. *Science*, **317**, 1360–1366.

Higham, T. F. G., Compton, T., Stringer, C., Jacobi, R., Shapiro, B., Trinkaus, E., Chandler, B., Gröning, F., Collins, C., Hillson, S., O'Higgins, P., Fitzgerald, C. & Fagan, M. 2011. The earliest evidence for anatomically modern humans in northwestern Europe. *Nature*, **479**, 521–524.

Higham, T. F. G., Jacobi, R. M. & Ramsey, C. B. 2006. AMS radiocarbon dating of ancient bone using ultrafiltration. *Radiocarbon*, **48**, 179–195.

Hill, C., Soares, P., Mormina, M., Macaulay, V., Clarke, D., Blumbach, P. B., Vizuete-Forster, M., Forster, P., Bulbeck, D., Oppenheimer, S. & Richards, M. 2007. A mitochondrial stratigraphy for island Southeast Asia. *American Journal of Human Genetics*, 80, 29–43.

Hill, K. R., Walker, R. S., Božičević, M., Eder, J., Headland, T., Hewlett, B., Hurtado, A. M., Marlowe, F., Wiessner, P. & Wood, B. 2011. Co-residence patterns in hunter-gatherer societies show unique human social structure. *Science*, **331**, 1286–1289.

Ho, S. Y. W. & Larson, G. 2006. Molecular clocks: When times are a-changin'. *Trends in Genetics*, **22**, 79–83.

Hoffecker, J. F. 2005. *A prehistory of the north: Numan settlement of the higher latitudes*. New Brunswick: Rutgers University Press.

Hoffecker, J. F. 2009. The spread of modern humans in Europe. *Proceedings of the National Academy of Sciences of the United States of America*, 106, 16040–16045.

Hoffecker, J. F. & Elias, S. 2007. *The human ecology of Beringia*. New York: Columbia University Press.

Hoffecker, J. F., Holliday, V. T., Anikovich, M. V., Sinitsyn, A. A., Popov, V. V., Lisitsyn, S. N., Levkovskaya, G. M., Pospelova, G. A., Forman, S. L. & Giaccio, B. 2008. From the Bay of Naples to the River Don: The Campanian Ignimbrite eruption and the Middle to Upper Palaeolithic transition in Eastern Europe. *Journal of Human Evolution*, **55**, 858–870.

Hood, B. C. 2009. The circumpolar zone. *In*: B. Cunliffe, C. Gosden & R. A. Joyce (eds.) *The Oxford handbook of archaeology*. Oxford: Oxford University Press.

Hoskins, J. 1998. *Biographical objects: How things tell the story of people's lives*. New York: Routledge.

Housley, R. A., Gamble, C. S., Street, M. & Pettitt, P. 1997. Radiocarbon evidence for the Lateglacial human recolonisation of Northern Europe. *Proceedings of the Prehistoric Society*, **63**, 25–54.

Hublin, J.-J., Weston, D., Gunz, P., Richards, M., Roebroeks, W., Glimmerveen, J. & Anthonis, L. 2009. Out of the North Sea: The Zeeland Ridges Neandertal. *Journal of Human Evolution*, **57**, 777–785.

Hudjashov, G., Kivisild, T., Underhill, P. A., Endicott, P., Sanchez, J. J., Lin, A. A., Shen, P., Oefner, P., Renfrew, C., Villems, R. & Forster, P. 2007. Revealing the prehistoric settlement of Australia by Y chromosome and mtDNA analysis. *Proceedings of the National Academy of Sciences of the United States of America*, **104**, 8726–8730.

Hunt, T. L. & Lipo, C. P. 2006. Late colonization of Easter Island. *Science*, **311**, 1603–1606.

Hutchins, E. 1995. *Cognition in the wild*. Cambridge, MA: MIT Press.

Huxley, T. H. 1863. *Man's place in nature and other anthropological essays*. London: Macmillan.

Imbrie, J. & Imbrie, K. P. 1979. *Ice Ages: Solving the mystery*. London: Macmillan.

Ingold, T. 1983. The significance of storage in hunting societies. *Man*, 18, 553–571.

Irwin, G. 1992. *The prehistoric exploration and colonisation of the Pacific*. Cambridge: Cambridge University Press.

Isaac, G. L. 1972. Early phases of human beaviour: Models in lower palaeolithic archaeology. In: D. L. Clarke (ed.) Models in archaeology. London: Methuen.

Isaac, G. L. (ed.) 1997. Koobi Fora research project. Oxford: Clarendon Press.

Jablonski, N. & Chaplin, G. 2010. Human skin pigmentation as an adaptation to UV radiation. Proceedings of the National Academy of Sciences of the United States of America, 107, 8962–8968.

Jablonski, N. & Chaplin, G. 2012. Human skin pigmentation, migration and disease susceptibility. Philosophical Transactions of the Royal Society of London B, 367, 785–792.

Jacobi, R. M. & Higham, T. F. G. 2008. The "Red Lady" ages gracefully: New ultrafiltration AMS determinations from Paviland. Journal of Human Evolution, 55, 898–907.

James, W. 2003. The ceremonial animal: A new portrait of anthropology. Oxford: Oxford University Press.

Jaubert, J., Lorblanchet, M., Laville, H., Slott-Moller, R., Turq, A. & Brugal, J. 1990. Les Chasseurs d'Aurochs de La Borde. Paris: Documents d'Archeologie Française.

Jiménez-Arenas, J. M., Santonja, M., Botella, M. & Palmqvist, P. 2011. The oldest handaxes in Europe: Fact or artefact? Journal of Archaeological Science, 38, 3340–3349.

Johnsen, S. J., Clausen, H. B., Dansgaard, W., Fuhrer, K., Gundestrup, N., Hammer, C. U., Iversen, P., Jouzel, J., Stauffer, B. & Steffensen, J. P. 1992. Irregular glacial interstadials recorded in a new Greenland ice core. Nature, 359, 311–313.

Jöris, O. & Street, M. 2008. At the end of the 14C time-scale: The Middle to Upper palaeolithic record of western Eurasia. Journal of Human Evolution, 55, 782–802.

Keegan, W. F. 1994. West Indian archaeology. 1. Overview and foragers. Journal of Archaeological Research, 2, 255–284.

Keegan, W. F. 2010. Island shores and "long pauses". In: S. M. Fitzpatrick & A. H. Ross (eds.) Island shores, distant pasts: Archaeological and biological approaches to the Pre-Columbian settlement of the Caribbean. Gainesville: University Press of Florida.

Keegan, W. F. 2012. Now bring me that horizon. Australian Archaeology, 74, 22–23.

Keegan, W. F. & Diamond, J. 1987. Colonization of islands by humans: A biogeographic perspective. Advances in Archaeological Method and Theory, 10, 49–92.

Kelly, R. L. 1983. Hunter-gatherer mobility strategies. Journal of Anthropological Research, 39, 277–306.

Kelly, R. L. 1995. The foraging spectrum: Diversity in hunter-gatherer lifeways. Washington: Smithsonian Institution Press.

Kelly, R. L. & Todd, L. C. 1988. Coming into the country: Early paleoindian hunting and mobility. American Antiquity, 53, 231–244.

Kephart, W. M. 1950. A quantitative analysis of intragroup relationships. American Journal of Sociology, 55, 544–549.

Khalke, R.-D. 1994. Die Entstehungs-, Entwicklungs- und Verbreitungsgeschichte des oberpleistozänen Mammuthus-Coelodonta Faunenkomplexes in Eurasien

(Großsäuger). *Abhandlungen der Senckenbergischen Naturforschenden Gesellschaft*, **546**, 1–164.

Killingsworth, M. A. & Gilbert, D. A. 2010. A wandering mind is an unhappy mind. *Science*, **330**, 932–933.

King, G. & Bailey, G. 2006. Tectonics and human evolution. *Antiquity*, **80**, 265–286.

Kingdon, J. 1993. *Self-made man and his undoing*. London: Simon and Schuster.

Kingston, J. 2007. Shifting adaptive landscapes: Progress and challenges in reconstructing early hominid environments. *Yearbook of Physical Anthropology*, **50**, 20–58.

Kirch, P. V. 1984. *The evolution of the Polynesian chiefdoms*. Cambridge: Cambridge University Press.

Kirch, P. V. 2002. *On the road of the winds: An archaeological history of the Pacific Islands before European contact*. Berkeley: University of California Press.

Kivisild, T. 2007. Complete mtDNA sequences: Quest on "Out-of-Africa" route completed? *In*: P. Mellars, O. Bar-Yosef, C. Stringer & K. V. Boyle (eds.) *Rethinking the human revolution*. Cambridge: McDonald Institute.

Klein, R. G. 1999. *The human career: Human biological and cultural origins*. Chicago: University of Chicago Press.

Klein, R. G. 2008. Out of Africa and the evolution of human behaviour. *Evolutionary Anthropology*, **17**, 267–281.

Klütsch, C. F. C. & Savolainen, P. 2011. Geographical origin of the domestic dog. *Encyclopedia of Life Sciences*. Chichester: John Wiley, online.

Knapp, A. B. 2010. Cyprus's earliest prehistory: Seafarers, foragers and settlers. *Journal of World Prehistory*, **23**, 79–120.

Knappett, C. 2011. *An archaeology of interaction: Network perspectives on material culture and society*. Oxford: Oxford University Press.

Kozlowski, J. K. (ed.) 1982. *Excavation in the Bacho Kiro cave, Bulgaria*. Warsaw: Paristwowe Wydarunictwo, Naukowe.

Kozlowski, J. K. 2010. The Middle to Upper Palaeolithic transition north of the continental divide: Between England and the Russian Plain. *In*: K. V. Boyle, C. Gamble & O. Bar-Yosef (eds.) *The Upper Palaeolithic revolution in global perspective: Papers in honour of Sir Paul Mellars*. Cambridge: McDonald Institute.

Krause, J., Fu, Q., Good, J. M., Viola, B., Shunkov, M. V., Derevianko, A. P. & Pääbo, S. 2010. The complete mitochondrial DNA genome of an unknown hominin from southern Siberia. *Nature*, **464**, 894–897.

Krause, J., Orlando, L., Serre, D., Viola, B., Prüfer, K., Richards, M. P., Hublin, J.-J., Hänni, C., Derevianko, A. P. & Pääbo, S. 2007. Neanderthals in Central Asia and Siberia. *Nature*, **449**, 902–904.

Kuhn, S. L. 1992. On planning and curated technologies in the Middle Palaeolithic. *Journal of Anthropological Research*, **48**, 185–214.

Kuhn, S. L. 1995. *Mousterian lithic technology: An ecological perspective*. Princeton: Princeton University Press.

Kuman, K. 1998. The earliest South African industries. *In*: M. D. Petraglia & R. Korisettar (eds.) *Early human behaviour in global context*. London: Routledge.

Kuman, K., Field, A. & McNabb, J. 2005. La préhistoire ancienne de l'Afrique méridionale: Contribution des sites à hominids d'Afrique du Sud. *In*: M. Sahnouni (ed.) *Le Paléolithique en Afrique: L'histoire la plus longue*. Paris: Artcom.

Kuzmin, Y. V. 2007. Chronological framework of the Siberian Palaeolithic: Recent achievements and future directions. *Radiocarbon*, **49**, 757–766.

Kuzmin, Y. V. 2009. The Middle to Upper Palaeolithic transition in Siberia: Chronological and environmental aspects. *Eurasian Prehistory*, **5**, 97–108.

Kuzmin, Y. V. & Orlova, L. A. 2000. The neolithization of Siberia and the Russian Far East: Radiocarbon evidence. *Antiquity*, **74**, 356–364.

Lahr, M. M. & Foley, R. 1994. Multiple dispersals and modern human origins. *Evolutionary Anthropology*, **3**, 48–60.

Lahr, M. M. & Foley, R. 2004. Human evolution writ small. *Nature*, **431**, 1043–1044.

Lakoff, G. & Johnson, M. 1980. *Metaphors we live by*. Chicago: University of Chicago Press.

Lakoff, G. & Johnson, M. 1999. *Philosopy in the flesh: The embodied mind and its challenge to Western thought*. New York: Basic Books.

Lalueza-Fox, C., Calderón, F. L., Calafell, F., Morera, B. & Bertranpetit, J. 2001. MtDNA from extinct Tainos and the peopling of the Caribbean. *Annals of Human Genetics*, **65**, 137–151.

Lalueza-Fox, C., Gilbert, M. T. P., Martinez-Fuentes, A. J., Calafell, F. & Bertranpetit, J. 2003. Mitochondrial DNA from pre-Columbian Cibneys from Cuba and the prehistoric colonization of the Caribbean. *American Journal of Physical Anthropology*, **121**, 97–108.

Lambeck, K., Purcell, A., Flemming, N. C., Vita-Finzi, C., Alsharekh, A. M. & Bailey, G. N. 2011. Sea level and shoreline reconstructions for the Red Sea: Isostatic and tectonic considerations and implications for hominin migration out of Africa. *Quaternary Science Reviews*, **30**, 3542–3574.

Larick, R., Ciochon, R. L., Zaim, Y., Sudijono, S., Rizal, Y., Aziz, F., Reagan, M. & Heizler, M. 2001. Early Pleistocene 40AR/39Ar ages for Bapang Formation hominins, Central Jawa, Indonesia. *Proceedings of the National Academy of Sciences of the United States of America*, **98**, 4866–4871.

Larson, G., Cucchi, C., Fujita, M., Matisoo-Smith, E., Robins, J., Anderson, A., Rolett, B., Spriggs, M., Dolman, G., Kim, T. H., Thuy, N. T., Randi, E., Doherty, M., Awe Due, R., Bollt, R., Djubiantono, T., Griffin, B., Intoh, M., Keane, E., Kirch, P., Li, K.-T., Morwood, M., Pedriña, L. M., Piper, P., Rabett, R., Shooter, P., Van den Bergh, G., West, E., Wickler, S., Yuan, J., Cooper, A. & Dobney, K. 2007. Phylogeny and Ancient DNA of Sus provides insights into Neolithic Expansion in Island South East Asia and Oceania. *Proceedings of the National Academy of Sciences of the United States of America*, **104**, 4834–4839.

Lawler, A. 2010. Beyond Kon-Tiki: Did Polynesians sail to South America? *Science*, **328**, 1344–1347.

Leach, E. R. 1970. *Lévi-Strauss*. London: Fontana.

Leakey, M. D. 1971. *Olduvai Gorge: Excavations in Beds I and II 1960–1963*. Cambridge: Cambridge University Press.

Leakey, R. E. F. & Walker, A. 1976. *Australopithecus, Homo erectus* and the single species hypothesis. *Nature*, **261**, 572–574.

Leavesley, M. G. & Chappell, J. 2004. Buang Merabek: Additional early radiocarbon evidence of the colonisation of the Bismarck Archipelago, Papua New Guinea. *Antiquity*, 78, 1–4.

LeDoux, J. 1998. *The emotional brain*. London: Orion Books.

Lee, R. B. & DeVore, I. (eds.) 1976. *Kalahari hunter-gatherers: Studies of the !Kung San and their neighbours*. Cambridge, MA: Harvard University Press.

Lee-Thorp, J. & Sponheimer, M. 2006. Contributions of biogeochemistry to understanding hominin dietary ecology. *Yearbook of Physical Anthropology*, 49, 131–148.

Lehmann, J., Korstjens, A. & Dunbar, R. I. M. 2007. Group size, grooming and social cohesion in primates. *Animal Behaviour*, 74, 1617–1629.

Leonard, W. R. & Robertson, M. L. 2000. Ecological correlates of home range variation in primates: Implications for hominid evolution. *In*: S. Boinski & P. A. Garber (eds.) *On the move: How and why animals travel in groups*. London: University of Chicago Press.

Lepre, C. J., Roche, H., Kent, D. V., Harmand, S., Quinn, R. L., Brugal, J.-P., Texier, P.-J., Lenoble, A. & Feibel, C. S. 2011. An earlier origin for the Acheulian. *Nature*, 477, 82–85.

Lienhardt, G. 1985. Self: Public, private. Some African representations. *In*: M. Carrithers, S. Collins & S. Lukes (eds.) *The category of the person: Anthropology, philosophy, history*. Cambridge: Cambridge University Press.

Lindenfors, P. 2005. Neocortex evolution in primates: The "social brain" is for females. *Biology Letters*, 1, 407–410.

Lisiecki, L. E. & Raymo, M. E. 2005. A Pliocene–Pleistocene stack of 57 globally distributed benthic delta O-18 records. *Paleoceanography*, 20, PA1003.

Lordkipanidze, D., Jashashvili, T., Vekua, A., Ponce de Léon, M. S., Zollikofer, C. P. E., Rightmire, P., Pontzer, H., Ferring, C. R., Oms, O., Tappen, M., Bukhsianidze, M., Agusti, J., Kahlke, R., Kiladze, G., Martinez-Navarro, B., Mouskhelishvili, A., Nioradze, M. & Rook, L. 2007. Postcranial evidence from early *Homo* from Dmanisi, Georgia. *Nature*, 449, 305–310.

Lovejoy, C. O. 1981. The origin of man. *Science*, 211, 341–350.

Lowe, J. J., Barton, N., Blockley, S., Bronk Ramsey, C., Cullen, V. L., Davies, W., Gamble, C., Grant, K., Hardiman, M., Housley, R., Lane, C. S., Lee, S., Lewis, M., MacLeod, A. A., Menzies, M. A. A., Mueller, W. A., Pollard, M. A., Price, C. A., Roberts, A. P. A., Rohling, E. J. A., Satow, C. A., Smith, V. C. A., Stringer, C. A., Tomlinson, E. L. A., White, D. A., Albert, P. G. A., Arienzo, I. A., Barker, G. A., Boric, D. A., Carendente, A. A., Civetta, L. A., Ferrier, C. A., Guadelli, J.-L. A., Karkanas, P. A., Koumouzelis, M. A., Mueller, U. C. A., Orsi, G. A., Pross, J. A., Rosi, M. A., Shalamanov-Korobar, L. A., Sirakov, N. A. & Tzedakis, P. C. A. 2012. Volcanic ash layers illuminate the resilience of Neanderthals and early Modern Humans to natural hazards. *Proceedings of the National Academy of Sciences of the United States of America*, 109, 13532–13537.

Lowe, J. J., Rasmussen, S. O., Björck, S., Hoek, W. Z., Steffensen, J. P., Walker, M. J. C. & Yu, Z. C. 2008. Synchronisation of palaeoenvironmental events in the North Atlantic region during the Last Termination: A revised protocol recommended by the INTIMATE group. *Quaternary Science Reviews*, 27, 6–17.

Lowe, J. J. & Walker, M. J. C. 1997. *Reconstructing quaternary environments*. Harlow: Longman.

Lycett, S. J. & Bae, C. J. 2010. The Movius line controversy: The state of the debate. *World Archaeology*, 42, 521–544.

Lycett, S. J. & Norton, C. J. 2010. A demographic model for Palaeolithic technological evolution: The case of East Asia and the Movius line. *Quaternary International*, 211, 55–65.

MacArthur, R. H. & Wilson, E. O. 1967. *The theory of island biogeography*. Princeton: Princeton University Press.

Macaulay, V., Hill, C., Achilli, A., Rengo, C., Clarke, D., Meehan, W., Blackburn, J., Semino, O., Scozzari, R., Cruciani, F., Taha, A., Shaari, N. K., Raja, J. M., Ismail, P., Zainuddin, Z., Goodwin, W., Bulbeck, D., Bandelt, H.-J., Oppenheimer, S., Torroni, A. & Richards, M. 2005. Single, rapid coastal settlement of Asia revealed by analysis of complete mitochrondrial genomes. *Science*, 308, 1034–1036.

Macaulay, V. & Richards, M. 2008. Mitochondrial genome sequences and their phylogeographic interpretations. *Encyclopedia of life sciences*. Chichester: John Wiley.

MacGregor, N. 2010. *The history of the world in 100 objects*. London: British Museum Press.

MacLarnon, A. M. & Hewitt, G. P. 1999. The evolution of human speech: The role of enhanced breathing control. *American Journal of Physical Anthropology*, 109, 341–363.

MacLarnon, A. M. & Hewitt, G. P. 2004. Increased breathing control: Another factor in the evolution of human language. *Evolutionary Anthropology*, 13, 181–197.

Maddison, A. 2001. *The world economy: A millennial perspective*. Groningen: Economic History Services OECD.

Makeyev, V., Pitul'ko, P. & Kasparov, A. 1992. Ostrova De-Longa: An analysis of palaeoenvironmental data. *Polar Record*, 28, 301–306.

Markgraf, V. (ed.) 2001. *Interhemispheric climate linkages*. San Diego: Academic Press.

Marks, A. E. (ed.) 1983. *Prehistory and palaeoenvironments in the Central Negev, Israel. Volume III*. Dallas: Southern Methodist University Press.

Marks, A. E. 1990. The Middle and Upper Palaeolithic of the Near East and the Nile Valley: The problem of cultural transformations. In: P. Mellars (ed.) *The emergence of modern humans: An archaeological perspective*. Edinburgh: Edinburgh University Press.

Martin, P. S. 1967. Pleistocene overkill. In: P. S. Martin & H. E. Wright (eds.) *Pleistocene extinctions: The search for a cause*. New Haven: Yale University Press.

Martin, P. S. 1973. The discovery of America. *Science*, 179, 969–974.

Martin, P. S. & Klein, R. (eds.) 1984. *Quaternary extinctions: A prehistoric revolution*. Tucson: University of Arizona Press.

Martinon-Torres, M., Dennell, R. W. & Bermudez de Castro, J. M. 2010. The Denisova hominin need not be an out of Africa story. *Journal of Human Evolution*, online.

Marwick, B. 2003. Pleistocene exchange networks as evidence for the evolution of language. *Cambridge Archaeological Journal*, 13, 67–81.

Mascie-Taylor, C. G. N. & Lasker, G. W. (eds.) 1988. *Biological aspects of human migration*. Cambridge: Cambridge University Press.

Maslin, M. A. & Christensen, B. 2007. Tectonics, orbital forcing, global climate change, and human evolution in Africa. *Journal of Human Evolution*, 53, 443–464.

Mason, S., Hather, J. & Hillman, G. 1994. Preliminary investigation of the plant macro-remains from Dolní Vestonice II and its implications for the role of plant foods in Palaeolithic and Mesolithic Europe. *Antiquity*, 68, 48–57.

Maxwell, M. S. 1985. *Prehistory of the Eastern Arctic*. Orlando: Academic Press.

McBrearty, S. 2007. Down with the revolution. *In*: P. Mellars, O. Bar-Yosef, C. Stringer & K. V. Boyle (eds.) *Rethinking the human revolution*. Cambridge: McDonald Institute.

McBrearty, S. & Brooks, A. S. 2000. The revolution that wasn't: A new interpretation of the origin of modern humans. *Journal of Human Evolution*, 39, 453–563.

McBrearty, S. & Jablonski, N. 2005. First fossil chimpanzee. *Nature*, 437, 105–108.

McBrearty, S. & Stringer, C. 2007. The coast in colour. *Nature*, 449, 793–794.

McBryde, I. 1988. Goods from another country: Exchange networks and the people of the Lake Eyre basin. *In*: J. Mulvaney & P. White (eds.) *Archaeology to 1788*. Sydney: Waddon Associates.

McBurney, C. B. M. 1950. The geographical study of the older Palaeolithic stages in Europe. *Proceedings of the Prehistoric Society*, 16, 163–183.

McGhee, R. 1996. *Ancient people of the Arctic*. Vancouver: University of British Columbia Press.

McGhee, R. 2009. When and why did the Inuit move to the eastern Arctic? *In*: H. Maschner, O. Mason & R. McGhee (eds.) *The northern world, AD 900–1400*. Salt Lake City: University of Utah Press, pp. 155–163.

McGrew, W. C. 1992. *Chimpanzee material culture: Implications for human evolution*. Cambridge: Cambridge University Press.

McNabb, J. 2001. The shape of things to come. A speculative essay on the role of the Victoria West phenomenon at Canteen Koppie, during the South African Earlier Stone Age. *In*: S. Milliken & J. Cook (eds.) *A very remote period indeed: Papers on the Palaeolithic presented to Derek Roe*. Oxford: Oxbow Books.

Mellars, P. A. 1973. The character of the Middle–Upper Palaeolithic transition in south-west France. *In*: C. Renfrew (ed.) *The explanation of culture change: Models in prehistory*. London: Duckworth.

Mellars, P. A. 2006a. Going east: New genetic and archaeological perspectives on the modern human colonization of Eurasia. *Science*, 313, 796–800.

Mellars, P. A. 2006b. A new radiocarbon revolution and the dispersal of modern humans in Eurasia. *Nature*, 439, 931–935.

Mellars, P. A. 2006c. Why did modern human populations disperse from Africa ca. 60,000 years ago? A new model. *Proceedings of the National Academy of Sciences of the United States of America*, 103, 9381–9386.

Mellars, P. A. 2007. Response to Smith, Tacon, Curnoe and Thorne. *Science*, 315, 598.

Mellars, P. A., Bar-Yosef, O., Stringer, C. & Boyle, K. V. (eds.) 2007. *Rethinking the human revolution*. Cambridge: McDonald Institute.

Mellars, P. A. & Stringer, C. (eds.) 1989. *The human revolution: Behavioural and biological perspectives on the origins of modern humans*. Edinburgh: Edinburgh University Press.

Meltzer, D. J. 2009. *First peoples in a New World: Colonizing Ice Age America*. Berkeley: University of California Press.

Mercader, J., Barton, H., Gillespie, J., Harris, J. W. K., Kuhn, S., Tyler, R. & Boesch, C. 2007. 4,300-year-old chimpanzee sites and the origins of percussive stone technology. *Proceedings of the National Academy of Sciences of the United States of America*, **104**, 3043–3048.

Merrick, H. V. & Brown, F. H. 1984. Obsidian sources and patterns of source utilization in Kenya and northern Tanzania: Some initial findings. *African Archaeological Review*, **2**, 129–152.

Mijares, A. S., Détroit, F., Piper, P., Grun, R., Bellwood, P., Aubert, M., Champion, G., Cuevas, N., De Leon, A. & Dizon, E. 2010. New evidence for a 67,000-year-old human presence at Callao cave, Luzon, Philippines. *Journal of Human Evolution*, **59**, 123–132.

Milham, P. & Thompson, P. 1976. Relative antiquity of human occupation and extinct fauna at Madura cave, Southeastern Western Australia. *Mankind*, **10**, 175–180.

Miller, D. 2008. *The comfort of things*. London: Polity Press.

Mitchell, P. 2004. Towards a comparative archaeology of Africa's islands. *Journal of African Archaeology*, **2**, 229–250.

Mithen, S. 1996. *The prehistory of the mind*. London: Thames and Hudson.

Mochanov, U. A. 1977. *The earliest stages of the peopling of northeastern Asia*. Novosibirsk: Nauka.

Mochanov, U. A., Fedoseeva, S. A. & Alexeev, V. P. 1983. *Archaeological sites of Yakut. The Adlan and Ol'okma basins*. Novosibirsk: Nauka.

Mol, D., Post, K., Reumer, J. W. F., van der Plicht, J., de Vos, J., van Geel, B., van Reenen, G., Pals, J. P. & Glimmerveen, J. 2006. The Eurogeul – First report of the palaeontological, palynological and archaeological investigations of this part of the North Sea. *Quaternary International*, **142–143**, 178–185.

Montenegro, A., Araujo, A., Eby, M., Ferreira, L. F., Hetherington, R. & Weaver, A. J. 2006. Parasites, paleoclimate, and the peopling of the Americas. *Current Anthropology*, **47**, 193–200.

Montenegro, A., Avis, C. & Weaver, A. J. 2008. Modeling the prehistoric arrival of the sweet potato in Polynesia. *Journal of Archaeological Science*, **35**, 355–367.

Moore, M. W. & Brumm, A. 2007. Stone artifacts and hominins in Island Southeast Asia: New insights from Flores, Eastern Indonesia. *Journal of Human Evolution*, **52**, 85–102.

Mora, S. & Gnecco, C. 2003. Archaeological hunter-gatherers in tropical forests: A view from Colombia. In: J. Mercader (ed.) *Under the canopy: The archaeology of tropical rain forests*. New Brunswick: Rutgers University Press.

Morey, D. F. & Wiant, M. D. 1992. Early Holocene domestic dog burials from the North American Midwest. *Current Anthropology*, **33**, 224–229.

Morisaki, K. 2012. The evolution of lithic technology and human behaviour from MIS3 to MIS2 in the Japanese Upper Palaeolithic. *Quaternary International*, **248**, 56–69.

Morphy, H. 1989. From dull to brilliant: The aesthetics of spiritual power among the Yolngu. *Man*, **24**, 21–40.

Morwood, M. J., Soejono, R. P., Roberts, R. G., Sutikna, T., Turney, C. S. M., Westaway, K. E., Rink, W. J., Zhao, J.-X., van den Bergh, G. D., Due, R. A., Hobbs, D. R., Moore, M. W., Bird, M. I. & Fifield, L. K. 2004. Archaeology and age of a new hominin from Flores in eastern Indonesia. *Nature*, **431**, 1087–1091.

Moutsiou, T. 2011. The obsidian evidence for the scale of social life during the palaeolithic. PhD thesis, Royal Holloway, University of London.

Movius, H. L. 1948. The Lower Palaeolithic cultures of southern and eastern Asia. *Transactions of the American Philosophical Society*, **38**, 239–426.

Movius, H. L. 1953. The Mousterian cave of Tehik-Tash, southeastern Uzbekistan, Central Asia. *American School of Prehistoric Research*, **17**, 11–71.

Mudelsee, M. & Stattegger, M. 1997. Exploring the structure of the mid-Pleistocene revolution with advanced methods of time-series analysis. *International Journal of Earth Sciences*, **86**, 499–511.

Mulcahy, N. J. & Call, J. 2006. Apes save tools for future use. *Science*, **312**, 1038–1040.

Müller, U. C., Pross, J., Tzedakis, P. C., Gamble, C., Kotthoff, U., Schmiedl, G., Wulf, S. & Christanis, K. 2010. The role of climate in the spread of modern humans into Europe. *Quaternary Science Reviews*, online.

Mulvaney, D. J. 1976. "The chain of connection": The material evidence. *In*: N. Peterson (ed.) *Tribes and boundaries in Australia*. Canberra: AIAS.

Musil, R. 2000. Evidence for the domestication of wolves in central European Magdalenian sites. *In*: S. L. Crockford (ed.) *Dogs through time: An archaeological perspective*. Oxford: BAR International Series 889.

Mussi, M. & Zampetti, D. 1997. Carving, painting, engraving: Problems with the earliest Italian design. *In*: M. W. Conkey, O. Soffer, D. Stratmann & N. G. Jablonski (eds.) *Beyond art: Pleistocene image and symbol*. San Francisco: Wattis Symposium Series in Anthropology, Memoirs of the California Academy of Sciences Number 23.

Muttoni, G., Scardia, G., Kent, D. V., Morsiani, E., Tremolada, F., Cremaschi, M. & Peretto, C. 2011. First dated human occupation of Italy at ~0.85Ma during the late Early Pleistocene climate transition. *Earth and Planetary Science Letters*, online.

Napierala, H. & Uerpmann, H.-P. 2012. A "New" Palaeolithic dog from Central Europe. *International Journal of Osteoarchaeology*, **22**, 127–137.

Nelson, R. K. 1973. *Hunters of the northern forest*. Chicago: University of Chicago Press.

Nettle, D. 1998. Explaining global patterns of language diversity. *Journal of Anthropological Archaeology*, **17**, 354–374.

Nettle, D. 2007. Language and genes: A new perspective on the origins of human cultural diversity. *Proceedings of the National Academy of Sciences of the United States of America*, **104**, 10755–10756.

Newsom, L. A. 1993. Native West Indian plant use. PhD thesis, University of Florida.

Newsom, L. A. & Wing, E. S. 2004. *On land and sea: Native American uses of biological resources in the West Indies*. Tuscaloosa: University of Alabama Press.

Nielsen, R. & Beaumont, M. 2009. Statistical inferences in phylogeography. *Molecular Ecology*, **18**, 1034–1047.

Nygaard, S. 1989. The stone age of northern Scandinavia: A review. *Journal of World Prehistory*, **3**, 71–116.

Oberg, K. 1973. *The social economy of the Tlingit Indians*. Seattle: University of Washington Press.

O'Connell, J. F. & Allen, J. 1998. When did humans first arrive in Greater Australia and why is it important to know? *Evolutionary Anthropology*, **8**, 132–146.

O'Connell, J. F. & Allen, J. 2004. Dating the colonization of Sahul (Pleistocene Australia–New Guinea): A review of recent research. *Journal of Archaeological Science*, **31**, 835–853.

O'Connell, J. F. & Allen, J. 2012. The restaurant at the end of the universe: Modelling the colonisation of Sahul. *Australian Archaeology*, **74**, 5–31.

O'Connell, J. F., Hawkes, K. & Blurton Jones, N. G. 1999. Grandmothering and the evolution of *Homo erectus*. *Journal of Human Evolution*, **36**, 461–485.

O'Connor, S., Ono, R. & Clarkson, C. 2011. Pelagic fishing at 42,000 years before the present and the maritime skills of modern humans. *Science*, **334**, 1117–1121.

Odling-Smee, F. J. 1993. Niche construction, evolution and culture. *In*: T. Ingold (ed.) *Companion encyclopedia of anthropology: Humanity, culture and social life*. London: Routledge.

Oldfield, F. & Thompson, R. 2004. Archives and proxies along the PEP III transect. *In*: R. W. Batterbee, F. Gasse & C. E. Stickley (eds.) *Past climate variability through Europe and Africa*. Dordrecht: Springer.

Olivieri, A., Achilli, A., Pala, M., Battaglia, V., Fornarino, S., Al-Zahery, N., Scozzari, R., Cruciani, F., Behar, D. M., Dugoujon, J.-M., Coudray, C., Santachiara-Benerecetti, A. S., Semino, O., Bandelt, H.-J. & Torroni, A. 2006. The mtDNA legacy of the Levantine early Upper Palaeolithic in Africa. *Science*, **314**, 1767–1770.

Oppenheimer, C. 2011. *Eruptions that shook the world*. Cambridge: Cambridge University Press.

Oppenheimer, S. 2003. *The peopling of the world*. London: Constable.

Oppenheimer, S. 2004a. The "Express train from Taiwan to Polynesia": On the congruence of proxy lines of evidence. *World Archaeology*, **36**, 591–600.

Oppenheimer, S. 2004b. *Out of Eden: The peopling of the world*. London: Robinson.

Oppenheimer, S. 2006. *The origins of the British: A genetic detective story*. London: Constable and Robinson.

Oppenheimer, S. 2009. The great arc of dispersal of modern humans: Africa to Australia. *Quaternary International*, **202**, 2–13.

O'Regan, H. J., Turner, A., Bishop, L. C., Elton, S. & Lamb, A. L. 2011. Hominins without fellow traveller? First appearance and inferred dispersals of Afro-Eurasian large-mammals in the Plio–Pleistocene. *Quaternary Science Reviews*, **30**, 1343–1352.

Ortner, S. B. 1973. On key symbols. *American Anthropologist*, **75**, 1338–1346.

Osborne, A. H., Vance, D., Rohling, E. J., Barton, N., Rogerson, M. & Fello, N. 2008. A humid corridor across the Sahara for the migration of early modern humans out of Africa 120,000 years ago. *Proceedings of the National Academy of Sciences of the United States of America*, **105**, 16444–16447.

Oswalt, W. H. 1973. *Habitat and technology: The evolution of hunting*. New York: Holt, Rinehart and Winston.

Oswalt, W. H. 1976. *An anthropological analysis of food-getting technology*. New York: John Wiley.

Ovodov, N. D., Crockford, S. J., Kuzmin, Y. V., Higham, T. F. G., Hodgins, G. W. L. & van der Plicht, J. 2011. A 33,000 year old incipient dog from the Altai Mountains of Siberia: Evidence of the earliest domestication disrupted by the Last Glacial Maximum. *PLoS ONE*, 6, e22821

Pala, M., Olivieri, A., Achilli, A., Accetturo, M., Metspalu, E., Reidla, M., Tamm, E., Karmin, M., Reisberg, T., Kashani, B. H., Perego, U. A., Carossa, V., Gandini, F., Pereira, J. B., Soares, P., Angerhofer, N., Rychkov, S., Al-Zahery, N., Carelli, V., Sanati, M. H., Houshmand, M., Hatina, J., Macaulay, V., Pereira, L., Woodward, S. R., Davies, W., Gamble, C., Baird, D., Semino, O., Villems, R., Torroni, A. & Richards, M. B. 2012. Mitochondrial DNA signals of Late Glacial recolonization of Europe from Near Eastern refugia. *The American Journal of Human Genetics*, 90, 915–924.

Pappu, S., Gunnell, Y., Akhilesh, K., Braucher, R., Taieb, M., Demory, F. & Thouveny, N. 2011. Early Pleistocene presence of Acheulian hominins in South India. *Science*, 331, 1596–1599.

Parfitt, S., Barendregt, R. W., Breda, M., Candy, I., Collins, M. J., Coope, G. R., Durbridge, P., Field, M. H., Lee, J. R., Lister, A. M., Mutch, R., Penkman, K. E. H., Preece, R., Rose, J., Stringer, C., Symmons, R., Whittaker, J. E., Wymer, J. J. & Stuart, A. J. 2005. The earliest record of human activity in Northern Europe. *Nature*, 438, 1008–1012.

Parker, A. G. 2012. Pleistocene climate change in Arabia: Developing a framework for hominin dispersal over the last 350ka. *In*: M. D. Petraglia & J. I. Rose (eds.) *The evolution of human populations in Arabia: Palaeoenvironments, prehistory and genetics*. Berlin: Springer.

Parker-Pearson, M. (ed.) 2010. *Pastoralists, warriors and colonists: The archaeology of Southern Madagascar*. Oxford: British Archaeological Reports, S2139.

Patnaik, R. & Chauhan, P. 2009. India at the cross-roads of human evolution. *Journal of Biosciences*, 34, 729–747.

Pavlov, P., Roebroeks, W. & Svendsen, J. I. 2004. The Pleistocene colonization of northeastern Europe: A report on recent research. *Journal of Human Evolution*, 47, 3–17.

Pavlov, P., Svendsen, J. I. & Indrelid, S. 2001. Human presence in the European Arctic nearly 40,000 years ago. *Nature*, 413, 64–67.

Perera, H. N. 2010. *Prehistoric Sri Lanka*. Oxford: British Archaeological Reports International Series 2142.

Petchey, F., Spriggs, M., Leach, F., Seed, M., Sand, C., Pietrusewsky, M. & Anderson, K. 2011. Testing the human factor: Radiocarbon dating the first peoples of the South Pacific. *Journal of Archaeological Science*, 38, 29–44.

Petraglia, M. D., Haslam, M., Fuller, D. Q., Boivin, N. & Clarkson, C. 2010. Out of Africa: New hypotheses and evidence for the dispersal of *Homo sapiens* along the Indian Ocean rim. *Annals of Human Biology*, 37, 288–311.

Petraglia, M. D., Korisettar, R., Boivin, N., Clarkson, C., Ditchfield, P. W., Jones, S., Koshy, J., Lahr, M. M., Oppenheimer, C., Pyle, D., Roberts, R., Schwenninger, J.-L., Arnold, L. & White, K. 2007. Middle Palaeolithic assemblages from the

Indian subcontinent before and after the Toba super-eruption. *Science*, **317**, 114–116.

Pettitt, P. B. 2011. *The Palaeolithic origins of human burial*. London: Routledge.

Pettitt, P. B., Davies, S. W. G., Gamble, C. S. & Richards, M. B. 2003. Radiocarbon chronology: Quantifying our confidence beyond two half-lives. *Journal of Archaeological Science*, **30**, 1685–1693.

Pickering, R., Dirks, P. H. G. M., Jinnah, Z., De Ruiter, D. J., Churchill, S. E., Herries, A. I. R., Woodhead, J. D., Hellstron, J. C. & Berger, L. R. 2011. *Australopithecus sediba* at 1.977Ma and implications for the origins of the genus *Homo*. *Science*, **333**, 1421–1423.

Pitulko, V. V., Nikolsky, P. A., Girya, E. Y., Basilyan, A. E., Tumskoy, V. E., Koulakov, S. A., Astakhov, S. N., Pavlova, E. Y. & Anisimov, M. A. 2004. The Yana RHS site: Humans in the Arctic before the Last Glacial Maximum. *Science*, **303**, 52–56.

Plummer, T. W., Ditchfield, P. W., Bishop, L. C., Kingston, J. D., Ferraro, J. V., Braun, D. R., Hertel, F. & Potts, R. 2009. Oldest evidence of toolmaking hominins in a grassland-dominated ecosystem. *PLos ONE*, **4**, e7199, 1–8.

Pope, G. 1989. Bamboo and human evolution. *Natural History*, **10**, 48–57.

Pope, M. & Roberts, M. 2005. Observations on the relationship between Palaeolithic individuals and artefact scatters at the Middle Pleistocene site of Boxgrove, UK. In: C. Gamble & M. Porr (eds.) *The individual hominid in context: Archaeological investigations of Lower and Middle Palaeolithic landscapes, locales and artefacts*. London: Routledge.

Potts, R. 1998a. Environmental hypotheses of hominin evolution. *Yearbook of Physical Anthropology*, **41**, 93–136.

Potts, R. 1998b. Variability selection in hominid evolution. *Evolutionary Anthropology*, **7**, 81–96.

Powell, A., Shennan, S. & Thomas, M. G. 2009. Late Pleistocene demography and the appearance of modern human behavior. *Science*, **324**, 1298–1301.

Powers, W. R. & Hoffecker, J. F. 1989. Late Pleistocene settlement in the Nenana Valley, Central Alaska. *American Antiquity*, **54**, 263–287.

Praslov, N. D. & Rogachev, A. N. (eds.) 1982. *Palaeolithic of the Kostenki–Borshevo area on the Don River, 1879–1979* [in Russian]. Leningrad: Nauka.

Proctor, R. N. 2003. Three roots of human recency: Molecular anthropology, the refigured Acheulean, and the UNESCO response to Auschwitz. *Current Anthropology*, **44**, 213–239.

Raichlen, D. A., Pontzer, H. & Sockol, M. D. 2008. The Laetoli footprints and early hominin locomotor kinematics. *Journal of Human Evolution*, **54**, 112–117.

Rainbird, P. 2004. *The archaeology of Micronesia*. Cambridge: Cambridge University Press.

Rappaport, R. A. 1968. *Pigs for the ancestors*. New Haven: Yale University Press.

Rasmussen, M. 2010. Ancient human genome sequence of an extinct Palaeo-Eskimo. *Nature*, **463**, 757–762.

Rasmussen, M. 2011. An Aboriginal Australian genome reveals separate human dispersals into Asia. *Science*, **334**, 94–98.

Read, D. 2010. From experiential-based to relational-based forms of social organisation: A major transition in the evolution of *Homo sapiens*. In: R.

Dunbar, C. Gamble & J. A. J. Gowlett (eds.) *Social brains and distributed mind*. Oxford: Oxford University Press.

Reed, D. L., Smith, V. S., Hammond, S. L., Rogers, A. R. & Clayton, D. H. 2004. Genetic analysis of lice supports direct contact between modern and archaic humans. *PLos Biology*, 2, 1972–1983.

Reich, D., Green, R. E., Kircher, M., Krause, J., Patterson, N., Durand, E. Y., Viola, B., Briggs, A. W., Stenzel, U., Johnson, P. L. F., Maricic, T., Good, J. M., Marques-Bonet, T., Alkan, C., Fu, Q., Mallick, S., Li, H., Meyer, M., Eichler, E. E., Stoneking, M., Richards, M., Talamo, S., Shunkov, M. V., Derevianko, A. P., Hublin, J.-J., Kelso, J., Slatkin, M. & Pääbo, S. 2010. Genetic history of an archaic hominin group from Denisova Cave in Siberia. *Nature*, 468, 1053–1060.

Renfrew, C. 1987. *Archaeology and language: The puzzle of Indo-European origins*. New York: Cambridge University Press.

Renfrew, C. 1996. The sapient behaviour paradox: How to test for potential? *In*: P. Mellars & K. Gibson (eds.) *Modelling the early human mind*. Cambridge: McDonald Institute for Archaeological Research.

Renfrew, C. 2007. *Prehistory: Making of the human mind*. London: Weidenfeld and Nicolson.

Renfrew, C. & Cooke, K. L. (eds.) 1979. *Transformations: Mathematical approaches to culture change*. New York: Academic Press.

Renfrew, C. & Scarre, C. (eds.) 1998. *Cognitive storage and material culture: The archaeology of symbolic storage*. Cambridge: McDonald Institute.

Revedin, A., Aranguren, B., Becattini, R., Longo, L., Marconi, E., Lippi, M. M., Skakun, N., Sinitsyn, A. A., Spiridodonova, E. & Svoboda, J. 2010. Thirty thousand-year-old evidence of plant food processing. *Proceedings of the National Academy of Sciences of the United States of America*, 107, 18815–18819.

Révillion, S. & Tuffreau, A. (eds.) 1994. *Les industries laminaires au Paleolithique moyen*. Paris: CNRS.

Rhode, D. L. T., Olson, S. & Chang, J. T. 2004. Modelling the recent common ancestry of all living humans. *Nature*, 431, 562–566.

Richards, M., Harvati, K., Grimes, V., Smith, C. A., Smith, T., Hublin, J.-J., Karkanas, P. & Panagopoulou, E. 2008. Strontium isotope evidence of Neanderthal mobility at the site of Lakonis, Greece using laser-ablation PIMMS. *Journal of Archaeological Science*, 35, 1251–1256.

Richards, M., Macaulay, V., Hickey, E., Vega, E., Sykes, B., Guida, V., Rengo, C., Sellitto, D., Cruciani, F., Kivisild, T., Villems, R., Thomas, M., Rychkov, S., Rychkov, O., Rychkov, Y., Gölge, M., Dimitrov, D., Hill, E., Bradley, D., Romano, V., Cali, F., Vona, G., Demaine, A., Papiha, S., Triantaphyllidis, C., Stefanescu, G., Hatina, J., Belledi, M., Di Rienzo, A., Novelletto, A., Oppenheim, A., Nørby, S., Al-Zaheri, N., Santachiara–Benerecetti, S., Scozzari, R., Torroni, A. & Bandelt, H. J. 2000. Tracing European founder lineages in the Near Eastern mtDNA pool. *American Journal of Human Genetics*, 67, 1251–1276.

Richards, M., Pettitt, P., Trinkaus, E., Smith, F. H., Paunovic, M. & Karavanic, I. 2000. Neanderthal diet at Vindija and Neanderthal predation: The evidence from stable isotopes. *Proceedings of the National Academy of Sciences of the United States of America*, 97, 7663–7666.

Richards, M. & Trinkaus, E. 2009. Isotopic evidence for the diets of European Neanderthals and early modern humans. *Proceedings of the National Academy of Sciences of the United States of America*, 106, 16034–16039.

Richerson, P. J. & Boyd, R. 2005. *Not by genes alone: How culture transformed human evolution*. Chicago: University of Chicago Press.

Richter, D., Tostevin, G. & Skrdla, P. 2008. Bohunician technology and thermoluminescence dating of the type locality of Brno-Bohunice (Czech Republic). *Journal of Human Evolution*, 55, 871–885.

Rightmire, G. P. 2004. Brain size and encephalization in early to Mid-Pleistocene *Homo*. *American Journal of Physical Anthropology*, 124, 109–123.

Rightmire, G. P., Lordkipanidze, D. & Vekua, A. 2006. Anatomical descriptions, comparative studies and evolutionary significance of the hominin skulls from Dmanisi, Republic of Georgia. *Journal of Human Evolution*, 50, 115–141.

Rizzolatti, G., Fogassi, L. & Gallese, V. 2006. Mirrors in the mind. *Scientific American*, 295, 54–61.

Roberts, M. B. & Parfitt, S. A. 1999. *Boxgrove: A Middle Pleistocene hominid site at Eartham Quarry, Boxgrove, West Sussex*. London: English Heritage.

Roberts, M. B., Stringer, C. B. & Parfitt, S. A. 1994. A hominid tibia from Middle Pleistocene sediments at Boxgrove, UK. *Nature*, 369, 311–313.

Roberts, R. G., Jones, R. & Smith, M. A. 1990. Thermoluminescence dating of a 50,000 year old human occupation site in northern Australia. *Nature*, 345, 153–156.

Roberts, S. G. B. 2010. Constraints on social networks. *In*: R. Dunbar, C. Gamble & J. A. J. Gowlett (eds.) *Social brain, distributed mind*. Oxford: Oxford University Press, Proceedings of the British Academy 158.

Robson, S. L. & Wood, B. 2008. Hominin life history: Reconstruction and evolution. *Journal of Anatomy*, 212, 394–425.

Rodseth, L., Wrangham, R. W., Harrigan, A. & Smuts, B. B. 1991. The human community as a primate society. *Current Anthropology*, 32, 221–254.

Roebroeks, W., Mussi, M., Svoboda, J. & Fennema, K. (eds.) 2000. *Hunters of the golden age: The mid Upper Palaeolithic of Eurasia 30,000–20,000 BP*. Leiden: European Science Foundation and University of Leiden.

Roebroeks, W. & van Kolfschoten, T. 1994. The earliest occupation of Europe: A short chronology. *Antiquity*, 68, 489–503.

Roebroeks, W. & van Kolfschoten, T. (eds.) 1995. *The earliest occupation of Europe*. Leiden: European Science Foundation and University of Leiden.

Rogers, J. & Anichtchenko, E. 2013. Maritime archaeology of the Arctic Ocean and Bering Sea. *In*: C. Smith (ed.) *Springer encyclopedia of global archaeology*. Berlin: Springer.

Rohde, D. L. T., Olson, S. & Chang, J. T. 2004. Modelling the recent common ancestry of all living humans. *Nature*, 431, 562–566.

Rohling, E. J. & Pälike, H. 2005. Centennial-scale climate cooling with a sudden cold event around 8,200 years ago. *Nature*, 434, 975–979.

Rose, J. I. 2010. New light on human prehistory in the Arabo-Persian Gulf oasis. *Current Anthropology*, 51, 849–883.

Rouse, I. 1986. *Migrations in prehistory: Inferring population movement from cultural remains*. New Haven: Yale University Press.

Rouse, I. & Allaire, L. 1978. The Caribbean. In: R. E. Taylor & C. W. Meighan (eds.) Chronologies in New World archaeology. New York: Academic Press.

Ruff, C. B., Trinkaus, E. & Holliday, T. W. 1997. Body mass and encephalization in Pleistocene Homo. Nature, 387, 173–176.

Sablin, M. V. & Khlopachev, G. A. 2002. The earliest Ice Age dogs: Evidence from Eliseevichi 1. Current Anthropology, 43, 795–799.

Said, E. W. 1978. Orientalism: Western conceptions of the Orient. London: Penguin Books.

Sathiamurthy, E. & Voris, H. K. 2006. Maps of Holocene sea level transgression and submerged lakes on the Sunda Shelf. The Natural History Journal of Chulalongkorn University, Supplement 2, 1–44.

Satterthwait, L. D. 1979. A comparative analysis of Australian Aboriginal food procurement technologies. PhD thesis, UCLA.

Satterthwait, L. D. 1980. Aboriginal Australia: The simplest technologies? Archaeology and Physical Anthropology in Oceania, 15, 153–156.

Sauer, C. O. 1967. Land and life: A selection from the writings of Carl Ortwin Sauer. Berkeley: University of California Press.

Schalansky, J. 2010. Atlas of remote islands. London: Penguin Books.

Schoeninger, M. J. 2011. In search of the australopithecines. Nature, 474, 43–44.

Schreve, D. C. 2001. Differentiation of the British late Middle Pleistocene interglacials: The evidence from mammalian biostratigraphy. Quaternary Science Reviews, 20, 1693–1705.

Schreve, D. C. 2006. The taphonomy of a Middle Devensian (MIS3) vertebrate assemblage from Lynford, Norfolk, UK, and its implications for Middle Palaeolithic subsistence strategies. Journal of Quaternary Science, 21, 543–565.

Schreve, D. C. 2012. The vertebrate assemblage from Lynford: Taphonomy, biostratigraphy and implications for Middle Palaeolithic subsistence strategies. In: W. A. Boismier, C. S. Gamble & F. Coward (eds.) Neanderthals among mammoths: Excavations at Lynford Quarry, Norfolk. London: English Heritage Monographs.

Schurr, T. G. 2004. The peopling of the New World: Perspectives from molecular anhropology. Annual Review of Anthropology, 33, 551–583.

Semaw, S., Renne, P., Harris, J. W. K., Feibel, C. S., Bernor, R. L., Fesseha, N. & Mowbray, K. 1997. 2.5 million-year-old stone tools from Gona, Ethiopia. Nature, 385, 333–336.

Senut, B. 2010. Upper Miocene hominoid distribution and the origin of hominids revisited. Historical Biology, 22, 260–267.

Sepulchre, P., Ramstein, G., Fluteau, F., Schuster, M., Tiercelin, J.-J. & Brunet, M. 2006. Tectonic uplift and Eastern African aridification. Science, 313, 1419–1423.

Serangeli, J. & Bolus, M. 2008. Out of Europe: The dispersal of a successful European hominin form. Quartär, 55, 83–98.

Sharma, K. K. 1984. The sequence of uplift of the Himalaya. In: R. Whyte (ed.) The evolution of the East Asian environment. Hong Kong: University of Hong Kong, Centre of Asian Studies.

Shea, J. J. 2007. The boulevard of broken dreams: Evolutionary discontinuity in the Late Pleistocene Levant. In: P. Mellars, O. Bar-Yosef, C. Stringer & K. V. Boyle (eds.) Rethinking the human revolution. Cambridge: McDonald Institute.

Shea, J. J. 2011. *Homo sapiens* is as *Homo sapiens* was: Behavioural variability versus "behavioural modernity" in Palaeolithic archaeology. *Current Anthropology*, **52**, 1–35.

Shennan, S. 2000. Population, culture history, and the dynamics of culture change. *Current Anthropology*, **41**, 811–835.

Shennan, S. 2001. Demography and cultural innovation: A model and its implications for the emergence of modern human culture. *Cambridge Archaeological Journal*, **11**, 5–16.

Sherratt, A. 1997. *Economy and society in prehistoric Europe: Changing perspectives.* Edinburgh: Edinburgh University Press.

Shryock, A. & Smail, D. L. (eds.) 2011a. *Deep history: The architecture of past and present.* Berkeley: University of California Press.

Shryock, A. & Smail, D. L. 2011b. Introduction. *In:* A. Shryock & D. L. Smail (eds.) *Deep history: The architecture of past and present.* Berkeley: University of California Press.

Shryock, A., Trautmann, T. & Gamble, C. 2011. Imagining the human in deep time. *In:* A. Shryock & D. L. Smail (eds.) *Deep history: The architecture of past and present.* Berkeley: University of California Press.

Shultz, S. & Dunbar, R. I. M. 2007. The evolution of the social brain: Anthropoid primates contrast with other vertebrates. *Proceedings of the Royal Society of London B*, **274**, 2429–2436.

Shunkov, M. 2005. The characteristics of the Altai (Russia) Middle Palaeolithic in regional context. *Indo-Pacific Prehistory Association Bulletin*, **25**, 69–77.

Siddall, M., Rohling, E. J., Almogi-Labin, A., Hemleben, C., Meischner, D., Schmelzer, I. & Smeed, D. A. 2003. Sea-level fluctuations during the last glacial cycle. *Nature*, **423**, 853–858.

Sigurdsson, G. 2008. The North Atlantic expansion. *In:* S. Brink & N. S. Price (eds.) *The Viking world.* London: Routledge.

Sigurdsson, J. V. 2008. Iceland. *In:* S. Brink & N. S. Price (eds.) *The Viking world.* London: Routledge.

Silk, J. B. 2007. Social components of fitness in primate groups. *Science*, **317**, 1347–1351.

Simpson, G. G. 1940. Mammals and land bridges. *Journal of the Washington Academy of Sciences*, **30**, 137–163.

Slimak, L. & Giraud, Y. 2007. Circulations sur plusiers centaines de kilomètres durant le Paléolithique moyen. Contribution à la connaissance des sociétés néanderthaliennes. *Comptes Rendus Palevol*, **6**, 359–368.

Slimak, L., Svendsen, J. I., Mangerud, J., Plisson, H., Heggen, H. P., Brugere, A. & Pavlov, P. Y. 2011. Late Mousterian persistence near the Arctic Circle. *Science*, **332**, 841–845.

Smail, D. L. 2008. *On deep history and the brain.* Berkeley: University of California Press.

Smith, A. 1759. *The theory of moral sentiments.* London: A. Millar.

Smith, M. A. 1987. Pleistocene occupation in arid central Australia. *Nature*, **328**, 710–711.

Smith, M. A. 1989. The case for a resident human population in the central Australian ranges during full glacial aridity. *Archaeology in Oceania*, **24**, 93–105.

Smith, M. A. 2005. Moving into the southern deserts: An archaeology of dispersal and colonisation. *In*: M. A. Smith & P. Hesse (eds.) 23°S: *Archaeology and environmental history of the southern deserts*. Canberra: National Museum of Australia Press.

Smith, M. A. 2009. Late Quaternary landscapes in Central Australia: Sedimentary history and palaeoecology of Puritjarra rock shelter. *Journal of Quaternary Science*, 24, 747–760.

Smith, M. A 2013. *The archaeology of Australia's deserts*. Cambridge: Cambridge University Press.

Soares, P., Achilli, A., Semino, O., Davies, W., Macaulay, V., Bandelt, H.-J., Torroni, A. & Richards, M. B. 2010. The archaeogenetics of Europe. *Current Biology*, 20, 174–183.

Soares, P., Alshamali, F., Pereira, M., Fernandes, V., Silva, N. M., Afonso, C., Costa, M. D., Musilova, E., Macaulay, V., Richards, M. B., Cerny, V. & Pereira, L. 2012. The expansion of mtDNA haplogroup L3 within and out of Africa. *Molecular Biology and Evolution*, 29, 915–927.

Soares, P., Ermini, L., Thomson, N., Mormina, M., Rito, T., Röhl, A., Salas, A., Oppenheimer, S., Macaulay, V. & Richards, M. B. 2009. Correcting for purifying selection: An improved human mitochondrial molecular clock. *The American Journal of Human Genetics*, 84, 740–759.

Soares, P., Rito, T., Trejaut, J., Mormina, M., Hill, C., Tinkler-Hundal, E., Braid, M., Clark, D. J., Loo, J.-H., Thomson, N., Denham, T., Donohue, M., Macaulay, V., Lin, M., Oppenheimer, S. & Richards, M. 2011. Ancient voyaging and Polynesian origins. *American Journal of Human Genetics*, 88, 1–9.

Soffer, O. 1985. *The Upper Palaeolithic of the Central Russian Plain*. New York: Academic Press.

Soffer, O. 1991. Storage, sedentism and the Eurasian palaeolithic record. *Antiquity*, 63, 719–732.

Soffer, O. & Praslov, N. D. (eds.) 1993. *From Kostenki to Clovis: Upper Palaeolithic–Paleo-Indian adaptations*. New York: Plenum Press.

Speth, J. D. 1983. *Bison kills and bone counts*. Chicago: University of Chicago Press.

Speth, J. D. & Spielmann, K. 1983. Energy source, protein metabolism and hunter-gatherer subsistence strategies. *Journal of Anthropological Archaeology*, 2, 1–31.

Sponheimer, M., Passey, B. H., De Ruiter, D. J., Guatelli-Steinberg, D., Cerling, T. E. & Lee-Thorp, J. A. 2006. Isotopic evidence for dietary variability in the early hominin *Paranthropus robustus*. *Science*, 314, 980–982.

Spoor, F. 2011. Malapa and the genus *Homo*. *Nature*, 478, 44–45.

Spriggs, M. 2000. The Solomon Islands as bridge and barrier in the settlement of the Pacific. *In*: A. Anderson & T. Murray (eds.) *Australian archaeologist: Collected papers in honour of Jim Allen*. Canberra: Coombs Academic.

Stanner, W. E. H. 1965. Aboriginal territorial organisation: Estate, range, domain and regime. *Oceania*, 36, 1–26.

Steadman, D. W., Vargas, C. & Cristino, F. 1994. Stratigraphy, chronology, and cultural context of an early faunal assemblage from Easter Island. *Asian Perspectives*, 33, 79–96.

Steele, J., Adams, J. & Sluckin, T. J. 1998. Modelling palaeoindian dispersals. *World Archaeology*, 30, 286–305.

Steele, J., Sluckin, T. J., Denholm, D. R. & Gamble, C. S. 1996. Simulating hunter-gatherer colonization of the Americas. *Analecta Praehistorica Leidensia*, **28**, 223–227.

Stewart, J. R. & Lister, A. M. 2001. Cryptic northern refugia and the origins of the modern biota. *Trends in Ecology and Evolution*, **16**, 608–613.

Stiner, M. C. 2002. Carnivory, coevolution, and the geographic spread of the genus *Homo*. *Journal of Archaeological Research*, **10**, 1–64.

Stiner, M. C., Barkai, R. & Gopher, A. 2009. Cooperative hunting and meat sharing 400–200kya at Qesem Cave, Israel. *Proceedings of the National Academy of Sciences of the United States of America*, **106**, 13207–13212.

Storey, A., Ramirez, J. M., Quiroz, D., Burley, D. V., Addison, D. J., Walter, R., Anderson, A. J., Hunt, T. L., Athens, J. S., Huynen, L. & Matisoo-Smith, E. 2007. Radiocarbon and DNA evidence for a pre-Columbian introduction of Plynesian chickens to Chile. *Proceedings of the National Academy of Sciences*, **104**, 10335–10339.

Storey, A., Spriggs, M., Bedford, S., Hawkins, S. C., Robins, J. H., Huynen, L. & Matisoo-Smith, E. 2010. Mitochondrial DNA from 3000-year old chickens at the Teouma site, Vanuatu. *Journal of Archaeological Science*, **37**, 2459–2468.

Stout, D., Quade, J., Semaw, S., Rogers, M. J. & Levin, N. E. 2005. Raw material selectivity of the earliest stone toolmakers at Gona, Afar, Ethiopia. *Journal of Human Evolution*, **48**, 365–380.

Strasser, T. F., Panagopoulou, E., Runnels, C. N., Murray, P. M., Thompson, N., Karkanas, P., McCoy, F. W. & Wegmann, K. W. 2010. Stone age seafaring in the Mediterranean: Evidence from the Plakias region for Lower Palaeolithic and Mesolithic habitation of Crete. *Hesperia*, **79**, 145–190.

Strasser, T. F., Runnels, C. N., Wegmann, K. W., Panagopoulou, E., McCoy, F. W., Digregorio, C., Karkanas, P. & Thompson, N. 2011. Dating Palaeolithic sites in southwestern Crete, Greece. *Journal of Quaternary Science*, online.

Street, M. 2002. Ein Wiedersehen mit dem Hund von Bonn-Oberkassel. *Bonner zoologische Beiträge*, **50**, 269–290.

Stringer, C. 2006. *Homo britannicus: The incredible story of human life in Britain.* London: Penguin Books.

Stringer, C. 2011. *The origin of our species.* London: Allen Lane.

Stringer, C. & Gamble, C. 1993. *In search of the Neanderthals: Solving the puzzle of human origins.* London: Thames and Hudson.

Strum, S. S. & Latour, B. 1987. Redefining the social link: From baboons to humans. *Social Science Information*, **26**, 783–802.

Stuart, A. J., Kosintsev, P. A., Higham, T. F. G. & Lister, A. M. 2004. Pleistocene to Holocene extinction dynamics in giant deer and woolly mammoth. *Nature*, **431**, 684–689.

Summerhayes, G. R. 2009. Obsidian network patterns in Melanesia: Sources, characterisation and distribution. *IPPA Bulletin*, **29**, 109–123.

Summerhayes, G. R., Leavesley, M., Fairbairn, A., Mandui, H., Field, J., Ford, A. & Fullagar, R. 2010. Human adaptation and plant use in Highland New Guinea 49,000 to 44,000 years ago. *Science*, **330**, 78–81.

Sutcliffe, A. J. 1985. *On the track of ice age mammals.* London: Natural History Museum.

Sutherland, P. 2008. Norse and natives in the Eastern Arctic. *In:* S. Brink & N. S. Price (eds.) *The Viking world.* London: Routledge.

Sutton, P. 1990. The pulsating heart: Large scale cultural and demographic processes in Aboriginal Australia. *In:* B. Meehan & N. White (eds.) *Hunter-gatherer demography: Past and present.* Sydney: University of Sydney.

Suwa, G., Asfaw, B., Kono, R. T., Kubo, D., Lovejoy, C. O. & White, T. D. 2009. The Ardipithecus ramidus skull and its implications for hominid origins. *Science,* **326,** 68e1–68e7.

Suzuki, H. & Hanihara, K. 1982. *The Minatogawa man: The Upper Pleistocene man from the island of Okinawa.* Tokyo: University Museum, University of Tokyo Bulletin.

Svoboda, J. 1994. *Paleolit Moravy a Slezska.* Brno: Dolnovesonické studies 1.

Svoboda, J., Lozek, V. & Vleck, E. 1996. *Hunters between east and west: The Palaeolithic of Moravia.* New York: Plenum Press.

Swisher, C. C., Curtis, G. H., Jacob, T., Getty, A. G., Suprijo, A. & Widiasmoro 1994. Age of the earliest known hominids in Java, Indonesia. *Science,* **263,** 1118–1121.

Szabo, B. J., McHugh, W.P., Schaber, G.G., Haynes, C.V. & Breed C.S. 1989. Uranium-series dated authigenic carbonates and Acheulian sites in southern Egypt. *Science,* **243,** 1053–1056.

Tanabe, K., Mita, T., Jombart, T., Eriksson, A., Horibe, S., Palacpac, N., Ranford-Cartwright, L., Sawai, H., Sakihama, N., Ohmae, H., Nakamura, M., Ferreira, M. U., Escalente, A. A., Prugnolle, F., Björkman, A., Färnert, A., Kaneko, A., Horii, T., Manica, A., Kishino, H. & Balloux, F. 2010. *Plasmodium falciparum* accompanied the human expansion out of Africa. *Current Biology,* online.

Tchernov, E., Horowitz, L. K., Ronen, A. & Lister, A. 1994. The faunal remains from the Evron Quarry in relation to other Lower Palaeolithic hominid sites in southern Levant. *Quaternary Research,* **42,** 328–339.

Tchernov, E. & Valla, F. F. 1997. Two new dogs and other Natufian dogs, from the Southern Levant. *Journal of Archaeological Science,* **24,** 65–95.

Thieme, H. 2005. The Lower Palaeolithic art of hunting: The case of Schöningen 13 II-4, Lower Saxony, Germany. *In:* C. Gamble & M. Porr (eds.) *The individual hominid in context: Archaeological investigations of Lower and Middle Palaeolithic landscapes, locales and artefacts.* London: Routledge.

Thierry, B., Iwaniuk, A. N. & Pellis, S. M. 2000. The influence of phylogeny on the social behaviour of macaques (Primates: Cercopithecidae, genus Macaca). *Ethology,* **106,** 713–724.

Thomas, J. 2004. *Archaeology and modernity.* London: Routledge.

Thorne, A. G., Grun, R., Mortimer, G., Spooner, N. A., Simpson, J. J., McCulloch, M., Taylor, L. & Curnoe, D. 1999. Australia's oldest human remains: Age of the Lake Mungo 3 skeleton. *Journal of Human Evolution,* **36,** 591–612.

Thorsby, E. 2012. The Polynesian gene pool: An early contribution by Amerindians to Easter Island. *Philosophical Transactions of the Royal Society of London B,* **367,** 812–819.

Tilley, C. 1999. *Metaphor and material culture.* Oxford: Blackwell.

Torrence, R. 1983. Time budgeting and hunter-gatherer technology. *In:* G. Bailey (ed.) *Hunter-gatherer economy in prehistory.* Cambridge: Cambridge University Press.

Torrence, R. (ed.) 1989. *Time, energy and stone tools*. Cambridge: Cambridge University Press.

Torrence, R. 2000. Hunter-gatherer technology: Macro- and microscale approaches. *In:* C. Panter-Brick, R. H. Layton & P. Rowley-Conwy (eds.) *Hunter-gatherers: An interdisciplinary perspective*. Cambridge: Cambridge University Press.

Torroni, A., Achilli, A., Macaulay, V., Richards, M. & Bandelt, H.-J. 2006. Harvesting the fruit of the human mtDNA tree. *Trends in Genetics*, 22, 339–345.

Trauth, M. H., Larrasoana, J. C. & Mudelsee, M. 2009. Trends, rhythms and events in Plio–Pleistocene African climate. *Quaternary Science Reviews*, 28, 399–411.

Trauth, M. H., Maslin, M. A., Deino, A. L., Streker, M. R., Bergner, A. G. N. & Dühnforth, M. 2007. High- and low-latitude forcing of Plio–Pleistocene East African climate and human evolution. *Journal of Human Evolution*, 53, 475–486.

Trigger, B. G. 2006. *A history of archaeological thought (2nd edition)*. Cambridge: Cambridge University Press.

Trinkaus, E. 2003. An early modern human from the Peçstera cu Oase, Romania. *Proceedings of the National Academy of Sciences of the United States of America*, 100, 11231–11236.

Turner, J. H. 2000. *On the origins of human emotions: A sociological inquiry into the evolution of human affect*. Stanford: Stanford University Press.

Turvey, S. M., Weksler, M., Morris, E. L. & Nokkert, M. 2010. Taxonomy, phylogeny, and diversity of the extinct Lesser Antillean rice rats (Sigmodontinae: Oryzomyini), with description of a new genus and species. *Zoological Journal of the Linnean Society*, 160, 748–772.

Ugan, A. & Byers, D. 2007. Geographic and temporal trends in proboscidean and human radiocarbon histories during the late Pleistocene. *Quaternary Science Reviews*, 26, 3058–3080.

Underhill, P. A., Passarino, G., Lin, A. A., Shen, P., Lahr, M. M., Foley, R., Oefner, P. J. & Cavalli-Sforza, L. L. 2001. The phylogeography of Y chromosome binary haplotypes and the origins of modern human populations. *Annals of Human Genetics*, 65, 43–62.

Valentin, F., Buckley, H. R., Herrscher, E., Kinaston, R., Bedford, S., Spriggs, M., Hawkins, S. C. & Neal, K. 2010. Lapita subsistence strategies and food consumption patterns in the community of Teouma (Efate, Vanuatu). *Journal of Archaeological Science*, 37, 1820–1829.

Valla, F. 1975. La sepulture H104 de Mallaha (Eynan) et le probleme de la domestication du chien en Palestine. *Paléorient*, 3, 287–292.

Van Andel, T. H. & Davies, W. (eds.) 2003. *Neanderthals and modern humans in the European landscape during the last glaciation*. Cambridge: McDonald Institute Monographs.

van der Made, J. 2011. Biogeography and climate change as a context to human dispersal out of Africa and within Eurasia. *Quaternary Science Reviews*, 30, 1353–1367.

Van Peer, P. & Vermeersch, P. M. 2007. The place of Northeast Africa in the early history of modern humans: New data and interpretations on the Middle Stone Age. *In:* P. Mellars, O. Bar-Yosef, C. Stringer & K. V. Boyle (eds.) *Rethinking the human revolution*. Cambridge: McDonald Institute.

Vasil'ev, S. A., Kuzmin, Y. V., Orlova, L. A. & Dementiev, V. N. 2002. Radiocarbon-based chronology of the Palaeolithic in Siberia and its relevance to the peopling of the New World. *Radiocarbon*, 44, 503–530.

Veltre, D. W. & Smith, M. A. 2010. Historical overview of archaeological research in the Aleut region of Alaska. *Human Biology*, **82**, 487–506.

Vermeersch, P., Paulissen, E., Stokes, S., Charlier, C., Van Peer, P., Stringer, C. & Lindsay, W. 1998. A Middle Palaeolithic burial of a modern human at Taramsa Hill, Egypt. *Antiquity*, **72**, 475–484.

Veth, P. 2010. The dispersal of modern humans into Australia. In: K. V. Boyle, C. Gamble & O. Bar-Yosef (eds.) *The Upper Palaeolithic revolution in global perspective: Papers in honour of Sir Paul Mellars*. Cambridge: McDonald Institute.

Veth, P., Smith, M., Bowler, J., Fitzsimmons, K., Williams, A. & Hiscock, P. 2009. Excavations at Parnkupirti, Lake Gregory, Great Sandy Desert: OSL ages for occupation before the Last Glacial Maximum. *Australian Archaeology*, **69**, 1–10.

Veth, P., Spriggs, M., Jatmiko, A. & O'Connor, S. 1998. Bridging Sunda and Sahul: The archaeological significance of the Aru Islands, southern Moluccas. In: G.-J. Bartstra (ed.) *Bird's Head approaches: Irian Jaya studies – A programme for interdisciplinary research*. Rotterdam: A. A. Balkema.

Vidal, L. & Arz, H. 2004. Oceanic climate variability at millennial time-scales: Models of climate connections. In: R. W. Batterbee, F. Gasse & C. E. Stickley (eds.) *Past climate variability through Europe and Africa*. Dordrecht: Springer.

Vrba, E. S. 1985. Ecological and adaptive changes associated with early hominid evolution. In: E. Delson (ed.) *Ancestors: The hard evidence*. New York: Alan R. Liss.

Vrba, E. S. 1988. Late Pliocene climatic events and hominid evolution. In: F. E. Grine (ed.) *Evolutionary history of the "robust" Australopithecines*. New York: Aldine de Gruyter.

Wadley, L. 2001. What is cultural modernity? A general view and a South African perspective from Rose Cottage Cave. *Cambridge Archaeological Journal*, **11**, 201–221.

Walker, A. & Leakey, R. (eds.) 1993. *The Nariokotome Homo erectus skeleton*. Cambridge, MA: Harvard University Press.

Wallace, B. 2008. The discovery of Vinland. In: S. Brink & N. S. Price (eds.) *The Viking world*. London: Routledge.

Wang Chiyuen, Yaolin, S. & Wenhu, Z. 1982. Dynamic uplift of the Himalaya. *Nature*, **298**, 553–556.

Warmuth, V., Eriksson, A., Bower, M. A., Barker, G., Barrett, E., Hanks, B. K., Li, S., Lomitashvili, D., Ochir-Goryaeva, M., Siznov, G. V., Soyonov, V. & Manica, A. 2012. Reconstructing the origin and spread of horse domestication in the Eurasian steppe. *Proceedings of the National Academy of Sciences of the United States of America*, **109**, 8202–8206.

Waters, M. R., Forman, S. L., Jennings, T. A., Nordt, L. C., Driese, S. G., Feinberg, J. M., Keene, J. L., Halligan, J., Linfquist, A., Pierson, J., Hallmark, C. T., Collins, M. B. & Wiederhold, J. E. 2011. The Buttermilk Creek complex and the origins of Clovis at the Debra L. Friedkin site, Texas. *Science*, **331**, 1599–1603.

Waters, M. R. & Stafford, T. W. 2007. Redefining the age of Clovis: Implications for the peopling of the Americas. *Science*, **315**, 1122–1126.

Waters, M. R., Stafford, T. W., McDonald, H. G., Gustafson, C., Rasmussen, M.,
Cappellini, E., Olsen, J. V., Szklarczyk, D., Jensen, L. J., Gilbert, M. T. P. &
Willerslev, E. 2011. Pre-Clovis mastodon hunting 13,800 years ago at the Manis
site, Washington. *Science*, **334**, 351–353.

Watson, P. 1983. *This precious foliage*. Sydney: Oceania Monograph 26.

Weaver, A. H. 2005. Reciprocal evolution of the cerebellum and neocortex in fossil
humans. *Proceedings of the National Academy of Sciences*, **102**, 3576–3580.

Webb, S. 2006. *The first boat people*. Cambridge: Cambridge University Press.

Wells, J. C. K. & Stock, J. T. 2007. The biology of the colonizing ape. *Yearbook of
Physical Anthropology*, **50**, 191–222.

Wheeler, P. E. 1984. The evolution of bipedality and loss of functional body hair in
hominids. *Journal of Human Evolution*, **13**, 91–98.

Wheeler, P. E. 1988. Stand tall and stay cool. *New Scientist*, **118**, 62–65.

White, M. J. 2012. The lithic assemblage from Lynford Quarry and its bearing on
Neanderthal behaviour in late Pleistocene Britain. *In*: W. A. Boismier, C. S.
Gamble & F. Coward (eds.) *Neanderthals among mammoths: Excavations at
Lynford Quarry, Norfolk*. London: English Heritage Monographs.

White, M. J. & Schreve, D. C. 2000. Island Britain – Peninsula Britain:
Palaeogeography, colonisation, and the Lower Palaeolithic settlement of the
British Isles. *Proceedings of the Prehistoric Society*, **66**, 1–28.

White, R. 1993. Technological and social dimensions of "Aurignacian-age" body
ornaments across Europe. *In*: H. Knecht, A. Pike-Tay & R. White (eds.) *Before
Lascaux: The complex record of the Early Upper Paleolithic*. Boca Raton: CRC
Press.

White, R. 1997. Substantial acts: From materials to meaning in Upper Palaeolithic
representation. *In*: M. W. Conkey, O. Soffer, D. Stratmann & N. G. Jablonski
(eds.) *Beyond art: Pleistocene image and symbol*. San Francisco: Wattis
Symposium Series in Anthropology, Memoirs of the California Academy of
Sciences Number 23.

White, R. 2007. Systems of personal ornamentation in the Early Upper Palaeolithic:
Methodological challenges and new observations. *In*: P. Mellars, O. Bar-Yosef,
C. Stringer & K. V. Boyle (eds.) *Rethinking the human revolution*. Cambridge:
McDonald Institute.

Whiting, J. W. M., Sodergren, J. A. & Stigler, S. M. 1982. Winter temperature as a
constraint to the migration of preindustrial peoples. *American Anthropologist*,
84, 279–298.

Wiessner, P. 1982. Risk, reciprocity and social influences on !Kung San economics.
In: E. Leacock & R. Lee (eds.) *Politics and history in band societies*. Cambridge:
Cambridge University Press.

Wilmsen, E. N. 1989. *Land filled with flies: A political economy of the Kalahari*.
Chicago: University of Chicago Press.

Wilmshurst, J. M., Anderson, A. J., Higham, T. F. G. & Worthy, T. H. 2008.
Dating the late prehistoric dispersal of Polynesians to New Zealand using the
commensal Pacific rat. *Proceedings of the National Academy of Sciences*, **105**,
7676–7680.

Wilson, S. 2007. *The archaeology of the Caribbean*. Cambridge: Cambridge
University Press.

Wing, E. S. 2001. The sustainability of resources used by Native Americans of four Caribbean islands. *International Journal of Ostearchaeology*, 11, 112–126.

Winney, B. J., Hammond, R. L., Macasero, W., Flores, B., Boug, A., Biquand, V., Biquand, S. & Bruford, M. W. 2004. Crossing the Red Sea: Phylogeography of the hamadryas baboon, *Papio hamadryas hamadryas*. *Molecular Ecology*, 13, 2819–2827.

Wobst, H. M. 1978. The archaeo-ethnology of hunter gatherers or the tyranny of the ethnographic record in archaeology. *American Antiquity*, 43, 303–309.

Wobst, H. M. 1990. Minitime and megaspace in the Palaeolithic at 18K and otherwise. *In:* O. Soffer & C. Gamble (eds.) *The world at 18,000 BP. Volume 2: High latitudes.* London: Unwin Hyman.

Wood, B. 2010. Reconstructing human evolution: Achievements, challenges, and opportunities. *Proceedings of the National Academy of Sciences of the United States of America*, 107, 8902–8909.

Wood, B. & Lonergan, N. 2008. The hominin fossil record: Taxa, grades and clades. *Journal of Anatomy*, 212, 354–376.

Woodburn, J. 1980. Hunters and gatherers today and reconstruction of the past. *In:* E. Gellner (ed.) *Soviet and western anthropology.* London: Duckworth.

Wrangham, R. W. 1980. An ecological model of female-bonded primate groups. *Behaviour*, 75, 262–299.

Wrangham, R. W. 2009. *Catching fire: How cooking made us human.* London: Profile Books.

Wrangham, R. W., Jones, J. H., Laden, G., Pilbeam, D. & Conklin-Brittain, N. 1999. The raw and the stolen: Cooking and the ecology of human origins. *Current Anthropology*, 40, 567–594.

Wynn, T. 2002. Archaeology and cognitive evolution. *Behavioral and Brain Sciences*, 25, 389–438.

Wynn, T. & Coolidge, F. L. 2004. The skilled Neanderthal mind. *Journal of Human Evolution*, 46, 467–487.

Wynn, T. & Coolidge, F. L. 2012. *How to think like a Neanderthal.* Oxford: Oxford University Press.

Yamei, H., Potts, R., Baoyin, Y., Zhengtang, G., Deino, A., Wei, W., Clark, J., Guangmao, X. & Weiwen, H. 2000. Mid-Pleistocene Acheulean-like stone technology of the Bose Basin, South China. *Science*, 287, 1622–1626.

Yellen, J. & Harpending, H. 1972. Hunter-gatherer populations and archaeological inference. *World Archaeology*, 3, 244–252.

Yesner, D. R. 2001. Human dispersal into interior Alaska: Antecedent conditions, mode of colonization, and adaptations. *Quaternary Science Reviews*, 20, 315–327.

Yi, S. & Clark, G. A. 1983. Observations on the Lower Palaeolithic of Northeast Asia. *Current Anthropology*, 24, 181–202.

Young, C. R. 2012. Coalescent theory. http://bio.classes.ucsc.edu/bio107/Class%20 pdfs/W05_lecture14.pdf

Zeder, M., Emshwiller, E., Smith, B. D. & Bradley, D. G. 2006. Documenting domestication: The intersection of genetics and archaeology. *Trends in Genetics*, 22, 139–155.

Zerega, N. J. C., Ragone, D. & Motley, T. J. 2004. Complex origins of breadfruit (*Artocarpus altilis*, Moraceae): Implications for human migrations in Oceania. *American Journal of Botany*, **91**, 760–766.

Zhou, W.-X., Sornette, D., Hill, R. A. & Dunbar, R. 2004. Discrete hierarchical organization of social group sizes. *Proceedings of the Royal Society of London B*, **272**, 439–444.

Zilhão, J. 2007. The emergence of ornaments and art: An archaeological perspective on the origins of behavioural "modernity". *Journal of Archaeological Research*, **15**, 1–54.

Zilhão, J., Angelucci, D. E., Badal-Garcia, E., d'Errico, F., Daniel, F., Dayet, L., Douka, K., Higham, T. F. G., Martinez-Sánchez, M. J., Montes-Bernárdez, R., Murcia-Mascarós, S., Pérez-Sirvent, C., Roldán-Garcia, C., Vanhaeren, M., Villaverde, V., Wood, R. & Zapata, J. 2010. Symbolic use of marine shells and mineral pigments by Iberian Neandertals. *Proceedings of the National Academy of Sciences of the United States of America*, Early Edition.

Zilhão, J., Trinkaus, E., Constantin, S., Milota, S., Gherase, M., Sarcina, L., Danciu, A., Rougier, H., Quilès, J. & Rodrigo, R. 2007. Petera cu Oase people, Europe's earliest modern humans. *In*: P. Mellars, O. Bar-Yosef, C. Stringer & K. V. Boyle (eds.) *Rethinking the human revolution*. Cambridge: McDonald Institute.

Index

Printed in Great Britain
by Amazon